AF743366

Perspectives on Global Development 2017

INTERNATIONAL MIGRATION IN A SHIFTING WORLD

OECD DEVELOPMENT CENTRE

This work is published under the responsibility of the Secretary-General of the OECD. The opinions expressed and arguments employed herein do not necessarily reflect the official views of the member countries of the OECD or its Development Centre.

This document and any map included herein are without prejudice to the status of or sovereignty over any territory, to the delimitation of international frontiers and boundaries and to the name of any territory, city or area.

Please cite this publication as:
OECD (2016), *Perspectives on Global Development 2017: International Migration in a Shifting World*, OECD Publishing, Paris.
http://dx.doi.org/10.1787/persp_glob_dev-2017-en

ISBN 978-92-64-26253-9 (print)
ISBN 978-92-64-26568-4 (PDF)
ISBN 978-92-64-26646-9 (epub)

The statistical data for Israel are supplied by and under the responsibility of the relevant Israeli authorities. The use of such data by the OECD is without prejudice to the status of the Golan Heights, East Jerusalem and Israeli settlements in the West Bank under the terms of international law.

Photo credits: Cover design by the OECD Development Centre.

Corrigenda to OECD publications may be found on line at: *www.oecd.org/publishing/corrigenda.*

© OECD 2016

You can copy, download or print OECD content for your own use, and you can include excerpts from OECD publications, databases and multimedia products in your own documents, presentations, blogs, websites and teaching materials, provided that suitable acknowledgment of the source and copyright owner is given. All requests for public or commercial use and translation rights should be submitted to *rights@oecd.org*. Requests for permission to photocopy portions of this material for public or commercial use shall be addressed directly to the Copyright Clearance Center (CCC) at *info@copyright.com* or the Centre français d'exploitation du droit de copie (CFC) at *contact@cfcopies.com*.

Foreword

Since its initiation in 2010, the OECD Development Centre's Perspectives on Global Development *series has investigated the increasing economic weight of developing countries in the world economy, a phenomenon we refer to as "shifting wealth". Each edition has examined the effect of this trend on development, focusing on different policy concerns, from social cohesion (2012) and industrial policy (2013) to productivity and the middle-income trap (2014).*

This edition of Perspectives on Global Development *focuses on the issue of international migration and development in the context of shifting wealth. The report builds on a growing body of research carried out by the Development Centre that looks at the drivers and impacts of migration in developing countries, South-South migration, and the interrelations between public policies, migration and development.*

The main purpose of this report is to enrich the debate on migration and development by:

- *highlighting the main trends and drivers of international migration;*
- *analysing the impact of migration on developing countries of origin and destination;*
- *discussing illustrative potential scenarios on the future of migration;*
- *making recommendations to governments in origin and destination countries, as well as to the international community, about policies that could help to improve the contribution of migration to development.*

Acknowledgements

The 2017 edition of the OECD's *Perspectives on Global Development* was prepared by the OECD Development Centre under the direction of Mario Pezzini, Director. The team was led by Carl Dahlman, Head of the Thematic Division, and David Khoudour, Head of the Migration and Skills Unit. The report was drafted by Lisa Andersson, Amandine Aubry, Martha Baxter, Marcus Böhme, Hannah Bull, Carl Dahlman, Jason Gagnon, Shinyoung Jeon, David Khoudour, Sarah Kups, Hyeshin Park and Martin Wermelinger. Significant inputs to the chapters were provided by Amy Hong, Bram Dekker, Gaëlle Ferrant, Nina Galanska, Sam Mealy, Joanne Tang and Alejandra Urrea. Statistical assistance was provided by Vararat Atisophon and administrative support by Myriam Andrieux. The report was edited by Meg Bortin and Stephen Jessel and the Development Centre's publications team, in particular Delphine Grandrieux and Elizabeth Nash, turned the draft into a publication. Jill Gaston proof-read the report. Aida Buendia designed the cover.

The authors are thankful to the speakers of the two experts' meetings and scenarios workshops that were organised for the preparation of the report : Rolando Avendano (OECD), Michel Beine (University of Luxembourg), Richard Black (SOAS University of London), Simon Buckle (OECD), Lisa Chauvet (DIAL/IRD), Michael Clemens (Center for Global Development), Jeff Dayton-Johnson (MIIS), Jean-Christophe Dumont (OECD), Ambassador Pierre Duquesne (OECD), Giovanni Facchini (University of Nottingham), Douglas Frantz (OECD), Yoshifumi Fukunaga (RIETI), Sarah Gammage (ICRW), François Gemenne (IDDRI, CEDEM), Flore Gubert (IRD/DIAL), Camilla Hagstroem (European Commission), Nicola Harrington (UN Volunteers), Bela Hovy (UNPD), Dina Ionesco (IOM), Christina Jespersen (UNHCR), Devesh Kapur (University of Pennsylvania), Yevgeny Kuznetsov (World Bank), Michelle Leighton (ILO), Thomas Liebig (OECD), Ramón Mahía (Universidad Autónoma de Madrid), Mathilde Maurel (CNRS, FERDI), Anna Maria Mayda (Georgetown University), Erik Melander (Uppsala University), Sandrine Mesplé-Somps (IRD/DIAL), Jean-Baptiste Meyer(IRD), El Mouhoub Mouhoud (Université Paris-Dauphine), Rainer Münz (Hamburg Institute of International Economics), Sebastian Nieto Parra (OECD), Ceri Oeppen (University of Sussex), Çağlar Özden (World Bank), Natalia Popova (ILO), Lant Pritchett (Harvard Kennedy School), Guna Sankar Ramasamy Kone (Superu), Gabriela Ramos (OECD), Hillel Rapoport (Paris School of Economics), Ambassador Mithat Rende (OECD) Cécile Riallant (the Joint Migration and Development Initiative), Markus Reisle (Swiss Agency for Development and Cooperation), Jan Rieländer (OECD), Indrajit Roy (University of Oxford), Marco Salvi (Avenir Suisse), Rachel Scott (OECD), Melissa Siegel (Maastricht University), Alice Szczepanikova (European Commission), Alessandra Venturini (Migration Policy Center), Jackline Wahba (University of Southampton), Serge Weber (UPEM), Alan Whaites (National School of Government International), Catherine Wihtol de Wenden (CNRS, Sciences Po), Andrew Wyckoff (OECD), Theodora Xenogiani (OECD), Hui Xu (Beijing Normal University), Juan Yermo (OECD) and the delegates from the Centre's Governing Board. Many thanks to Raphaël Beziz (YOUMEO), Deirdre Culley (OECD) and Martin Mayer (YOUMEO) for helping design and moderate the scenario sessions.

The team is also grateful to all the speakers who took part in the "DEV talk" seminar series on migration that contributed to their thinking: Michael Clemens (Center for Global Development), Frédéric Docquier (FNRS, Université catholique de Louvain), François Gemenne (IDDRI, CEDEM), Robert Holzmann (University of New South Wales), Dina Ionesco (IOM), Yevgeny Kuznetsov (World bank), Sandrine Mesplé-Somps (IRD/DIAL), Daria Mokhnacheva (IOM), Hillel Rapoport (Paris School of Economics) and Cécile Riallant (the Joint Migration and Development Initiative).

The team also gratefully acknowledges written contributions for the report by: Anna Boucher (Univesity of Sydney), Caroline Caplan (Université Paris Descartes), Michael Clemens (Center for Global Development), Jean Luc Demonsant (Toulouse School of Economics), Giovanni Facchini (the University of Nottingham), Anna Maria Mayda (Georgetown University), Cécile Riallant (the Joint Migration and Development Initiative), and Soonhwa Yi (World Bank).

The report benefited from helpful comments on drafts from Development Centre colleagues Federico Bonaglia, Juan de Laiglesia, Jan Rieländer, Linda Smiroldo Herda and Felix Zimmerman, and colleagues from other directorates: Jean-Christophe Dumont and the International Migration Division of the OECD Employment, Labour and Social Affairs Directorate; Catherine Mann and the OECD Economics Department; and Anne-Lise Prigent and Sue Kendall-Bilicki from the Public Affairs and Communications Directorate.

Finally the Development Centre gratefully acknowledges the direct financial contribution for this report by the Government of Switzerland and the Government of Italy; as well as the contribution from the EU for the research projects IPPMD and ECLM on migration in developing countries carried out by the Migration and Skills Unit of the Development Centre, which are the basis for much of Chapters 7 and 8.

Table of contents

Tables

Figures

Boxes

Follow OECD Publications on:

http://twitter.com/OECD_Pubs

http://www.facebook.com/OECDPublications

http://www.linkedin.com/groups/OECD-Publications-4645871

http://www.youtube.com/oecdilibrary

http://www.oecd.org/oecddirect/

This book has... *StatLinks*

A service that delivers Excel® files from the printed page!

Look for the *StatLinks* at the bottom of the tables or graphs in this book. To download the matching Excel® spreadsheet, just type the link into your Internet browser, starting with the *http://dx.doi.org* prefix, or click on the link from the e-book edition.

Acronyms and abbreviations

AEC	ASEAN Economic Community
ALMPs	Active Labour Market Policies
AMERM	Association Marocaine d'Etudes et de Recherche en Migrations
ASEAN	Association of Southeast Asian Nations
ASM	Academy of Sciences of Moldova
BRIC	Beirut Research and Innovation Center
BRIICS	Brazil, Russian Federation, India, Indonesia, China and South Africa
CCT	Conditional Cash Transfer
CEPII	Centre d'Etudes Prospectives et d'Informations Internationales
CIS	Commonwealth of Independent States
DEMIG	Determinants of International Migration
DIBP	Department of Immigration and Border Protection, Australia
DIOC	Database on Immigrants in OECD countries
DIOC-E	Database on Immigrants in OECD and Non-OECD Countries
DKNs	Diaspora Knowledge Networks
ECEC	Early Childhood Education and Care
ECOWAS	Economic Community of West African States
EU	European Union
FDI	Foreign Direct Investment
FIIAPP	Fundación Internacional y para Iberoamérica de Administración y Políticas Públicas
FISDL	Fund for Local Development, El Salvador
FSU	Former Soviet Union
GATT	General Agreement on Trade and Tariffs
GCC	Gulf Cooperation Council
GDP	Gross Domestic Product
GFMD	Global Forum on Migration and Development
GIZ	Deutsche Gesellschaft für Internationale Zusammenarbeit
GMG	Global Migration Group
GNI	Gross National Income
GSP	Global Skills Partnerships
GVCs	Global Value Chains

HDI	Human Development Index
HI countries	High-Income by 1995 countries
HTAs	Hometown Associations
HWWI	Hamburg Institute of International Economics, Hamburg
IBRD	International Bank for Reconstruction and Development, World Bank
ICJ	International Court of Justice
ICMPD	International Centre for Migration Policy Development
ICT	Information and Communications Technology
IDPs	Internally Displaced Persons
IFR	International Federation of Robotics
ILO	International Labour Organization
IMF	International Monetary Fund
IOM	International Organization for Migration
IPCC	Intergovernmental Panel on Climate Change
IPPMD	Interrelations between Public Policies, Migration and Development
ISSP	International Social Survey Programme
KNOMAD	Global Knowledge Partnership on Migration and Development
LEED	Local Economic and Employment Development
LRAs	Local and Regional Authorities
MERCOSUR	Mercado Común del Sur
MR	Multilateral Resistance
NAFTA	North American Free Trade Agreement
NEVRHA	Nepal Earthquake Victims Research and Help Association
NGOs	Non-governmental Organisations
NRSBL	New Rural Bank of San Leonardo, the Philippines
OAU	Organisation of African Unity
ODA	Official Development Assistance
ODI	Overseas Development Institute
OECD	Organisation for Economic Co-operation and Development
OPEC	Organization of the Petroleum Exporting Countries
PAN	Partido de Acción Nacional, Mexico
PEPs	Public Employment Programmes
PICT	Scientific and Technological Research Projects, Argentina
PISA	Programme for International Student Assessment
PPML	Poisson Pseudo-Maximum Likelihood
PPPs	Purchasing Power Parities
REP	Return Expert Programme, Malaysia
RW countries	Rest of the World
R&D	Research and Development

SCMD	Sub-Committee on Migration and Development
SEDESOL	Ministry of Social Development, Mexico
SIGI	Social Institutions and Gender Index
SIPRI	Stockholm International Peace Research Institute
SDGs	Sustainable Development Goals
SG countries	High and Sustained Growth countries
TRIPS	Trade-Related Aspects of Intellectual Property Rights
TTIP	Transatlantic Trade and Investment Partnership
TVET	Technical and Vocational Education and Training
TWG	Thematic Working Group
UCDP	Uppsala Conflict Data Program
UN	United Nations
UNCTAD	United Nations Conference on Trade and Development
UNHCR	United Nations High Commissioner for Refugees
UNDESA	United Nations Department of Economic and Social Affairs
UNDP	United Nations Development Programme
UNPD	United Nations Population Division
UNRWA	United Nations Relief and Works Agency
UNSCR	United Nations Security Council resolution
USSR	Union of Soviet Socialist Republics
VAT	Value-Added Tax
WEF	World Economic Forum
WPP	World Population Prospects
WTO	World Trade Organization

Editorial: Realising the potential of migration and development

International migration holds the potential to improve the lives of migrants and advance welfare in countries of origin and destination alike provided the right public policies are put in place. Yet, in a context of rising anti-immigration sentiment, migration has become a sensitive issue on most policy agendas. While immediate humanitarian concerns linked to the current refugee crisis need to be addressed and resolved, more coherent policies and strengthened international co-operation are required to enhance the contribution of migration to development.

Against this backdrop, the 2017 edition of *Perspectives on Global Development*, prepared by the OECD's Development Centre, focuses on international migration from the perspective of developing countries. It firstly examines to what extent and how the shifting of economic activity to developing countries has affected migration patterns, and secondly the many ways that international migration contributes to development. Ultimately, it aims to help policy makers take stock of what we know, what we can expect and what we can do.

What we know

The proportion of people who live outside their countries of birth has increased in the last 20 years, from 2.7% of the world population in 1995 to 3.3% in 2015. People move in search of better jobs, better incomes and, more broadly, a better quality of life. Yet, migration is costly and the decision to migrate is rarely taken lightly. Costs are not only financial – the cost of travel and settling in – but also social and psychological – moving away from home, leaving friends and family behind.

While the overall percentage of migrants from developing countries in the world's total has only increased from 79% to 80% in the last two decades, the share of migrants heading to high-income countries has increased from 36% to 51%. Despite rapid economic growth in many developing economies, the absolute difference between what an individual can earn in a low or middle-income country and in a high-income country has increased, making the latter even more attractive. In addition, although developing countries have made significant progress on various dimensions of well-being, such as access to education, health and social protection as well as the quality of institutions, the gaps with high-income countries remain large.

Migration can have both positive and negative effects on countries of origin as well as those of destination. For countries of origin, benefits are linked to its effect on taking pressure off the labour market and on contributing finance and knowledge through remittances, diasporas and return migration. But emigration can come with economic, human and social costs, such as labour shortages, loss of educated and skilled workers and social repercussions, especially for family members left behind. These costs need to be addressed by policy makers.

Countries of destination can also benefit from migration to make up for shortages of workers in key sectors. Skilled workers, in particular, can help low and middle-income countries move up the value chain. Countries with ageing populations such as Brazil, the People's Republic of China and the Russian Federation, which will face declining labour forces in the future, can rely on immigration to help offset the reduction in their labour forces and help finance their pension systems. However immigrants may also compete with locals for jobs (particularly low skilled workers); stretch the capacity of public services such as education, social protection and infrastructure, particularly for subnational regions where they concentrate; and put pressure on social cohesion. Policies in countries of destination therefore need to address these concerns as well as recognise that there are geographic asymmetries within countries in the effects of immigration, and strengthen subnational governments' capacities to help deal with them.

What we can expect

Looking from now to 2030, migration from developing counties is likely to continue to increase because of persisting economic and well-being gaps with developed countries. Population pressures and climate change are likely to further fuel emigration from developing countries. On the other hand, the tightening of migration policies in high-income countries may encourage people to migrate to those developing countries which possess higher incomes and better living conditions.

Aside from labour migration, continuing instability in the Middle East and increasing conflicts around the world may create new refugee spikes. 87% of refugees are currently hosted in low and middle-income countries, stretching their already-limited resources. Greater international assistance for these countries is essential.

What we can do

Better policies can help improve the benefits of migration to origin and destination countries, as well as for migrants. In countries of origin, policy objectives should include providing support to families who stay behind, lowering the costs of remittances and channelling them towards productive investment, attracting back and reintegrating return migrants, and bringing diasporas into development initiatives. If countries are concerned about high rates of emigration, efforts need to be redoubled to improve conditions at home, in particular creating decent jobs and improving well-being. The donor community can play a role in supporting countries improve development outcomes.

In countries of destination, migrant integration is vital for ensuring social cohesion and empowering migrants. Besides protecting immigrants' rights, regardless of their migratory status, destination countries can better benefit from the contribution immigrants can make to development by improving the functioning of labour markets, the quality of education and the access to social protection and health. Effective integration policies in countries of destination also have potential beneficial effects on the countries of origin as they may foster productive linkages between the diaspora and the country of origin. Better data and further research on the impacts of migration will enable a thorough understanding of the costs and benefits of migration, and help design better policies. Public information campaigns based on this evidence can then contribute to dispelling the myths surrounding migration and changing existing attitudes.

It is also essential to improve international co-operation on regular migration and on handling refugee crises, thereby working towards an effective international migration architecture. Enhanced co-operation between origin and destination countries would lead to better managed and mutually beneficial migration. Mechanisms to govern migration at the global level are also limited, not least because of questions of sovereignty over national borders. Greater co-ordination of mobility is needed to meet the policy challenges that the international community faces. This is particularly important in a context where immigration is increasingly seen as a threat by public opinion and by many policy makers. The successful inclusion of migration-related targets in the Sustainable Development Goals should help establish commitments that can be monitored multilaterally, regionally and nationally. Improved co-operation can span areas such as visa agreements, mutual skills recognition and qualification framework agreements, skills partnerships, and the protection of migrants' rights, among others. The proposed Global Compact for Safe, Orderly and Regular Migration is a positive step towards more effective international co-operation. More timely, bold and innovative efforts to address the refugee crisis are also needed: in this respect, the Global Compact on Refugees will be an important element towards creating a robust framework to deal with future refugee crises.

The OECD and its Development Centre stand ready to help move this agenda forward with analysis, policy dialogue and advice and to support governments in maximising the potential contribution of migration to sustainable development.

Angel Gurría
Secretary-General, OECD

Executive summary

Global economic development is boosting migration

Some 243 million people were living outside their country of birth in 2015, accounting for 3.3% of the world's population, up from 2.7% in 1995. The shift in global economic activity towards developing countries (low- and middle-income countries) in the last two decades has not led to a parallel shift in migration towards these countries. Using a new three-way classification of countries to explore the impact of shifting wealth on migration, this report shows that migrants are instead increasingly attracted to traditional, high-income destination countries. Between 1995 and 2015, the share of immigrants to these countries increased by 13 percentage points to nearly two-thirds of the world total. Furthermore, economic development in developing countries has boosted international migration as more people have the financial resources needed to migrate.

People are drawn to these destinations not just by higher incomes but also by higher levels of well-being. Despite progress in many developing economies, the gap in incomes with high-income countries has been increasing and differences in well-being remain large. The presence of migrant networks (family, friends and community) already living in traditional destination countries also helps to reduce the costs of migration, thereby reinforcing the concentration in a few preferred destinations.

Public policies also influence migration. A broad array of policies, beyond migration policies, influence migration flows and patterns in many, often complex ways. Understanding them is central to maximise the benefits and minimise the costs of migration for both origin and destination countries and migrants themselves.

While most international migrants move voluntarily, some are forced by armed conflict or violence. By the end of 2015, refugee numbers totalled 16.1 million. Contrary to other international migrants, most refugees – 87% – are accommodated in developing countries.

Making migration a driver of development

International migration presents an opportunity for countries of origin and destination and for migrants themselves. However, the benefits from migration are not yet fully realised and more needs to be done to reap the gains from an increasingly mobile world. In a context where more people are aspiring to migrate than can actually do so, a three-pronged approach is needed to ensure that migration can be a driver of development.

The first prong: Designing policies that incorporate the development dimension

Migration is not a prerequisite for development, yet it can contribute significantly to the development of countries of both origin and destination. Policy makers should design migration and development strategies to minimise the costs induced by human mobility and maximise its benefits.

In countries of origin, policy objectives include lowering the costs of remittances and channelling them towards productive investments, bringing diasporas into development initiatives, attracting back and reintegrating emigrants, and providing support to families who stay behind. If countries are concerned about high rates of emigration, efforts need to be redoubled to improve conditions at home, in particular creating decent jobs and improving well-being.

In countries receiving migrants, measures include improving labour markets, reducing the size of the informal sector, expanding the fiscal base, and strengthening financial markets to maximise the economic benefits of immigration, promoting integration and social cohesion by providing language training, education and health benefits to immigrants, protecting immigrants' rights regardless of their migratory status, and designing communication strategies to change public attitudes on immigration.

Policy makers across sectors also need to take better account of the interrelations between migration policy and other public policies by integrating migration into their development strategies.

The second prong: Fostering policy and institutional coherence

Policy makers should aim to promote a better co-ordination of public initiatives to enhance the contribution of migration to development. Better policy coherence can help balance policy trade-offs in a way that is sensitive to the needs and well-being of all stakeholders, especially migrants.

Achieving policy and institutional coherence at the domestic level requires adopting mechanisms to facilitate intra-governmental co-ordination, encouraging local initiatives since local authorities are often at the forefront of managing immigration, and promoting consultation and partnerships with non-governmental actors who have a stake in migration and development.

Policies in one country also have spillover effects on other countries. For example, trade protectionism in high-income countries, especially in the agricultural and textile sectors, constitutes a barrier to the development of low-wage countries and therefore contributes indirectly to increasing migration pressures from developing countries. Therefore policy makers need to take into account these trade-offs to have more coherent policies.

The third prong: Strengthening international co-operation

The international community needs to strengthen co-operation mechanisms to address the present and future shared migration challenges.

Bilateral agreements can improve the benefits and efficiency of migration. Examples are visa agreements to adjust the number of visas to the changing situation in both countries, mutual skills recognition and qualification framework agreements, partnerships to develop skills, and pension portability.

To encourage regional mobility, countries could include free mobility in their regional trade agreements and regional employment agencies could provide workers with information about jobs available in other countries.

The global governance of international migration is currently limited. The inclusion of migration-related targets in the Sustainable Development Goals should establish commitments that can be monitored multilaterally, regionally and nationally. The Global Compact on Refugees and a Global Compact for Safe, Orderly and Regular Migration that are scheduled to be adopted in 2018 would be further welcome additions to the global governance architecture.

Responding to refugee crises requires greater international solidarity. High-income countries should help refugee host countries by providing more financing, by developing resettlement agreements and by increasing access to alternative pathways for refugees (e.g. labour migration, student visas).

Migration is an important dimension of globalisation and will become more important in the future. Better data, more research and evidence-based policy action are needed. The international community must find durable solutions that will address the future challenges of an increasingly mobile world and to resolve situations that precipitate spikes of desperate people seeking escape from wars. Much more needs to be done to foster sustainable development and harness the contributions of migration to it.

Perspectives on Global Development 2017
International Migration in a Shifting World
© OECD 2016

Chapter 1

Overview: International migration and development in a shifting world

This overview chapter summarises the key findings and sets out the policy recommendations of this edition of Perspectives on Global Development *which focuses on international migration. The report helps dispel the myths and enrich the debate on migration and development by highlighting the main trends and drivers of international migration in the context of shifting wealth; analysing the impact of migration on developing countries of origin and destination; making recommendations to governments in origin and destination countries, as well as to the international community, about policies that could help to improve the contribution of migration to development; and discussing potential scenarios on the future of migration. The overview chapter finishes by presenting a brief roadmap that describes the rest of the report.*

This is the fifth report in the series *Perspectives on Global Development*. As is the custom, the report starts with an overview of global development from the perspective of developing countries, with an emphasis on shifting wealth – the movement of economic activity to developing countries. The rest of the report then focuses on the relationship between shifting wealth and international migration.

International migration has become a very sensitive issue on most policy agendas. This is the case in Europe, where recurrent images of individuals trying to cross terrestrial or maritime borders irregularly has raised concerns about the capacity of host countries to deal with large inflows of foreigners. Concerns exist in many parts of the world where immigrants are seen as competitors in the labour market, a cost for public finances, and a threat to social cohesion and security. The increase in terrorist attacks, which many citizens associate with a failure of integration policies, also has contributed to reinforcing negative perceptions and feeding the global surge in anti-immigration sentiment.

This problem of perception is strengthened by the fact that many people, including policy makers, overestimate the size of the migrant population in their country. They also tend to misunderstand the effects of migration, both in countries of origin and destination. Public opinion usually overstates the costs of migration for countries of origin – such as the exodus of highly skilled individuals, the so-called brain drain – and the lack of integration in countries of destination. Conversely, citizens usually underestimate the benefits of migration, for instance those related to the remittances sent by emigrants to their home countries or the fiscal contribution of immigrants in host countries.

The purpose of *Perspectives on Global Development 2017* is to help dispel the myths and enrich the debate on migration and development by:

- highlighting the main trends and drivers of international migration in the context of shifting wealth
- analysing the impact of migration on developing countries of origin and destination
- making recommendations to governments in origin and destination countries, as well as to the international community, about policies that could help to improve the contribution of migration to development
- discussing potential scenarios on the future of migration.

The main message of this report is that migration can be expected to become an increasingly important matter, requiring greater attention from policy makers in developing and developed countries. Global migration is likely to increase, both in absolute numbers and as a proportion of the world population. The confluence of demographic trends, prospects for job creation and environmental changes point to an uncertain picture for the future of global migration, but one in which better management of migration becomes imperative. Policy makers will have to take into account the impact of migration and non-migration policies on development and vice versa. Key destination countries are likely to keep attracting migrants because of continued higher income and better quality of life. Scope exists for improving the benefits of migration to origin countries, destination countries and the migrants themselves, but it will require better policies in both origin and destination countries and greater co-ordination within and across countries. Ultimately, the goal should be to improve quality of life in developing countries by better understanding and integrating migration into policy making.

This overview chapter summarises key findings and sets out policy recommendations before presenting a brief roadmap that describes the rest of the report.

Summary of key findings

Global economic activity is still shifting to developing countries, but at a slower rate

Emerging and developing countries have grown faster than advanced countries since the 2000s. The difference in gross domestic product (GDP) growth rates between advanced countries and emerging and developing countries began to rise surely and steadily in the 2000s, peaking in 2009 during the financial crisis, when advanced economies contracted by 3.4% and emerging and developing economies achieved 3.5% growth (OECD, 2014).

Shifting wealth has led to good progress in improving livelihoods. It has prompted a massive expansion of productive employment in the developing world. Millions of people have emerged from extreme poverty, unskilled workers have seen real increases in their wages, life expectancy has risen and literacy is more widespread than ever.

However, the period of rapid growth in the emerging world may be over. The growth differential between Organisation for Economic Co-operation and Development (OECD) and non-OECD countries has narrowed in recent years, after its peak in 2009. This development is largely the result of a slowdown in some large developing economies, particularly the People's Republic of China, and countries that export natural resources, such as Brazil and the Russian Federation. Global growth prospects are further weakened by several converging trends, including lower commodity prices and weak investment and total factor productivity.

Furthermore, shifting wealth has improved per capita incomes in developing economies, but the income gap with advanced economies has not narrowed greatly and may remain wide in the years to come. For example, countries such as Colombia, Peru, Thailand and Turkey trimmed their income gap with OECD countries by around 10 percentage points between 1990 and 2014, but income in these countries remains below 40% of the OECD average. Job creation has not been fast enough to cope with quickly expanding working-age populations in most developing regions. For every ten additional working-age people, only seven new jobs were created in Southeast Asia and the Pacific, sub-Saharan Africa, and Latin America and the Caribbean. And although wages have been growing faster in developing economies than in advanced economies, they are on average still more than three times lower.

It is against this backdrop of shifting wealth that this year's *Perspectives on Global Development* report investigates the topic of international migration. The large-scale economic transformations witnessed over the last two decades are likely to have an impact on migration. The movement of people is a core component of globalisation, together with the free movement of capital, goods, services and ideas.

To explore whether and how shifting wealth has affected patterns of international migration, this report proposes a new typology that divides countries into three groups based on income level and economic growth performance (Table 1.1). The typology identifies the developing and emerging economies that have experienced extended periods of fast economic growth and thus have contributed to the shifting wealth phenomenon. These countries are referred to as High and Sustained Growth (SG) countries. The migration dynamics of this group are examined in contrast with those of the other two groups: "High-Income by 1995" (HI) countries, many of which can be considered traditional destination countries for migrants, and "Rest of the World" (RW), the group of developing countries that has not experienced high and sustained economic growth.

Table 1.1. **Definition of country classifications**

Category	Income criteria	Economic growth criteria
High-Income by 1995 (HI countries)	Classified as a high-income country in 1995	Experienced sufficient economic growth to be classified as a high-income country in 2016
High and Sustained Growth (SG countries)	Not classified as a high-income country in 1995	Experienced a period of high and sustained economic growth (see criteria described in Annex A
Rest of the World (RW countries)	Not classified as a high-income country in 1995	Did not experience a period of high and sustained economic growth

Migration is increasingly from SG countries to HI countries

Some 243 million people were living outside their country of birth in 2015, accounting for 3.3% of the world's population, up from 2.7% in 1995. Over the last 20 years, the trajectories of migrants have changed.

Countries experiencing high and sustained economic growth should theoretically become more attractive for migrants and potentially divert migration away from traditional corridors. However, this evolution has not occurred. Instead, migration is increasingly concentrated in HI countries. Traditional destination countries accounted for 64% of total migration in 2015, an increase of 13% from 1995 (Figure 1.1). In 2015, all top ten destination countries except Russia were HI countries. The United States remained the most attractive destination for migrants.

Figure 1.1. **Share of global migration by three categories of countries, 1995 versus 2015**

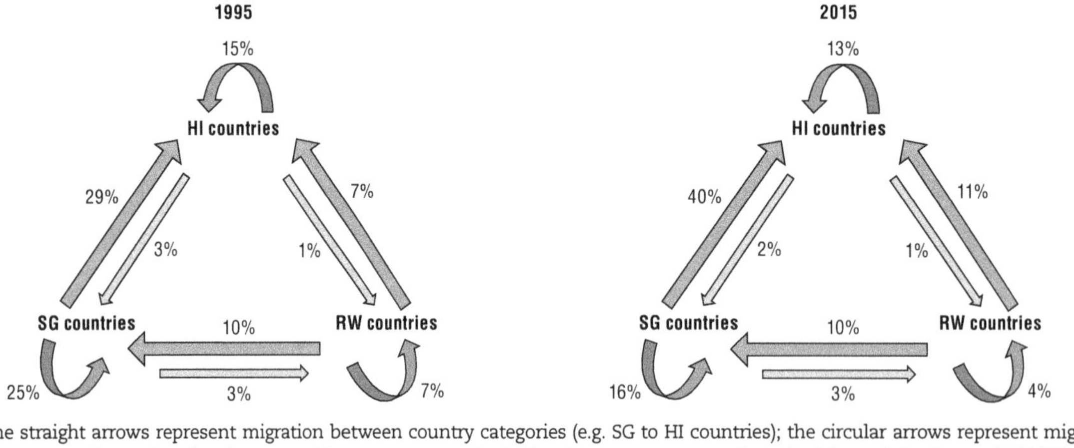

Note: The straight arrows represent migration between country categories (e.g. SG to HI countries); the circular arrows represent migration within a category (e.g. migration from one SG country to another). The shares are computed on the bilateral database of UN (2016) and include 89% of total migration in 1995 and 87% in 2015.

Source: Authors' calculations based on UNDESA (2015), *International Migration Flows to and from Selected Countries: The 2015 Revision* (database), and a new three-way country classification.

Contrary to expectations, high and sustained growth has coincided with an increase in migration from SG countries towards HI countries. In 2015, expatriates from India made up the largest diaspora in the world, accounting for 15.6 million migrants.

This growing migration from SG countries to HI countries is reflected in the top migration corridors. One-fifth of total migration is concentrated among the top 15 country pairs. All of these corridors involved at least one SG country. The corridor between Mexico and the United States remains the largest in terms of the number of migrants. Migration from India to the United Arab Emirates was the second largest corridor in 2015. This corridor is a recent phenomenon, beginning to form in 2005, and exemplifies the effect of recent economic transformations and the evolution of migration policies.

The characteristics of migrants have also changed over the past 20 years. Most migrants belong to the working-age population and are increasingly educated, with roughly equal numbers of men and women.

Migration is driven by differences in income, well-being and migrant networks

The shifting of economic weight of the world towards countries that have undergone recent periods of high and sustained growth has changed the trajectories of migrants. Historical ties, common languages and geographical proximity between countries tend to increase migration flows, and these links continue to influence migration patterns. But shifting wealth has changed other drivers of migration over the past few decades, transforming migration patterns.

Emigration from SG countries to HI countries has increased over the past 20 years. This is in part because, despite their rapid growth, average per capita income differences between SG countries and HI countries have increased.

Migration is also driven by differences in levels of well-being between countries. Well-being worldwide has significantly improved over the past half century, but the gaps between HI and other countries remain large. HI countries score better in such indicators of well-being as political freedom and the extent of democratic institutions.

Even in the absence of economic change, established migration corridors are reinforced by the presence of personal connections between countries of origin and countries of destination. Family, friends and communities abroad attract new migrants by providing funds, information and other forms of support. These migrant networks continue to divert migration away from SG countries and towards HI countries.

Income gains, high levels of well-being and social ties have continued to drive migration towards HI countries over the past two decades. But, more surprisingly, most of the increase in immigration towards HI countries is due to the growing number of emigrants from SG countries. Why is this? Many people across the world aspire to move permanently abroad, but most of those who aspire to migrate do not do so. One reason is that migration is costly. Economic improvements in SG countries have helped many people in these countries to overcome financial constraints and turn their aspirations into reality. An inverted U-shape pattern exists between the percentage of the population outside a developing country relative to its population as the country's per capita income increases. This helps to explain why emigration from SG countries has been rising rather than falling. It also has implications for expectations about the potential future supply of emigration, since many developing countries are below the point at which emigration rates begin to decrease.

New opportunities provided by high and sustained growth particularly help those without a tertiary degree, as highly educated people are more likely already to have the means to migrate. High and sustained growth has coincided with a large increase in educational attainment, which facilitates migration. Nonetheless, economic growth does not necessarily increase the emigration rate of tertiary-educated people. Better opportunities in the country of origin may eventually slow the high emigration rates of people with a tertiary education (Figure 1.2).

Figure 1.2. **GDP per capita affects the proportion of emigrants relative to the population of the origin country by educational achievement, 2010**

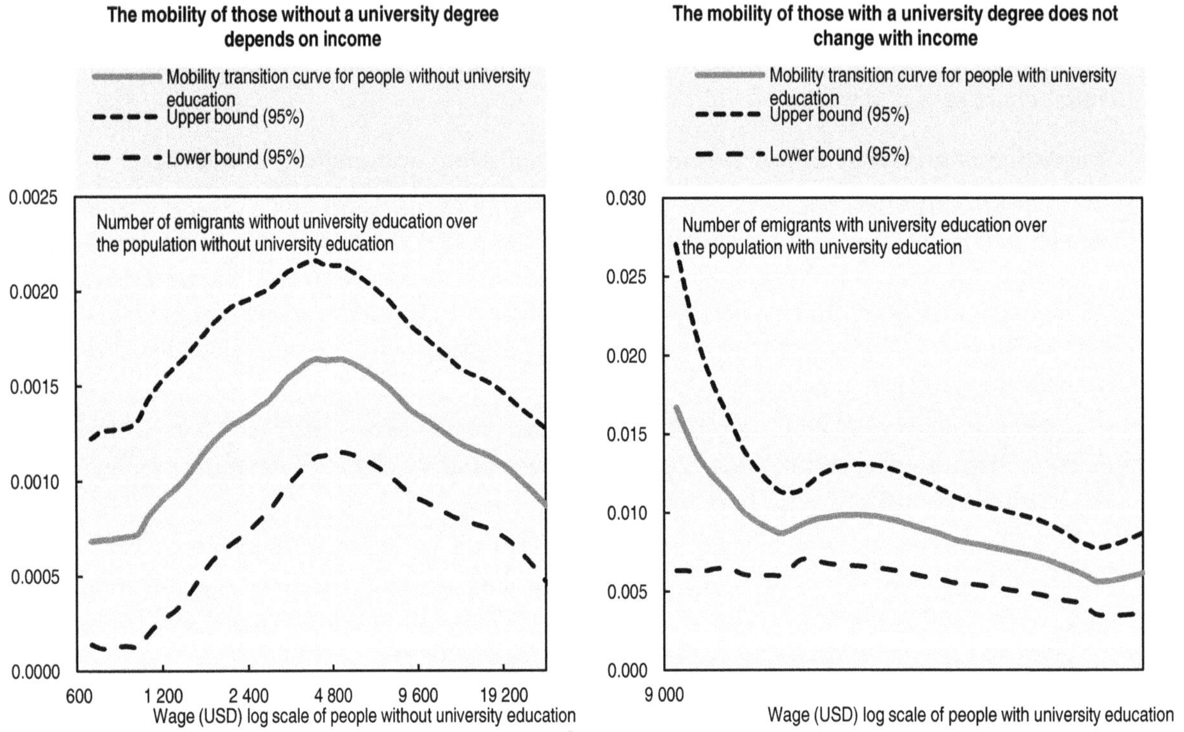

Note: The curve represents the relation between the GDP per capita (logarithmic scale) and the proportion of emigrants in the population of the origin country (specifically, the curve is computed with an Epanechnikov kernel density function that is detailed in Aubry (2016), "Recent economic transformations and migration patterns", *Mimeo*).

Source: Authors' calculations based on data from OECD (2015), *Connecting with Emigrants: A Global Profile of Diasporas 2015*, *http://dx.doi.org/10.1787/9789264239845-en* and World Bank (2016), *World Development Indicators* (database), *http://data.worldbank.org/indicator*.

StatLink http://dx.doi.org/10.1787/888933422067

Public policies affect migration directly and indirectly

Migration policies, as well as other policies that affect migration, are complex and may have contradictory effects on migration flows. One key challenge is the coherence of policy objectives and the integration of migration into development policy strategies.

Contrary to common belief, most countries of destination have not implemented policies to lower immigration. In fact, most have loosened migration policies over the past 20 years and have seen an increase in immigration. Nevertheless, after the 2008/09 economic crisis, a number of HI and SG countries tightened migration policies. Changes in migration policy often coincide with economic change, which simultaneously affects the number of migrants (Figure 1.3).

Figure 1.3. **Yearly average change in migration policy restrictiveness, 1995-2013**

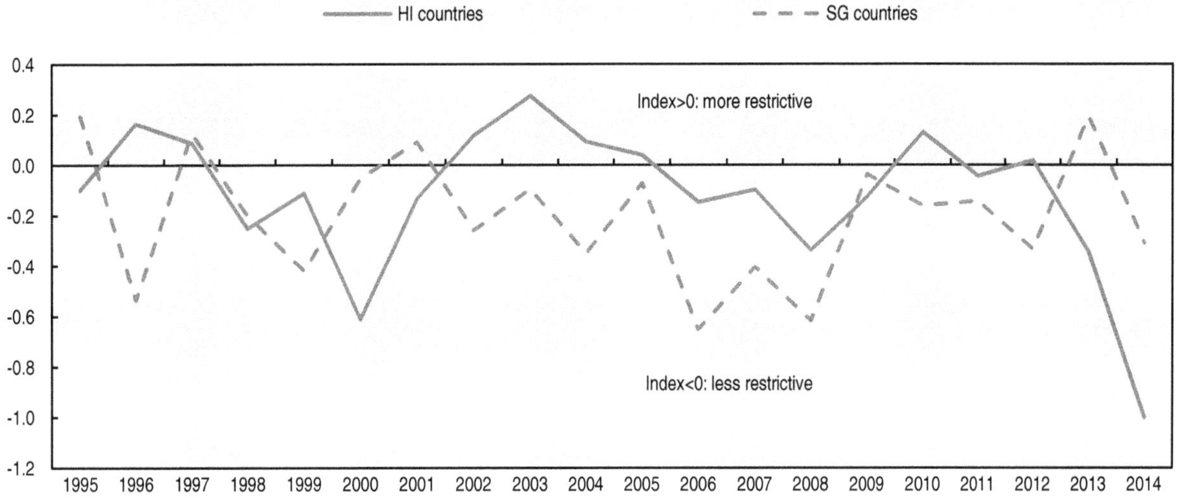

Note: The figure depicts average yearly changes in migration policy restrictiveness for 40 countries from 1995 to 2013. The average is taken across countries and types of policies within a country. A restrictive policy takes the value 1, no change in restrictiveness is coded by the value zero and a less restrictive policy takes the value -1. A score above zero means that the number of restrictive policy changes was larger than the number of less restrictive policy changes. The average should be treated with caution, as for some years the database contains only a small number of recorded policy changes.

Source: Authors' calculations based on DEMIG (2015), *Determinants of International Migration: A Theoretical and Empirical Assessment of Policy, Origin and Destination Effects* (database), *www.imi.ox.ac.uk/data/demig-data/demig-policy-1* and de Haas, Natter and Vezzoli (2014), "Growing restrictiveness or changing selection? The nature and evolution of migration policies", *International Migration Institute Working Papers.*

StatLink http://dx.doi.org/10.1787/888933422079

Policies involving skills and family reunification are becoming more selective across the world. In HI and SG countries, policies increasingly target migrants based on skills, with an increased selection of highly educated workers. Family reunification policies are a major channel of entry for migrants towards OECD countries, but such policies there are tightening. In contrast, family reunification policies are loosening in SG countries.

Other public policies that do not explicitly target migration can nevertheless affect migration patterns. Labour market policies such as government employment agencies and public employment programmes can improve job prospects in developing countries, reducing incentives to emigrate. Technical and vocational training plays a crucial role in building a labour force capable of fulfilling the needs of the domestic economy, but vocational training also can lead to more emigration by facilitating employment abroad. The quality of the education system can be a driver of migration. Parents with school-aged children may decide to migrate to provide a better education for their children. Cash transfers that are conditional on children attending school can deter migration.

Risk and uncertainty can push people to migrate towards destination countries with strong social safety nets. Health care, work-related benefits and formal labour contracts improve well-being and play an important role in decisions on whether to migrate or to remain in the country of birth. While the provision of social security in origin countries can free up funds for individuals who may use the extra money to migrate, evidence shows that more public social spending is likely to reduce emigration.

Refugee numbers are reaching historically high levels

Armed conflict and the threat of violence have driven millions of people from their homes and across international borders in search of safety. By the end of 2015, refugee numbers totalled 16.1 million, with a further 3.2 million asylum seekers (UNHCR, 2016). This new era of high refugee numbers is being driven largely by the conflict in the Syrian Arab Republic (hereafter "Syria"), although refugee crises are by no means limited to the Middle East-to-Europe corridor that is currently dominating the headlines. Nevertheless, a handful of countries account for the majority of the world's refugees. More than 50% of current refugees are from just three countries: Syria, Afghanistan, and Somalia.

People fleeing conflict and violence overwhelmingly seek refuge in neighbouring countries, often following the route of previous migration flows. Beyond their search for safety, their decisions about where to flee are influenced by social, cultural and, to a lesser extent, economic factors. Contrary to other international migrants, most refugees are accommodated in developing countries: 87% of refugees live in low- and middle-income countries. Turkey, Pakistan and Lebanon host the largest numbers of refugees.

Refugee situations are tending to last longer due to slow progress in the three sustainable solutions: return, resettlement and integration. Refugees are often marginalised economically, socially and geographically, yet they bring with them knowledge and skills that they could contribute to their host country if their integration is prioritised.

Migration can have both positive and negative development impacts

Emigration can have positive effects on countries whose citizens move abroad. While losing labour can damage an economy, in certain cases the loss relieves pressure in an over-crowded market, helping to increase wages and reduce unemployment in countries of origin. Emigration can also have a "brain gain" effect by encouraging those left behind to study longer, hence increasing the stock of human capital. Furthermore, emigration brings with it remittances – a stable source of finance that reduces poverty and adds to investment opportunities – while diasporas can contribute to development through innovative financing mechanisms, such as microfinance, collective remittances, long-distance entrepreneurship, diaspora bonds or participation in knowledge networks. Finally, returning migrants bring back with them financial, human and social capital that can help spur development.

But emigration can come with economic, human and social costs. Evidence suggests the main costs are related to labour shortages, negative impacts in terms of human capital and the social repercussions of emigration, especially for those left behind.

Developing countries may also receive significant numbers of immigrants. About 35% of international migrants live at present in low- or middle-income countries. As countries of destination, developing countries may have limited ability to benefit fully from immigration. Imperfect capital and insurance markets, a shortage of fiscal resources and the large share of workers in the informal sector reduce the ability to adapt to change. On the other hand, immigration offers an opportunity for developing countries to expand their skills base, advance their technological development and increase their trade and investment with other countries.

The recommendations section below proposes policies that can minimise the costs of migration and maximise the potential benefits.

Possible future scenarios show that migration will require more policy attention

What might the next decades hold for international migration? Put simply, it is very difficult to know. Some observers may look to the large numbers of young people about to enter the job market in sub-Saharan Africa and South Asia and conclude that unless enough employment can be created, people will move to other countries – perhaps to ageing countries in need of workers – in search of better prospects. Other observers may note that the proportion of the world's population who are migrants has remained fairly stable despite the transformation of the global economy, and conclude that the scale of migration is unlikely to change drastically.

Given the differing views on future trends and the challenges of forecasting, this report develops scenarios to explore alternative futures for migration. Scenarios are not predictions or projections, but rather structured, well thought-out stories that challenge existing world views and assumptions so as to better anticipate plausible, alternative futures.

All the scenarios demonstrate that migration is likely to become an even more important issue in the future as many developing countries, particularly in sub-Saharan Africa and South Asia, are expected to show historically high population growth over the next 15 years, and climate change is likely to create greater migration pressures in the longer term.

Implications of the key findings

The main implication of the findings is that migration is likely to become far more important and will require greater attention from policy makers in developed and developing countries because of the following trends:

- The number of migrants relative to the population of developing countries increases as their per capita income rises. Therefore, the potential supply of migrants relative to the rising populations of developing countries is likely to increase at a rate faster than the growth of their populations.
- The majority of migrants from developing countries tend to go to developed countries. This is because of continuing large gaps in income and well-being between developed and developing countries, and the impact of migrant networks. As noted, a strong tendency is seen for migration from SG and RW countries to HI countries.
- Finally, the number of refugees also may increase, both because of the changing nature of warfare and due to the risk of instability in some developing countries if they cannot productively employ their rapidly growing labour forces.

Policies in both destination countries and developing countries of origin will influence the extent to which these trends lead to an actual increase in emigration, and will help determine the benefits of migration for origin and destination countries, and for the migrants themselves.

The proposals that follow take into account these implications and aim to help policy makers harness migration as an engine for development.

Migration and development: A three-pronged approach

International migration presents an opportunity for countries of origin and destination and for the migrants themselves. In a context where growing numbers are aspiring to migrate, a better policy framework is needed to face today's migration challenges. This report proposes a three-pronged approach:

- First, it is important that countries of origin and destination design policies that incorporate the development dimension.
- Second, policy makers should aim to promote policy and institutional coherence to enhance the contribution of migration to development.
- Third, the international community needs to strengthen co-operation mechanisms to address shared migration challenges.

The first prong: Designing policies that incorporate the development dimension

Migration is not a prerequisite for development, yet it can contribute significantly to the development of countries of both origin and destination. Policy makers should design migration and development strategies to minimise the costs induced by human mobility and maximise its benefits.

Beyond policies directly oriented towards migration, sectoral policies can play a significant role. Yet ministries in charge of these sectors are frequently unaware of the effects of migration on their areas of competency and, conversely, of the effects of their policies on different migration outcomes (OECD, 2016). It is not enough for a government that wants to enhance the contribution of migration to development to adopt migration and development policies. Policy makers across sectors need to take better account of the interrelations between migration policy and other public policies by integrating migration into their development strategies.

Migration and development in countries of origin

The effects of emigration on the development of countries of origin depend widely on the public policies in place. Emigrants represent an opportunity for the countries of origin to accumulate financial and human capital. Remittances can help beneficiaries invest in the education of children and create new businesses or sustain current activities. Diasporas can use their savings to invest in their countries of origin. In some cases, they can even save in their countries of origin, for instance through diaspora bonds. Returning migrants bring back with them the human and financial capital they have accumulated abroad. Policy makers need to implement policies to take advantage of these opportunities. Here are some examples of what could be done.

Lower the costs of remittances and channel them towards productive investment. An important step towards maximising the benefits of remittances was taken with the adoption of the 2015 Addis Ababa Action Agenda (United Nations, 2015a). The agenda includes commitments to ensure that adequate and affordable financial services are available to migrants and their families in countries of origin and destination, and that they can benefit from financial literacy and inclusion.

Remittances are private sources of funding, and policy makers cannot decide how individuals and households spend their money. However, public policies can play an important role in helping migrants and recipients maximise the sending and use of remittances.

The high cost of sending remittances has been one of the main areas of policy intervention. Remittances sent through informal channels limit the ability of households to save and borrow money in the formal financial system. In addition, un-banked households are often subject to higher costs when accessing basic financial services. For such reasons, policies to lower the costs of remittances should promote greater information on the availability and cost of money transfers and try to avoid restrictions and taxes on the remittance inflows as well as any kind of exclusive partnerships with money transfer operators. Initiatives such as the 2014 G20 Leaders' Call to Action on Remittances and the subsequent G20 National Remittance Plans (G20, 2014) are important examples of how governments can engage in making remittances work for development.

To make financial services more available, policy makers need to increase competition among service providers, change regulatory frameworks and expand service provision. They also can invest in improving technology through online and mobile money transfer systems. Priority should be given to initiatives fostering financial inclusion among migrants and remittance recipients, in particular through financial literacy training on topics like banking services, savings and investments.

Migration and development policies should channel remittances towards more productive investments. They can adopt tax exemptions for remittance-related investments and create incentives to attract diaspora investments, for instance through savings accounts in foreign currency, diaspora bonds and matching grants targeting the diaspora, such as Mexico's *Tres por Uno* programme.

Policies to make the financial sector more accessible to all parts of the population can boost the amount of remittances sent and channel them into formal financial systems. It is important that financial inclusion and access to credit extends beyond migrant households, as households without migrants also receive remittances from family and friends, and non-receiving households can benefit from multiplier effects from remittances. Particular emphasis should be put on access to financial services by women, as they play a key role in remittance investments, but often face higher barriers.

Bring diasporas into development initiatives. Because diasporas can play an active role in the development of their countries of origin, many governments have tried to strengthen links with their nationals abroad. But policy efforts are not always successful. Emigrants who left their countries in difficult economic or political times do not always look favourably at governmental initiatives. The issue of trust is at the core of any relationship between public institutions and diasporas. In addition, policy makers need to take into account the multiplicity of associations and networks that compose diasporas.

Matching grants schemes, where the national and local authorities of home communities add funds to the collective remittances sent by hometown associations (HTAs), represents an opportunity for migrants to contribute not only to the welfare of their own families, but also to economic and social development projects. The government can benefit from the involvement of the diaspora in their local communities to increase public investment in other areas that need it more.

Similarly, public authorities can help strengthen scientific diasporas. Highly skilled emigrants can contribute to research projects that are linked to the development of their home countries. Diaspora knowledge networks (DKNs) are a way to consolidate links with members of the scientific community abroad and can help transfer technology and knowledge, even in developing countries with weak research institutions (Meyer, 2015). India, for example, used diaspora investments to develop its software industry, even without a strong innovation policy (Devane, 2006).

Make return sustainable by attracting emigrants back and reintegrating them. Because return migration can hold great potential for development in origin countries, return policies in developing countries should focus on two main objectives:

- attract nationals abroad back to the country of origin through both direct and indirect incentives for return
- support the adjustment and resettlement of returning migrants through policies for the productive use of financial, human and social capital acquired abroad.

Financial and non-financial benefits provided to return migrants increase the incentives to go home. These benefits can include tax and duty exemptions related to the transport of personal belongings (offered in, among other countries, Jamaica and Malaysia), salary subsidies (Thailand) or capital provided for the start of micro businesses (Cabo Verde, Georgia and the Philippines).

Armenia is a good example of a country that promotes return migration. It runs a bilingual website with comprehensive information for potential returning migrants. Armenia also organises job fairs in countries where it has strong ties with diaspora networks to help emigrants willing to return find positions in the Armenian labour market.

Sectoral policies also can contribute to creating a favourable environment. Returning migrants need access to jobs that correspond to their skills or the possibility to make productive investments. They also need access to housing and adequate social protection, and their children need a quality education. In other words, the success of return policies depends on the existence of public policies that create favourable conditions to guarantee the long-term sustainability of return migration.

Make the overall enabling environment attractive, especially education. The overall country enabling environment impacts the extent to which people want to emigrate, or to return or invest in the country. Most migrants leave in search of better opportunities. The overall environment affects whether they decide to return or otherwise contribute to their home country.

Education can play an important role in the decision to migrate. Skilled individuals are more likely to migrate, since international demand for them is high. In the short run this can represent a cost to the country, particularly if the education is publicly financed. However, educated migrants may send back more remittances and contribute human and financial capital that can offset the cost of the brain drain. In addition, the emigration of persons with higher education may entice more people to seek higher education in the hope of emigrating. Since most of them may not emigrate, the country could experience a net gain. On the other hand, if education and skills correspond to the needs of the domestic labour market, the probability of finding a good job locally increases and fewer people will be interested in moving abroad. In addition, an increase in the demand for educational services from remittance-receiving households requires investments in the supply of educational services. Thus, as part of their development strategy, governments need to weigh the relationship between education and migration. Stronger co-operation is required among policy makers, educational institutions and employers.

Provide support to those who stay behind. When countries of origin try to build a migration and development strategy, they usually focus on the positive effects of emigration, but tend to forget the costs. Policy makers in origin countries must understand the costs of emigration on family members left behind, and adjust their policies.

Family members staying behind deserve special attention, as do carers for the migrants' children – and, increasingly, parents. Policy makers can provide legal, social and financial assistance to households with absent parents, as is the case in the Philippines and Sri Lanka, and psychological support can be offered to people left behind who suffer from mental health issues and depression. Specific support can be given to those who remain in charge of the household and need to deal with new responsibilities. This is the case for women, especially in countries affected by high gender discrimination, but also for men who also have to deal with new responsibilities. Targeted training, including financial literacy, can help empower them and bring them actively into local development.

Migration and development in countries of destination

Although a growing number of developing countries have become countries of destination, policies for maximising the economic contribution of immigration and for facilitating integration remain limited. This section focuses on recommendations for developing countries of destination – the subject of the OECD Development Centre's recent research. However, most policies suggested below are relevant for developed countries of destination too, and draw on the OECD's long-standing work on policies for OECD countries of destination, including policies for integration (see, for example, OECD, 2014).

Policy makers often do not see the need for specific integration policies in countries of destination. They might consider it better to use scarce financial resources for the native population rather than for immigrants. However, integration is important even in the poorest countries. The lack of inclusion might generate serious problems of social cohesion, which in some cases can even translate into riots and political turmoil.

Non-migration policies play a key role in countries of destination. First, the policy environment can strengthen the attractiveness of the destination, which is important for countries that need foreign labour to fill skills shortages. Second, public policies can help leverage the impact of immigration on the host country's economy. Third, public policies can ease the integration process.

Non-migration policies can determine the types of individuals who immigrate to the country and whether those immigrants are channelled in the best way. As many developing countries suffer from the loss of skilled workers, attracting and retaining educated workers is key to sustained growth. In this respect, education and social protection systems are an important complement to the job opportunities and wages offered by the labour market.

Key considerations include: designing communication strategies to change perceptions about immigration, maximising immigration's impact on development, creating an environment that facilitates integration and protecting the rights of immigrants regardless of their migratory status.

Design communication strategies to change perceptions about immigrants. The 2015 Addis Ababa Action Agenda (UN, 2015a) emphasises the importance of adopting communication strategies to explain how migrants contribute to development. This is particularly important in countries of destination, where the positive role of immigrants is often overlooked while negative impacts tend to be overestimated. Changing perceptions about migrants implies, first, that local populations know more about the real weight of immigration in their countries.

Negative feelings about immigration often are related to misperceptions about the real dimension of the migration phenomenon. Most people tend to overestimate the importance of immigration in their countries. In a 2015 survey conducted by Ipsos MORI in 33 countries (22 OECD member countries and 11 non-member countries),[1] interviewees from all countries, except Israel and Saudi Arabia, considered that the population born abroad (as a share of total population) was above real numbers. The gap between estimates and actual figures was huge in some countries, especially Argentina (30% according to the public, 5% in reality), Brazil (25% versus 0.3%) and South Africa (29% versus 5%).

A second step towards changing perceptions requires acknowledging an economy's need for foreign workers and recognising the economic contributions immigrants make to the host country. Most countries need immigrants to fill temporary labour shortages or more structural skills gaps. Even countries with a long emigration tradition face shortages. This is the case of countries like the Dominican Republic and Lebanon, where a significant number of people have emigrated in search of better wages and job opportunities, but where local populations do not want to occupy vacant jobs, particularly the dirtiest and most dangerous and demeaning ones.

To be credible, a communication strategy needs to address the costs associated with immigration, in particular the potential negative effects on social cohesion. This is precisely why it is so important to protect immigrants' rights and to implement concrete integration and anti-discrimination policies.

Maximise the impact of immigration on development. The impact of immigration on the development of destination countries varies. In some countries, immigration can have a negative impact on the wages of native workers, especially the lowest skilled, while in others the impact is positive. This depends a lot on the skills of local and foreign labour forces. In this respect, public policies to select the type of migrants that complement rather than compete with the domestic population can help reduce the potential negative effects of immigration.

Labour market policies can help both native and immigrant workers find the jobs that best correspond to their skills by developing better information systems, through an extended network of employment agencies, and by avoiding restrictions on labour mobility. This includes allowing migrants to change employers. Education and skills policies can provide increased training opportunities and better matching of jobs and skills.

Taxation and expenditure policies also affect the net contribution of immigrants. In many developing countries, immigrants are overrepresented in informal sectors. To maximise the fiscal contribution of immigrants, destination countries should foster growth of the formal sector, or strengthen tax and contribution payments from the informal one.

Create an environment that facilitates integration. The success of integration does not always rely on specific integration policies, but rather on the fact that public services have universal coverage, including for immigrants. Likewise, if the conditions for access to credit and investment are the same for native and immigrant populations, specific policies targeting immigrants are not always required.

The well-being of immigrants is essential both to their human development and to their potential as broader agents of development (Rudiger and Spencer, 2003). For example, if skilled migrants do not master the language of the host country, they will be less likely to find a job that corresponds to their real competencies. As a result, the host society will experience brain waste: a loss in potential assets for its development. Lack of integration, in a context of racism and discrimination, can also translate into more problems of marginalisation and violence in a society.

Education represents one of the main keys to integration, for both the first generation of immigrants and the second. The main challenge for developing countries is to address the financial cost of this investment, above all when native children do not always benefit from good education standards. Host countries also should adopt housing strategies to avoid concentrating migrants in the poorest areas so as to promote economic and social inclusion and the second generation's social mobility.

Countries of destination should also consider mechanisms to better manage immigration taking into account the needs of the country and the rights of migrants. This can include more visas for low-skilled work depending on market needs, expanding temporary visas for seasonal work in sectors such as agriculture and tourism, allowing migrants to extend their visas when conditions warrant it (UNDP, 2009). Countries of destination should allow immigrants to establish businesses and provide them with training and financial support to do so. In some cases, migrant entrepreneurship emerges from the difficulties foreign workers face in finding a job that corresponds to their skills. Finally, countries of destination should consider pathways to allow immigrants to convert temporary visas into permanent residency based on some years of a good job performance and no criminal convictions. Permanent residency can eventually be converted into citizenship after a reasonable period of time to be determined by the country. Dual citizenship also should be allowed to help immigrants maintain the link with their countries of origin while becoming full citizens of their host countries.

Protect immigrants' rights, regardless of their migratory status. The need to protect the rights of migrants and their families is based on the normative principle that the dignity of migrants is a fundamental goal in itself. It rests on the idea that the respect for migrants' rights contributes to economic development. When host countries adopt active policies to protect migrants' socio-economic and political rights, the well-being of immigrants increases, which helps foster human capital (Kerwin, 2013).

Against this backdrop, countries of destination should provide comprehensive health care and education to all migrants, regardless of status and time spent in the country. Immigrants should have access to the labour market and be allowed to join trade unions and form associations. Not just national but also local authorities can help protect immigrants' rights. One effective measure is to establish local redress mechanisms that provide immigrants with support, especially legal aid, and with information about rights and procedures, and assistance in reporting abuses.

In addition, countries of destination can sign bilateral agreements with the countries of origin to implement standardised contracts for migrant workers that cover basic rights, working conditions, wages, pension portability, etc. They need to adopt concrete measures to combat racism and discrimination, which represent serious obstacles to the integration of immigrants.

Countries of origin also have important responsibilities in ensuring that emigrants' rights are respected. Emigration comes with many risks for those who migrate without documents, who are victims of human trafficking or who leave their children with other people. Information campaigns in schools and in the media, especially social media, and pre-departure courses are efficient ways of making potential migrants aware of such risks. Countries of emigration should develop their consular activities abroad so that emigrants can benefit from adequate protection in the countries of destination. Some countries, such as Colombia, have appointed labour and/or social attachés in their consulates to advise migrants about their rights.

Finally, origin countries should contribute to the integration of their citizens in host countries. By developing mechanisms in partnership with the main countries of destination, such as mutual recognition agreements and qualifications frameworks, countries of origin help their citizens gain access to the labour market in host countries. Like countries of destination, origin countries should allow their citizens to have dual citizenship to guarantee that they will be able to integrate in the best conditions into their host societies, while contributing to the development of their home communities.

The second prong: Fostering policy and institutional coherence

Mainstreaming migration into development planning does not mean that policies are coherent. In several countries, different ministries across sectors have tried to integrate the migration dimension into their strategies. That was the case until recently in the Philippines where the departments in charge of labour, education and social affairs, as well as the Central Bank, all had programmes targeting emigrants and their families. Yet no formal co-ordination mechanism was in place to ensure that public policies did not overlap or even conflict with each other. Only in 2014 did Philippine authorities create a Sub-Committee on Migration and Development (SCMD) for better co-ordination of public initiatives on migration.

Policy coherence is an essential tool for helping policy makers harness migration as an engine for development. While incoherence can increase the likelihood of unfulfilled development commitments and result in financial costs and wasted resources (OECD, 2009), coherence can help balance policy trade-offs in a way that is sensitive to the needs and well-being of all stakeholders, especially migrants. Pursuing coherence can lead to increased efficiency and foster an environment in which partners share a strengthened consensus on policy priorities, a more holistic understanding of migration issues and an enhanced sense of "being in it together" (Hong and Knoll, 2016).

In this respect, the Global Knowledge Partnership on Migration and Development (KNOMAD) has a Thematic Working Group (TWG) on Policy and Institutional Coherence – currently chaired by the OECD Development Centre and the UN Development Programme (UNDP) – that seeks to address the need for improved coherence in the realm of migration and development in countries of origin and destination.[2] The TWG developed a dashboard of indicators for measuring policy and institutional coherence for migration and development (Khoudour and Meddeb, 2015).

Policy and institutional coherence implies not just co-ordinating actions at the domestic level, but also taking account of the spillover effects of domestic policies on the development of other countries.

Better co-ordination at the domestic level

Achieving policy and institutional coherence at the intra-governmental level, i.e. within one government, requires commitment to migration and development objectives, clarity around the distinct roles and interests of different policy fields, and strong horizontal and vertical co-ordination and co-operation between actors with a stake in migration and development (GFMD, 2012).

Adopt mechanisms to facilitate intra-governmental co-ordination. Policy and institutional coherence across public authorities is crucial for enhancing the contribution of migration to development. As far as institutional set-ups go, countries may draw on different types of co-ordination mechanisms (Hong and Knoll, 2016).

Policy makers can take a centralised or decentralised approach. Generally, under decentralisation, the migration and development dossier is divided among different ministries or agencies, each of which has its own specific migration-related responsibilities. Under this approach, strong co-ordination, for example through inter-ministerial working groups, is indispensable. Meanwhile, within centralised set-ups, one entity, such as a migration ministry, is responsible for overseeing and co-ordinating the implementation of migration and development policies.

Ideally, both types of set-up complement each other so that centralised responsibility is combined with a common understanding of policy and institutional coherence among all institutions and partners with a stake in migration and development. Each country should determine what kind of approach fits its system of government better.

Encourage local initiatives. An exclusive national lens does not take into account the broadly varied local migratory contexts within countries. In a world marked by rapid urbanisation, the majority of migrants and displaced populations are moving to urban areas. The direct consequence is that the drivers and impacts of migration are mostly felt at the local level, through effects on the labour market, the size and demographics of local populations, and the need for public service provision.

Cities and other local and regional authorities thus find themselves directly and increasingly responsible for a wide range of issues related to integration, reintegration, access to the labour market, legal protection, education, economic development and health. The Joint Migration and Development Initiative,[3] which started operations in 2008, has shown that initiatives that are strongly anchored with local and regional authorities (LRAs) and local development priorities have a more far-reaching and sustainable development impact.

LRAs need to carry out mapping exercises, consultations with pertinent actors, migrants and their families, and needs-based assessments to adjust local policies to respond to the specific migratory context. This has been achieved most successfully where LRAs facing high migration flows have engaged firmly in improving policy coherence in local development planning.

Promote dialogue with non-governmental actors. Coherence requires mechanisms for consultation and partnerships with civil society, trade unions, media, the private sector and migrants themselves. Widespread consultations can strengthen coherence in two ways. First, they foster co-operation among a range of actors around common objectives. Second, the unique insights of different stakeholders on how certain policies affect the migration-development nexus – and can benefit or disadvantage migrants – can systematically feed back into policy making and act as an external accountability check for governments (GFMD, 2012).

Although not all stakeholders pursue the same objectives or align their interests to sustainable development goals, peaceful disagreement among stakeholders over divergent interests is a normal feature of democratic societies (Ashoff, 2005). While some conflicts of interest and objectives may be irresolvable, compromise-based solutions may be better than having no engagement whatsoever among different stakeholders (Hong and Knoll, 2016).

Sharper focus on the repercussions of policy decisions on migrants and their countries of origin

Policies in one country not only have repercussions in the country itself, but also have spillover effects on other countries. This particularly applies in the field of migration and development, first because sectoral policies can increase migration pressures from developing countries and second because migration policies that have been cobbled together over time with different objectives and in response to different conditions may not be coherent.

In seeking to reduce immigration, consider the effects of policies like development assistance. Even though the links between aid and migration are not always straightforward, it might seem inconsistent to reduce development assistance while trying to control immigration (OECD, 2011). A more coherent co-operation policy could focus on helping developing countries enhance their social protection systems to provide universal access for local populations. Policies aimed at creating stable jobs and training people based on the needs of the labour markets of the countries of origin, along with better social protection systems in those countries, could be more efficient in controlling migration flows than migration policies themselves.

Likewise, trade protectionism, especially in the agricultural and textile sectors, constitutes a barrier to the development of low-wage countries (Cervantes-Godoy and Dewbre, 2010). Such policies therefore contribute indirectly to increasing migration pressures from developing countries (Anderson, Cockburn and Martin, 2011). From the perspective of trying to reduce migration flows, it would be coherent to try to lower tariffs in the sectors where developing countries have comparative advantages so that workers have more employment opportunities at home. However, protectionism is driven by specific sectoral interests, so the trade-offs between different interests and policy objectives need to be factored in.

Re-examine the coherence of migration policies. Sometimes migration policies work at cross purposes, and the effect of restrictions can be different than intended. For example, worker shortages that migrants could fill in some sectors may go unfilled when overall migration policies are tightened. And the tightening of formal immigration requirements can lead to increased undocumented migration, since migrants already in the country may overstay their visas because they know it will be harder to get back in.

In the last two decades, migration policies have often been determined in response to economic and political shocks. For instance, migration policies were tightened following the 2008/09 economic crisis (OECD, 2012). After 2013, when the economic situation progressively improved, fewer changes were made. When the reasons behind migration policies change, however, their objectives may no longer be appropriate (for example, restrictions or selection of particular migrants). Mismatches and changes in migration policies are costly. Such changes may alter the effect of other migration policies and consequently threaten the coherence of the country's overall migration strategy.

Restrictive policies can also have a large financial cost. Policies for reinforcing border controls require large resources. Restrictive migration policies in response to crises have a human cost as well, as they affect people who are not responsible for the crisis. People aspiring to better economic and social prospects may decide to choose a dangerous pathway to realise their objectives. In such circumstances, migrants are more liable to be victims of human trafficking and labour exploitation. The number of people who die trying to cross borders is related to migration policies. According to the Missing Migrants Project,[4] implemented by the International Organization for Migration (IOM), 4 320 migrant deaths were recorded worldwide between 1 January and 12 September 2016. In the Mediterranean region alone, 3 207 individuals died during this period trying to reach Europe's shores.

The third prong: Strengthening international co-operation

The Addis Ababa Action Agenda (United Nations, 2015a) and the 2030 Agenda for Sustainable Development (United Nations, 2015b) recognise international migration as "a multidimensional reality of major relevance for the development of countries of origin, transit and destination". In this respect, the Sustainable Development Goals (SDGs) highlight the needs to protect the rights of migrants (Goal 8.8), facilitate migration through well-managed migration policies (Goal 10.7) and reduce to less than 3% the costs of sending remittances by 2030 (Goal 10.c).

The global consensus around the role of international migration in fuelling development represents an opportunity to boost international co-operation. The 2006 and 2013 High-Level Dialogues on Migration and Development, and the Global Forum on Migration and Development (GFMD), held annually since 2007, have been the space where policy makers have shared country-specific experiences and discussed good practices. Yet because their recommendations are not binding, these meetings have not translated into international agreements or normative decisions. The new development agenda might thus create momentum for increased international co-ordination mechanisms on migration issues.

International co-operation can be strengthened by rethinking and improving the global governance of migration, developing bilateral agreements between destination and origin countries, encouraging global skills partnerships, fostering regional mobility, addressing environment-related migration and sharing refugee responsibility.

Rethinking and improving the international governance of migration

In the New York Declaration for Refugees and Migrants adopted during the UN Summit on Refugees & Migrants held on 19 September 2016, the General Assembly stressed the need for collaboration to maximise the positive impact of migration and ensure that the human rights of migrants are respected and protected regardless of their status (United Nations, 2016). Similarly, Peter Sutherland (2013), the UN Secretary-General's special representative for international migration and development, has stressed the role of international co-operation in achieving "triple wins" – positive outcomes for countries of origin, countries of destination and for migrants themselves. The current refugee crisis has revealed the limits of international co-operation, as many countries have decided not to assume the common responsibility of hosting asylum seekers on their soil. The General Assembly proposed to support countries receiving and hosting large numbers of refugees and migrants by implementing a new framework that sets out the responsibility of the different stakeholders.

At present, the "governance" of international migration is characterised by a significant lack of co-operation. While trade and finance have been greatly integrated, migration policies have not. A significant gap in the field of international migration persists at the multilateral level (OECD, 2011). The Global Migration Group (GMG), an inter-UN agency initiative, and the state-led GFMD are important initiatives that underpin a more coherent global approach to migration and development. Yet they remain informal arrangements: follow-up of their recommendations cannot be enforced. The IOM, which in July 2016 became a "related organisation" of the United Nations, neither co-ordinates nor supervises migration policies (as, for example, the World Trade Organization regulates trade negotiations). It rather focuses on providing migration services to member states and migrants, such as recruitment, selection, orientation and, in some cases, repatriation.

The main reason for the difficulty in co-operating on migration is linked to the big income differentials between the main receiving and destination countries. While workers from low-wage countries may want to migrate to high-wage countries, few from high-wage countries wish to migrate to low-wage countries except to access special high-paying jobs that may be available there. As a result of the asymmetry in benefits, no organised lobby group in the high-wage countries is willing to defend the right for workers to access labour markets outside their country. Negotiation on international migration thus lacks an overarching goal, namely the free movement of people (OECD, 2011; Hatton and Williamson, 2005).

However, the lack of reciprocity is more illusory than real. As highlighted above, restrictive migration policies are costly not only for the migrants themselves, but also for the countries that implement restrictions. They are also counterproductive, as strict border controls tend to generate high levels of irregular immigration. On the other hand, immigrants contribute to the development of countries of destination. There is more room for co-operation than is generally recognised.

The governance of international migration is limited by the fact that most countries do not want to abandon sovereignty over who can enter their territory. Yet greater co-ordination is needed to meet the big challenges that the international community will face regarding increasing pressure for international migration in the next decades. The successful inclusion of migration-related targets in the recently adopted SDGs should, in theory, help establish commitments that can be monitored multilaterally, regionally and nationally. This could open the door to a new governance framework, as suggested during the UN Summit on Refugees & Migrants in 2016 (United Nations, 2016), with strengthened collaboration between the GFMD, the GMG and the UN system as a whole.

Developing bilateral agreements between destination and origin countries

Bilateral agreements constitute a way to increase efficiency in regulating flows while maximising the contribution of migration to development, both in the countries of origin and destination. One common type of mutually beneficial accord involves visa agreements that can reduce the cost of migration and adjust the number of visas to the changing situation in both countries. Another is mutual skills recognition and qualification framework agreements that help certify the skills and qualification of migrants.

Bilateral agreements also can encourage circular mobility by giving migrants the opportunity to cross the border several times. Such arrangements generate benefits for the host country, since immigrants can come in when labour demand is high, particularly for seasonal activities, and tend to return frequently to their home countries. Circular migration also benefits the countries of origin, as migrants can still contribute to local activities, like agriculture. It helps migrants, through the savings they accumulate, develop productive projects in their home communities (OECD, 2011).

Bilateral agreements should also address family reunification, which is a basic right for all migrants but has become a sensitive issue in many countries. Likewise, social and pension portability agreements help migrants circulate more easily, as they know that they are not going to lose their rights if they decide to return home, temporarily or permanently. In this respect, granting permanent visas to immigrants who have worked for at least one decade in the host country is a way to enable them to circulate more easily between the two countries.

Encouraging global skills partnerships

Global skills partnerships (GSP) represent a new way to make skilled migration more beneficial to destination countries, origin countries and migrants (Clemens, 2015). A GSP is an up-front agreement between employers and/or governments in destination countries and professional training centres in origin countries. These parties agree on a practical and equitable way for the benefits of migrants' professional service at the destination to finance training at the origin, for both migrants and non-migrants. Such an agreement allows mutual gains by taking advantage of large international differences in both professional earnings and training costs.

The destination country must work directly with employers to understand their unmet needs and design training around those needs; craft visa policy that allows graduates to enter the country reliably; and co-operate to seek repayment from any graduates who might not fulfil post-graduation work commitments. Both governments must collaborate to ensure that graduates' qualifications and skills are recognised at the destination, with positive effects on the quality of training in the origin country as facilities conform to the destination country's training standards.

Nursing offers one example of a field where a GSP could be arranged. Other forms of technical training could also be suitable, including basic information technology services and skilled trades such as heating systems maintenance. This idea could be adopted by many country pairs where wage and training cost differentials are more than large enough to power a GSP. Designed correctly, a GSP can provide good jobs and professionals without harming the public coffers of the country of origin. This is a better way to strengthen developing nations' employment markets than blocking the migration of skilled people (Clemens, 2015).

Fostering regional mobility

Labour mobility can play an important role as an adjustment mechanism at the regional level. Some mobility agreements exist today. The ASEAN Economic Community (AEC), one of three pillars on which the Association of Southeast Asian Nations is built, established freer mobility of skilled labour in 2015. The agreement allows for labour movement in eight skilled professions across the ten member states. South America's common market, Mercosur, also took greater steps towards freer mobility in 2009. Member-country nationals may reside and work for a period of two years in a host state, and may stay longer if they can prove a legitimate means of living. The agreement has also been ratified by countries outside the Mercosur group.

Regional mobility represents a way to promote a better allocation of human resources and help smooth business cycles, through temporary movements between the countries affected by economic slowdowns and those experiencing rapid growth. By enabling economies to adjust to asymmetric shocks, regional labour mobility contributes to reducing the social costs of economic crises.

To encourage regional mobility, countries should not only include free mobility in their regional trade agreements, but also make sure that people can really move from one country to another. This implies that there are no barriers to work and that citizens can benefit from social protection in any country of the area.

Given that in many developing countries the best jobs are in the public sector, workers from neighbouring countries should be allowed to work as civil servants, at least when they could contribute to reducing skills gaps. This is the case, for instance, for language teachers.

To facilitate labour mobility, regional employment agencies could provide workers with information about available jobs in other countries. Finally, student mobility should be encouraged as a way of overcoming the lack of financial resources in many universities in developing countries. Universities could develop specialties, with students moving to countries where they can specialise. A system of grants could support student mobility across countries (OECD, 2011).

Addressing environment-related migration

Environment-related migration is likely to become a more serious problem as the effects of climate change become more pronounced. Because the environment is a global public good, the international community should collectively address the situation of people affected by natural disasters and environmental changes, for example the problem of rising seawater for island states. In the absence of an adequate international response, a large number of stateless individuals could be denied legal entry to other countries and thus become irregular immigrants. It is therefore urgent to develop appropriate admission policies at the global level (Martin, 2010).

Sharing the refugee responsibility

Refugees fleeing from conflict areas are placed in an inextricable situation. They often endanger their lives to reach safe countries, which many times do not want to receive them and do not respect their basic human rights. Countries that do not want to host refugees often have strengthened border controls, developed detention centres and in some cases erected walls to prevent foreigners from entering their territories. Even countries willing to host large numbers of refugees, such as Germany and Sweden, now face a situation where the huge inflow has created a bottleneck in terms of capacity and might, in the long run, make integration more challenging.

Solutions exist, but they require a more co-ordinated approach. First, it is important to acknowledge that the refugee crisis affects developing countries first and foremost. Some 87% of refugees are hosted in low- and middle-income countries. High-income countries can help these countries of first arrival through financial support and by ensuring safe and legal channels for people to escape from violence and conflict.

Financing for forced displacement requires ensuring that there are sufficient resources of the right type to deliver the expected results, and increasing efficiency – making those resources go further. There is scope for increasing the financing by maintaining and potentially increasing funds from traditional donors alongside efforts to grow newer funding sources such as new donors, private giving, social finance and the private sector. Financial flows also need to be properly layered, matching the needs and risks of different forced displacement situations to the right type of finance. As part of this, the push towards multi-annual funding based on true multi-annual plans has been suggested as an effective approach. Finally, there is also the need to reduce the cost of responses, and recognise that the current financing model is most likely unsustainable. Shifting to greater conflict prevention and preparedness could go some way to reducing the costs of forced displacement situations.

High-income countries also need to develop resettlement agreements with the main countries where refugees first arrive. Resettlement agreements should be discussed at a global level to make sure that all countries assume their responsibilities, based on their population and income per capita. Alternative pathways include labour migration; international study, family migration and humanitarian visas; and private sponsorship arrangements (OECD, 2016).

Countries hosting refugees also need to invest in their economic and social integration. Measures that can help refugees include: shortening their stays in refugee camps; giving them the right to work legally; offering training targeted to local market needs; mainstreaming public service delivery to refugee populations; and taking refugee populations into account in national and local development planning. The OECD Secretary-General, Angel Gurría, stressed the importance of addressing the tension between short-term measures and durable solutions such as the local integration of migrants.

Preparing for greater migration

All of the above proposals can help both to improve the contribution of migration to development and to deal with the humanitarian crises caused by violence and environmentally driven migration. However, in the next 15 years, as has been argued in this report, the potential supply of migrants from developing countries is likely to be large. This has four implications.

First, greater study is needed of trends in migration and its impact on development. This report aims to contribute to this objective, but more needs to be done. Migration is a highly complex and political topic. Also global data are very poor. It is therefore critical to collect data on immigration and emigration more systematically, to ensure that the information is comparable across countries and to support more studies of migration.

Second, emerging countries are likely to receive more immigrants. So far the bulk of the increase in migration is going to HI countries. However, given rapidly increasing populations in many developing countries and the limits to the absorption capacity of developed countries, this pattern may shift. As noted in this report, most developing countries have not created sufficiently comprehensive strategies to deal with migration. They can learn a lot from the experience of developed countries. However, they are more fiscally constrained than developed countries, have very large informal sectors and must address the many pressing needs of their own populations. Therefore, they will need to be more innovative in developing policies that can maximise the benefits of migration for development.

Third, much more needs to be done by the international community to avoid the dire situations that spark refugee crises. Europe is currently seeing the impact of refugees fleeing from war-torn Syria, Afghanistan, Somalia and other countries in strife. But as noted above, nearly 90% of the world's refugees are hosted in low- and middle-income countries, whose resources are being stretched. Thus the international community must try to do more to resolve situations that precipitate spikes of desperate people seeking escape from wars or failed states.

Fourth, much more needs to be done to foster sustainable development. Pressures for migration will ultimately be alleviated only by improving conditions in developing countries. The main reason people migrate is to seek better lives. Working to achieve the Sustainable

Development Goals is critical to improve global well-being. It is likely that, in the short run, greater development will lead to more emigration from developing countries. However, better development policies in those countries can help reduce the need for people to migrate.

Roadmap to the report

The report is structured as follows.

Chapter 2 provides an overview of shifting wealth: the increasing movement of economic activities to developing countries. It also presents a new three-way classification of countries, based on income level and economic growth performance, to explore the links between shifting wealth and migration. Chapter 3 provides a quick overview of the history of migration and summarises trends in migration between 1995 and 2015. Chapter 4 examines the key drivers of migration to explain the evolution of migration patterns between 1995 and 2015, using the new three-way classification defined in this report. It highlights the extent to which not just income differences but quality of life and social ties matter in people's decisions about whether and where to migrate. Chapter 5 examines the impact of migration polices, which seek to increase or decrease immigration through visas, border controls and selection criteria; and non-migration policies, such as those affecting labour markets, the level of social welfare, education, health or subsidies to agriculture, in both the origin and destination countries. Chapter 6 puts the spotlight on refugees, a special case of migration that deserves separate treatment.

Chapters 7 and 8 explore the impact of migration on development. Chapter 7 analyses migration and development from the perspective of developing countries as countries of origin. It uses a new analysis just completed by the OECD Development Centre on ten developing countries, and shows the impact of migration on development and the importance of creating policies to maximise the benefits and reduce the costs of migration. Chapter 8 analyses migration and development from the perspective of developing countries as countries of destination. It summarises the literature, which has been primarily devoted to developed countries, and presents initial findings from the Development Centre on developing countries.

Finally, because migration is such a complex topic and since predicting the future is so uncertain, Chapter 9 explores four potential future scenarios for the year 2030. Its aim is to raise awareness of what is at stake and to sensitise policy makers to some of the issues they may need to confront in the near future.

Notes

1. The Ipsos Perils of Perception Survey ran 25 556 interviews in October 2015. More details on the survey can be found on the survey web page: *www.slideshare.net/IpsosMORI/the-perils-of-perception-in-2015-ipsos-mori* (accessed 21 July 2016).
2. More information about the activities of the KNOMAD Thematic Working Group on Policy and Institutional Coherence project can be found here: *www.oecd.org/dev/migration-development/knomad.htm*.
3. The Joint Migration and Development Initiative is a European Commission and Swiss-funded global programme led by UNDP and implemented in close co-operation with the IOM, the International Labour Organization, UNHCR, UN Women, the United Nations Institute for Training and Research and the United Nations Population Fund.
4. Details of the Missing Migrants Project and updated numbers can be found on the IOM webpage: *http://missingmigrants.iom.int/* (accessed 13 September 2016).

References

Anderson, K., J. Cockburn and W. Martin (2011), "Would freeing up world trade reduce poverty and inequality? The vexed role of agricultural distortions", *World Bank Policy Research Working Paper*, No. 5603, World Bank, Washington, DC.

Ashoff, G. (2005), "Enhancing policy coherence for development: Justification, recognition and approaches to achievement", German Development Institute, Bonn, *http://edoc.vifapol.de/opus/volltexte/2012/3799/pdf/Studies_11.pdf*.

Cervantes-Godoy, D. and J. Dewbre (2010), "Economic importance of agriculture for poverty reduction", *OECD Food, Agriculture and Fisheries Working Papers*, No. 23, OECD Publishing, Paris, *http://dx.doi.org/10.1787/5kmmv9s20944-en*.

Clemens, M. (2015), "Global Skill Partnerships: A proposal for technical training in a mobile world", *IZA Journal of Labour Policy*, Vol. 4(2), Clemens; licensee Springer, *http://dx.doi.org/10.1186/s40173-014-0028-z*.

De Haas, H., K. Natter and S. Vezzoli (2014), "Growing restrictiveness or changing selection? The nature and evolution of migration policies", *International Migration Institute Working Papers*, No. 96, International Migration Institute, Oxford, *www.imi.ox.ac.uk/publications/wp-96-14*.

DEMIG (2015), *Determinants of International Migration: A Theoretical and Empirical Assessment of Policy, Origin and Destination Effects* (database), International Migration Institute, University of Oxford, *www.imi.ox.ac.uk/data/demig-data/demig-policy-1 (accessed 17 June 2016)*.

Devane, R. (2006), "The dynamics of diaspora networks: Lessons of experience", in Y. Kuznetsov (ed.), *Diaspora Networks and the International Migration of Skills*, Washington, DC, pp. 59-67.

G20 (2014), "G20 plan to facilitate remittance flows", *www.g20australia.org/sites/default/files/g20_resources/library/g20_plan_facilitate_remittance_flows.pdf*.

GFMD (2012), "Expert workshop report", GFMD Ad-hoc Working Group on Policy Coherence, Data and Research; Promoting Policy Coherence for Development in International Migration Issues, *Global Forum on Migration and Development*, Brussels, 26 June, *www.gfmd.org/files/documents/GFMD_coherence_workshop_report_260612.pdf*.

Hong, A. and A. Knoll (2016), "Strengthening the migration-development nexus through improved policy and institutional coherence", *KNOMAD Working Paper*, No. 15, World Bank Group, Washington, DC.

Hatton, T.J. and J.G. Williamson (2005), *Global Migration and the World Economy: Two Centuries of Policy and Performance*, The MIT Press, Boston, *https://mitpress.mit.edu/books/global-migration-and-world-economy*.

Kerwin, D. (2013), "Does respect for migrant rights contribute to economic development?", *Policy Brief*, No. 1, Migration Policy Institute, Washington, DC.

Khoudour, D. and R. Meddeb (2015), "Operationalising a dashboard of indicators for measuring policy and institutional coherence for migration and development", PowerPoint presentation, 8th *Global Forum on Migration and Development*, Istanbul.

Martin, S. (2010), "Climate change, migration and governance", *Global Governance: A Review of Multilateralism and International Organizations*, Vol. 16(3), Lynne Rienner Publishers, Inc., pp. 397-413, *http://journals.rienner.com/doi/pdf/10.5555/ggov.2010.16.3.397*.

Meyer, J.-B. (ed.) (2015), *Diaspora: Towards the New Frontier*, IRD UDELAR, *http://horizon.documentation.ird.fr/exl-doc/pleins_textes/divers15-11/010065854.pdf*.

OECD (2016), *International Migration Outlook 2016*, OECD Publishing, Paris, *http://dx.doi.org/10.1787/migr_outlook-2016-en*.

OECD (2015), *Connecting with Emigrants: A Global Profile of Diasporas 2015*, OECD Publishing, Paris, *http://dx.doi.org/10.1787/9789264239845-en*.

OECD (2014), *International Migration Outlook 2014*, OECD Publishing, Paris, *http://dx.doi.org/10.1787/migr_outlook-2014-en*.

OECD (2012), *International Migration Outlook 2012*, OECD Publishing, Paris, *http://dx.doi.org/10.1787/migr_outlook-2012-en*

OECD (2011), *Tackling the Policy Challenges of Migration: Regulation, Integration, Development*, Development Centre Studies, OECD Publishing, Paris, *http://dx.doi.org/10.1787/9789264126398-en*.

OECD (2009), *Building Blocks for Policy Coherence for Development*, OECD Publishing, Paris, *www.oecd.org/pcd/44704030.pdf*.

Rudiger, A. and S. Spencer (2003), "Social integration of migrants and ethnic minorities: Policies to combat discrimination", paper delivered to the conference *The Economic and Social Aspects of Migration*, jointly organised by the European Commission and the OECD, Brussels, 21-22 January.

Sutherland, P. (2013), "A decalogue for the UN Migration Summit", *Project Syndicate*, 1 October, *www.project-syndicate.org/commentary/peter-sutherlandten-commitments-on-migration-that-governments-should-make*.

UNDESA (2015), *International Migration Flows to and from Selected Countries: The 2015 Revision* (database), United Nations Department of Economic and Social Affairs, Population Division, New York, *www.un.org/en/development/desa/population/migration/data/empirical2/migrationflows.shtml*.

UNDP (2009), *Human Development Report – Overcoming Barriers: Human Mobility and Development*, United Nations Development Programme, New York, *http://hdr.undp.org/sites/default/files/reports/269/hdr_2009_en_complete.pdf*.

UNHCR (2016), *Statistical Yearbook 2015*, United Nations High Commissioner for Refugees, *http://popstats.unhcr.org/en/overview#_ga=1.261217871.393378321.1447865158* (accessed 20 June 2016).

United Nations (2016), "New York Declaration for Refugees and Migrants", *http://refugeesmigrants.un.org/declaration*.

United Nations (2015a), *The Addis Ababa Action Agenda of the Third International Conference on Financing for Development*, *www.un.org/esa/ffd/wp-content/uploads/2015/08/AAAA_Outcome.pdf*.

United Nations (2015b), *Resolution Adopted by the General Assembly on 25 September 2015*, *www.ipu.org/splz-e/unga16/2030-e.pdf*.

United Nations (2013), "Secretary-General's remarks to High-Level Dialogue on International Migration and Development", *www.un.org/sg/statements/index.asp?nid=7175*.

Perspectives on Global Development 2017
International Migration in a Shifting World
© OECD 2016

Chapter 2

Shifting wealth: Trends, implications and prospects

This edition of Perspectives on Global Development *examines international migration in the context of the phenomenon of "shifting wealth" and an increasingly interconnected world economy. Laying the groundwork for the following chapters on migration, this chapter revisits shifting wealth trends and implications, and it outlines some prospects for the future. The first section looks at the economic factors that have driven shifting wealth, highlighting in particular the role of China as its engine, the recent commodity price boom, massive capital investment, the increasing interdependencies of the world economy and technological change. It illustrates how the shifting wealth process is slowing. The second section records how the phenomenon has benefited living conditions around the world, particularly with respect to jobs, wages and incomes. However, it also illustrates that current challenges to growth and trends in other areas, such as demography and inequality, risk undoing some of the recent achievements. The final section posits the hypothesis that the shifting wealth phenomenon has influenced patterns of international migration. It introduces a new typology of countries to help explore this question.*

Emerging and developing countries have grown faster than advanced countries since the 2000s. This shifting weight of global economic activity that is referred to as shifting wealth,[1] has largely been driven by China and, to a lesser extent, India. It has prompted a massive expansion of productive employment in the developing world. Millions of people have emerged from extreme poverty, unskilled workers have seen real increases in their wages, life expectancy has improved and literacy is more widespread than ever.

However, there is a risk that the period of rapid growth in the emerging world is over. The growth differential between Organisation for Economic Co-operation and Development (OECD) and non-OECD countries has narrowed in recent years after its peak in 2009 during the global financial and economic crisis. This development is largely the result of a slowdown in some large developing economies, particularly China, and countries that export natural resources, such as Brazil and the Russian Federation. China is moving gradually towards a lower growth path, sometimes called the "new normal". Moreover, many people's livelihoods around the world remain vulnerable because of a number of other emerging trends that are affecting the globally integrated world system and posing a threat to continued convergence of per capita incomes and other improvements made in recent decades.

This edition of *Perspectives on Global Development* examines international migration in the context of the phenomenon of "shifting wealth". This chapter revisits shifting wealth trends and implications, and it outlines some prospects for the future. In so doing, it lays the groundwork for the following chapters covering migration issues in the context of current and future shifting wealth. The first section looks at economic factors that have driven past shifting wealth, highlighting in particular the role of China as its engine, the recent commodity price boom, massive capital investment and the increasing interdependencies of the world economy as well as technological change. The section also illustrates that the shifting wealth process is slowing and points to some risks for an even more significant slowdown than that currently projected by international institutions. The second section highlights how shifting wealth has benefited livelihoods around the world, particularly with respect to jobs, wages and incomes. However, it also illustrates that current growth challenges and trends in other areas, such as demography and inequality, risk undoing some of the recent achievements. The final section posits the hypothesis that the shifting wealth phenomenon has influenced patterns of international migration. It introduces a new typology of countries to help explore this question.

Slower shifting wealth or much slower shifting wealth?

Since the early 2000s, developing economies have experienced greatly accelerated economic growth compared with OECD countries. In 2010, non-OECD countries accounted for more than 50% of the world's GDP (expressed in purchasing power parities [PPPs]), up from around 40% in 2000 (Figure 2.1). The difference in GDP growth rates between advanced countries and emerging and developing countries began to rise surely and steadily in the 2000s, peaking in 2009 during the financial crisis when advanced economies contracted by

3.4% and emerging and developing economies achieved 3.5% growth (OECD, 2014). Since then the growth differential between OECD and non-OECD countries has narrowed. Shifting wealth was made possible by a combination of factors, some of them more structural and others more cyclical, but now they all show signs of fading away.

Figure 2.1. **Shifting weight in global economic activity is likely to continue, although at a slower pace, mostly because of the slowdown in China**

Share in global GDP (in %): 2000-15

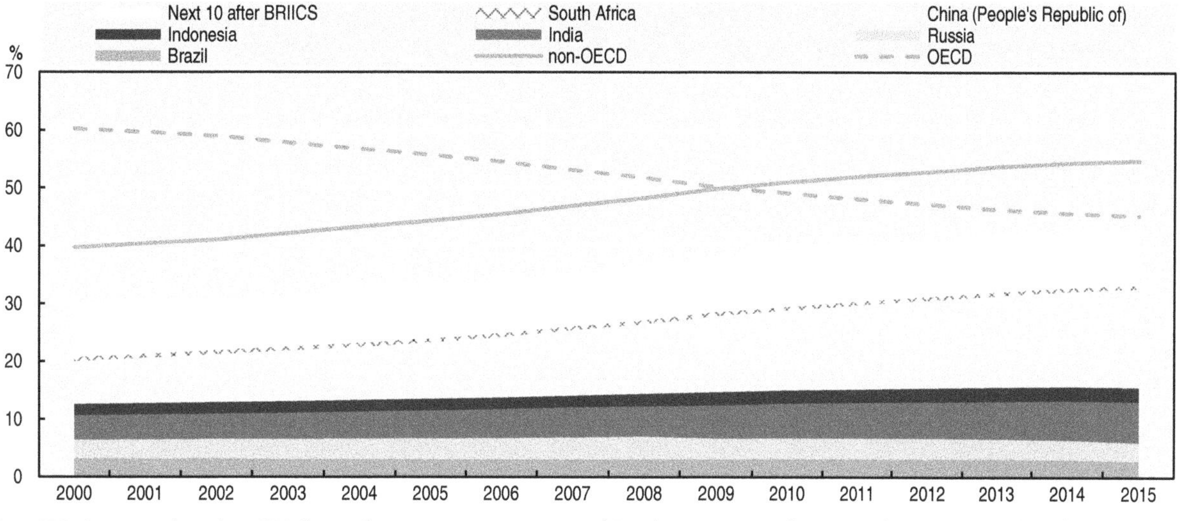

Note: GDP shares are based on GDP figures in current PPPs. In terms of GDP in PPPs terms, the next 10 largest economies after the BRIICS (Brazil, Russian Federation, India, Indonesia, China and South Africa) and the OECD are: Saudi Arabia, Iran, Chinese Taipei, Nigeria, Thailand, Egypt, Argentina, Pakistan, Malaysia and the Philippines.

Source: Authors' calculations based on IMF (2016), *World Economic Outlook, Too Slow for Too Long*, April, *www.imf.org/external/pubs/ft/weo/2016/01/*.

StatLink http://dx.doi.org/10.1787/888933422089

The overall shift of the concentration of economic activity is to a large extent attributable to the rise of China. China's share in global GDP (in PPPs) was around 7% in 2000 and jumped to almost 17% by 2015 (Figure 2.1). China has experienced a unique growth spurt since the start of the economic reform process in the late 1970s. Economic reforms introducing market principles began in 1978 and were carried out in two rounds. First, in the late 1970s and early 1980s, the decollectivisation of agriculture, the opening up of the country to foreign investment, and permission for entrepreneurs to start businesses were introduced, while most industry remained state-owned. The second round of reforms, in the late 1980s and 1990s, involved the privatisation and contracting out of much state-owned industry and the lifting of price controls, protectionist policies, and regulations, although state monopolies in sectors such as banking and petroleum remained. From 1978 until the recent global financial and economic crisis, unprecedented growth occurred, with the economy recording increases of almost 10% each year. China also managed to maintain growth during the crisis.

China's "new normal" and slowdowns in other large emerging economies mean that the shifting wealth process will be slower regardless of other factors

After three decades of extraordinary economic development, China is moving gradually towards a lower growth path, sometimes called the "new normal". Growth reached a peak of around 14% before the crisis in 2007 and has been slowing since then to slightly below 7% in 2015 (Figure 2.2). Even optimistic forecasts foresee growth at below 7% in the coming years (OECD, 2016a). China's new normal is consistent with its transition towards a broad-based growth model, ensuring greater stability over the longer run, with a wider spread of the benefits of growth across society and less stress on a highly polluted environment.

Figure 2.2. **The growth differential between China and more advanced countries is narrowing**

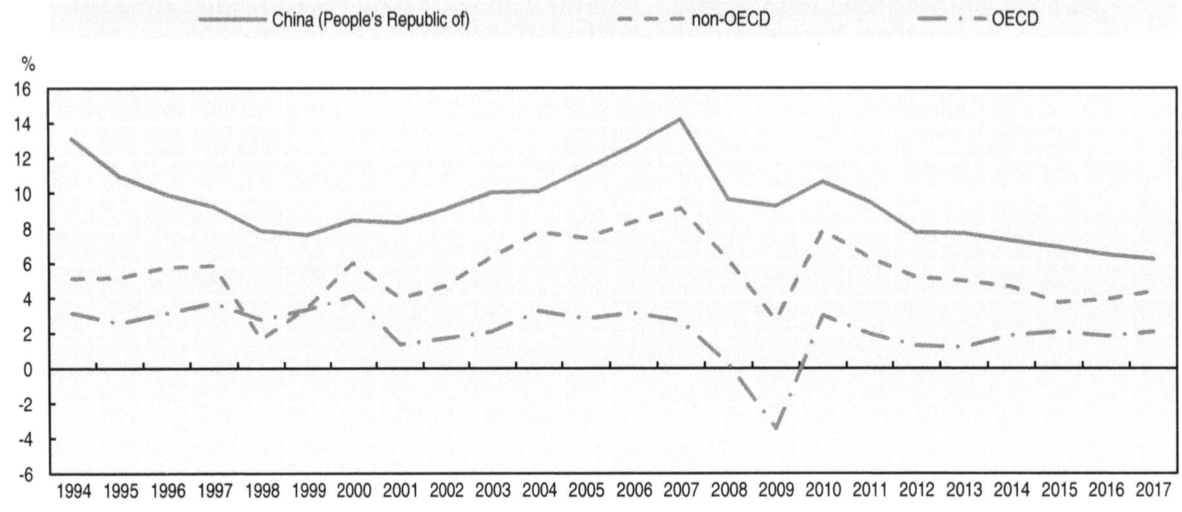

Note: The figures for 2016 and 2017 are projections.

Source: OECD (2016), *OECD Economic Outlook* (June), *www.oecd.org/eco/economicoutlook.htm*.

StatLink http://dx.doi.org/10.1787/888933422095

Risks exist that the slowdown in China may be much faster than expected. Rapid investment growth in China came with strong credit growth, including in non-bank financial institutions, and has raised financial stability concerns as investment efficiency is losing ground (Bank for International Settlements, 2014; IMF, 2014). Caps on bank deposit rates led investors to search for higher-yielding assets at the same time as bank lending was constrained by the regulated loan-to-deposit ratio. As a result, lending outside the traditional banking sector towards riskier "shadow bank" lending surged (Elliott, Kroeber and Qiao, 2015). Corporate credit risk is further rising in China as exports are dropping rapidly relative to GDP, large companies are highly leveraged, anti-corruption campaigns reduce business activities and property prices are falling (Wong, 2014). The latter is a particular risk as special "shadow bank" vehicles used by local governments use land as collateral (Vandenberg and Zhuang, 2015). Recent stock market turbulences in China illustrate increasing market uncertainties about China's transition towards more balanced growth, including, among others, concerns with respect to over-investment in certain sectors accompanied with a huge expansion of debt (Wolf, 2015). Beyond economic challenges, China faces inequality and environmental concerns that, if not addressed in time, could trigger a middle-income trap (Dahlman and Wermelinger, forthcoming).

Other large emerging economies have also slowed down. Beyond China, strong growth spells in the other five BRIICS (Brazil, Russian Federation, India, Indonesia and South Africa) in the 2000s contributed to an acceleration of the shifting wealth process but only India managed decisively to expand its share in global economic activity, from around 4% in 2000 to 7% in 2015 (Figure 2.1). All five countries have now much lower growth rates compared with their peak periods in the 2000s. In Brazil and the Russian Federation, entrenched in political crises for very different reasons, growth came to a halt or even turned negative and prospects are very uncertain for the future. Political difficulties themselves are a barrier to growth, because of significant uncertainties for business, but they also make needed structural reforms more difficult (OECD, 2014). Additionally, both countries have benefited from the recent commodity price boom through their exports of agricultural and mineral commodities and are now facing lower export prices (see section below). South Africa will also suffer from lower prices and demand for commodities and is likely to report lower growth in the coming years. India and Indonesia are the potential trump cards for a continuously robust shifting wealth process. In spite of considerable challenges to the implementation of reforms in these countries, there is reason to hope that the leaderships of the new governments can make possible major reforms and thus stronger and more sustained growth in India and Indonesia.

Nor should political developments be ruled out. In June 2016 the United Kingdom (UK) voted in a referendum by 52% to 48% to leave the European Union (EU), against the advice of the chief political parties. How this departure will take place, and what the timeframe will be, are completely uncertain, but there is widespread agreement that there will be an effect on global growth as one of the world's ten largest economies withdraws from the EU single market. Developed economies, including those of the OECD, are likely to be hardest hit, including those of the UK, the EU and the United States (US). The effect may be to reduce the growth differential between OECD and non-OECD countries while overall global growth may slow.

Lower commodity prices and demand have an impact on growth prospects in developing countries

Shifting wealth was supported by stronger commodity demand from China. The exceptional growth performance of China was among other things the result of major investment in heavy industries. The development of these industries is partly the outcome of local authorities' growth-seeking behaviour as they competed to offer low-cost or free land, cheap credit, tax concessions and other subsidies to attract investment. Cheap energy has led to the massive development of energy-intensive industries – where China does not have a comparative advantage as it is a net importer of coal and oil (OECD, 2015a). All this drove strong Chinese import demand for minerals – particularly iron ore, coking coal, manganese ore and bauxite – as well as agricultural products and other natural resources. China's share of global mineral imports increased from around 5% in 2000 to almost 50% in recent years, while the world imported six to seven times as many minerals (nominal dollar value) in recent years as compared with the late 1990s and early 2000s (Figure 2.3, Panel A). For exporters in all world regions, the supply of minerals to China has become increasingly important and the regions have benefited from surging mineral export revenues. Total mineral exports tripled in all regions, while sub-Saharan Africa and Latin America benefited most with increases by a factor of seven between 2000 and 2014 (Figure 2.3, Panel B).

Stronger commodity demand from China and other emerging economies has led to a commodity price boom. Besides increased demand, the surge in commodity export revenues around the globe in the 2000s can be attributed to strong commodity price hikes. This holds for agricultural, metal and energy commodities (Figure 2.4). The rise in these prices supported export revenues not only for raw materials themselves but also exported products using these commodities as inputs into production.

Figure 2.3. **China imports almost 50% of worldwide traded minerals**

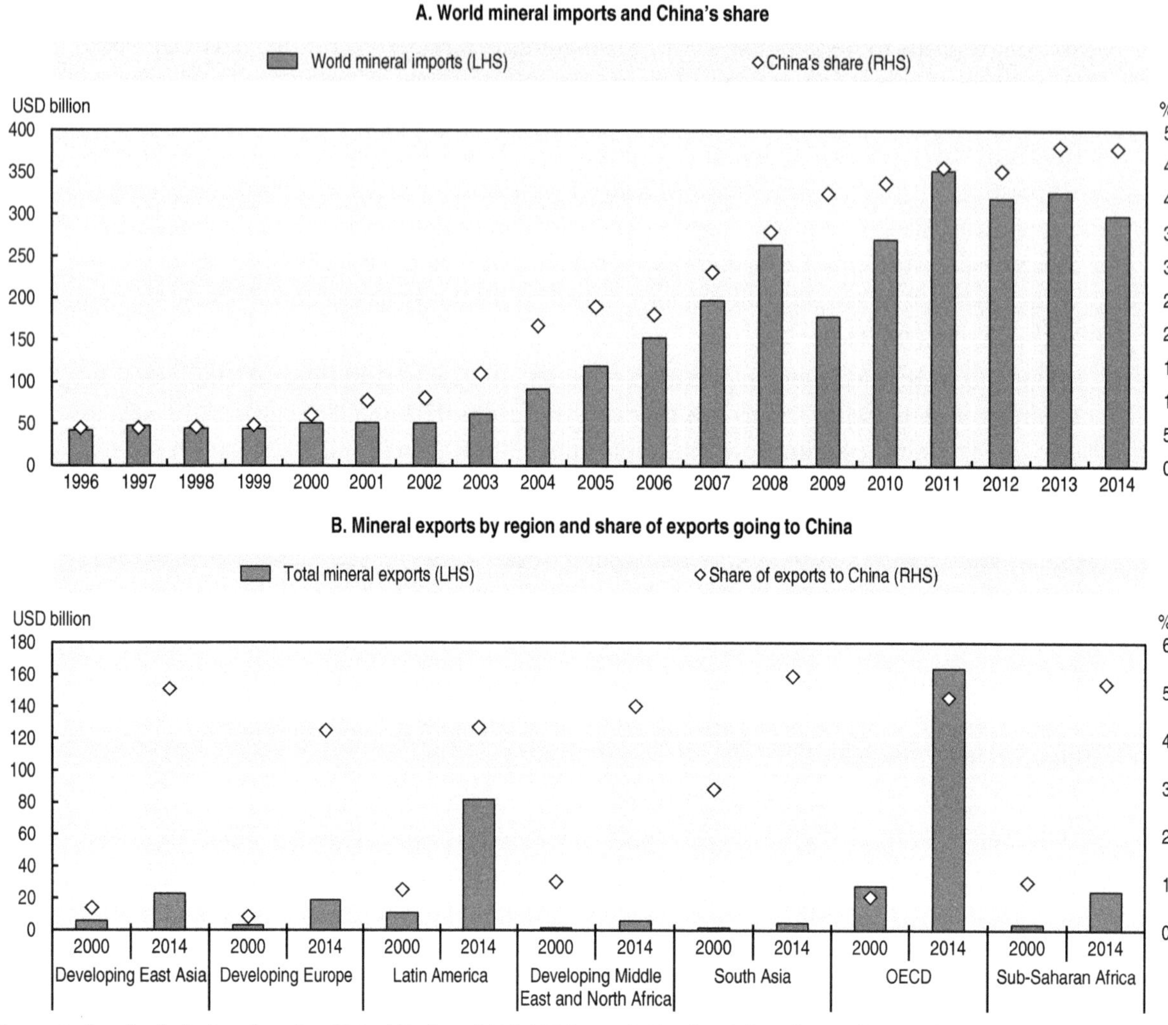

Source: Authors' calculations based on United Nations (2016), *UN Comtrade* (database), *http://comtrade.un.org/*.

StatLink *http://dx.doi.org/10.1787/888933422107*

Commodity prices have been falling more recently and are likely to stay low for some time. By 2015, energy and metal prices had fallen by 40% since the peak in 2011 (Figure 2.4). Similarly, prices of agricultural commodities dropped by 30% over the same period. The falling prices may be attributed to the US shale-energy boom or OPEC's unwillingness to agree on supply restrictions. That the drop in prices is so broad in terms of type of commodities suggests that more macroeconomic factors are also at play. The most natural explanation is the global economic slowdown. The slowdown of the Chinese economy has particularly contributed to the end of the so-called "commodity super cycle". Adjustment in heavy industries implies lower imports of iron ore, coking coal, manganese ore and bauxite. By contrast growth in the US is robust and yet it is particularly in the US that commodity prices have been falling. One additional explanation for the drop in prices was that monetary tightening has been expected in the US. The Federal Reserve ended quantitative easing in October 2014 and accordingly interest rate increases were expected. However, the Federal Reserve has been reluctant to increase rates during recent months. Real interest rates may affect real commodity prices through four channels (Frankel, 2014): higher interest rates reduce the price of storable commodities by increasing the incentive for extraction today rather than tomorrow; higher rates reduce firms' desire to carry inventories; portfolio investors respond to higher interest rates by shifting out of commodity contracts and into treasury bills; and finally, high interest rates strengthen the domestic currency and thereby reduce the price of internationally traded commodities in domestic terms. These more macroeconomic explanations suggest that prices could stay low for some years and potentially drop even more.

Figure 2.4. **Shifting wealth was to a great extent a result of the commodity price boom**

Commodity price indices in USD, real, 2010=100

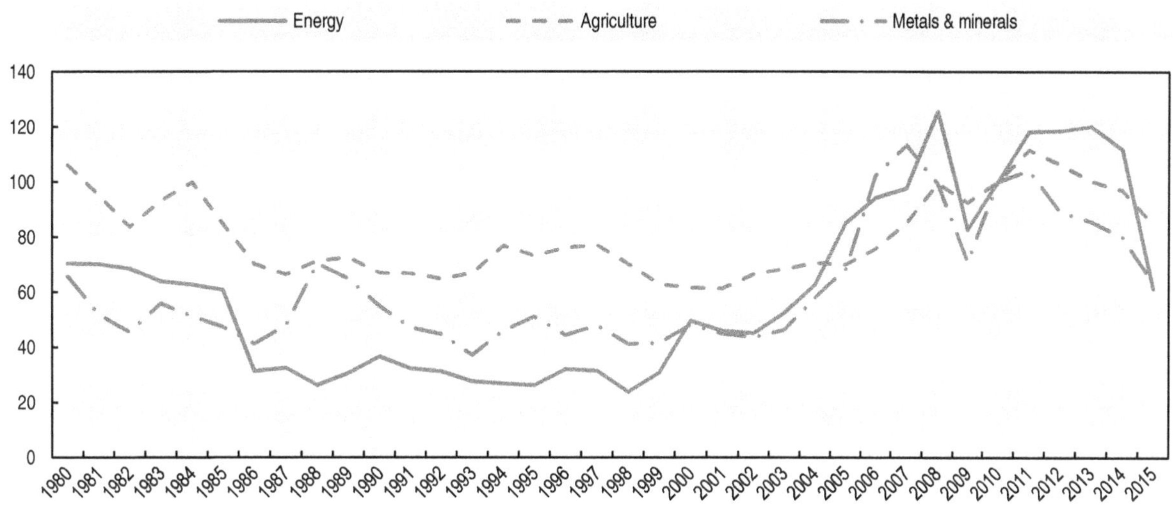

Source: World Bank (2016a), *Commodity Markets Outlook*, June, *www.worldbank.org/en/research/commodity-markets*.

StatLink *http://dx.doi.org/10.1787/888933422116*

Lower commodity prices challenge the growth prospects of those that benefited from the higher levels. The drop in commodity prices is not only a possible factor in the global economic slowdown, but it also further challenges growth prospects for all the many exporters of natural resources that benefited from the price and demand boom in the 2000s. Among them are countries as diverse as Australia, Brazil, Canada, the Gulf States, Kazakhstan, Myanmar, the Russian Federation, South Africa and Venezuela. Meanwhile, net commodity importers, such as India and most European countries, are gaining.

Global trade and investment patterns are changing and affect the shifting wealth process

The recent slowdown in the developing world, and thus the global economic slowdown, are largely due to slowdowns in investment and total factor productivity. Global flows of foreign direct investment (FDI) in both OECD and non-OECD countries have also slowed and remain around 30% below the pre-crisis peak (year 2007) in nominal terms. It should however be noted that 2007 was an exceptional peak year. In the event, post-crisis FDI flows moved quickly back to average global FDI flows reported over the three years before the crisis (2005-07), but are now slowing again. Growth of FDI inflows stood at around 5% in non-OECD economies and 3% in OECD economies during recent years, down from rates above 30% during the pre-crisis period (Figure 2.5, Panel C). While the contribution of foreign investment to total capital accumulation decreased, overall gross capital formation (including domestic and foreign investments) has also slowed since the crisis. In OECD economies, gross capital formation came to a halt, while the accumulation of capital in non-OECD countries slowed from around 20% in the early 2010s to just 10% in recent years. The low total factor productivity is explained by the slowdown in trade (OECD, 2016a). The latest World Trade Organization (WTO) forecasts suggest 2016 will be the fifth year running that global merchandise trade volumes grow by less than 3%, barely at – or below – the rate of GDP growth (WTO, 2016). Before the crisis, trade was growing faster than GDP. The recent OECD economic outlook shows that growth of non-OECD imports even turned negative in 2015 (OECD, 2015b). In nominal terms, the differential growth rate of exports of goods and services between non-OECD and OECD countries was at around 8% on average during the pre-crisis period, but has been declining to below 5% in recent years (Figure 2.5, Panel A). The decrease of international trade slows down the technology and knowledge diffusion leading to decreased total factor productivity.

A structural shift in the international division of labour has taken place with the rise of global value chains (GVCs). The revolutions in information and communications technology (ICT), the Internet, transport and other services, coupled with the development of ever more complex products, have allowed firms to establish chains that are geographically dispersed across the globe. The fragmentation of production enabled firms to combine multiple channels – imports, exports, FDI, movement of business personnel, services, data and licences – to optimise their international business strategies. Firms produce each component of a product and source each pre-production and post-production service to wherever host economies can offer the best cost advantages. In a world of GVCs, trade and investment are complements to enhance business opportunities for firms (Helpman, 1984; Helpman and Krugman, 1985; OECD/WTO/World Bank Group, 2014; and for an overview of the empirical literature Go, Wong and Tham, 2013). Developed countries still exhibit higher participation rates in GVCs than developing countries, but these countries have been catching up (OECD/World Bank Group, 2015).

Over the past two decades, global economic growth has increasingly been supported by international trade in global value chains. Multinational enterprises' co-ordinated GVCs account for 80% of global trade (OECD/WTO/UNCTAD, 2013). Around one-third of world trade is intra-firm trade (OECD, 2011). In nominal terms, global trade has increased more than fourfold since the mid-1990s. OECD countries still commanded the largest share of global exports, namely around 60%. However, all other regions have seen their exports growing at a faster pace than the OECD over the last one and a half decades. Most remarkably, the BRIICS countries (Brazil, Russian Federation, India, Indonesia, China and South Africa) have jointly multiplied their export revenues by a factor of five, expanding their share of global exports from 7% to almost 20% since 2000 (Figure 2.5, Panel A). Although the developing world, without the BRIICS, has also greatly expanded exports over the last 15 years, their combined share of global exports remains small at 13%, up from 8% in 2000. In the developing world, the share of exports in GDP has increased from around 25% in the early 1990s to above 40% in pre-crisis years, but has been contracting since then. Much of the increase in global trade can be explained by the emergence of GVCs; illustrated particularly by increased trade in intermediate and capital goods (Figure 2.6) and by a high trade-to-income elasticity. On the contrary, the decrease in trade of intermediates and the slowdown of capital goods trade since 2011 can be interpreted as a contraction of GVCs. Also, the recent reduction of exports' share in GDP in developing countries illustrates that the slowdown of shifting wealth is partly driven by decelerated trade.

Figure 2.5. **The boost of global integration in the developing world is slowing**

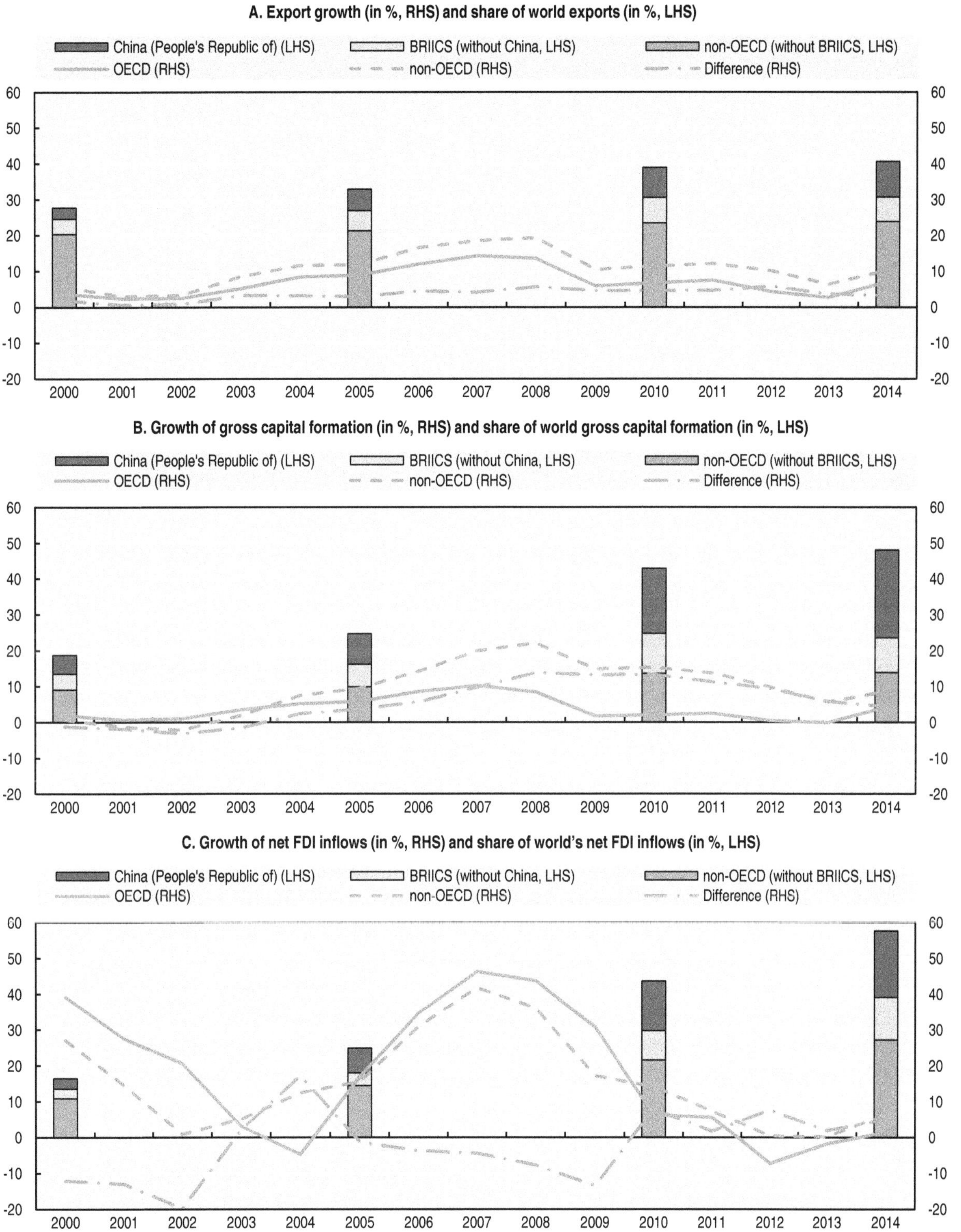

Notes: Growth rates for exports (of goods and services), gross capital formation and net FDI inflows are five-year moving averages. All values are in current terms.

Source: Authors' calculations based on World Bank (2016b), *World Development Indicators* (database), *http://databank.worldbank.org/data/reports.aspx?source=world-development-indicators.*

StatLink http://dx.doi.org/10.1787/888933422125

Figure 2.6. **Declining global imports of intermediates point to a process of GVC contraction**
Global imports by product groups, in current USD billion

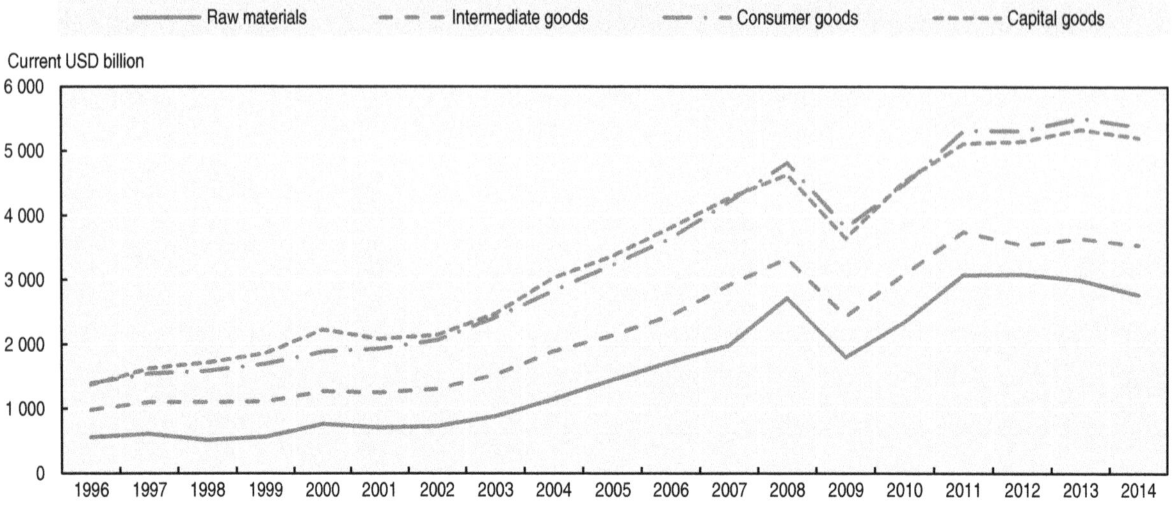

Source: Authors' calculations based on United Nations (2016), *UN Comtrade* (database), *http://comtrade.un.org/*.

StatLink http://dx.doi.org/10.1787/888933422133

The interconnected world economic system also challenges global financial stability, a particular risk in the emerging world. The sharp fall in trade at the outbreak of the global financial crisis underscores significant global interconnectedness through GVCs, but also how the global financial system is connected to the real economy (Dahlman et al., 2015). The stability of the global financial system remains at risk. Following the easy monetary policies brought on by the crisis, financial markets have rallied strongly while companies that undertake capital spending do not appear to see the same opportunities for value creation. Moreover, current low interest rates regimes may feed price bubbles (Roubini, 2015) and with rising longevity this could be a concern for the solvency position of pension funds and life insurance companies (OECD, 2015c). Global capital flows, including bank transactions, portfolio investment and FDI, remain below pre-crisis levels. Global capital flows were at 6% of global GDP on average over the period 2008-12; down from 13% over the period 2000 to 2007, or 60% below their pre-crisis peak. The current slowdown of growth and investment in China has drastic implications on growth around the world. If investment shrank more drastically as demand and balance-sheet constraints bite, the negative effects on the world economy would be even more dramatic (Wolf, 2015; Summers, 2015). Uncertainty about the robustness of growth in emerging economies as well as about more robust growth in the United States and expectations about interest rate hikes by the Federal Reserve are factors that have already led to a slowdown in overall capital inflows into emerging markets and developing regions and accelerated capital outflows from these regions (Figure 2.7). Net cross border capital flows to emerging markets and developing economies are expected to be negative in 2015, causing depreciation of emerging market currencies and thus a further slowdown.

Advances in ICTs and technology have made possible the integration of developing countries into the global trading system, but are now challenging these countries' growth model.

The foundation of current GVCs, and particularly the rising share of services inputs in global production networks, is greatly determined by advances in ICTs. During the past decade, progress in communication networks and the fall of unit prices favoured the massive uptake of the Internet and increases in connection speed and in the volume of data traffic across borders. This progress allowed firms to develop and upgrade their globally fragmented supply chains, including in the emerging world (OECD, 2014). While ICTs and the Internet have become key enablers of the integration into GVCs for producers of any type of good or service, some developing countries, particularly India, actually established a comparative advantage specifically in ICT-enabled services, such as call centres or software programming.

Figure 2.7. **Inflows of capital have slowed whereas outflows have accelerated in emerging markets and developing regions**

Emerging markets and developing regions

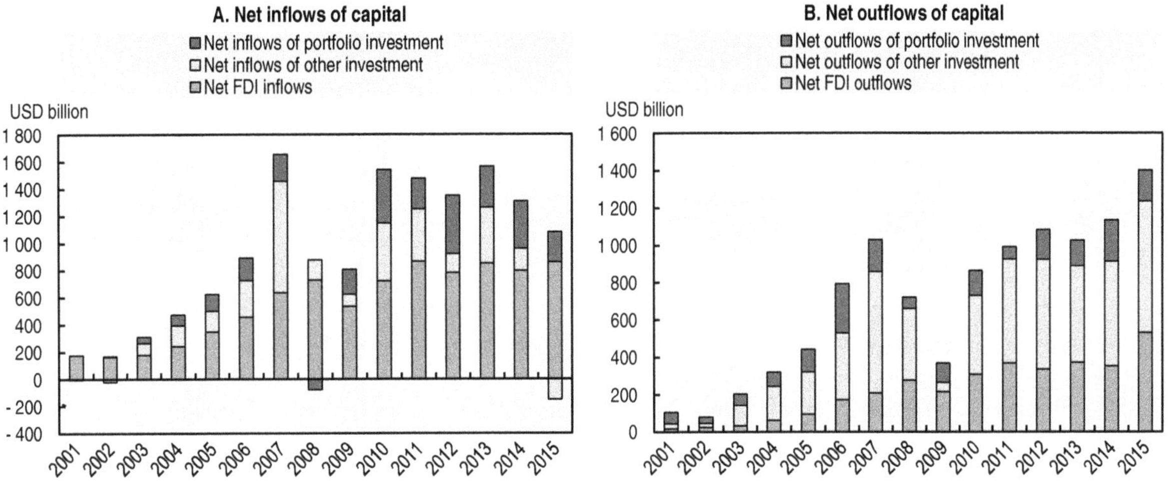

Note: Data are based on balance of payment figures taken from IMF's *World Economic Outlook*, April 2016 revision.

Source: Authors' calculations based on IMF (2015), *World Economic Outlook: Adjusting to Lower Commodity Prices*, *www.imf.org/external/pubs/ft/weo/2015/02/*.

StatLink http://dx.doi.org/10.1787/888933422149

Technological progress including in ICTs continues and is reshaping the current model of global value chains. ICT technologies are still a leading area in innovation as well as an engine for innovative activity performed in other technology domains, such as robotics and 3-D printing, artificial intelligence appliances, or nano-technology and bio-technology. ICTs also contribute to the reshaping of products, processes, the organisation of economic activities and societal behaviours; the sharing or peer-to-peer economy is an illustration of such change. Moreover, data growth is very rapidly growing and has the potential to unleash a new spiral of innovation and growth, independent of location. Over 2.5 quintillion bytes of data are created each day; 90% of the world's stored data was created in the last two years alone (WEF, 2015). It is estimated that the data universe (digital data created, replicated or consumed) will grow by a factor of 30 from 2005 to 2020, doubling every two years. Much of this data growth is transported and stored over Internet technologies. Internet-related data traffic is estimated to grow threefold between 2012 and 2017. The analysis of this data opens new opportunities for value creation and fostering new products, processes and markets, as well as for empowering autonomous machines and systems that can learn and make decisions independently of human involvement (OECD, 2015d).

In this way new and technologically enhanced business models mean that parts of firms' global supply chains will be consolidated. This could take place through automated processes, the use of artificial intelligence appliances or an increase in ICT-enabled service components in goods and more traditional services. Signs of increased automation through robotics exist. For example, in 2014 alone world sales of industrial robots increased by 29% to around 230 000

(IFR, 2015). In 2003 global sales stood at just about 70 000. Increased automation is not limited to highly advanced countries: China is the biggest market for industrial robots in the world and has considerably expanded its leading position in recent years with a share of 25% of the total supply in 2014. This consolidation may also involve reshoring, a process in which companies repatriate jobs to home markets (Reshoring Initiative, 2015). In the US, for example, 60 000 manufacturing jobs were added in 2014, versus 12 000 in 2003, either through reshoring, or FDI. By contrast, as many as 50 000 jobs were "offshored" last year, a decline from about 150 000 in 2003.

This technologically-driven shift of global businesses may challenge growth and job prospects around the world, but particularly in some developing regions with lower technological readiness. In order to tap into technologically-enhanced business models while creating new jobs and alternative types of economic activity, countries need to develop and implement effective strategies to foster cutting edge technological skills and infrastructure and create other incentives – e.g. funding or innovation clusters – for people and firms to invest and participate in new value creation. Latin America, Southeast Asia and many developed regions, which have ageing and often relatively well-educated populations, may be better placed to jump on the bandwagon of new generation supply chains. On the other hand, consolidated and technologically-enhanced value chains create a particular challenge for regions with fast-growing working age populations, such as sub-Saharan Africa or South Asia. These regions have a great need to accelerate job creation in order to reap their demographic dividend.

The challenge is to sustain improvements of livelihoods in the emerging world

The shifting wealth process has been accompanied by improvements in livelihoods. Millions of people have emerged from extreme poverty in recent decades, particularly in China and in East Asia. In general the proportion of people living in extreme poverty has fallen in all developing regions (Figure 2.8). People in developing regions have seen real increases in their incomes and wages, life expectancy has improved, and literacy is more widespread than ever (OECD, 2015e). Despite these significant improvements, many people remain vulnerable. The recent economic and financial crisis already destabilised many people's livelihoods. A more sustained slowdown of shifting wealth, demographic shifts and other challenges may challenge further improvements to livelihoods.

Figure 2.8. **Extreme poverty has been massively reduced in East Asia and the Pacific**

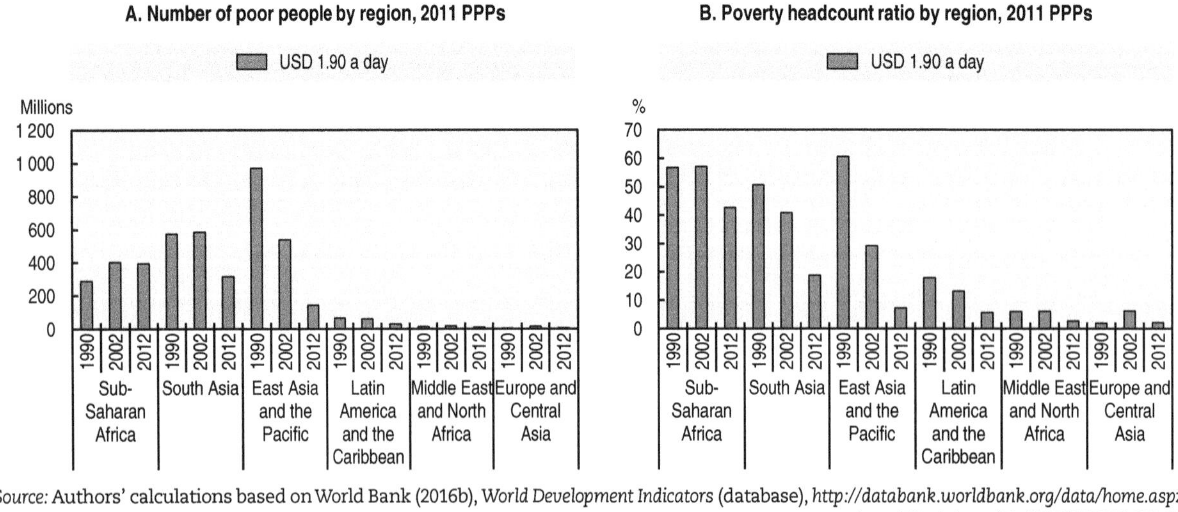

Source: Authors' calculations based on World Bank (2016b), *World Development Indicators* (database), *http://databank.worldbank.org/data/home.aspx*.

StatLink http://dx.doi.org/10.1787/888933422158

Shifting wealth corresponds to an increase in per capita incomes in developing economies, but the income gap with advanced economies has not reduced much and may remain high in the years to come

Many developing countries have experienced a period of impressive economic growth and improvement in per capita income (Figure 2.9, for an illustration of selected countries in Africa, Latin America and Asia). GDP per capita can be decomposed into labour productivity (defined by GDP per person employed) and labour utilisation (defined by total number of employees as a ratio of total population). The decomposition shows that growth over the past one and a half decades has in many developing economies been due to both improvements in labour productivity and increases in employment relative to their population growth. The catch-up in labour productivity was – with some exceptions (e.g. Azerbaijan, China, India, Indonesia and the Russian Federation) – relatively weak (see more detailed productivity analysis in OECD, 2014). The rapid rise in GDP per capita in many non-OECD economies in the 2000s was partly linked to improvements in labour utilisation (as measured by number of persons employed as a ratio of total population). Growth in labour utilisation was high in most countries in Latin America, Africa and Asia.

Figure 2.9. **Some emerging economies have greatly improved per capita incomes through productivity improvements**

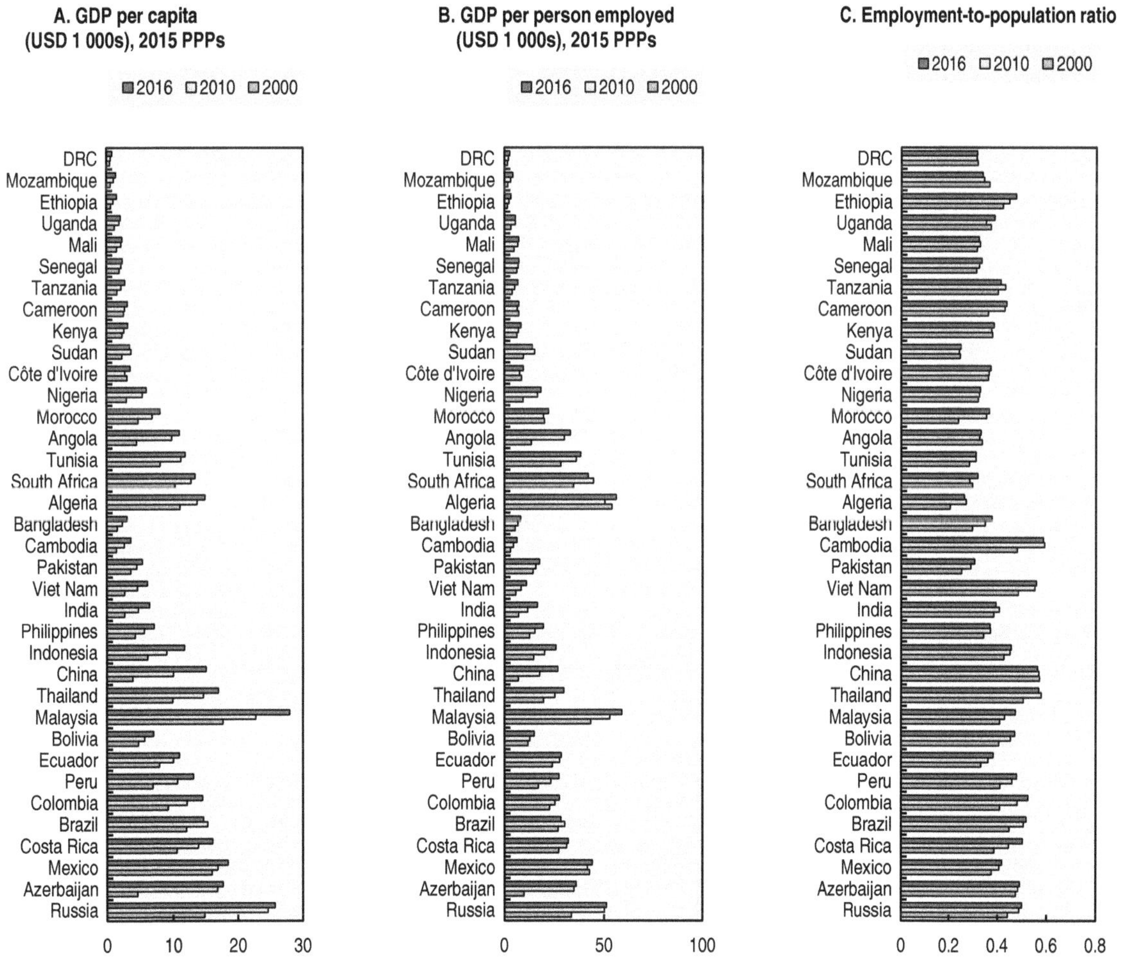

Note: For methodological details, see: *https://www.conference-board.org/data/economydatabase/*. GDP figures are in 2015 prices using updated 2011 PPP indices.

Source: Authors' calculations based on the Conference Board (2016), *Total Economy Database*.

StatLink http://dx.doi.org/10.1787/888933422165

The gap in per capita income levels of many middle-income countries, particularly in the upper bracket, with advanced economies has not been much reduced over the last quarter of a century. Brazil, Mexico and South Africa did not make progress in terms of convergence with OECD incomes between 1990 and 2014; in Mexico and South Africa the gap even widened slightly (Figure 2.10). Their proportion of OECD incomes stood at around 35% to 40%. Other countries, such as Colombia, Peru, Thailand and Turkey, reduced the gap by around 10 percentage points over the same period but their incomes remain clearly below 40% of the OECD average. Countries such as Kazakhstan and Malaysia were more successful and have managed to reduce the gap since 1990, reaching about 55% of OECD incomes (in PPPs) by 2014. Most impressive is the growth spurt of China. The country started with an OECD income proportion below 6% in 1990 and reduced this gap to around 30% of OECD incomes by 2014. As mentioned above, much of the reduction in the income gap has been driven by China's boost in productivity.

Figure 2.10. **Many upper middle-income countries struggle to close the income gap with OECD economies**

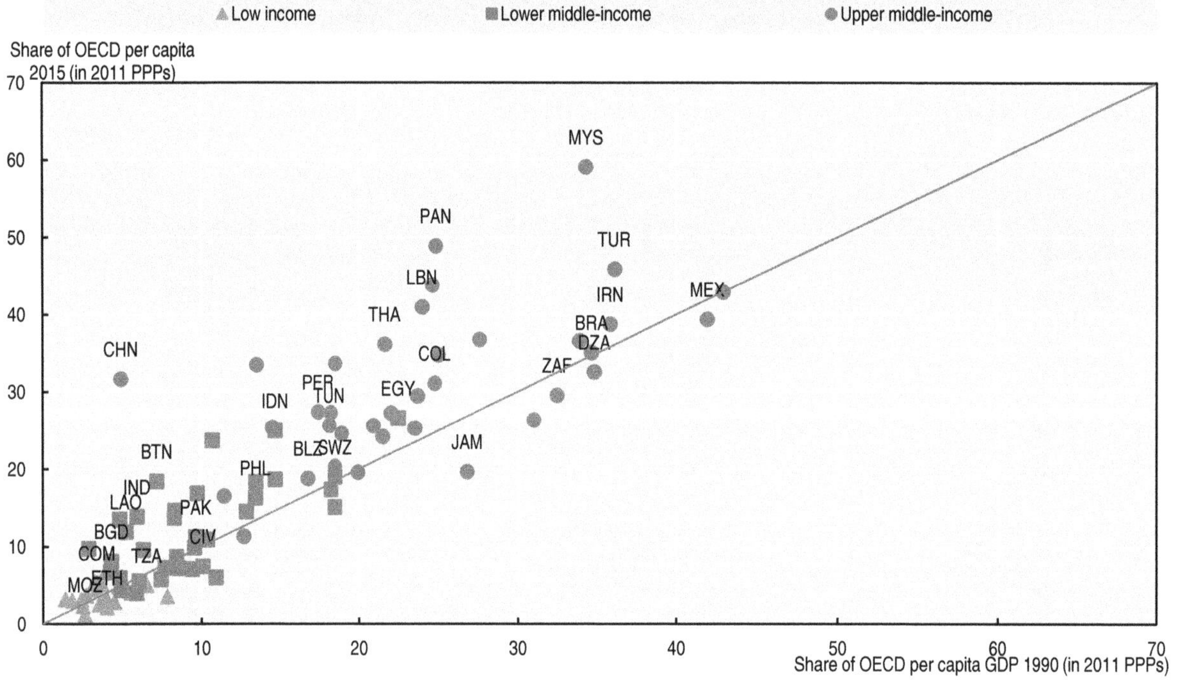

Note: GDP per capita figures in current 2011 PPPs are used.

Source: Authors' calculations based on IMF (2016), *World Economic Outlook: Too Slow for Too Long*, *www.imf.org/external/pubs/ft/weo/2016/01/*.

StatLink http://dx.doi.org/10.1787/888933422175

The convergence process of per capita incomes with OECD incomes continues to be slow. The difference in the rate of growth between OECD and non-OECD countries has narrowed recently. Based on current IMF projections shifting wealth will continue, although at a slower pace; however, these projections may even be too optimistic, as outlined in the first section. Despite continued shifting wealth, many poor and emerging countries, such as Brazil, Mexico and South Africa (Figure 2.11), may not improve their per capita incomes relative to the OECD by the 2030s. The position of Argentina may even worsen. By contrast, some large emerging economies, such as China, India and Indonesia, are expected to catch up considerably over the next 15 years.

Figure 2.11. **The convergence of per capita incomes between OECD and developing economies is likely to be very slow over the next 15 years**

GDP per capita (in constant 2015 PPPs) projections: 2015 versus 2030

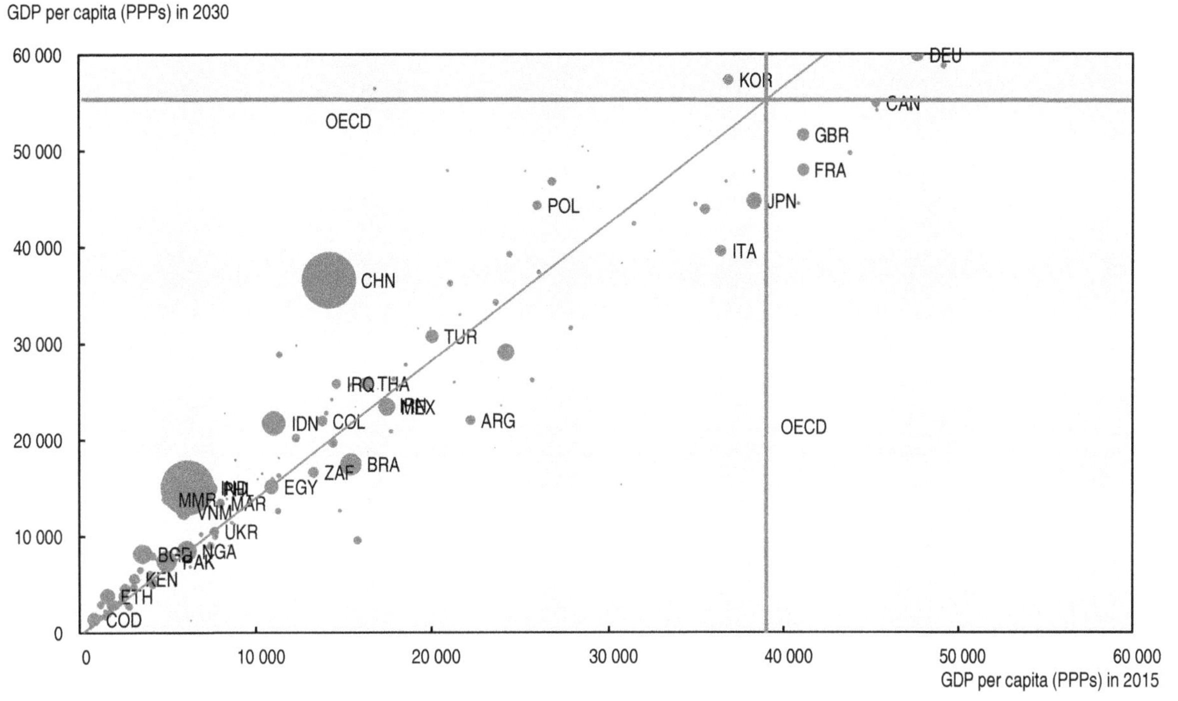

Note: The bubble size represents the projected size of the working age population in 2030. IMF projections for GDP (in current PPPs) and UN projections for working age population size and total population are used. IMF's GDP projections are only done over 2015-20. Projections for 2030 are based on extrapolations using the compound average growth rates over 2010-20. Calculated GDP per capita (in current PPPs) are deflated with IMF projections of the US GDP deflator. For many countries, these extrapolations are most likely to be too optimistic.

Source: Authors' calculations based on IMF (2016), *World Economic Outlook: Too Slow for Too Long*, April, *www.imf.org/external/pubs/ft/weo/2016/01/ and UN (2015), 2015 Revision of World Population Prospects, http://esa.un.org/unpd/wpp/.*

StatLink http://dx.doi.org/10.1787/888933422189

Job creation has not been fast enough to cope with fast expanding working age populations in most developing regions

Shifting economic activity to the developing world over the last two decades made possible a rapid expansion of employment in all developing regions. Increased employment is an important contributory factor in poverty reduction (OECD, 2015e). The significant reduction of poverty around the globe was made possible by the creation of millions of new productive jobs, particularly in the developing world. According to ILO estimates, South Asia has created more than 220 million wage-paying jobs since 1992, corresponding to a 50% increase (ILO, 2016). Sub-Saharan Africa doubled employment and has created over 170 million jobs within the same period according to these estimates. East Asia has increased employment by 20% since the early 1990s. High growth rates of employment have been made possible by new job opportunities provided by off-shoring activities of multinational enterprises as well as emerging jobs for upstream businesses. However, it is striking that some regions, which – beyond exports of natural resources and services – are still only marginally integrated into the global trading and investment system (e.g. sub-Saharan Africa, South Asia and Latin America), also managed to boost employment.

However, job creation around the world was lower than the expansion of the working age populations. In most developing regions, working age populations expanded considerably between 1992 and 2015; the expansion over that period was higher than 80% in the Middle East and sub-Saharan Africa, and higher than 60% in North Africa, South Asia and Southeast Asia and the Pacific (Figure 2.12). The expansion of working age populations was considerably higher than the speed of job creation in all regions of the world.[2] While the speed of job creation is higher in some developing regions compared with advanced regions, for example, the job deficit is much more alarming for developing regions with fast expanding working age populations, such as sub-Saharan Africa and South Asia (Figure 2.12).

Figure 2.12. **In South Asia and sub-Saharan Africa, working age populations will increase by more than 200 million people between 2015 and 2030**

Past and projected future change in working age populations by region: 1992-2015 and 2015-2030

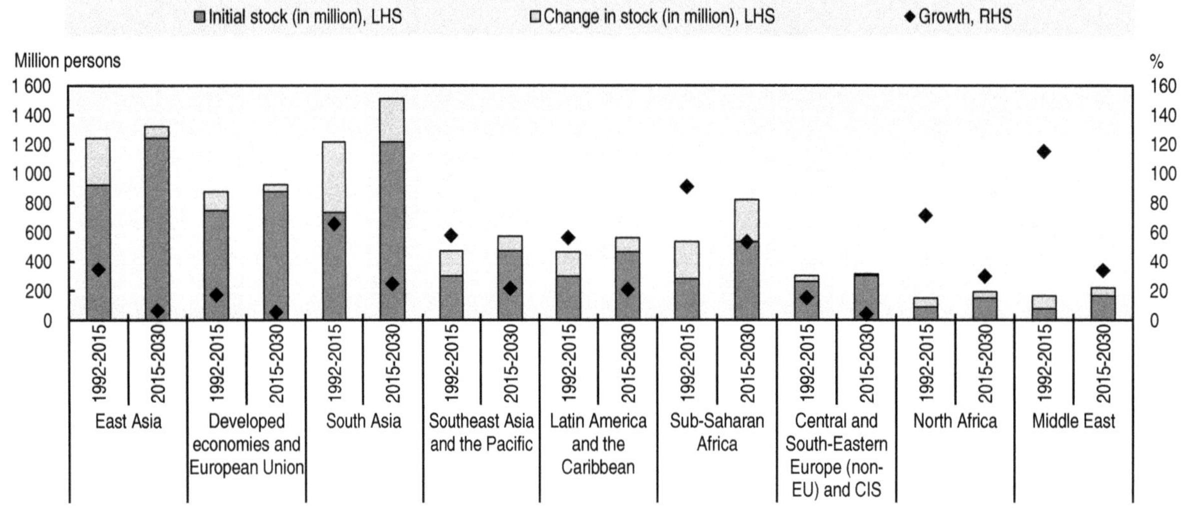

Note: Projections of working age populations retrieved from ILO Trends database and based on UN projections.

Source: Authors' calculations based on ILO (2016), *Employment Trends*, *www.ilo.org/empelm/units/employment-trends/lang--en/index.htm*.

StatLink http://dx.doi.org/10.1787/888933422194

Wages in emerging economies remain far behind levels in more advanced economies. Using average monthly wages in PPPs and population data to compute the world wage distribution shows that the difference in wage levels between the developing economies (on the left side of the distribution) and the developed economies (on the right) is substantial. Average wages in the developing world are still more than three times lower than in the developed world (Figure 2.13). However, the difference in wage levels has decreased over time. Between 2000 and 2012 the wage distribution shifted to the right and became more compressed; this implies that in real terms average wages grew across the world, but they grew by more in emerging economies.

In order to sustain existing wages in emerging economies, skills need to better match labour market demand. According to current wage levels in the emerging world (including in China), there is still significant room for these economies to compete in economic activities that require mid-range skills, also illustrated by their low proportions of tertiary-educated employees. Nonetheless, it is important that these skills are well aligned with market demand. While education attainment has improved markedly in recent years and returns to education appear high in many emerging economies, there is increasing evidence that the knowledge taught and the skills nurtured in school do not always match labour market requirements; in particular vocational skills are often not sufficiently acquired in secondary education (OECD, 2015f: OECD, 2014). For example, the proportion of firms that perceive an inadequately educated workforce as a major constraint is on average higher in emerging middle-income countries than in low-income and high-income countries (Figure 2.14).

Figure 2.13. **The wage gap of developing countries with more advanced economies remains significant**

Global monthly average wage distribution in 2000 and 2012 (2012 PPP$)

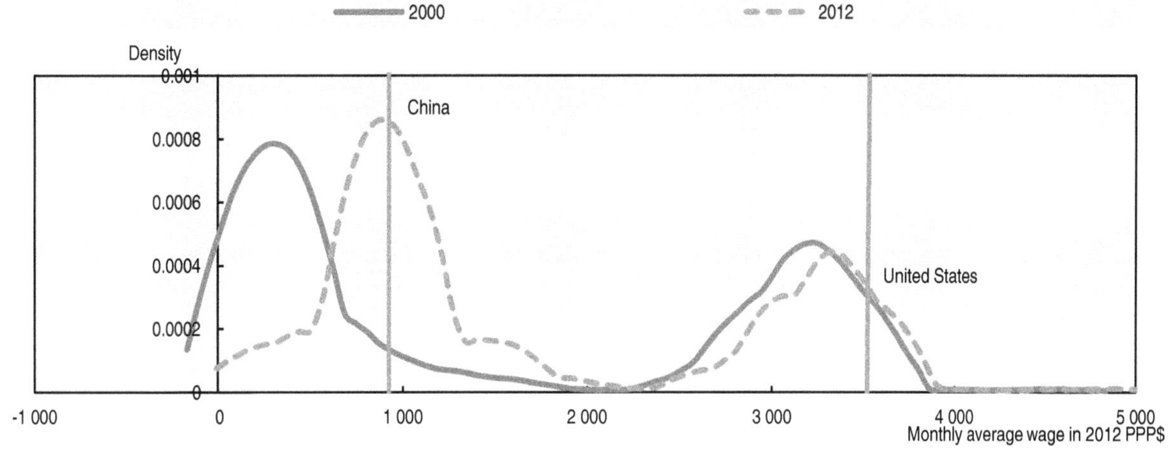

Notes: Figure is based on ILO calculations and refers to countries for which wage levels for 2000 and 2012 are available and covers 83 countries which represent 73% of the world's employees. Wage levels are converted to constant 2012 PPPs. The figure shows the distribution of average wages, weighted by population, in 2012 PPPs for the 83 countries in the sample. The grey vertical lines are the average wages in China and the United States in 2012.

Source: ILO (2015), *Global Wage Report 2014/15: Wages and Income Inequality, www.ilo.org/global/publications/books/WCMS_324678/lang--en/index.htm.*

StatLink *http://dx.doi.org/10.1787/888933422203*

Figure 2.14. **An inadequately educated workforce seems to be more of a business constraint in middle-income economies as compared to low- and high-income countries**

Percentage of firms that believe an inadequately educated workforce is a major constraint on their operations, by country and income per capita

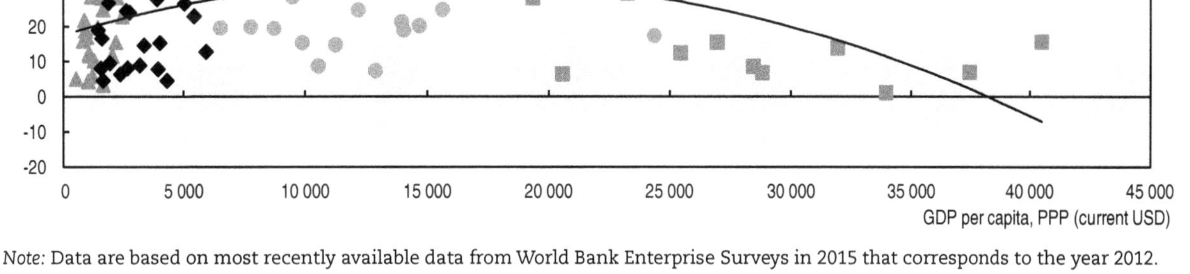

Note: Data are based on most recently available data from World Bank Enterprise Surveys in 2015 that corresponds to the year 2012.

Source: OECD (2015f), *Latin American Economic Outlook 2015: Education, Skills and Innovation for Development.*

StatLink *http://dx.doi.org/10.1787/888933422219*

Moreover, increasing wage costs can only be afforded if the economic environment is sufficiently conducive to innovation and the development of more sophisticated skills. These ingredients will be required for the production of goods and services with higher added value. Some emerging economies are already developing innovation capacity. China, for example, is becoming a more important supplier of added value to other countries' production or of final products with higher added value. Domestic firms are taking on the competition in areas such as mobile phones, tablets, laptops, solar panels, commuter trains as well as automobiles (Vandenberg and Zhuang, 2015).

Increasing inequalities and environmental concerns put livelihoods, social cohesion and trust in government at risk

While income and wage inequalities across countries have marginally decreased with shifting wealth, economic growth has not always been shared inclusively within developing countries. Although many developing economies have reduced poverty over recent decades, inequality in income per capita has often increased within countries. In China and India, income groups in the upper brackets have increased their incomes proportionately more than those in the lower brackets (OECD, 2014). China's Gini coefficient for disposable income has risen to above 40, up from around 35 in the early 1990s (Figure 2.15). (The higher the Gini coefficient, the more unequally income is distributed.) Other big emerging economies, such as India, Indonesia and South Africa, have also seen increasing inequality during the last two decades. The biggest exception to this upward trend is Latin America and the Caribbean (see Annex A, Table A.1), as a result, among other things, of the expansion of education, public transfers to the poor (UNDP, 2014) and labour force participation (as in Brazil). However, these countries still have comparatively high levels of inequality. Many emerging economies managed significantly to reduce poverty and to expand the middle class (whose lower threshold can be defined as people living at USD 10 a day) over the last decade. Nonetheless, in China and India, fewer than 10% of the population reached these "middle-class" income levels. Also, the proportion of people on vulnerable incomes (here regarded as those individuals with incomes or consumption spending between USD 2 and USD 10) remains significant and sometimes increased. In all BRIICS economies, the proportion of people on vulnerable incomes remains at 50% or above. As these low-income households have little to spend, the emergence of large consuming societies may be delayed (OECD, 2015e).

While income and wage inequalities across some countries decreased with shifting wealth, there are reasons to think that inequality can increase further given the trend towards the knowledge economy and offshoring activities, which will widen the gap between the highly educated and the lower-skilled, particularly in developed countries. Skills-biased technological change has outpaced educational attainment and per capita income growth, both of which have an equalising effect and tend to lower earnings dispersion. Moreover, greater disparity in earnings among high- and medium-income earners lends support to recent evidence that technology replaces medium-skilled jobs, leading to polarisation of earnings. Offshoring has and continues to contribute to increased job polarisation and wage inequality, in particular in industrialised countries (Rojas-Romagosa, 2011). Job polarisation describes the phenomenon that employment increases relatively faster at both extremes of the skill distribution – for highly paid professionals and low paid personal services – while employment for the middle skill range decreases, including manufacturing and office workers who are paid around the mean wage (Becker, Jansen and Muendler, 2011; OECD, 2015g). On the other hand, improving access for firms in developing and developed economies to take part in the globally integrated economic system accelerates productivity for individual firms and improves the wages of their employees. If more firms could take part in this, it is likely to also reduce wage and income inequality (see ongoing OECD work on skills, jobs and GVCs: OECD, forthcoming). Policy options are available to contribute to decreasing income inequality, including policies for employment promotion and good-quality jobs; fostering women's participation in economic life; strengthening quality education and skills development; and improving the design of tax and benefit systems for a more efficient redistribution for instance.

Figure 2.15. **Some large emerging economies saw distribution of income among their populations worsen, others saw it improve**

Gini coefficient (0-100)

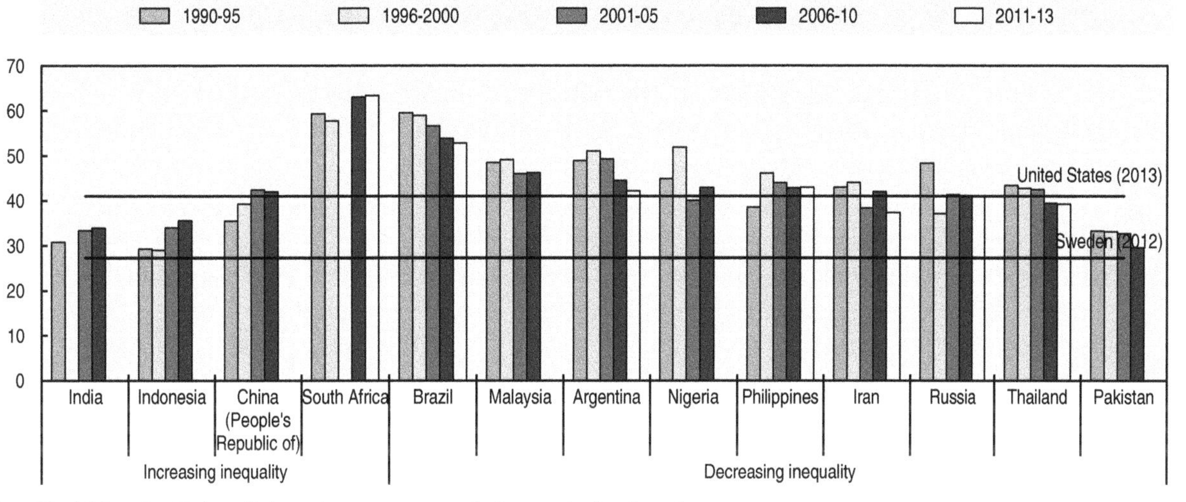

Note: The higher the Gini coefficient, the more unequally income is distributed.

Source: Authors' calculations based on World Bank (2016b), *World Development Indicators* (database), *http://data.worldbank.org/data-catalog/world-development-indicators.*

StatLink http://dx.doi.org/10.1787/888933422227

Economic inequalities lead to frustration, social unrest and mistrust in public institutions. Discontent created by the worsened relative economic situation of many citizens in developing and developed countries and resentment against politico-administrative sources of inequality, including those related to health and education services, are consequences of economic inequality. This may lead to social tensions, as increasingly seen in emerging economies, and in developed countries. Most fundamentally, these inequalities can lead to a fall in trust in public institutions putting economic prospects at risk. Trust in public institutions has received heightened political attention. Today, only 40% of citizens worldwide have trust in their government (OECD, 2015e). The significant erosion in trust in a number of OECD and emerging countries has implications for the effectiveness of policy making and the successful implementation of reforms. Rebuilding trust requires more efficient and more reactive public action, greater transparency and a sustained fight against political misconduct and corruption.

Moreover, environmental concerns are increasing and challenge livelihoods and social cohesion, particularly in developing economies. The costs of inaction on climate change, including economic and social burdens, will increase with time. Continued disturbances to ecosystems could pass a tipping point beyond which damage is irreversible. In the short term, it is mostly extreme weather events and natural disasters, driven largely by climate change, which challenge economies and livelihoods (Global Commission on the Economy and Climate, 2014). An increasing number of extreme weather events such as floods and hurricanes, directly caused by the global warming process, can be observed. Sea level rise is another threat, affecting agriculture productivity, creating health hazards and generating large migrations. Coastal zones are particularly exposed to climate change impacts, especially those that are densely populated. Climate changes in the coming decade, such as severe droughts or flood, particularly affect developing regions including those that have most benefited from the shifting wealth process, such as China, India and Latin American countries. Droughts can contribute to higher food prices, famine and social unrest, with strong destabilising effects for the countries involved. A recent survey by the World Economic Forum (WEF, 2015) revealed that water crises are judged to be a global risk with the greatest potential impact, and that this risk will be even more acute in ten years' time.

The human impact of environmental challenges is worsening as populations increase. Hundreds of millions of people are now exposed to dramatic situations caused by climate change. A common claim in policy circles is that more than 100 million people will be climate change refugees in the coming decades, cited by bodies such as the Intergovernmental Panel on Climate Change (IPCC), the Stern Review on the Economics of Climate Change, NGOs such as Friends of the Earth, and intergovernmental organisations such as the Council of Europe. Slow-onset and rapid-onset environmental changes can alter the relative safety level and ability to earn a living in different regions and will thus influence migration flows. Moreover, many countries that have taken part of the shifting wealth process have done so at the cost of the environment and created heavily polluted cities. In China, for example, coal has been a key source of energy and has created pollution reaching hazardous levels in not only industrial but also residential areas. Pollution may aggravate social tensions in the country.

Has shifting wealth affected international migration?

This chapter has shown that the global economy has experienced a major transformation over the last two decades that has seen the economic centre of gravity shift from developed towards developing countries. This shift may now be slowing down, but today's global economic geography already differs profoundly from the situation in the 1980s and 1990s.

Such large-scale economic transformations are likely to have an impact on international migration. The movement of people is a core component of globalisation, together with the free movement of capital, goods, services and ideas. Changes in differences in income levels between countries, for example, should alter the incentives for people to migrate. As income and other conditions improve, people in rapidly growing economies may not be as interested in emigrating. Perhaps rapidly growing economies will become new poles attracting migrants from other developing countries. For example, China may increasingly compete for particular skills to fill gaps in its labour markets as the country's working age population shrinks and the elderly, dependent population grows. Moreover, improvement in livelihood can also change the decision to migrate or return. Some emigrants from emerging economies may return in light of improved living conditions at home, as observed during episodes of mass migration in the 19th and 20th centuries (Hatton and Williamson, 2005). This report aims to clarify these hypotheses by examining the impact of shifting wealth on patterns of international migration in the last two decades.

A new typology of countries

This report proposes a new typology that divides countries into one of three groups depending on income level and economic growth performance (Table 2.1). The concept of "shifting wealth" aims at including developing countries that have gained a significant weight in the global economy resulting from structural transformations. The growing complexity of the global economy makes it difficult to classify countries according to economic and political reforms in countries. However, the duration of growth is positively related to export orientation (with higher propensities to export manufactured goods), greater openness to FDI and macroeconomic stability (Hausmann, Pritchett and Rodrik, 2005; Berg, Ostry and Zettelmeyer, 2012). The report uses the criterion of high and sustained economic growth to distinguish between developing countries that experienced sustained economic growth (capturing economic and political reforms) (see Annex A and Aubry, 2016 for further details on the methodology to group the countries). These countries contributing to the shifting wealth process are referred to as "High and Sustained Growth" (SG) countries. In the ensuing chapters, the migration dynamics of this group will be examined in contrast with those of the two other groups: "High Income by 1995" (HI) countries, many of which can be considered traditional destination countries for migrants, and "Rest of the World" (RW), the group of developing countries that has not experienced high and sustained economic growth. The sample includes 144 countries. For the purposes of the analysis, only countries with sufficient data on both GDP and migration were classified, and countries with a population of less than 1 million in 1995 were also excluded. Table A.2, in the Annex, presents the full list of countries by category.

Table 2.1. **Criteria for country classifications**

Category	Income criteria	Economic growth criteria
High Income by 1995 (HI)	Classified as a high-income country in 1995	Experienced sufficient economic growth to be classified as a high-income country in 2016
High and Sustained Growth (SG)	Not classified as a high-income country in 1995	Experienced a period of high and sustained economic growth (see criteria below)
Rest of the World (RW)	Not classified as a high-income country in 1995	Did not experience a period of high and sustained economic growth

Countries in the SG category have experienced very different development trajectories from RW countries. The SG economies have undergone transformations that could be expected to have an impact on patterns of migration. The impressive growth performance of SG countries has also helped put them on the path towards convergence with HI countries. In contrast, RW countries – which had levels of GDP per capita similar to those of SG countries at one stage – did not experience the economic "take off" that SG countries such as China or India have seen in the last two decades.

The criterion "High and Sustained Growth" reflects economic reforms. SG countries have increased their integration into the global economy and have become more open to trade since 1980. They have also attracted more foreign direct investment than RW countries.

Most SG countries changed income group as classified by the World Bank between 1995 and 2015.[3] All of the countries that changed income category have moved upward to a higher level of income classification. These countries are spread across the world: 34 % are in Asia, 27% are located in Europe and 17% in Africa.

Using the new typology, the next chapter examines changes in patterns of international migration between 1995 and 2015. Chapter 4 then identifies the drivers of international migration that explain these patterns.

Notes

1. Shifting wealth is used as shorthand for shifting economic activity from developed to developing countries although the former is a stock concept and the latter is a flow concept. This expression refers to the concept defined for the Perspectives on Global Development series.
2. Moreover, many countries experienced a rapid increase in female labour force participation increasing the labour participation of the population (see OECD, 2016b).
3. The countries are analysed over the period 1995-2015 because the migration data are only available from 1990 and the year 1990 is disregarded because many former USSR countries were not classified by income in 1990. Serbia is not considered because it was included in an income group only from 2006.

References

Aubry, A. (2016), "Recent economic transformations and Migration patterns", *Mimeo.*

Bank for International Settlements (2014), "Debt and the financial cycle: domestic and global", in *84th Annual Report 2013/4*, Basel.

Becker, S., M. Jansen and M. Muendler (2011), "Making globalisation work for workers", Centre for Economic Policy Research, *www.voxeu.org/article/making-globalisation-work-workers.*

Berg, A., J.D. Ostry and J. Zettelmeyer (2012), "What makes growth sustained?", *Journal of Development Economics*, Volume 98(2), July, pp. 149-166, DOI:*10.1016/j.jdeveco.2011.08.002.*

Conference Board (2016), *Total Economy Database, https://www.conference-board.org/data/economydatabase/.*

Dahlman, C. and M. Wermelinger (forthcoming), "Dealing with the "new normal": Can China avoid the middle-income trap?", *Development Centre Working Paper*, OECD Publishing, Paris.

Dahlman, C. et al. (2015), "A call for enhanced dialogue on major challenges and opportunities to prioritise collaborative action of the G20", Global Governance and Open Economy - 2015 G20 Think Tank Summit, Beijing.

Elliott, D., A. Kroeber and Y. Qiao (2015), "Shadow banking in China: A primer", *Economic Studies at Brookings*, The Brookings Institution, Washington, DC.

Frankel, J. (2014), "Why are commodity prices falling?", Project Syndicate, *https://www.project-syndicate.org/commentary/commodities-oil-falling-prices-by-jeffrey-frankel-2014-12.*

Global Commission on the Economy and Climate (2014), *The New Climate Economy*, Global Commission on the Economy and the Climate, *http://newclimateeconomy.report.*

Go, S.K., K.N. Wong and S.Y. Tham (2013), "Trade linkages of inward and outward FDI: Evidence from Malaysia", *Economic Modelling* 35, pp. 224-230.

Hatton, T.J. and J.G. Williamson (2005), "Global migration and the world economy: Two centuries of policy and performance", MIT Press, Boston.

Hausmann, R., L. Pritchett and D. Rodrik (2005), "Growth Accelerations", *Journal of Economic Growth*, 10, pp. 303-329.

Helpman, E. (1984), "A simple theory of trade with multinational corporations", *Journal of Political Economy* 92, pp. 451-471.

Helpman, E. and P. Krugman (1985), *Market Structure and Foreign Trade*, MIT Press, Cambridge, MA.

IFR (2015), *World Robotics 2015 Industrial Robots, www.ifr.org/industrial-robots/statistics/.*

ILO (2016), *Employment Trends*, International Labour Organization, Geneva, *www.ilo.org/empelm/units/employment-trends/lang--en/index.htm.*

ILO (2015), *Global Wage Report 2014/15: Wages and Income Inequality*, International Labour Organization, Geneva, *www.ilo.org/global/publications/books/WCMS_324678/lang--en/index.htm.*

IMF (2016), *World Economic Outlook: Too Slow for Too Long*, International Monetary Fund, April, *www.imf.org/external/pubs/ft/weo/2016/01/*.

IMF (2015), *World Economic Outlook: Adjusting to Lower Commodity Prices*, International Monetary Fund, October, *www.imf.org/external/pubs/ft/weo/2015/02/*.

IMF (2014), Article IV Consultation, Staff Report, Washington, DC.

OECD (forthcoming), *Skills Outlook 2017: Skills and Global Value Chains*, OECD Publishing, Paris.

OECD (2016a), *OECD Economic Outlook, Volume 2016 Issue 1*, OECD Publishing, Paris, *http://dx.doi.org/10.1787/eco_outlook-v2016-1-en*.

OECD (2016b), "Closing gender gaps in the labour markets of emerging economies: The unfinished job", in *OECD Employment Outlook 2016*, OECD Publishing, Paris, *http://dx.doi.org/10.1787/empl_outlook-2016-8-en*.

OECD (2015a), *OECD Economic Surveys: China 2015*, OECD Publishing, Paris, *http://dx.doi.org/10.1787/eco_surveys-chn-2015-en*.

OECD (2015b), *OECD Economic Outlook, Interim Report September 2015*, OECD Publishing, Paris, *http://dx.doi.org/10.1787/eco_outlook-v2015-sup1-en*.

OECD (2015c), *OECD Business and Finance Outlook 2015*, OECD Publishing, Paris, *http://dx.doi.org/10.1787/9789264234291-en*.

OECD (2015d), *Data-Driven Innovation: Big Data for Growth and Well-Being*, OECD Publishing, Paris, *http://dx.doi.org/10.1787/9789264229358-en*.

OECD (2015e), *Securing Livelihoods for All: Foresight for Action*, Development Centre Studies, OECD Publishing, Paris, *http://dx.doi.org/10.1787/9789264231894-en*.

OECD (2015f), *Latin American Economic Outlook 2015: Education, Skills and Innovation for Development*, OECD Publishing, Paris, *http://dx.doi.org/10.1787/leo-2015-en*.

OECD (2015g), "Non-standard work, job polarisation and inequality", in *In It Together: Why Less Inequality Benefits All*, OECD Publishing, Paris, *http://dx.doi.org/10.1787/9789264235120-7-en*.

OECD (2014), *Perspectives on Global Development 2014: Boosting Productivity to Meet the Middle-Income Challenge*, OECD Publishing, Paris, *http://dx.doi.org/10.1787/persp_glob_dev-2014-en*.

OECD/World Bank Group (2015), *Inclusive Global Value Chains: Policy Options in Trade and Complementary Areas for GVC Integration by Small and Medium Enterprises and Low-Income Developing Countries*, report prepared for submission to G20 Trade Ministers Meeting, Istanbul, 6 October, *www.oecd.org/trade/OECD-WBG-g20-gvc-report-2015.pdf*.

OECD/WTO/UNCTAD (2013), *Implications of Global Value Chains for Trade, Investment, Development and Jobs*, report prepared for the G20 Leaders Summit, Saint Petersburg, Russian Federation, 2 September, OECD, World Trade Organization and United Nations Conference on Trade and Development, *www.oecd.org/trade/G20-Global-Value-Chains-2013.pdf*.

OECD/WTO/World Bank Group (2014), *Global Value Chains: Challenges, Opportunities and Implications for Policy*, report prepared for submission to the G20 Trade Ministers Meeting, Sydney, Australia, 19 July, OECD, World Trade Organization and World Bank Group, *www.oecd.org/tad/gvc_report_g20_july_2014.pdf*.

Reshoring Initiative (2015), *Reshoring Initiative* (database), *www.reshorenow.org/*.

Rojas-Romagosa, H. (2011), "Wage inequality in trade-in-tasks models", proceedings of *Globalization and Labour Market Outcomes* academic workshop, International Labour Organization, Geneva, 23-24 June.

Roubini, N. (2015), "The liquidity time bomb: Monetary policies have created a dangerous paradox", *The Guardian*, 1 June, *www.theguardian.com/business/2015/jun/01/the-liquidity-timebomb-fiscal-policies-have-created-a-dangerous-paradox*.

Summers, L. (2015), "The global economy: The case for expansion", *Financial Times*, 7 October, *www.ft.com/intl/cms/s/0/1e912316-6b88-11e5-8171-ba1968cf791a.html#axzz3ocUPcew5*.

UNDP (2014), *The 2014 Human Development Report: Sustaining Human Progress: Reducing Vulnerabilities and Building Resilience*, Human Development Report Office, United Nations Development Programme, New York, *http://hdr.undp.org/sites/default/files/hdr14-report-en-1.pdf*.

United Nations (2016), *UN Comtrade* (database), *http://comtrade.un.org/*.

United Nations (2015), *2015 Revision of World Population Prospects*, UN Department of Economic and Social Affairs, Population Division, *http://esa.un.org/unpd/wpp/*.

Vandenberg, P. and J. Zhuang (2015), "People's Republic of China: The challenge of the middle-income transition", *Asia Pathways*, Asian Development Bank Institute blog, *www.asiapathways-adbi.org/2015/03/peoples-republic-of-china-the-challenge-of-the-middle-income-transition/*.

WEF (2015), *Global Risks 2015: Insight Report*, 10th Edition, World Economic Forum, Geneva.

Wolf, M. (2015), "A new Chinese export: Recession risk", *Financial Times*, 15 September.

Wong, M.C.S (2014) "Analyzing corporate credit risk: The myths in China", invited talk, UK Chapter Meeting, Global Association of Risk Professionals, London.

World Bank (2016a), *Commodity Markets Outlook*, June, *www.worldbank.org/en/research/commodity-markets*.

World Bank (2016b), *World Development Indicators* (database), *http://databank.worldbank.org/data/reports.aspx?source=world-development-indicators*.

WTO (2016), "Trade growth to remain subdued in 2016 as uncertainties weigh on global demand", World Trade Organization, 7 April, *https://www.wto.org/english/news_e/pres16_e/pr768_e.htm*.

ANNEX 2.A1

Diverging trends

A country is said to have experienced a period of high and sustained growth if the following four conditions are met in the period between 1980 and 2011 (see Aubry, 2016 for further details):

1. period of rapid growth (more than 3.5% per annum for at least 6 years)
2. accelerated growth (the growth rate throughout the period of rapid growth must be at least two percentage points higher than in the previous 6 years)
3. post-growth output exceeds the output prior to the period of rapid growth (to prevent a growth acceleration episode that follows the collapse of an economy)
4. the growth must be sustained (growth rate of at least 2% during the ten years following the episode of rapid and accelerated growth).

This definition follows established approaches to identifying high and sustained growth episodes in economic literature (see, for example, Hausmann, Pritchett and Rodrik, 2005). The first year analysed is 1980. This allows for a sufficiently long period to identify SG countries according to the definition above. The end point is 2011, as this is the year of latest available data in the Penn Table at the time of writing. The Penn Table data enables the comparison of GDP across countries over time.

Perspectives on Global Development 2017
International Migration in a Shifting World
© OECD 2016

Chapter 3

Recent trends in international migration

International migration is receiving greater attention. This chapter provides a short overview of migration over the last 200 years to provide some context. It then describes the trends between 1995 and 2015 using data from the UNDESA released in 2016 and the new three-way classification of countries developed in this report. It highlights the main countries of origin and destination as well as the main migration corridors. It shows the impact of the 2008/09 economic crisis on migration flows. It highlights how country location and other specificities have a strong effect on the broad relationship between emigration rates and increasing GDP per capita in developing countries. Finally, it details the changes in the demographic and educational characteristics of migrants between 2000 and 2010, the last year for which such detailed information is available.

Migration has become a very sensitive topic, highlighted in the media, in the political debate in many countries and in policy discussions. This attention has been driven partly by the impact of the refugee crisis in the European Union (EU), but the issue is more general. International migration is a broader reflection of increasing globalisation. According to the United Nations, the number of people living outside their country of birth in 2015 was 244 million, up from 173 million in 2000 (UNDESA, 2015). Refugees represent less than 7% of that total, although they are a group that requires urgent and explicit attention, as will be developed in Chapter 6. While migration can benefit origin and destination countries as well as the migrants, there is a strong and growing anti-immigration movement in many countries, driven by concerns that migrants will compete for jobs with the domestic population, become a burden to the social services provided by the state, cause problems for social cohesion, and more recently, pose a threat to security. There are also frequent misperceptions on the size of immigrant flows.

Assessing the impact of migration on countries of origin and destination is not easy. The data on migration at the global level are poor and incomplete, and disagreements persist on the impact of migration on both origin and destination countries. Policy makers in origin countries worry about the brain drain. Policy makers in destination countries worry about integration, social cohesion and the extra pressure on public services, such as education and health. Even with respect to the impact on development, there is strong debate in academic circles between those who argue that relaxing controls on immigration into developed countries is one of the most effective policies for improving human welfare (Clemens, 2011; Prichett, 2006) and others who argue that emigration has a negative effect on the origin countries because they lose some of the best and more entrepreneurial of their population (Collier, 2013).

The objectives of this report are to examine migration from the perspective of developing countries and to provide analysis that will be useful to policy makers in developing and developed countries on the complex relationship between international migration and development. The report will examine recent trends in international migration, the link between shifting wealth and migration, and the links between migration and development and vice versa. It will analyse migration in a granular way and look in detail at the impact in developing countries, an area where not much empirical work has been carried out to date. This report benefits from recently completed detailed empirical research carried out by the OECD Development Centre on the relationship between international migration and development in ten developing countries. The aim is to identify factors and policies that can maximise the positive and minimise the negative impacts of migration. The report is by no means a definitive study because of the complexity of the topic and the poor quality of data. However, it identifies some of the critical issues for policy makers and identifies areas that need further work.

This chapter provides a broad overview of migration trends. This entails moving from the conventional geographic analysis of the Global North and the Global South, which has been common in much of the literature, to a more detailed analysis based on income categories and growth performance, as outlined in Chapter 2. This new typology is helpful in examining the relationship between shifting wealth and migration. It also provides better understanding of how the drivers of migration vary across different types of countries.

This chapter is structured as follows. Section 1 provides an overview of international migration over the last 200 years. This provides insights for understanding current patterns of migration and helps to anticipate some possible future trends, as developed in Chapter 9 on alternative future scenarios. Section 2 describes the broad changes in migration stocks between 1995 and 2015, based on the most recent data released by the United Nations in 2016 (UNDESA, 2015).[1] It shows that the relationship between shifting wealth and migration is the opposite of what may have been expected from the narrowing relative income gap between rapidly growing countries, higher-income countries and the rest of the world. Section 3 provides a more disaggregated picture of the main countries of destination and origin and the main migration corridors. It also presents more detail on some particularly important countries of migration. Section 4 shows the impact of the 2008/09 economic crisis on migration from developing countries to high-income countries. Section 5 highlights how country location and other specificities have a strong effect on the broad relationship between emigration rates and increasing GDP per capita in developing countries, with important implications for what may be expected in the future. Finally, Section 6 details the changes in the demographic and educational characteristics of migrants between 2000 and 2010, the most recent year for which this type of detail is available. Because refugees are a distinct class of migrants, they are analysed in more detail in Chapter 6, although they are included in the total figures given in this chapter.

History shows that international migration results from push-and-pull factors affected by policy

The history of international migration has been characterised by two complementary forces as well as the intermediating influence of migration policies. On the one hand, migration flows correspond to the incentives for migrants to improve their well-being by seeking out better livelihoods in countries with better economic, social and political conditions. On the other, variations in economic activity and demographic transitions, and country-specific shocks such as civil unrest and natural disasters, have caused cyclical fluctuations in long-term migration patterns. Migration policies, whether restrictive or liberal, have worked to allow, promote or temper the volume and composition of the flows during different periods.

Within a 200-year time frame, international migration during the early period mainly consisted of settlement of the New World by Europeans who could afford to emigrate, drawn to the large land resources and economic opportunities. In the 18th and 19th centuries, migration also included the coercive process of moving slaves within Africa and outside it. Slaves, especially in the Americas, helped develop the newly conquered territories after local populations were destroyed by both weapons and disease. With the abolition of slavery, huge demand for labour in land-rich, labour-scarce economies interacted with several other forces to precipitate the mass migration movements of the 19th century. Lower transportation costs opened up the possibility of migration to large sections of the working-class population. Rising incomes in European countries further expanded the potential pool of migrants. Finally, large-scale demographic transitions in origin countries brought about a bulge of young adults, the age group most susceptible to the incentives of migration (Hatton and Williamson, 2005). Compounding these socio-economic forces was a lack of restriction on the movement of people. In many countries there were active recruitment programmes, for example to bring indentured servants from Europe or Chinese labourers to the United States to work in mines or on the transcontinental railroad. Other countries, such as Argentina, Australia and South Africa, provided special subsides to attract immigrants. The lack of border controls, passports and visas helped contribute to the highest levels of international human migration in history, both in volume and as a share of the world population.

The period of 1870 to 1913 is referred to as a "golden age of globalisation" because of the unprecedented levels of trade openness, capital mobility and migration flows both from Europe to the New World and between countries in the developing world. Approximately 60 million Europeans departed their shores in search of new lands in the century following 1820 (Hatton and Williamson, 2005). The most popular destinations for European migrants were the United States, followed by Argentina, Canada, Brazil, New Zealand, Australia and South Africa. European emigration averaged about 300 000 annually in the middle three decades of the 19th century (following the Irish famine), rising to over 1 million per annum after the turn of the century (Hatton and Williamson, 2005). The predominant origin countries in the first half of the 19th century were Great Britain and Germany. These were joined by the modern Benelux and Scandinavian countries by mid-century. By the 1880s and 1890s, the major European origin countries included Austria-Hungary, Italy, Poland, Portugal, Spain and the Russian Federation.

Although overall incomes were rising in most European countries, poverty remained widespread and many people suffered from other social injustices, such as religious persecution. Moreover, rapid agricultural and industrial development in the New World "pulled" migrants to her shores. European countries recorded average annual growth rates of around 2% between 1870 and 1913; the corresponding figure for the New World was 3.5%. This growth differential, coupled with the labour shortage in the New World, created significant wage gaps that strongly contributed to the migration decision. In addition, there were active recruitment policies in both the New World and elsewhere, including programmes to import indentured servants and temporary workers.

Business cycles also played an important role in determining labour mobility. Expansion phases in destination countries produced significant emigration waves in Europe; inversely, periods of economic crisis in destination countries worked to restrain arrivals. For example, the economic boom of 1877-82 played a significant role in drawing a considerable number of migrants to American soil (789 000 in 1882, up from 142 000 in 1877). Conversely, the 1893-94 depression saw a large downturn in the number of emigrants to America. Overall, migration cycles were dictated by economic fluctuations both in sending and receiving countries. People were more attracted by growing markets when their countries of origin were facing periods of economic slowdown.

Mass migration in the Atlantic economies never regained the peaks it reached before the outbreak of the Great War in 1914

World War I led to a steep decline in international migration, and the interwar period, including the Great Depression, marked another sharp contraction. The development of tighter migration policies in the United States, including border controls and passport and visa requirements, occurred after the war. Congress enacted two laws in 1921 and 1924 designed to restrict immigrant numbers severely, except from North West Europe (Castles, De Haas and Miller, 2014). The global crisis of the 1930s marked the end of the period's mass migration movements, both as a result of the worldwide expansion of border control measures and as a direct consequence of the Depression itself.

Migration flows increased after 1945 because of the rapid growth in intra-regional refugee flows and the pressing need to rebuild economies following the Second World War. Large numbers of displaced persons and refugees flowed around Europe, and migration links between former colonies and metropolises increased. Quotas on immigrants were maintained in the United States (US) until 1965 (Immigration and Nationality Act of 1965), but immigration, especially from Mexico, continued to rise, partly as a result of the strong demand for labour. Immigrants were also sought through active recruitment schemes such as the Bracero Program (started in 1942) for Mexican agricultural labourers to work on US farms. In Europe, there was also active recruitment, such as the temporary worker programme in Germany to obtain workers from Turkey (Sander, Abel and Riosmena, 2008). South-South migration also increased significantly, partly driven by the partition of the British Indian Empire into the independent countries of India and Pakistan in 1947, which led to large migration flows between the two countries. And in 1971, the independence of Bangladesh from Pakistan led to flows between all three of these countries. But part of the increase was also "statistical migration", which results when countries are split up and the place of birth of a respondent is considered a different country because of the redefinition of borders.

With the oil shock of 1973 and the subsequent economic crisis, international migration flows significantly decreased until the mid-1980s. Restrictive migration policies expanded during this period, in particular in Europe, but they targeted mainly labour immigration. The doors for family reunification, asylum and temporary work remained open. In the second half of the 1980s, border controls remained, but immigration continued to grow and diversify, particularly in the United States, with more people arriving from Asia and Latin America. New countries of destination emerged, including the south of Europe, the Gulf countries and the new Asian emerging economies. The fall of the Berlin Wall in 1989 helped accelerate international flows. Even so, international migration levels still remain widely below their pre-1914 level.

This short history shows that migration is a dynamic and fast changing process that is affected by differences in economic and social opportunities as well as population asymmetries and migration policies in destination countries. Because of the importance of changing economic opportunities, there was an expectation that shifting wealth would lead to an increase in migration from other developing countries to the High and Sustained Growth (SG) countries, and a reduction of emigration from these countries to higher-income countries. However, this research has found that this is not the case.

The share of migration to developed countries increased significantly from 1995 to 2015

This section highlights the most recent global trends in the volume and characteristics of international migrants. It relies on the UN Global Migration Database (UNDESA, 2015), the most up-to-date dataset on estimates of international migrant stocks. This dataset covers 232 economic entities over the period from 1990 to 2015. However, the period used for the ensuing analysis is 1995 and 2015. The 1990-95 period is omitted because the collapse of the former Soviet Union in 1991 led to an arbitrary increase in migration stocks through a 15-fold increase in the number of countries over the same land mass (See Box 3.3 on immigration in the Russian Federation).

The number of migrants increased from 2.7% of the world's population in 1995 to 3.3% in 2015. That the ratio of migrants to total population increased by 22% in these two decades, while total world population increased, is a significant rise and, as will be argued later, suggests that international migration may continue to increase.

Many previous studies of international migration (UNDP, 2009; Gagnon and Khoudour-Castéras, 2011; UNDESA, 2013) have argued that migration from developing countries to other developing countries accounts for the bulk of global migration. However, they have tended to use broad geographical categories of the Global North as a proxy for developed countries and the Global South as a proxy for developing countries. Moreover, these studies have included the Gulf states and other high-income countries in the category of Global South. This has led to an overestimation of the flows to developing countries. The latest UN Migration Report (UNDESA, 2015) used the World Bank income categories to allocate countries to high-income, middle-income and low-income groups. It showed that high-income countries increased their share of total immigrants from 53% in 1995 to 66% in 2015, and that low- and middle-income countries (developing countries) were the origin of 80% of the migrants in 2015, a slight increase from 79% in 1995 (Table 3.1). Therefore while there has been stability of developing countries as the main source of migrants, at roughly 80%, what is interesting is the large increase (13 percentage points of total migrants) in the proportion of migrants from developing countries who are going to high-income countries.

Table 3.1. **The share of world immigration in high-income countries has increased between 1995 and 2015**

Share of world migration	1995	2015	Change
High-income countries			
• Immigration stocks	53%	66%	+13
• Emigration stocks	21%	20%	-1
Low- and middle-income countries			
• Immigration stocks	47%	34%	-13
• Emigration stocks	79%	80%	+1

Note: UNDESA (2015) uses the World Bank's country classification that is based on countries' gross national income (GNI) in 2014.
Source: Authors' calculations based on UNDESA (2015), *International Migration Flows to and from Selected Countries: The 2015 Revision* (database), *www.un.org/en/development/desa/population/migration/data/empirical2/migrationflows.shtml.*

The classification of countries presented in Chapter 2 helps clarify the relationship between shifting wealth and migration, as well as the changing orientation of migration. This report henceforth refers to three groups of countries (the precise definition of each group, as well as a table listing countries by classification, is provided in Annex Tables A.1 and A.2):

- **High-Income by 1995 (HI)** countries, which were classified as high-income countries by the World Bank in 1995.
- **High and Sustained Growth (SG)** countries, which have experienced a recent period of high and sustained growth. Countries in this group were not classified as high-income countries in 1995 by the World Bank, but many have since attained high-income status.
- **Rest of the World (RW)** which includes all other countries – those that have not experienced a recent period of high and sustained growth and that remain low- and middle-income countries.

These categories were applied to countries with populations above one million in 1995 and for which migration and GDP data were available since 1980 for purposes of the growth analysis. This yielded a total of 144 countries, which accounted for 98% of world GDP, 97% of world population and 89% of total world migration (see Annex Table A.2 for a full list of countries by category).[2]

Analysis indicates that the share of emigrants from SG countries has not changed in the aggregate and accounts for roughly three-fifths of total migration (Table 3.2). What have changed are the destination countries of these emigrants. The share of emigrants from SG countries going to high-income countries increased by 11 percentage points between 1995 and 2015 (from 29% to 40%), while the share going to other SG countries fell by 9 percentage points (from 25% to 16%) (Figure 3.1). At the same time, the share of emigration from RW to SG countries has not increased. Instead, the share of emigration from these countries to HI countries increased by 4 percentage points over the period (from 7% to 11%) (Figure 3.1). This is surprising because it could be expected that, with faster growth over the last two decades in SG countries than in HI countries (shifting wealth), there would be relatively more migration to other SG countries, particularly to those that are geographically close, and less to high-income countries (see Chapter 2 and Figure 3.2, which shows that, in PPP terms, SG countries surpassed HI countries' share of world GDP in 2010). The reasons for this change will be explored in the next chapter. The rest of this chapter will summarise other key trends in migration.

Table 3.2. **Changing share of immigration and emigration for three groups of countries, 1995-2015**

Share of world migration	1995	2015	Change
HI countries			
• Immigration stocks	51.2	64.4	+13.2
• Emigration stocks	18.0	15.6	-2.4
SG countries			
• Immigration stocks	38.0	27.9	-10.1
• Emigration stocks	58.0	58.9	+0.9
RW countries			
• Immigration stocks	10.8	7.7	-3.1
• Emigration stocks	24.0	25.5	+1.5

Note: Country categories as defined in Annex A.
Source: Authors' calculations based on UNDESA (2015) *International Migration Flows to and from Selected Countries: The 2015 Revision* (database), *www.un.org/en/development/desa/population/migration/data/empirical2/migrationflows.shtml*; World Bank (2016) country classification by income groups, and the data in Figure 3.1.

Figure 3.1. **Share of global migration by country category, 1995 versus 2015**

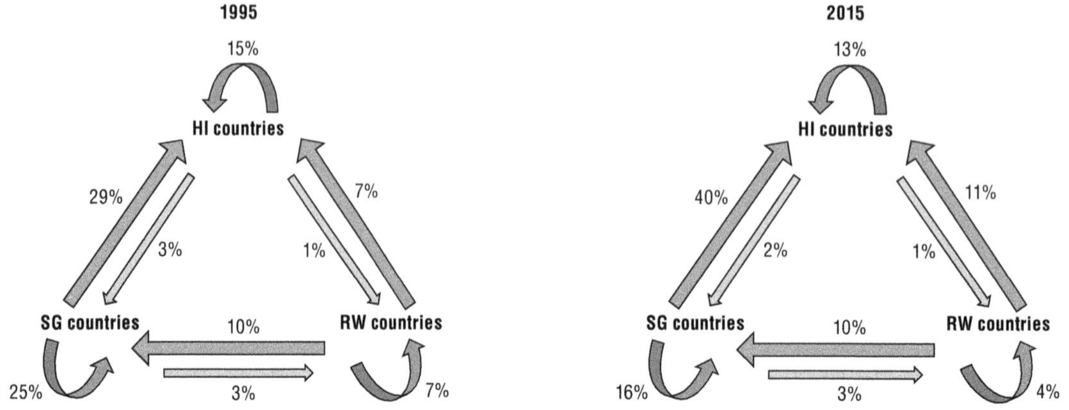

Note: The straight arrows represent migration between country categories (e.g. SG to HI); the circular arrows represent migration within a category (e.g. migration from one SG country to another). Shares are computed on the bilateral database of UNDESA (2015) and include 89% of total migration in 1995 and 87% in 2015.

Source: Authors' calculations based on UNDESA (2015), *International Migration Flows to and from Selected Countries: The 2015 Revision* (database), *www.un.org/en/development/desa/population/migration/data/empirical2/migrationflows.shtml* and a new three-way country classification.

Figure 3.2. **The shares of global GDP are changing by country category between 1995 and 2015**

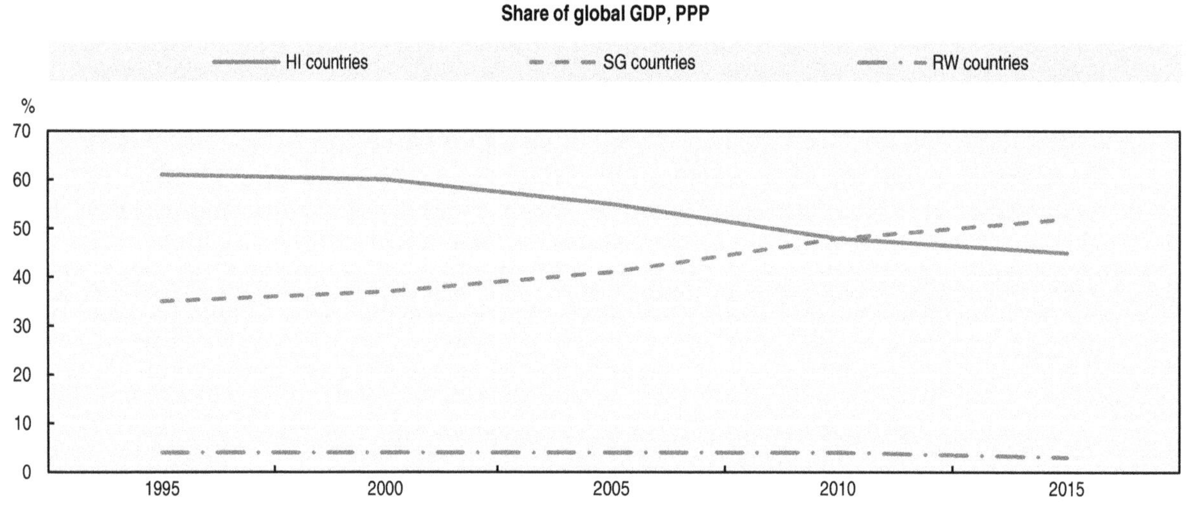

Source: Authors' calculations based on new country classification and GDP data in PPP from World Bank.

StatLink http://dx.doi.org/10.1787/888933422233

Concentration of migration has increased over the last two decades

The distribution of *immigrants* is concentrated in particular regions. More than three-fifths of the world's immigrants live in Europe (31%) and in Asia (31%). The share of the world's immigrants in Europe and Asia remained stable between 1995 and 2015. However, the share of the world's immigrants in North America increased from 18% in 1995 to 22% in 2015. In 2015, Africa hosted 9% of the world's immigrants, a decrease of two percentage points since 1995. In 2015, Latin America hosted 4% of the global immigrant population, and Oceania 2%.

The top 15 destination countries hosted 64% of the world's total stock of international immigrants in 2015, an increase of four percentage points since 1995 (Figure 3.4). Among the top ten destination countries, all but Russia are in the HI category. The United States remained the most attractive destination. The number of immigrants in the United States in 2015 was approximately 47 million, with an average 3% increase per annum. Other important destination countries for immigrants are Germany, the Russian Federation, Saudi Arabia and the United Kingdom. Except for India, the Russian Federation and Ukraine all of the top 15 destination countries experienced an increase in their stock of immigrants between 1995 and 2015 at a slightly faster rate than the average global increase in the stock of immigration. The global average increase in the number of immigrants per year was approximately 5.7% between 1995 and 2015, whereas the number of immigrants increased by 6.1% per annum in the top 15 destination countries over the same period. Spain, Thailand and the United Arab Emirates (UAE) experienced the largest annual growth rate, of above 17% between 1995 and 2015. Box 3.1 explores the rise of the Gulf states as major destination countries as the stock of immigrants to those countries increased by more than 10 million between 1995 and 2015.

The increase in migration to HI countries has led to an increase in the share of migrants in their population. In these countries, the average proportion of immigrants in the population increased by five percentage points between 1995 and 2015, to reach 13% (Figure 3.3). In the UAE and Saudi Arabia, oil-rich states where many migrants were attracted by job opportunities, the proportion of immigrants in the population reached 88% and 32% respectively. In Australia, Canada and Switzerland, the proportion of immigrants in the population surpassed 20%. In contrast, the immigrant proportion in SG countries has barely changed over the last 20 years, increasing from only 6% to 7%.

Figure 3.3. **Proportion of immigrants in the total population is largest and has increased most in high-income countries, 1995-2015**

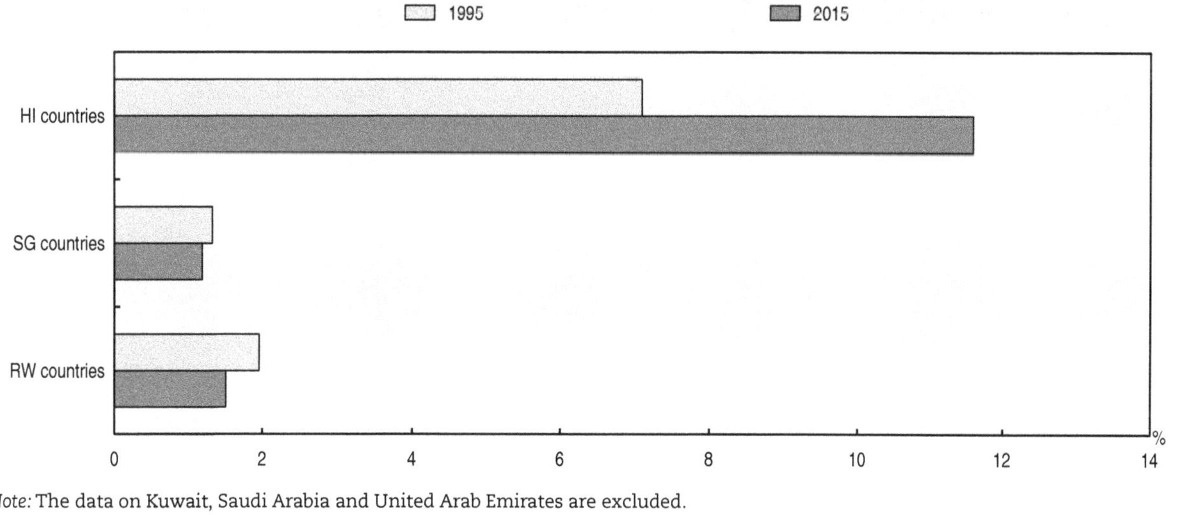

Note: The data on Kuwait, Saudi Arabia and United Arab Emirates are excluded.

Source: Authors' calculations based on UNDESA (2015), *International Migration Flows to and from Selected Countries: The 2015 Revision* (database), *www.un.org/en/development/desa/population/migration/data/empirical2/migrationflows.shtml.*

StatLink http://dx.doi.org/10.1787/888933422243

The distribution of *emigrants* is also concentrated in particular regions. In 2015, 43% of international emigrants were born in Asia, and this region also experienced the largest growth in the stock of emigration. The number of Asian emigrants increased by 4% between 1995 and 2015. Europe represents the second largest source of international emigrants, with 25% in 2015.

The top 15 origin countries accounted for 45% of total emigrants (Figure 3.4). All but two (Germany and the United Kingdom) are developing countries, and of the remaining 13, all are SG countries except for Afghanistan, Bangladesh and Syria. The high numbers of emigrants leaving Afghanistan and Syria are due to refugee flows rather than labour migration. With the exception of Russia, these 15 countries have all experienced an increase in the stock of emigrants since 1995. About 15.6 million individuals born in India were living in another country in 2015, making Indians the largest diaspora in the world. Mexico and Russia accounted for the second and third largest sources of emigrants in 2015. Poland experienced an average annual growth rate of 7% in its stock of emigrants between 1995 and 2015. India and China have seen their stocks of emigrants grow at 6% and 5% per annum, respectively, during the same period. Other countries with high and sustained growth, such as the Philippines and Thailand, also recorded a large increase in the volume of emigrants. Syria, a non-SG country, experienced the largest percentage increase in outflows of migrants because of the large increase in the number of refugees and asylum seekers leaving the country. Large numbers of asylum seekers have also left Afghanistan due to war.

Figure 3.4. **The top 15 destinations are high-income countries, and the top origin countries are SG countries**

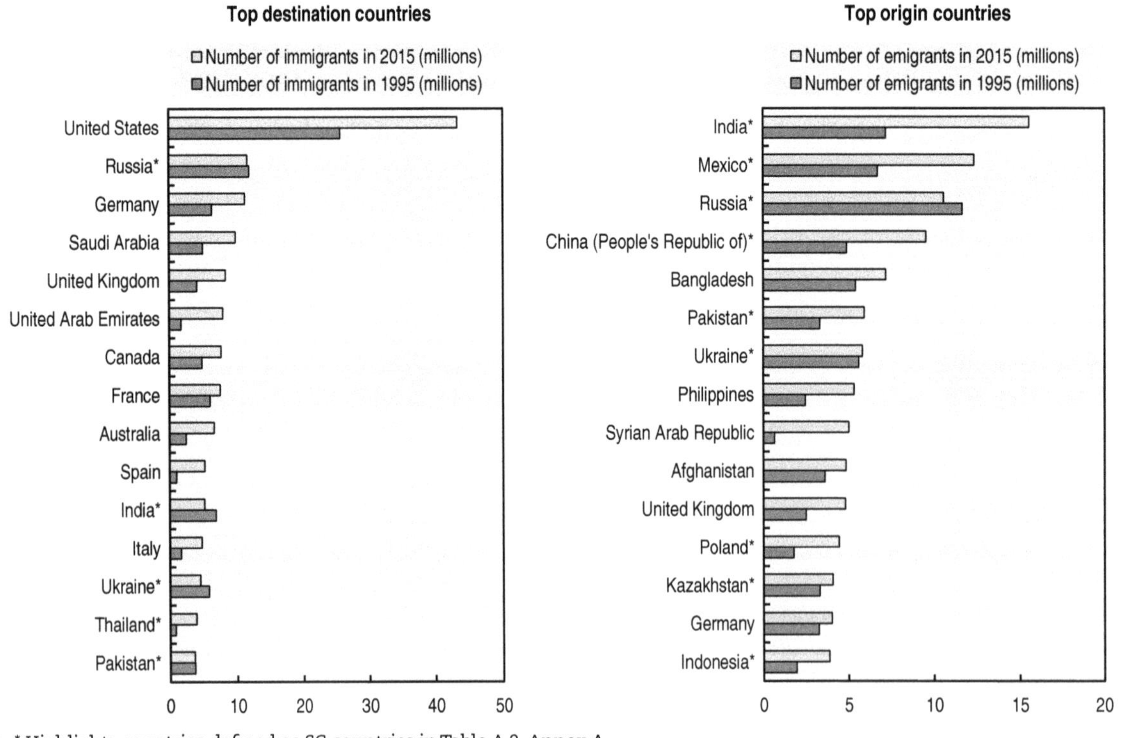

Note: * Highlights countries defined as SG countries in Table A.2, Annex A.

Source: Authors' calculations based on UNDESA (2015), *International Migration Flows to and from Selected Countries: The 2015 Revision* (database), *www.un.org/en/development/desa/population/migration/data/empirical2/migrationflows.shtml*.

StatLink http://dx.doi.org/10.1787/888933422257

One-fifth of total migration is concentrated among the top 15 country pairs

All of these migration corridors involve at least one SG country (Figure 3.5). The corridor between Mexico and the United States remains the largest in terms of volume of migrants. This corridor accounts for 5% of total global migration, with 12 million regular Mexican emigrants living in the United States in 2015 (Box 3.4). The United States is the destination of four country pairs. Four pairs involve the Russian Federation and other former Soviet Republics, in part because of the statistical problems noted above, but also because there have been large flows back and forth (Box 3.3). Four pairs involve India at one end or the other – three to India, in part due to the division of the country into India and Pakistan (Box 3.2), while the fourth is to the United States. Two involve emigration from China, to Hong Kong, China and the United States. Except for four corridors (Russian Federation to Ukraine and vice versa, India to Pakistan, and Bangladesh to India), there has been an increase in the number of migrants between 1995 and 2015. The 2004 enlargement of the European Union precipitated the migration flows from Poland to Germany, which increased by 41% from 2003 to 2004, and by 18% from 2004 to 2005.

Figure 3.5. **One-fifth of total migration is concentrated among 15 country pairs**

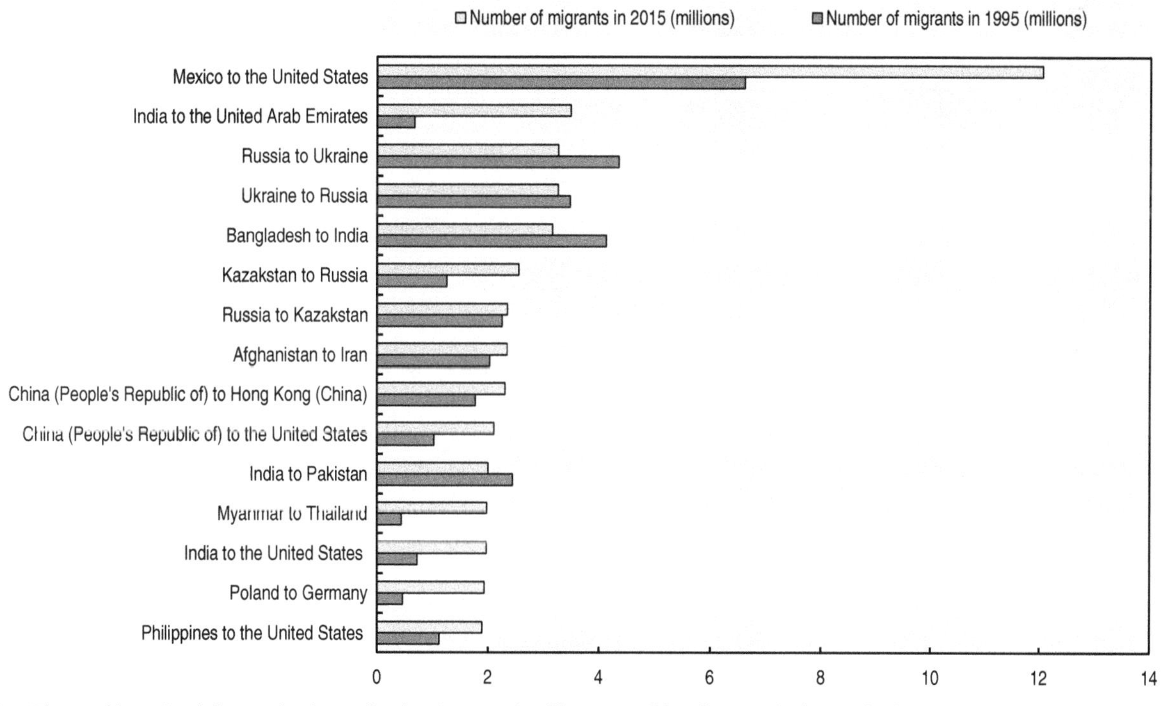

Note: The corridor Palestinian Authority-Jordan has been omitted because of data issues. The issue of refugees in this corridor is analysed in detail in Chapter 6. Otherwise this corridor is ranked 10th out of the 15 largest corridors.

Source: Authors' calculations based on UNDESA (2015), *International Migration Flows to and from Selected Countries: The 2015 Revision* (database), *www.un.org/en/development/desa/population/migration/data/empirical2/migrationflows.shtml.*

StatLink http://dx.doi.org/10.1787/888933422260

Box 3.1. **Migration in the Gulf countries**

Large migration flows to the Gulf Cooperation Council (GCC) countries – Bahrain, Kuwait, Oman, Qatar, Saudi Arabia and the United Arab Emirates – began during the 1970s' oil boom. The boom brought a rapid increase in demand for foreign labour, as domestic labour forces were too small and lacked the necessary skills. Since then, the immigrant population has continued to grow rapidly, with immigrants now making up more than 40% of the total population in GCC countries (Figure 3.6). Immigrants now account for almost 70% of the total population in Kuwait and more than 80% in Qatar and the UAE. The top six origin countries for immigrants to GCC countries are in Asia: Bangladesh, India, Indonesia, Nepal, the Philippines and Sri Lanka.

Figure 3.6. **Immigrant stocks and share of immigrants in total population of GCC countries**

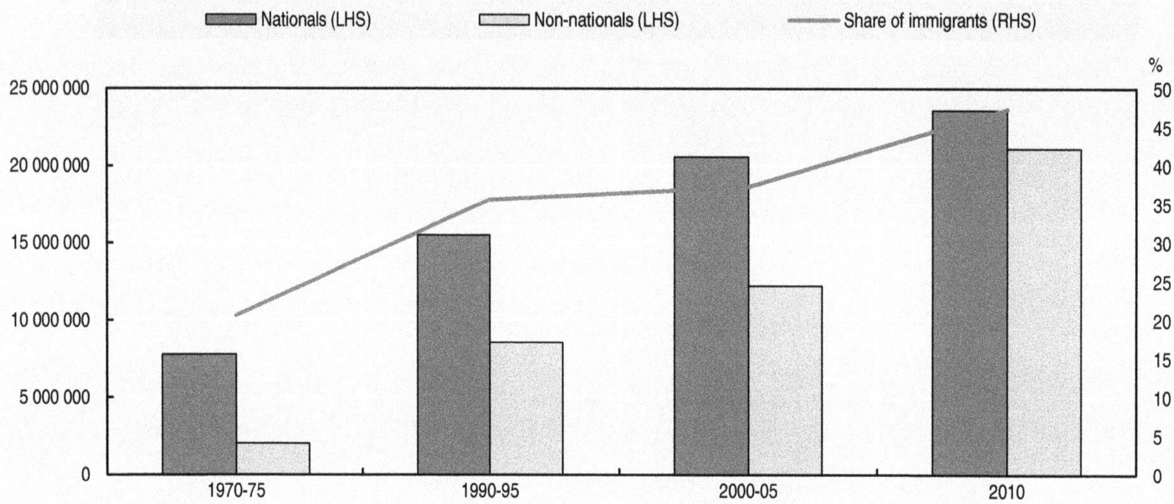

Source: GLMM (2016), *Demographic and Economic Module* (database), *http://gulfmigration.eu/glmm-database/demographic-and-economic-module/*.

StatLink http://dx.doi.org/10.1787/888933422272

The combination of high oil prices and small national populations quickly transformed the GCC countries into rentier states, where oil revenues accounted for 80% (and often more) of government revenue (Winckler, 2010). This facilitated the rise of a dual labour market, in which nationals are almost exclusively employed in the public sector while the majority of foreign workers are employed in the private sector. Liberal labour immigration policies and weak enforcement of labour regulations have made possible the rapid rise of immigrant labour in the GCC countries.

The 2008 global financial crisis affected the GCC countries in terms both of trade and finance, although they maintained spending levels despite a decline in oil revenues (Khamis and Senhadji, 2010). Immigration has continued during the global recession, although at a slower pace (UNDESA, 2015). This is because "governments of the GCC countries have significant fiscal capacity to withstand near-term impacts of oil price decline" (Ratha, 2016). However, GCC governments have begun to strengthen nationalisation policies and to enforce immigration laws more strictly. Declining oil prices are also expected to have a knock-on effect on construction projects in the region, affecting prospects for the large number of immigrants employed in this sector, with remittances projected to decline.

New emerging corridors are among these 15 country pairs

Migration from India to the United Arab Emirates represented the second largest corridor in 2015 (Figure 3.5). This corridor is a recent phenomenon, beginning to form in 2005 (Box 3.2). The number of migrants from India living in the United Arab Emirates grew by 126% between 2005 and 2010, to account for 22% of total Indian migrant stock in 2015, a large increase from 9% in 1995. Thus, although there is an increasing degree of concentration among the main destination countries and the main migration corridors, there is also some change over time, but in unexpected ways.

Box 3.2. **Indian migration in historical perspective**

The British withdrawal from India and the subsequent partition that created India and Pakistan in 1947 caused large-scale external migration. Approximately 14.5 million people migrated between 1947 and 1951 (Castles and Delgado Wise, 2008). This mass migration was politically triggered, uncoordinated and extremely chaotic. Hindus and Sikhs fled the newly-created Pakistan and moved to India, and Muslims left India for Pakistan (Bates, 2011).

Prospects for intra-regional migration in South Asia (from and to India) became limited after independence. Voluntary migration to other regions has increased considerably since the 1970s and it continues to be significant particularly to the Gulf countries, mainly Saudi Arabia and the UAE, and to some OECD countries, particularly Australia, Canada, the United Kingdom and the United States (Castle and Delgado Wise, 2008).

There are currently an estimated 14.2 million Indian migrants worldwide, making the Indian diaspora the largest in the world, ahead of Mexico and Russia. The top destination for Indian migrants is Pakistan (1 396 000), the UAE (2 852 000), Saudi Arabia (1 762 000), and the United States (2 061 000), (Zong and Batalova, 2015).

The number of Indian immigrants in the United States rose sharply in the 1990s and has continued to rise steadily since then (Figure 3.7.). Indians are the second largest immigrant group in the United States after Mexicans, accounting for 4.7% of the 41.3 million foreign-born population (Zong and Batalova, 2015). A significant portion of Indian immigrants in the United States are recent arrivals: 51% of the total Indian-born population arrived during or after 2000, compared to 36% of the foreign-born population as a whole (Migration Policy Institute, 2014).

Figure 3.7. **Stock of Indian immigrants in the United States, 1980-2013**

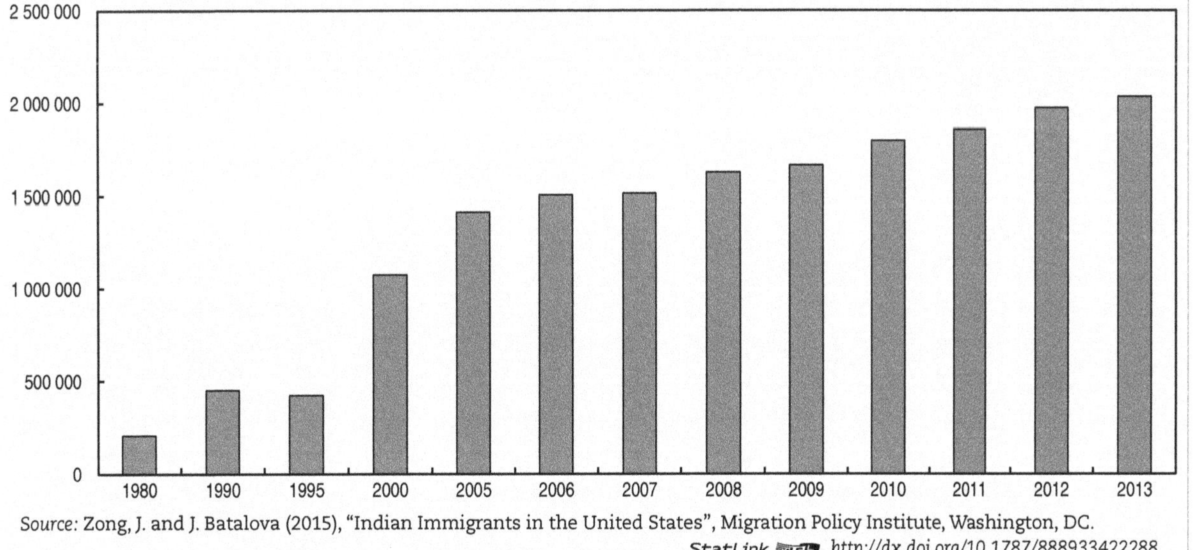

Source: Zong, J. and J. Batalova (2015), "Indian Immigrants in the United States", Migration Policy Institute, Washington, DC.

StatLink http://dx.doi.org/10.1787/888933422288

The destination countries of migrants from SG countries have evolved significantly over time

Emigration from China illustrates this evolution (Figure 3.8). In 1995, about 10% of migration from China was towards other SG countries. Since then, the proportion of migration from China towards SG countries has decreased, while the share of migration towards HI countries has increased. In 2015, more than 90% of migration from China was towards HI countries.

The evolution of migration from India illustrates still greater changes (Figure 3.8). The share of emigration from India to SG countries was about 45% of total emigration in 1995. This had fallen drastically, to 20%, by 2015, while migration increased sharply to HI countries, from 50% in 1995 to more than 75% by 2015, even despite the economic crisis. This change reflects not only the economic attractiveness of high-income countries, but a change in policies in the Saudi Arabia and United Arab Emirates, two countries that receive a large share (35%) of Indian migration. In 2006, India signed a bilateral agreement with the United Arab Emirates regarding labour recruitment, which led to a significant increase in emigration flows.

Figure 3.8. **Emigration from China and India shifted from SG countries to HI countries**

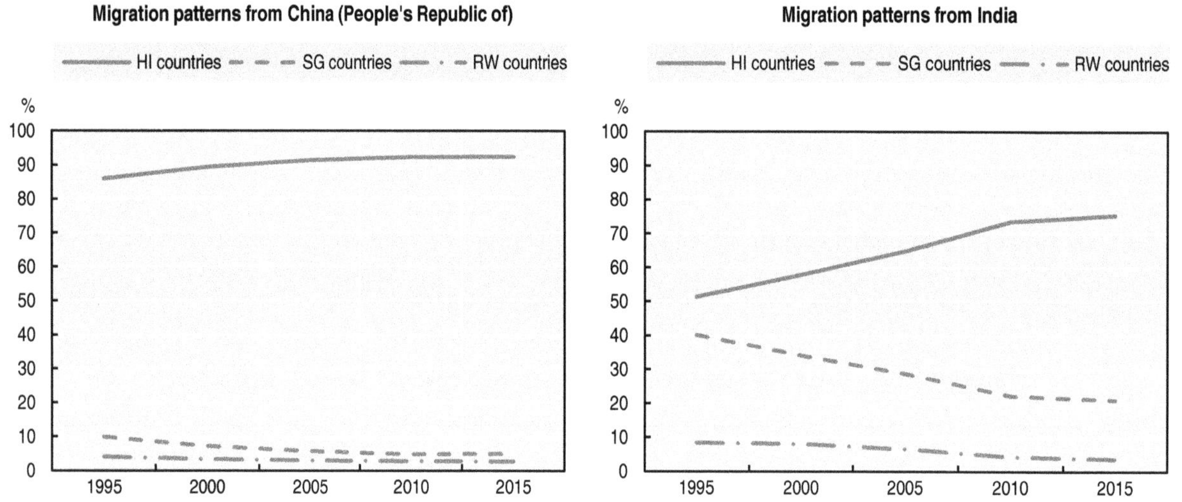

Source: Authors' calculations based on UNDESA (2015), *International Migration Flows to and from Selected Countries: The 2015 Revision* (database), *www.un.org/en/development/desa/population/migration/data/empirical2/migrationflows.shtml.*

StatLink http://dx.doi.org/10.1787/888933422291

However, there are some examples in which the share of emigration from SG countries to other SG countries did not decrease between 1995 and 2015. Such examples are generally SG countries with relatively low GDP per capita compared to other SG countries. For example, in Nigeria, the proportion of migration towards OECD countries has increased, but the proportion of migration towards other SG countries has remained constant. The proportion of emigration towards countries in the RW countries has markedly decreased.

Moreover, migrants from SG countries are choosing a more diverse range of destination countries. There are numerous examples of emigration flows from SG countries shifting from a historically large corridor towards a more diverse range of destinations. In 1995, nearly half of total migrants from Pakistan were in India, but in 2015, the proportion was only 19%. Some HI countries have been attracting more migrants as destination countries, and the proportion of emigration towards Saudi Arabia and the United Arab Emirates has grown. The same pattern can be observed for India. Over time, emigration from India has spread across destinations. Indeed, the number of countries of destination with a share of Indian migrants above 1% has increased from 8 to 13.

Although individuals in many SG countries migrate to an increasingly large number of destination countries, overall migration is concentrated in fewer destination countries. In other words, for a particular country, emigrants go to more destinations. However at the global level these destinations overlap (Czaika and de Haas (2014). For example, individuals from Pakistan migrated to more destination countries between 1995 and 2015. India and other countries experienced the same trend. However at the global level many of the HI destination countries are the same, so there is actually a concentration in a limited number of HI destination countries. The diversification of destination countries is a migration phenomenon which is observed at country level, while the convergence of destination countries is a migration phenomenon observed at an aggregate world level.

Box 3.3. **Migration in Russia was a reaction to post-Soviet economic and political conditions**

Migration in the Soviet era was strictly controlled: both voluntary and forced internal migrations were common. By the late Soviet era, internal migration was mostly voluntary but rigorously controlled by the authorities, while international migration was very limited (HWWI, 2010). The state encouraged internal migration of ethnic Russians to the other Soviet republics for political and economic purposes.

The dissolution of the Union of Soviet Socialist Republics (USSR) in 1991 changed the dynamics of migration, "causing what had been internal migration within one state to become migration across international borders" (Heleniak, 2001). From 1989 to 2002, Russia saw an inflow of 10.9 million migrants from other former Soviet republics (the current Commonwealth of Independent States, or CIS, and the Baltic states). During this same period, 4.1 million people migrated from Russia to former Soviet republics.

Figure 3.9 shows that the emigration flows have diminished considerably over time, from more than 670 000 people leaving Russia in 1991 to just over 33 000 people in 2010. Emigration from Russia to countries beyond the Former Soviet Union (FSU) has been mainly towards Germany, Israel and the United States. Emigration towards Israel and Germany has mainly taken place in the frame of ethnic repatriation programmes (IOM, 2008). Even though this type of emigration has not been as large as was expected once the restrictions on emigrating beyond the FSU states were lifted, the fact that many of these emigrants are highly skilled has represented a loss for Russia.

Figure 3.9. **Migration flows in Russia, 1991-2010**

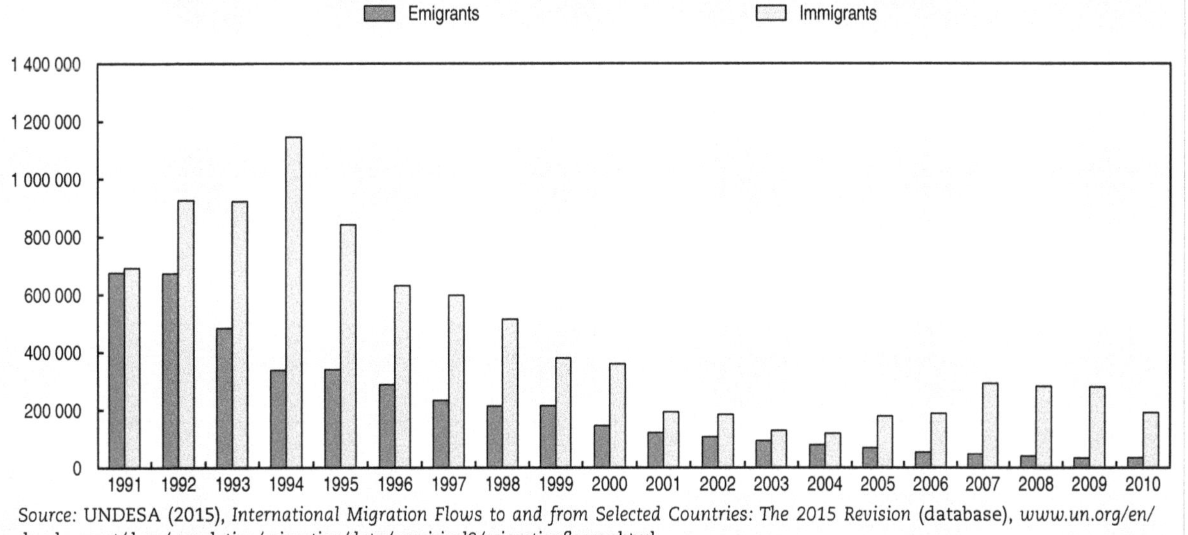

Source: UNDESA (2015), *International Migration Flows to and from Selected Countries: The 2015 Revision* (database), *www.un.org/en/development/desa/population/migration/data/empirical2/migrationflows.shtml.*

StatLink http://dx.doi.org/10.1787/888933422301

Box 3.3. **Migration in Russia was a reaction to post-Soviet economic and political conditions** *(cont.)*

One of the particularities of migration in Russia is that a large number of its foreign-born residents were born in other FSU states, while at the same time many people born in Russia reside in other FSU states. Hence, figures on the stock of emigrants and immigrants in the region reflect the change in geopolitical status of their country of birth, rather than actual international migration to and from Russia (IOM, 2008).

Russia's economic growth between 2000 and 2008 can partially explain the increase in immigration flows between 2004 and 2008. The global financial crisis and recession of 2008/09, as well as an increase in government repression and censorship, could also help explain a slight decrease in immigration numbers in Russia (Cooper, 2009).

The sanctions imposed on Russia following the 2014 annexation of Crimea and Russian involvement in the conflict in Ukraine, as well as the fall in oil prices, have had serious consequences for Russia's economy. When the increased repression on the part of the government is added, it is likely that the number of immigrants will remain at its current levels or become lower and that the number of emigrants will increase in the near future.

Immigration to HI countries decreased after the 2008 economic crisis

The broader picture on global migration flows is the following. Between 1995 and 2000, the global flow of migrants was 38.0 million.[3] It increased to 40.1 million for the next five-year period (2000-05), and to 45.1 million for the 2005-10 period, which included the economic crisis. As a result of the crisis, the flows declined over the next five year period to just 36.5 million largely because of the decline to HI countries.

The 2008 economic crisis brought a decrease in immigration to HI countries and fostered immigration to SG countries. Emigration flows from SG countries diminished by half, from nearly 16 million (2005-10) to 8 million (2010-15). Similarly, immigration flows to HI countries decreased from 22 million (2005-10) to 12 million (2010-15) (Figure 3.10).

Figure 3.10. **The 2008/09 economic slowdown sharply decreased migration to HI and fostered immigration to SG countries**

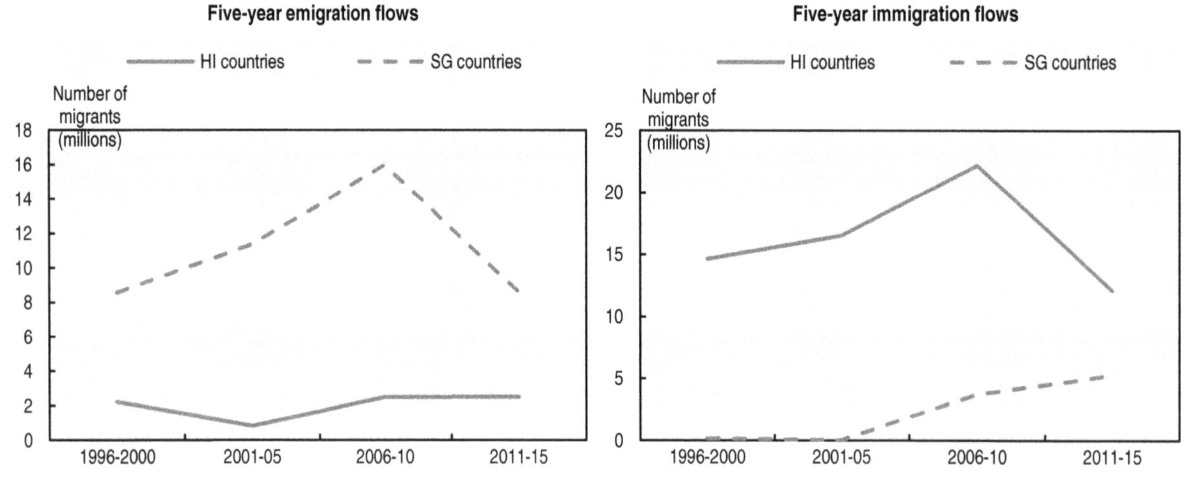

Note: Due to negative net immigration flows, the migration corridors between Russia and Ukraine, Pakistan and India, and Ethiopia and Sudan have been omitted in the calculation of immigration flows.

Source: Authors' calculations based on UNDESA (2015), *International Migration Flows to and from Selected Countries: The 2015 Revision* (database), *www.un.org/en/development/desa/population/migration/data/empirical2/migrationflows.shtml.*

StatLink http://dx.doi.org/10.1787/888933422316

In contrast, immigration flows to SG countries increased from 4 million (2005-10) to 5 million (2010-15). The 2008/09 economic crisis had a lighter impact on SG countries than on HI countries. The economies of high-income countries contracted by 4.6% between 2008 and 2009. Although SG economies contracted by 3% between 2008 and 2009, they returned to a strong growth path the following year, with an average annual growth rate of 3.1%.

The crisis led not only to lower migration from SG countries to HI countries, the group most strongly affected by the economic downturn, but also to return migration from those countries back to the origin countries. A good example is the case of Mexico (Box 3.4).

Box 3.4. **Mexico-United States: The largest migration corridor**

The history of Mexican migration to the United States can be traced back to before World War II. What began as temporary migration in the first half of the 20th century became a more permanent migration in the 1980s, mainly because of tougher border enforcement and more restrictive migration policies in the United States (which made temporary workers stay longer because it was more difficult to get back in), on the one hand, and poor socio-economic conditions in Mexico, on the other. As Canada, Mexico and the United States integrated economically through a preferential trade agreement (the North American Free Trade Agreement), the trend toward increased migration continued through the 1990s and early 2000s until a decline in flows after the 2008 economic crisis. From 3 million Mexican immigrants arriving between 1995 and 2000, the flow dropped to less than half that number, 1.4 million, between 2005 and 2010 (Figure 3.11) (Passel, Cohn and Gonzalez-Barrera, 2012).

Figure 3.11. **Stock of Mexican-born population in the United States**

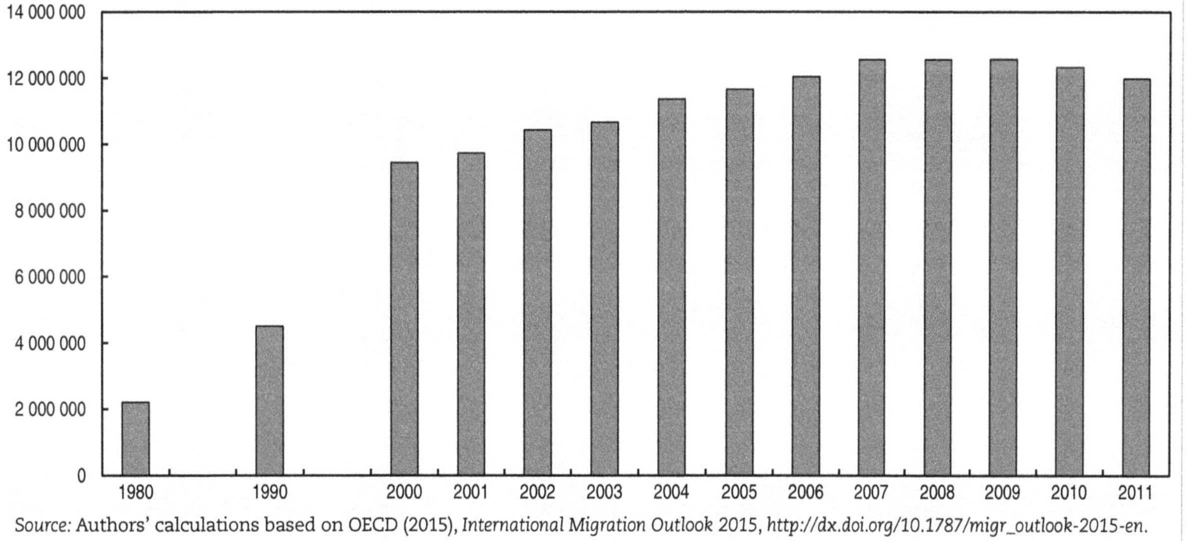

Source: Authors' calculations based on OECD (2015), *International Migration Outlook 2015, http://dx.doi.org/10.1787/migr_outlook-2015-en.*

StatLink http://dx.doi.org/10.1787/888933422323

The increase in inflows in 1995 can be viewed as a consequence of the downturn of the Mexican economy that began with the 1994 economic crisis. The decrease of inflows in 2001, according to some authors, is closely related to the security measures taken after the 9/11 attacks in the United States (namely border security and interior enforcement). The decline in the number of immigrants, both regular and irregular, since the mid-2010s is ascribed to increased border security, better educational and economic opportunities in Mexico, increasing abuses by smugglers and criminal organisations along the migrant routes, a decrease of the population growth rate in Mexico and the downturn of the US economy as a consequence of the 2008/09 economic crisis (Rosenblum et al., 2012). The US downturn led to a large flow of migrants returning to Mexico. This flow, which included US-born children of the Mexican immigrants, increased from 670 000 between 1995 and 2000 to 1.4 million from 2005 to 2010. Mexican immigrants are concentrated in low-skill sectors such as construction, which were the hardest hit by the recession.

Country specificities have a strong effect on the trajectory of migration

Economic growth has stimulated emigration from SG countries, but it has affected emigration patterns from these countries differently (Figure 3.12). For example, Brazil, Colombia and Mexico experienced similar growth patterns over the period 1960-2014, but they have divergent emigration patterns. In 1960, the proportion of emigrants in the total population was less than 2% in each of these countries. However, in 2015, the proportion of emigrants from Brazil remained around 1%, while the proportion from Colombia increased to 5.5% and from Mexico to nearly 10%.

Figure 3.12. **Emigration share of Brazil, Colombia and Mexico, 1960-2015**

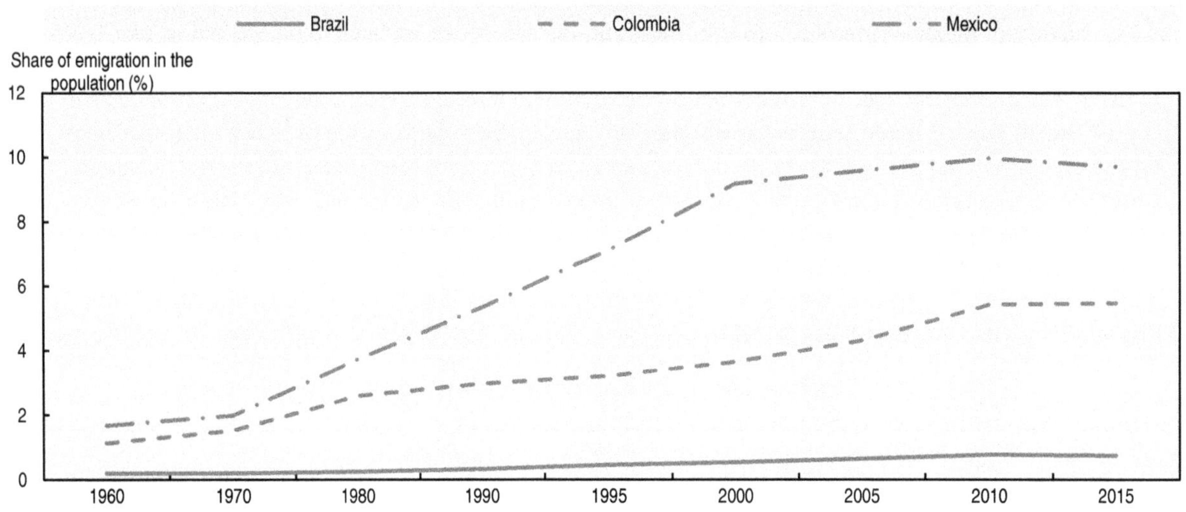

Source: Authors' calculations based on UNDESA (2015), *International Migration Flows to and from Selected Countries: The 2015 Revision* (database), *www.un.org/en/development/desa/population/migration/data/empirical2/migrationflows.shtml* and Özden et al. (2011), "Where on earth is everybody? The evolution of global bilateral migration 1960-2000", *World Bank Economic Review*.

StatLink http://dx.doi.org/10.1787/888933422330

The interdependence between country-specific factors and economic growth partly explains the difference in the evolution of migration in Brazil, Colombia and Mexico. The large increase in emigration from Mexico occurred when it started to liberalise its economy. Mexico joined the General Agreement on Trade and Tariffs (GATT) in 1986. The North American Free Trade Agreement (NAFTA) was signed in 1992, creating a trilateral trade bloc among Canada, Mexico and the United States (Box 3.4). This preferential trade agreement had direct and indirect effects, through explicit migration policy and by stimulating demand for Mexican labour on US farms. Geographic location is likely to be a central factor in the evolution of migration from the three countries. The US GDP per capita was five times that of Mexico in 2014. The United States borders Mexico, leading to lower migration costs. In contrast, Brazil and Colombia do not have the same large income differential with their neighbours and are also further away from the United States, so the cost of travelling there is much higher, particularly for Brazil.

It is also worth noting that, for these three developing countries, the emigration rate has increased as their GDP per capita has risen. Data over time for many developing countries for which that historical data is available show that emigration rates rise as the per capita income of the countries increases. The positive correlation of emigration rates with rising per capita income implies that migration is likely to rise faster than population growth for most developing countries. The factors behind this positive relationship, which tends to hold more generally for developing countries, will be analysed in more detail in the next chapter.

The gender of migrants and their education level vary across regions and country categories

Detailed data on age, gender and educational characteristics are available for a subset of 84 destination countries for 2010 at the time of writing of this report, and will be used to summarise some interesting trends comparing SG with HI countries.[4]

Most migrants belong to the working-age population and are increasingly educated, with roughly equal numbers of men and women, although demographic characteristics vary across regions and country categories. Structural changes and policy changes, partly induced by economic growth, have not only altered the demographic characteristics of migrants, but also the trajectory of migration. These changes include population growth, ageing, gender bias, and non-migration and migration policies.

Gender balance among migrants hides many disparities across regions and income levels

Emigration from HI countries tends to be slightly female-dominant on average, while emigration from middle- and low-income countries tends to be slightly male-dominant on average. There is wide variation in the share of female migration from SG countries, and much of this variation is due to regional specificities. While SG countries located in Africa tend to have male-dominated emigration, SG countries located in Europe and Latin America tend to have female-dominated emigration. Migration from Asian SG countries tends to be reasonably gender balanced.

The female-dominance of migration in Europe is partially explained by the age distribution of migrants across regions. In African SG countries, immigrants tend to be young and predominantly male (57% are male). On the other hand, in European SG countries, immigrants tend to be older and predominantly female (53%), particularly over 45 years of age. Immigration in Latin American SG countries is fairly gender balanced, and immigration in Asian SG countries is slightly male-dominant, with a 47% share of female migration.

Migrants are more educated than they used to be

Migrants in OECD countries were more educated in 2010 than they were in 2000. For this sample of countries, the proportion of tertiary-educated individuals among the total migrant population increased by two percentage points over the period 2000-10, to 29% on average. The proportion of migrants holding at best a non-tertiary degree has also increased on average, from 36% in 2000 to 38% in 2010. This category is often absent from discussions, despite an expected substantial deficit of mid-skills workers with this level of education in the coming decades. It is expected that 14 million mid-skills job vacancies will emerge in the United States from 2010 to 2018 (INSEAD, 2013). Additionally, an estimated 45 million individuals with mid-level vocational skills will be required to satisfy the economic needs of India, South Asia and Africa over the period 2010 to 2030 (McKinsey, 2012).

Education levels among migrants differ between SG and HI countries. About 25% of immigrants in SG countries have a tertiary education, slightly below the average share of all tertiary-educated immigrants present in the sample. In contrast, the proportion of educated migrants in OECD countries is fairly split between tertiary-educated immigrants (33%), migrants with at most a secondary degree (37%) and immigrants with a lower level of education (30%). Increasingly selective policies aimed at highly educated migrants likely explain the higher share of tertiary-educated migrants in OECD countries. The United States maintains a dominant position in attracting skilled migrants: 40% of the skilled migrants in OECD countries reside in the United States. However, the skills composition of migrants in the United States has barely changed since 2000/01.

In most countries, immigrants tend to have higher educational levels than the native population

In Latin America, for instance, 12% of the migrant and 8% of the native populations had completed a tertiary education in 2010/11. In Peru, 22% of the native population had a tertiary degree, compared to 49% of immigrants. In Colombia, there is an 18 percentage point difference between highly educated natives and immigrants. In contrast, in Argentina, Costa Rica and the Dominican Republic, the native population is more educated than immigrants.

Part of the increase in the level of education of migrants is due to general increases in education levels across the world. On average, 5.5% of the population in a particular country held a tertiary degree in 1995. The share was 7.7% in 2010 (Barro and Lee, 2014). Levels of education vary according to economic development. Shifting wealth coincides with development of human capital at a faster pace in SG countries than in other developing countries, but education levels in SG countries are still far below the average in high-income countries. The level of education also varies across regions (Figure 3.13). Sub-Saharan African countries have the lowest share of tertiary-educated individuals.

Figure 3.13. **Tertiary education is increasing across regions**

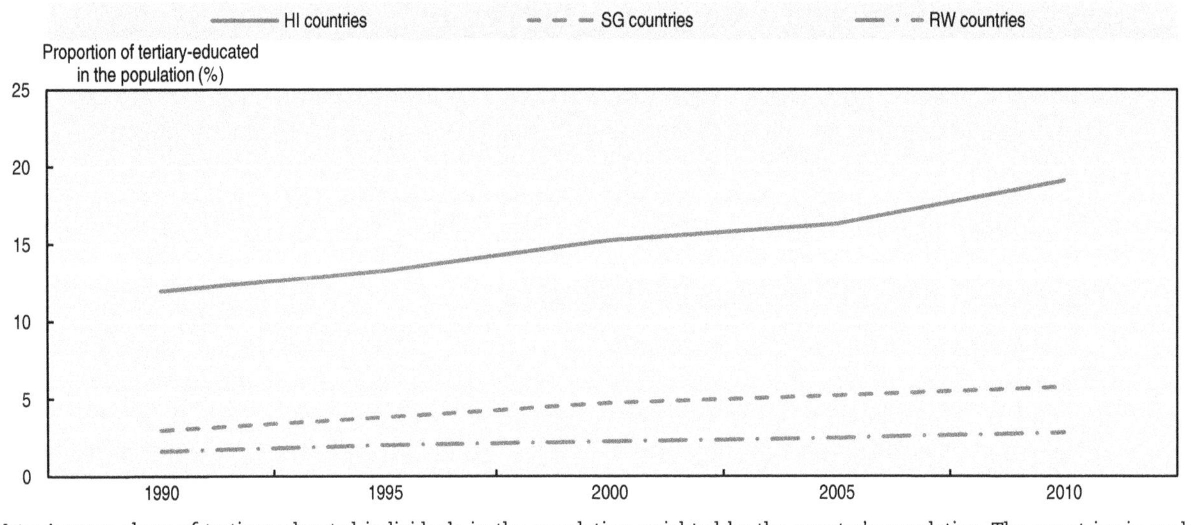

Note: Average share of tertiary-educated individuals in the population weighted by the country's population. The countries in each category are listed in Annex Table A.2.

Source: Authors' calculations based on Barro and Lee (2013), "A new data set of educational attainment in the world, 1950-2010", *Journal of Development Economics*.

StatLink http://dx.doi.org/10.1787/888933422346

Education levels provide information about the selective nature of migration. In most origin countries, the emigration rate for tertiary-educated migrants is higher than the rate for emigrants with other levels of education (Table 3.3). But this does not hold true for HI countries. Migrants from Europe are older than migrants elsewhere on average, and consequently may have lower educational attainment (OECD, 2015).

The emigration rate of individuals with a tertiary degree increased between 1995 and 2010 for all three categories of countries. SG countries display different emigration rates by level of education, reflecting the heterogeneity of these countries, but emigration rates are generally higher for the more educated in most countries. Mexico is an exception. Poorly educated Mexicans are six times more likely to emigrate than individuals with tertiary degrees. Kazakhstan and Russia also have higher emigration rates for the less educated. In contrast, most other SG countries that are also among the top origin countries recorded higher emigration rates for emigrants holding tertiary degrees than for those with lower education. And in RW countries the emigration rates among those holding tertiary degrees was even higher, increasing from 18% to 22% over the same period (Table 3.3).

Table 3.3. **Emigration rates by category of origin countries for migrants residing in OECD countries in 2000 and 2010**

Category of origin countries	2000 Emigration rate				2010 Emigration rate			
	Total	Primary education	Secondary education	Tertiary education	Total	Primary education	Secondary education	Tertiary education
High-Income by 1995 Countries	2.60%	5.40%	3.70%	6.00%	2.60%	7.90%	2.60%	6.20%
High and Sustained Growth Countries	1.20%	3.20%	1.90%	6.00%	1.50%	3.60%	2.00%	7.60%
Rest of the World Countries	1.70%	4.80%	6.10%	18.80%	1.90%	4.40%	5.00%	22.10%

Note: Because of data limitations, the emigration rates of emigrants can only be calculated for immigrants residing in OECD countries. For the same reasons, emigration rates are calculated using the population residing in the origin country. In other words, foreign-born residents of the origin countries are included. The population of the origin country refers to persons aged 15 and above.
Source: Authors' calculations based on OECD (2008), *A Profile of Immigrant Populations in the 21st Century: Data from OECD Countries, http://dx.doi.org/10.1787/9789264040915-en*; OECD (2015), *Connecting with Emigrants: A Global Profile of Diasporas 2015, http://dx.doi.org/10.1787/9789264239845-en*; and Barro and Lee (2010), "A new data set of educational attainment in the world, 1950-2010", *Journal of Development Economics*.

The emigration rate of tertiary-educated women from SG and RW countries was very high in 2010. Of the tertiary-educated women born in a low-income country, 20% were residing outside their home country in 2010. Emigration rates of highly educated females are particularly high in RW countries located in Latin America and in Africa. In 2010, 77% of tertiary-educated women born in Zambia were residing in another country. Of the 37 African countries included in the sample, 15 recorded an emigration rate for tertiary-educated women above 20%. In contrast, the emigration rate of European tertiary-educated women was 8% in 2010 (excluding Albania).

Conclusion

International migration as a share of the world's population has risen over the last two decades, from 2.7% in 1995 to 3.3% in 2015, and its composition and destination have changed. Migrants largely come from SG countries. Moreover, they have become increasingly concentrated in traditional destination countries that are HI countries. Immigration to these countries has increased relative to immigration to SG countries.

This concentration is reflected also by the share of the immigrant population relative to the total population. The average proportion of immigrants in HI countries has increased from less than 8%in 1995 to around 13% in 2015 (and for the Gulf states among them, the average share is around 50%). In SG and RW countries, the share averages around 2% or less. This evolution of the concentration of migration is puzzling, given that SG countries are characterised by strong economic growth. Economic development should make these countries more attractive for migrants, and should divert migration away from traditional corridors. Reasons for the absence of such a trend are explored in the next chapter.

However, this long-term evolution is not immutable. Indeed, the 2008/09 economic crisis affected this pattern. OECD economies that had a recession experienced a large decrease in immigration flows. In contrast, SG countries that responded better to the crisis recorded an increase in immigration flows.

The characteristics of migrants have also changed. The gender distribution of migrants varies by region. This imbalance is not fully driven by the gender distribution in principal origin countries, and shows a preference among female migrants for HI countries.

Overall, migrants are more skilled than they used to be. The distribution of educational attainment in the migrant population differs between HI countries and the other two country categories. Educational attainment is likely to play an important role in the opportunity to emigrate. Indeed, the emigration rate to high-income countries among the highly educated is highest in Africa. This phenomenon is even more pronounced for tertiary-educated women.

The concentration of migration to traditional destination countries despite the emergence of strong alternative economic poles in the world shows that migration is a complex phenomenon determined by many intertwined factors. Economic growth affects the income difference between the origin and the destination countries and has a direct impact on the volume of migration. However, shifting wealth also leads to structural and institutional changes that affect the characteristics of migrants and the possibility for people to emigrate. Moreover, the effect of these structural changes on the volume and the characteristics of international migration are altered by unexpected shocks such as the 2008 economic crisis. All of these interactions make it difficult to predict the future direction of change in the pattern of migration.

SG countries share the characteristic of high and sustained growth, but country specificities remain important in explaining variations in the evolution of migration. The distinguishing characteristics of SG countries are used in Chapter 4 to better understand the impact of economic and non-economic factors on the volume and the characteristics of international migration.

Notes

1. This UN data rather than data collected by the OECD Employment, Labour and Social Affairs Directorate (ELS) are used because the latter are not global in coverage. However ELS's data are used for the analysis of educational and demographic characteristics for immigrants coming into OECD countries because they are more detailed than the UN global data.
2. In 2015, the sample accounted for 95% of world GDP and population and 87% of world migration. Of the roughly 30 million migrants that were excluded because of small population or missing data, nearly half came from six countries where the problem was lack of sufficient economic data. They were: Palestinian Authority (3.5 million), Myanmar (2.9 million), Sudan (2.0 million), Puerto Rico (1.7 million), Republic of Croatia (1.0 million) and Serbia (0.9 million).
3. Data for five-year flows are from Guy J. Abel from the Wittgenstein Centre for Demography in Vienna, cited in an article by Mingels (2016).
4. The analysis of the characteristics of migrants relies on the OECD *Database on Immigrants in OECD and Non-OECD Countries* (DIOC-E) (Dumont, Spielvogel and Widmaier, 2010).

References

Barro, R. and J.-W. Lee (2014), "A new data set of educational attainment in the world, 1950-2010", *Journal of Development Economics*, Vol. 104, pp.184-198, Elsevier, BV.

Bates, C. (2011), "The Hidden Story of Partition and its Legacies", BBC, *http://www.bbc.co.uk/history/british/modern/partition1947_01.shtml*.

Castles, S., H. de Haas and M.J. Miller (2014), *The Age of Migration: International Population Movements in the Modern World*, Palgrave Macmillan.

Castles, S. and R. Delgado Wise (2008), "Migration and Development: Perspectives from the South", International Organization for Migration, Geneva, *http://publications.iom.int/system/files/pdf/md_perspectives_from_the_south.pdf*.

Clemens, M. (2011), "Economics and emigration: Trillion-dollar bills on the sidewalk?", *Journal of Economic Perspectives*, Vol. 25(3), pp. 83-106, *http://dx.doi.org/10.1257/jep.25.3.83*.

Collier, P. (2013), *Exodus: How Migration is Changing Our World*, Oxford University Press, Oxford.

Cooper, W. (2009), "Russia's economic performance and policies and their implications for the United States", Congressional Research Service, *https://www.fas.org/sgp/crs/row/RL34512.pdf*.

Czaika, M. and H. de Haas (2014), "The globalization of migration: Has the world become more migratory?", *International Migration Review*, Vol. 48(2), pp. 283-323.

Dumont, J.-C., G. Spielvogel and S. Widmaier (2010), "International migrants in developed, emerging and developing countries: An extended profile", *OECD Social, Employment and Migration Working Papers*, No. 114, OECD Publishing, Paris, *http://dx.doi.org/10.1787/5km4g1bk3r7h-en*.

Gagnon, J. and D. Khoudour-Castéras (2011), *Tackling the Policy Challenges of Migration: Regulation, Integration, Development*, OECD Publishing, Paris, *http://dx.doi.org/10.1787/9789264126398-en*.

GLMM (2016), *Demographic and Economic Module* (database), Gulf Labour Markets and Migration, *http://gulfmigration.eu/glmm-database/demographic-and-economic-module/*.

Hatton, T.J. and J.G. Williamson (2005), *Global Migration and the World Economy: Two Centuries of Policy and Performance*, The MIT Press, Boston, *https://mitpress.mit.edu/books/global-migration-and-world-economy*.

Heleniak, T. (2001), "Migration and restructuring in post-Soviet Russia", *Demokratizatsiya*, Vol. 9(4), pp. 531-549.

HWWI (2010), "Country profile: Russian Federation", *Focus Migration*, No. 20, Hamburg Institute of International Economics, Hamburg.

INSEAD (2013), *The Global Talent Competitiveness Index 2013*, Singapore, *http://global-indices.insead.edu/gtci/documents/INSEADGTCI2013REPORT.pdf*.

IOM (2008), "Migration in the Russian Federation: A country profile 2008", International Organization for Migration, Geneva, *http://publications.iom.int/system/files/pdf/russia_profile2008.pdf*.

Khamis, M. and A. Senhadji (2010), "Impact of the global financial crisis on the Gulf Cooperation Council countries and challenges ahead: An update", International Monetary Fund, Washington, DC, *https://www.imf.org/external/pubs/ft/dp/2010/dp1002.pdf*.

McKinsey (2012). "The world at work – Jobs, pay, and skills for 3.5 billion people", *http://www.mckinsey.com/~/media/McKinsey/Global%20Themes/Employment%20and%20Growth/The%20world%20at%20work/MGI%20Global_labor_Full_Report_June_2012.ashx*.

Migration Policy Institute (2014), "The Indian Diaspora in the United States", Migration Policy Institute, Washington DC.

Mingels, G. (2016), "Global migration? Actually the world is staying home", *Spiegel OnlineInternational*, 17 May (accessed 4 August 2016), *www.afr.com/news/politics/world/global-migration-actually-the-world-is-staying-home-20160523-gp1emd*.

OECD (2015), *International Migration Outlook 2015*, OECD Publishing, Paris, *http://dx.doi.org/10.1787/migr_outlook-2015-en*.

OECD (2008), *A Profile of Immigrant Populations in the 21st Century: Data from OECD Countries*, OECD Publishing, Paris, *http://dx.doi.org/10.1787/9789264040915-en*.

Özden, Ç., C. Parsons, M. Schiff and T. Walmsley (2011), "Where on earth is everybody? The evolution of global bilateral migration 1960-2000", *World Bank Economic Review*, Vol. 25(1), pp. 12-56.

Passel, J., V. Cohn and A. Gonzalez-Barrera (2012), "Net migration from Mexico falls to Zero – and perhaps less", Pew Hispanic Center, Washington, DC, *www.pewhispanic.org/2012/04/23/net-migration-from-mexico-falls-to-zero-and-perhaps-less/*.

Pritchett, L. (2006), *Let Their People Come: Breaking the Gridlock on Global Labor Mobility*, Center for Global Development, Washington, DC.

Ratha, D. (2016), "Will falling oil prices lead to a decline in outward remittances from GCC countries?", World Bank, Washington, DC, *http://blogs.worldbank.org/peoplemove/will-falling-oil-prices-lead-decline-outward-remittances-gcc-countries.*

Rosenblum, M. et al. (2012), "Mexican migration to the United States: Policy and trends", Congressional Research Service, *www.fas.org/sgp/crs/row/R42560.pdf.*

Sander, N., G. Abel and F. Riosmena (2008), "The future of international migration", in W. Lutz, W. Butz and K.C. Samir (eds.), *World Population and Human Capital in the 21st Century*, Oxford University Press, Oxford.

UNDESA (2015), *International Migration Flows to and from Selected Countries: The 2015 Revision* (database), United Nations Department of Economic and Social Affairs, Population Division, New York, *www.un.org/en/development/desa/population/migration/data/empirical2/migrationflows.shtml.*

UNDESA (2013), *International Migration Report 2013*, United Nations Department of Economic and Social Affairs, Population Division, New York, *www.un.org/en/development/desa/population/publications/pdf/migration/migrationreport2013/Full_Document_final.pdf.*

UNDP (2009), *Human Development Report 2009: Overcoming barriers: Human mobility and development*, United Nations Development Programme, New York, *http://hdr.undp.org/sites/default/files/reports/269/hdr_2009_en_complete.pdf.*

Winckler, O. (2010), "Labour migration to the GCC states: Patterns, scale and policies", in *Migration and the Gulf*, Middle East Institute, Washington, DC, *www.voltairenet.org/IMG/pdf/Migration_and_the_Gulf.pdf.*

World Bank (2016, "Country and lending group classification", *https://datahelpdesk.worldbank.org/knowledgebase/articles/906519-world-bank-country-and-lending-groups.*

Zong, J. and J. Batalova (2015), "Indian Immigrants in the United States", Migration Policy Institute, Washington, DC.

Perspectives on Global Development 2017
International Migration in a Shifting World
© OECD 2016

Chapter 4

Key drivers of recent international migration

Prosperous countries attract migrants but economic considerations are not the only factors driving people to leave their country of birth. Other drivers include factors like geographical and cultural distance, levels of educational achievement and the influence exerted by migrants who have already established themselves abroad. This chapter provides an overview of the major drivers both economic and otherwise that explain the evolution of migration patterns from 1995 to 2015. It investigates the conditions that continue to attract more migrants to developed countries than to economies that experienced high and sustained economic growth. And it describes how in these countries new opportunities provided by economic development have perhaps counterintuitively led to increased emigration.

Over the past few decades, many large developing countries have experienced high and sustained economic growth. A common belief is that such economic progress should decrease emigration and increase immigration. Economic development usually occurs hand-in-hand with major improvements in standards of living and the availability of jobs. If economic conditions significantly improve in a country, then one may expect that its people become less likely to leave in search of opportunities abroad. Furthermore, countries undergoing rapid and sustained economic development should become increasingly attractive for migrants due to their potential to become strong economic poles.

Migration trends over the past 20 years present strong evidence that this belief is inaccurate. This report proposes a framework for studying the effect of different countries' growth trajectories on the evolution of migration. The framework uses a classification of countries based on both income levels and economic growth performance. This report henceforth refers to three groups of countries (a precise definition of each group, and a table listing countries by their classification, can be found in Annex A):

High-Income by 1995 (HI) countries, which were classified as high-income countries by the World Bank in 1995.

High and Sustained Growth (SG) countries, which have experienced a recent period of high and sustained growth. Countries in this group were not classified as high-income countries in 1995 by the World Bank, but many have since attained high-income status.

Rest of the World (RW), which includes all other countries – those that have not experienced a recent period of high and sustained growth and that remain low- and middle-income countries.

Surprisingly, migrants living in HI countries are increasingly likely to have arrived from SG countries, to the detriment of immigration towards SG countries. Migration from SG countries is shifting away from other SG countries and towards HI countries. This is precisely the opposite pattern of what many expected to result from high and sustained economic growth. So why, if economic conditions at home are improving, are people from SG countries increasingly likely to make the difficult decision to move abroad? And why aren't more people migrating to rapidly growing countries? In order to answer such questions, the reasons why people decide to migrate and how they decide where to go must be understood.

Prosperous countries attract migrants, for obvious reasons. But economic considerations are not the only factors driving people to leave their country of birth. This chapter provides an overview of the major drivers, both economic and otherwise, that contribute to explaining the recent evolution of migration patterns over the last two decades.

Across almost all countries, factors increasing migration include large income differences between the countries of origin and destination, and the presence of a common language and social ties in destination countries. The latter is of particular importance for people born in RW countries. The growth in immigration towards HI countries, as opposed to SG countries, can be explained by the availability of larger economic gains and higher quality of life there, as well as by past migration flows.

The ability to turn the aspiration to migrate into reality plays an important role, and helps explain the increase in emigration rates from SG countries. In contrast, the slower growth in emigration from RW countries can be explained by the fact that international migration is costly, and many potential emigrants lack sufficient resources to migrate. Shifting wealth, which changes the income differential across countries, is accompanied by improvements in educational achievement. Greater wealth in SG countries has expanded emigration opportunities by simultaneously increasing educational achievements and the financial resources needed for migration.

Section 1 of this chapter revisits the effects of key drivers on recent bilateral migration. These drivers include both the income differential between destination and origin countries, and factors like geographical and cultural distance that may increase the difficulty of migration and affect the choice of destination country. The influence exerted by *migrant networks* – migrants already well established in the country of destination – is a crucial factor in decisions on whether to move and where to go. Section 2 investigates the conditions that continue to attract people to HI countries, including income opportunities and high quality of life. Section 3 describes how new opportunities provided by economic development, such as higher income or a greater level of education, have increased emigration from SG countries.

An empirical analysis shows how key drivers have affected migration from 1995 to 2015

Economic incentives play an important role in people's decisions to leave family and friends behind in order to seek opportunities abroad for themselves, their relatives and their descendants. Many migrants move to places where they expect to benefit from better job prospects and higher wages. Although economic factors are important determinants, other factors also affect the decision to migrate. International migration is costly. The costs are both monetary, such as the cost of travelling to and settling in another country, and non-monetary, such as the cost of navigating cultural differences. The psychological costs of quitting the home country and leaving family behind also affect the decision to migrate. However, personal contacts and connections to communities in the host country help people overcome the challenges of migration and decide where to move.

The international phenomenon of shifting wealth has led to economic convergence between some countries and economic divergence between others. To measure this convergence or divergence, the income differential is used, defined as the ratio of GDP per capita between destination and origin countries. Rapid economic growth in SG countries has decreased their income differential with HI countries, while the income differential between SG countries and the Rest of the World has increased. Such changes alter migration patterns. In deciding to migrate, people consider their future welfare. Economic convergence diminishes the economic gains from migrating that people can expect for themselves and their descendants. Consequently, individual actors motivated by economic considerations can be expected to seek to migrate between countries with large income differentials. An increase in the income differential between two countries should thus foster migration, and a decrease in the income differential should stimulate a fall in migration.

A global empirical analysis revisits the importance of key drivers of migration in 139 economies from 1995 to 2015 (the most recent period for which data are available at the global level). This analysis investigates how economic disparities between countries, as well migrant networks and factors inhibiting migration, have affected the individual decision to move abroad or to stay in the country of birth over the past two decades. This analysis complements the literature on determinants of migration flows between countries. The current literature mostly focuses on determinants of immigration in OECD countries and covers at most the period between 1980 and 2005 (Mayda, 2010; Ortega and Peri, 2013; Beine, Docquier and Özden, 2011; Beine, 2013) or in particular countries such as the immigration to the United States (Clark, Hatton and Williamson, 2007) or emigration from the Philippines (McKenzie, Theoharides and Yang, 2014). The most recent global analysis on the determinants of migration covers 166 destination and 137 origin countries for the period 1960 to 2000 (Beine and Parsons, 2015). The results found in this chapter are in line with the literature (see Beine, Bertoli and Moraga, 2016 for a summary of the literature). Income differentials have changed for the three groups of countries during this period due to differing economic growth performance. Moreover, the drivers of migration affect countries differently according to their economic performance. Consequently, the analysis of the impact of changing income differentials on migration is conducted on different groups of origin countries (Box 4.1).

The income differential plays an important role in determining the size of migration flows between two countries. An increase of 10% in the income differential between two countries increases the number of migrants between the two countries by 3.1%, on average (Figure 4.1 and the first column in Table 4.A1.1).[1] The effects of the income differential on migration from the different groups of origin countries do not differ significantly from each other (Figure 4.1).

Box 4.1. **Global analysis of the determinants of bilateral migration flows between 1995 and 2015**

Many interdependent factors affect the size of bilateral migration flows. A growing body of research literature has emerged on the economic, geographic and cultural determinants of bilateral migration flows (see Mayda, 2010). This literature has borrowed a model developed in the trade literature – called the gravity model (see Beine, Bertoli and Moraga, 2015) – that captures the effect of income differentials and other non-economic factors on the size of bilateral migration flows. The gravity framework models the individual decision to move abroad or to stay in the country of birth. The migration decision in this type of framework depends on average income in both the origin and destination countries (the income differential) as well as factors affecting migration costs. Migration costs usually include geographical and cultural distance, such as common land borders, a shared official language and shared historical or colonial ties. The model provides estimates of the magnitude and direction of the effect of economic and non-economic factors that contribute to the individual's decision to migrate (see Aubry, 2016a for further details on the econometric results and Table A.1 in Annex A).

The following equation is used to assess the impact of each key driver on migration flows between countries of origin (*o*) and destination (*d*) at time (*t*), keeping other factors constant.

$$\log(Migrant\ flow)_{odt} = \beta_1 \log\left(\frac{\overline{GDP / cap_{dt}}}{GDP / cap_{ot}}\right) + A_{ot} + A_d + \beta_2 \log(distance)_{od} + \beta_3\,(Shared border)_{od}$$
$$+ \beta_4\,(Colony)_{od} + \beta_5\,(Common language)_{od} + \beta_6\,(network)_{odt-10} + \varepsilon_{odt}$$

An increase in income differential between the two countries o and *d* at time t, $\left(\frac{\overline{GDP / cap_{dt}}}{GDP / cap_{ot}}\right)$, is expected to increase the gain of migrating to country d and consequently to increase the size of migration flows between the two countries. β_1 is thus expected to be positive. A_{ot} captures shocks in the origin country that affect the decision to migrate, for instance climate changes or political instability. A_{ot} also captures differences between migrants and non-migrants. A_d captures factors in the destination country, such as labour market

Box 4.1. Global analysis of the determinants of bilateral migration flows between 1995 and 2015 (*cont.*)

conditions or migration policies, that have not changed over the period 1995-2015. Geographical distance is expected to have a negative effect on the size of bilateral migration flow (i.e. $\beta_2 < 0$). Shared borders, colonial links and common language reflect geographical and cultural proximity and decrease migration costs. β_3, β_4 and β_5 are thus expected to be positive. Migrant networks are expected to provide help to migrants, also lowering the cost to migrate ($\beta_6 > 0$).

Most of the existing literature has focused on immigration flows to OECD countries, due to data limitations elsewhere. However, the analysis in this chapter takes advantage of the recent publication of worldwide data on migrant numbers gathered over the period 1990-2015 by the United Nations Department of Economic and Social Affairs (UNDESA, 2015a) to investigate the determinants of migration flows on a global scale.

Migration flows correspond to the difference between the numbers of migrants across five-year periods, as only the number of migrants by country of destination and by country of origin are available at the global level. However, there are various problems with this methodology – migrants who arrive and leave within a five-year period are not recorded. In case of a lower stock of migrants, it is not possible to distinguish a fall in the number of arrivals from deceased migrants or from those who leave and the intermediary trajectories of migrants are not captured. Nevertheless, due to the scarcity of data, migration flows can only be estimated using this method.

In order to identify whether the magnitude of the effect of different factors determining the bilateral migration flows differs across different categories of countries defined in Table A.2 in Annex A, empirical estimations are conducted on different subgroups of origin countries.

Figure 4.1. Greater income differentials increase migration flows, regardless of country category, 1995-2015

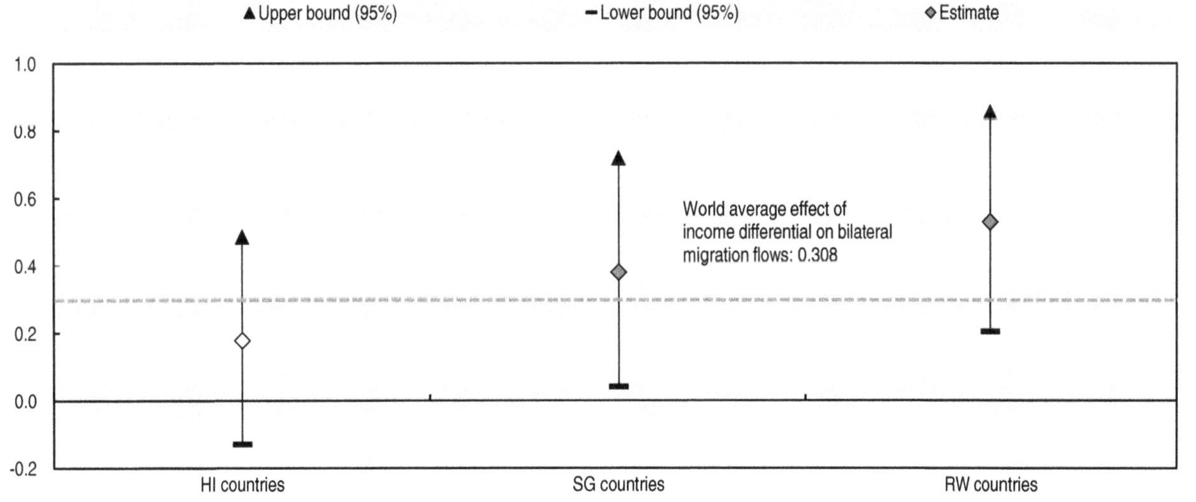

Note: See Table 4.A1.1 for detailed results. The values depicted on the vertical axis represent percentage change and the categories on the horizontal axis represent the category of economies of origin. *Read:* An increase of 1% in the income differential between two countries increases the volume of migration between these two countries by 0.31% on average, keeping other factors constant. The "Upper bound" and "Lower bound" define the 95% confidence interval. Regression uses the Poisson pseudo-maximum likelihood (PPML) estimator. Regressions include destination and time-origin fixed effects. The full sample consists of 94 018 observations corresponding to bilateral migration flows between 139 origin and destination economies. The migration flows between Chile and Venezuela have been excluded because of negative numbers of migrants in the raw data for the year 2015. The white dot is not significantly different from 0 (at 1%).

Source: Authors' calculations based on UNDESA (2015a), "Trends in international migrant stock: Migrants by destination and origin", *International Migration* (database), *www.un.org/en/development/desa/population/migration/data/estimates2/estimates15.shtml*; World Bank (2016), *World Development Indicators* (database), *http://data.worldbank.org/indicator*; Mayer and Zignago (2011), "Notes on CEPII's distances measures: the GeoDist Database", *CEPII Working Paper*, No. 2011-25, *www.cepii.fr/CEPII/en/publications/wp/abstract.asp?NoDoc=3877*.

StatLink http://dx.doi.org/10.1787/888933422356

Geographical distance has a negative impact on the size of bilateral flows. The further the distance between two countries, the higher the travel costs and the higher the costs of acquiring information about destination countries (Mayda, 2010). Geographical distance plays a more important role in the decision to migrate for people born in poorer countries, and matters less for migrants from HI and SG countries (Figure 4.2). This is likely to explain why countries belonging to the Rest of the World group are characterised by more regional migration.

Colonial links and shared languages reflect cultural proximity and decrease migration costs. They enable the collection of more information about the destination country and guarantee easier integration once in the host country. On average, migration flows from RW countries are larger if the origin and destination countries share past colonial ties. This is not the case for migration from HI countries. Surprisingly, migration flows are lower between a HI country and another country if they share past colonial ties. Characteristics associated with colonial ties, such as similar laws and institutions or ongoing conflict, have different relevance across groups of countries and should be investigated further. Country pairs sharing the same official language have, on average, flows of migrants 9.4% larger than country pairs that do not share the same language.

Countries sharing a common border have on average less migration than countries that do not share a common border (Figure 4.2 and Annex Table 4.A1.1.), keeping other factors constant. At first glance, this result is surprising and warrants further investigation. The interpretation of the effect of sharing a border on migration flows is difficult and different results are found in the literature (Mayda, 2010; Ortega and Peri, 2009; Beine and Parsons, 2015). In the analysis undertaken for this chapter the relationship was found to be positive without the inclusion of migrant networks as an explanatory variable. However, when migrant networks were added into the regression, the effect of a common border on migration flows became negative and significant. The variable accounting for migrant networks is likely to capture the proximity of two countries in terms of culture and availability of information. Thus, controlling for the effect of migrant networks, sharing a border may capture factors such as conflicts between the two countries, explaining the negative sign. A country has a limited number of neighbouring countries. Consequently, the number of country-pairs sharing a border is extremely small and only consists of 2% of the sample. As a result, the estimations for the effect of sharing a border may be imprecise.

The presence of family, friends and communities in the destination country encourages individuals to favour traditional corridors over newly emerging economic poles. Families and friends who have already moved abroad may provide funds and information that lessen migration and assimilation costs for the people in the home country (Beine, Docquier and Özden, 2011). Past migrants can provide information on job searching, cost of living, legal formalities or extra-legal channels of movements (Clemens, 2014). They can also provide a kind of insurance against risks, for example by hosting new migrants on arrival. Due to the effect of migrant networks, principal migration corridors are slow to change. The top destination for emigrants from each SG country did not change for 53 out of 66 SG countries between 2000 and 2010.

Migrant networks help explain why the already large number of migrants from SG countries is increasing in HI countries. Empirically, the effect of migrant networks on migration flows is strong. The extent of a migrant network can be measured by the number of people from the country of origin living in the host country. Increasing the number of people from a country of origin living in a particular destination country by 1 percentage point increases the flow of migrants between these countries by around 0.3 percentage points, if all other factors are constant (Figure 4.2, Table 4.A1.1). Migrant networks play a more important role in emigration from RW countries (Column 4, Table 4.A2.1). The costs of migration pose a greater constraint for individuals from poorer countries, explaining in part why people from RW countries rely more on social ties for successful migration.

Figure 4.2. **Migration costs differ by country category, 1995-2015**[2]

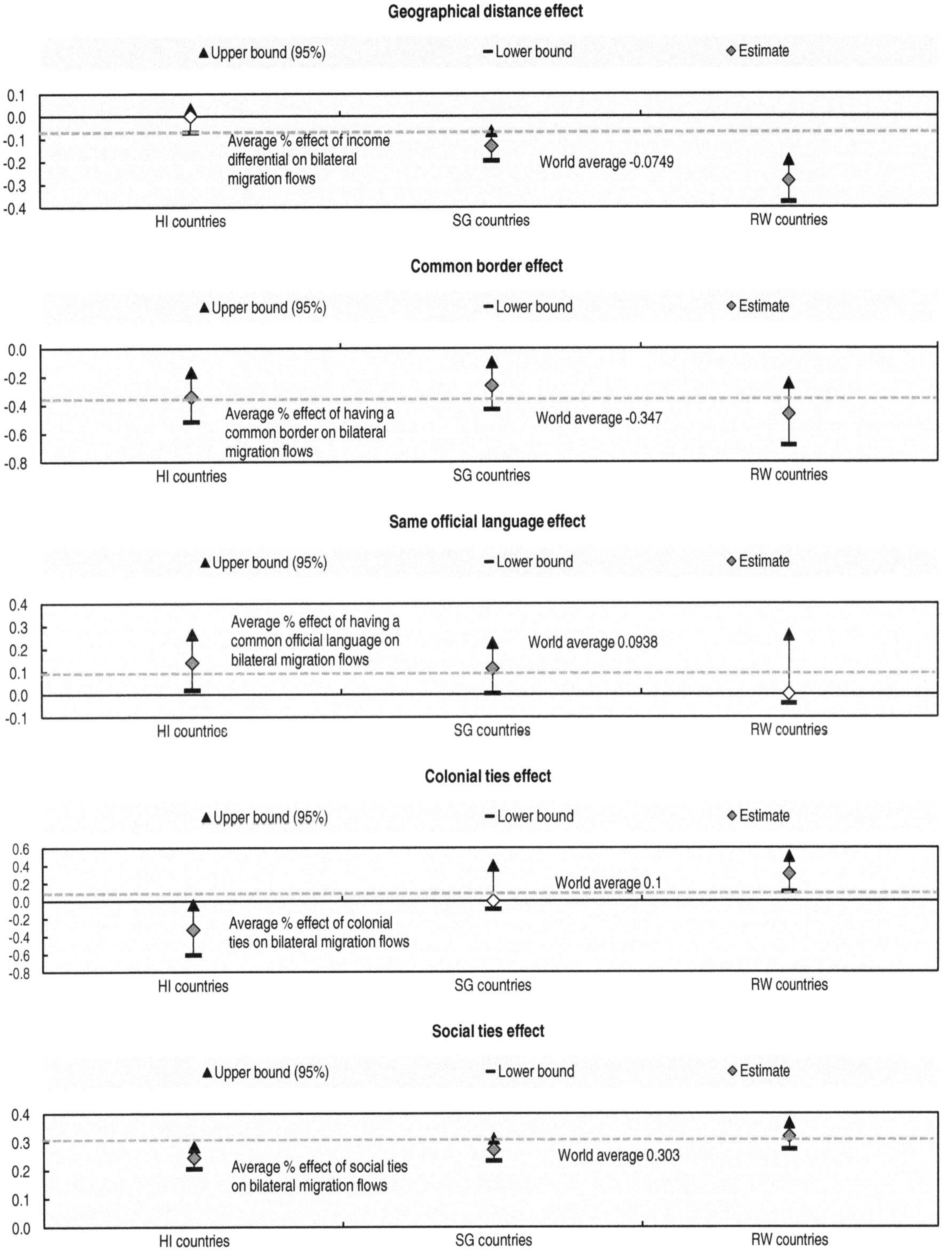

Figure 4.2. **Migration costs differ by country category, 1995-2015[2]** *(cont.)*

Note: See Table 4.A1.1 for detailed results. The results represent percentage effects. The categories on the horizontal axis represent the category of the country of origin. *Read:* An increase of 1% in geographical distance decreases the volume of migration from a High Income by 1995 country to a country of destination by 0.01% on average, keeping other factors constant. The "Upper bound" and "Lower bound" define the 95% confidence interval. Regression uses the Poisson pseudo-maximum likelihood (PPML) estimator. Regressions include destination and time-origin fixed effects. The full sample consists of 94 018 observations corresponding to bilateral migration flows between 139 origin and destination countries. The results of the global analysis are depicted by the horizontal line. The scatters represent the results decomposed by group of origin countries. The migration flows between Chile and Venezuela have been excluded due to negative numbers of migrants in the raw data for the year 2015. The white dots are not significantly different from 0 (at 1%).

Source: Authors' calculations based on UNDESA (2015a), "Trends in international migrant stock: Migrants by destination and origin", *International Migration* (database), *www.un.org/en/development/desa/population/migration/data/estimates2/estimates15.shtml*; World Bank (2016), *World Development Indicators* (database), *http://data.worldbank.org/indicator*; Mayer and Zignago (2011), "Notes on CEPII's distances measures: The GeoDist Database", *CEPII Working Paper*, No. 2011-25, *www.cepii.fr/CEPII/en/publications/wp/abstract.asp?NoDoc=3877*.

StatLink http://dx.doi.org/10.1787/888933422361

Past migration is a strong attractive force towards current migration flows. The country-pairs experiencing the largest flows of migrants between 1995 and 2015 often share the characteristic of having a large community of migrants already established in the destination country in 1995 (Table 4.1). Self-perpetuating migration flows generated by past migration already established in the destination country limit the scope of action for migration policies aiming at curbing migration flows (Beine, 2013).

While former colonial links are a major source of the development of large migrant networks, other sources play an important role. None of the large migration corridors in Table 4.1 share a common colonial past. Special bilateral agreements such as guest worker programmes, labour needs in the destination country and timing have been responsible of the constitution of recent large migrant networks (Beine, 2013). For instance, guest worker programmes existed between Mexico and the United States; Poland and the German Democratic Republic; and India and Saudi Arabia.

Table 4.1. **Large migration corridors between 1995 and 2015 share large past migration flows**

Country of origin	Country of destination	Number of migrants in 1995	Flow of migrants between 1995 and 2015	Ranking of the destination countries in 1995	Ranking of the destination countries in 2015
Mexico	United States	6 602 801	5 447 230	1	1
India	United Arab Emirates	667 853	2 831 484	4	1
Myanmar	Thailand	436 777	1 541 571	1	1
Poland	Germany	459 633	1 470 503	1	1
India	United States	721 728	1 247 558	3	3
China	United States	1 023 585	1 079 966	2	2
India	Saudi Arabia	929 709	964 671	2	4
Philippines	United States	1 118 021	778 010	1	1
Lao People's Democratic Republic	Thailand	205 957	763 310	1	1

Note: Flows between 1995 and 2015 are computed by taking the difference between the numbers of migrants in 1995 and 2015. Ranking of the destination corresponds to the rank of the destination country for each origin country in terms of number of migrants. For instance, the United States ranks 1 for Mexico, meaning that the largest number of migrants from Mexico, among all the destination countries, are in the United States.

Economic convergence and divergence of countries partially explains the evolution and the direction of migration flows. However, the economic convergence of SG countries towards HI countries goes only so far in explaining the growing concentration of migrants in HI countries, especially from SG countries. Due to rapid economic growth in SG countries, their income differentials with HI countries decreased by an average of 45% between 1995 and 2015. However, the volume of migration from SG countries to HI countries increased by 86% on average over the same period. Beyond economic reasons, migrant networks play an important role. Migrant networks have strengthened traditional migration corridors rather than diversifying migration corridors towards new poles of economic growth. Migrant networks better explain the growing migration from SG countries to HI countries. Social ties appear to have a still greater effect in increasing emigration from RW countries, where people face the difficulty of overcoming migration costs and need to rely on migrant networks.

Economic convergence slowly bridges the gap between regions and countries. Although SG economies are converging towards HI economies, there are still large economic and non-economic differences between these two categories. In deciding to migrate, people may rely more on the possibility of large economic gains in HI countries than on the prospect of better economic opportunities in SG countries. The future is uncertain, but current economic differences across countries are clear. Moreover, people take into account factors other than income, such as the expected quality of life and well-being, when making the decision to migrate.

Persistent inequalities between countries explain the recent evolution of migration

The strong economic performance of SG countries has been accompanied by many positive outcomes for people in these countries, for instance in terms of income or educational achievement, yet there remain significant inequalities between HI countries and SG countries. Such differences translate into current major economic and non-economic incentives to migrate towards HI countries, as opposed to SG countries. In deciding to migrate, people take current economic gains into account, and not just the prospect of strong future growth in their country of birth.

In some ways, the difference in GDP per capita between two countries can be considered a reflection of the current difference in average earnings between the two countries. This is, of course, an imprecise measure, as GDP per capita does not capture the distribution of wealth within an economy, nor is GDP per capita a measure of average wages, strictly speaking. Moreover, the wages of migrants can differ sharply from the average wages in a country. Nevertheless, differences in GDP per capita reveal persisting inequalities between countries. They are a reasonable indicator of the income gains to be expected from migrating and are also available for a large number of countries contrary to data on wage that are available for a limited number of countries.

The difference in GDP per capita between SG countries and HI countries remains very large, even after periods of high and sustained growth in SG countries. In 2015, the average difference in GDP per capita between SG countries and HI countries was around USD 35 000 (2011 PPP), on average, up from USD 20 000 in 1995. The average difference in GDP per capita between RW countries and HI countries was even larger, at around USD 40 000.

Furthermore, the difference in GDP per capita between SG countries and HI countries with the largest migration flows is even larger than the average difference between the two groups of countries.[3] In 2015, the average difference in GDP per capita across migration corridors from SG countries to HI countries was around USD 38 000. As an example, the migration corridor between India and the United States is one of the world's largest, and the difference in GDP per capita between these countries was around USD 54 000 in 2015.

Figure 4.3. **High and sustained growth has not yet closed the income gap between countries**

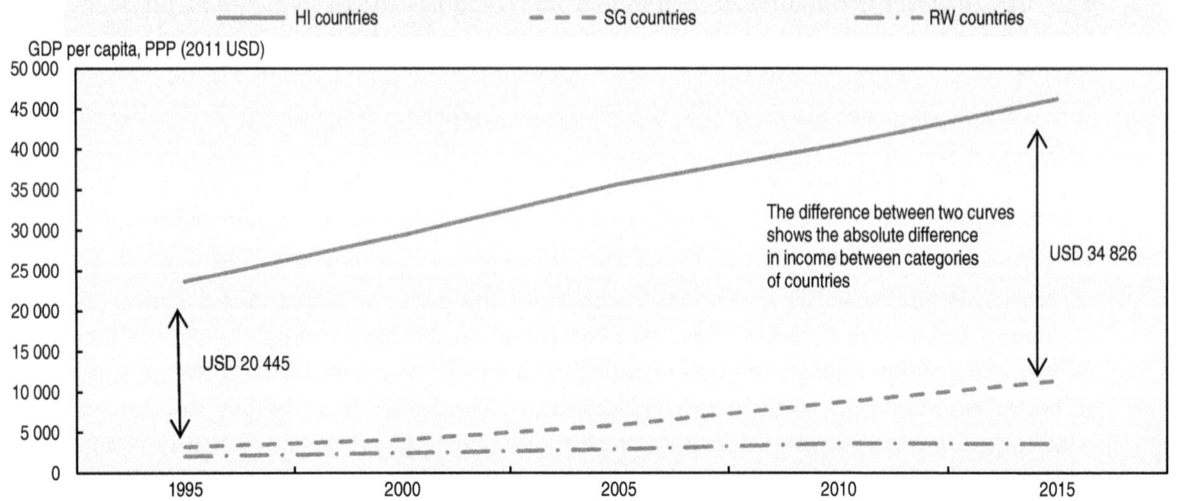

Note: The graph illustrates average GDP per capita in PPP (2011 USD) by country category, weighted by the country's population. Countries are classified according to the definition presented in Table A.1, Annex A.

Source: Authors' calculations based on World Bank (2016), *World Development Indicators* (database), *http://data.worldbank.org/indicator*.

StatLink http://dx.doi.org/10.1787/888933422376

Surprisingly, the proportion of total global migration from RW countries to SG countries has remained stable, even though the earning gains could be large. Expressed in current USD, the GDP per capita in Bangladesh (a country classified in the Rest of the World) was USD 1 212 in 2015. Three important destination countries for migrants from Bangladesh are India, Malaysia and the United States. In India, a SG country, the GDP per capita was USD 1 582. Malaysia, another SG country, had a GDP per capita of USD 9 766. On the other hand, the estimated GDP per capita in the United States was USD 55 837. Although each of these countries is attractive in terms of economic opportunity, the United States has by far the highest GDP per capita. The availability of alternative destinations with very high earning prospects partially explains why the proportion of migration from the Rest of the World to SG countries has not increased.

Economic inequalities between countries play an important role in explaining the recent evolution of global migration trends. The economic gains of migration to HI countries are extremely large and explain the growing proportion of total immigrants living in HI countries. Beyond economic factors, other elements such as well-being keep attracting international migrants to HI countries.

Beyond economic growth, well-being matters for migrants

People care about their quality of life, and not just about their earnings. They care about non-economic factors that contribute to their general well-being, such as health, environment, security and governance (OECD, 2014). Social institutions and gender equality also play a role (Box 4.2). GDP per capita is not a sufficient measure of well-being, as large economic gains may not fully translate into improvements in well-being.

A composite indicator of well-being produced by the OECD for each decade between 1820 and 2000 illustrates the relationship between well-being and the size of bilateral migration flows. The composite indicator is an equally weighted average of the following nine indicators: GDP per capita; real wages; inequality; life expectancy; height; education;

political freedom; mean species abundance; and homicide rates.[4] The well-being indicator is correlated with GDP per capita (the correlation was 81% in 2000), but it reveals additional information on the quality of life, which is determined by more than just income.

Box 4.2. **Female migration and well-being: The key role of discriminatory social institutions**

Female migration should not be explained only by wealth differences between countries. It also depends on well-being, including gender discrimination in social institutions. Social institutions are defined as the formal and informal laws, social norms and practices that play an important role in shaping or restricting the decisions, choices and behaviour of groups, communities and individuals. Discriminatory social institutions reduce women's well-being by restricting their rights and empowerment opportunities. As such, discriminatory social institutions, captured by the OECD Development Centre's Social Institutions and Gender Index (SIGI), influence female migration choices. Women's unequal status in familial, societal and cultural structures, and restrictions on their access to paid employment or public life, among other aspects, could be considered as migration barriers or incentives and affect their choice of destination country.

Women's motives for migrating may be explained by a desire to benefit from better social conditions with lower levels of gender-based discrimination. Gender-based discrimination in the labour market has been identified as an important factor driving female migration (Baudassé and Bazillier, 2014). Highly skilled women, who face greater gender-based discrimination and fewer occupational rewards in their home country than men do, are more likely to migrate than highly skilled men (Kanaiaupuni, 2000). Women may also migrate to escape sexual violence and abuse; single women, widows and divorcees may migrate to escape social stigma; and girls may migrate to escape restrictions on their freedom or pressure to marry or to remain chaste until marriage (Jolly and Reeves, 2005). There is evidence from Southeast Asia of women migrating in order to escape from involuntary marriages (Yeoh, Lam and Hoang, 2010).

Findings from the SIGI suggest that lower levels of discrimination in social institutions in the destination country parallel higher female immigration flows. Hence, greater parity in social institutions in the destination country than in the country of origin would appear to be attractive for women migrants seeking better social conditions and improved well-being. This suggests that more gender equality is a key element for female destination choices: women are more likely to migrate to a country where they can enjoy greater freedoms, empowerment opportunities and rights.

Although SG countries provide a wider range of employment opportunities for women due to sustainable growth over the last decades, discriminatory social institutions can counterbalance this incentive to migrate. For some women, migration towards SG countries may mean an increase in participation in the labour market. However, the attraction of SG countries also depends on their ability to offer to women increased social mobility, economic independence and relative autonomy.

The concentration of international immigration in HI countries is thus explained not only by economic opportunities but also by the well-being they offer. People in HI countries have the highest level of well-being, on average. Despite the improvement in well-being scores for developing countries, and in particular for SG countries, the gap between HI and other countries remains large, partially explaining the attractiveness of HI countries for migrants (Figure 4.4).

Figure 4.4. **Well-being is improving across the world, but differences persist**

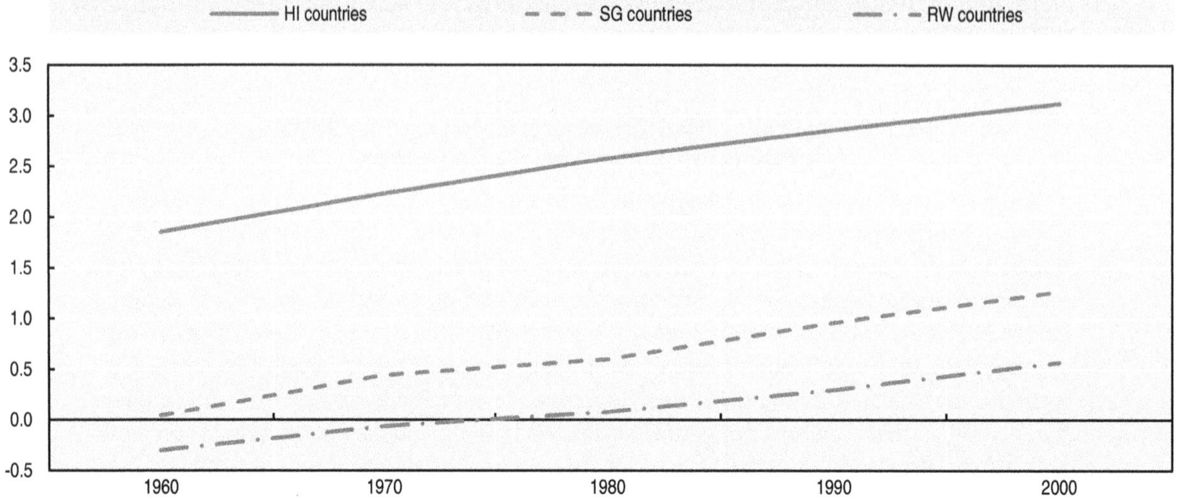

Note: Figure 4.4 shows the average composite indicator weighted by the decadal average country population. The well-being index is depicted on the vertical axis. A higher value of the index represents an increase in the average well-being of the population in a particular group of countries. The different groups of countries are defined in Table A.1, Annex A. For the purpose of comparison, the number of countries is kept constant over time. The sample includes 28 HI countries, 59 SG countries and 56 RW countries. The data on Congo are missing.

Source: Authors' calculations based on van Zanden et al. (eds.) (2014), *How Was Life? Global Well-being Since 1820*, *http://dx.doi.org/10.1787/9789264214262-en*.

StatLink *http://dx.doi.org/10.1787/888933422384*

SG economies are improving the well-being of their populations over time. However, they have lower well-being indicators than HI countries, which are principal destination countries for migrants (Figure 4.4). SG countries with a high value for the well-being index are generally located either in Asia or in Europe. Estonia and Latvia are among the SG countries with the highest well-being indicators, and these countries also belong to the countries with the highest proportion of immigrants in the population. In contrast, sub-Saharan African countries trail the ranking of SG countries in terms of well-being. Angola, Nigeria and Sudan Nigeria, Sudan and Angola have the lowest value for the well-being indicators among SG countries. These countries also have small numbers of foreign-born in the population.

The main difference between SG and HI countries in terms of well-being is the extent of their democratic institutions. Rapidly growing countries are improving the well-being of their populations in many respects (lower homicide rates, increased life expectancy, etc.), but they were not always enhancing democratic institutions by the year 2000. This potential democratic deficit leads to lower well-being indicators than in traditional migration destination countries. The well-being index is computed only until 2000. However, the Polity IV dataset (Marshall, Gurr and Jaggers, 2013) used to compute the well-being composite indicator is available until the year 2015 and enables observation of the recent evolution of democratic institutions in SG countries. In this dataset, each country is assigned a value ranging from -10 (fully autocratic) to 10 (fully democratic). HI countries scored around 7.9 over the 1995-2015 period. RW countries had an average score of only 0.6 over the same period. SG countries have shown improvement, with their average index on democratic institutions increasing by 2.1 points over the period, to 4.2 in 2015. However, despite this progress, the gap between SG countries and HI countries remains large.

The large gaps between countries highlighted in this section explain in part the growing attractiveness of HI countries for migrants. However, differences in income and in well-being do not fully explain why migrants towards HI countries are increasingly likely to come from SG countries. Emigration rates from SG countries are increasing much faster than rates in the other country categories. In SG countries, the number of emigrants is growing more than twice as fast as the population. In contrast, although populations are growing rapidly in Rest of the World countries, the number of emigrants from these countries is growing only slightly faster than their populations. One reason is that many people are inhibited from migrating due to financial and other constraints. The next section explores the transformations that have accompanied economic development, providing people in SG countries with more opportunities abroad.

Economic development boosts emigration opportunities

Economic development brings increased opportunities for migration. A large part of the world's population aspiring to migrate lacks the financial means to do so. While 3.3% of the world's population lived outside of their country of birth in 2015, 11% of people around the world aspired to move abroad permanently in 2013, according to Gallup (2012). Furthermore, in many countries, immigration policies are selective in terms of skills and qualifications, making migration even more difficult.

Recent economic transformations in growing economies help people hoping to migrate to realise their aspirations. Economic development provides additional resources that help individuals overcome migration costs. Additional revenue is more likely to help migrants with lower levels of education than highly-educated migrants who, in general, benefit from better financial situations and easier access to foreign labour markets. An empirical analysis estimates how the emigration rates by educational achievement change when people are provided with additional income (Box 4.3). Furthermore, economic progress generally coincides with an increase in the level of educational achievement of the population. People with a tertiary education are three to four times more likely to emigrate due, among other things, to increasingly selective policies in destination countries (Docquier, Peri and Ruyssen, 2014). Consequently, an increase in the number of highly educated individuals in the population in countries of origin is expected to increase the number of emigrants.

Aspirations to emigrate differ across groups of countries, depending on the geographic region or level of development. Individuals in SG countries are least likely to aspire to move permanently abroad, on average, even less so than people in HI countries (Figure 4.5). This result is surprising, as SG countries had the highest growth in emigration rates (i.e. the proportion of the population in the origin country that migrates) over the past two decades. A total of 9% of the population in SG countries reports an aspiration to move abroad permanently, compared to 23% of the population of RW countries (Figure 4.5). The proportion of people aspiring to migrate is particularly high in Africa, at 26% of the population of the 23 African low-income countries included in the 2013 sample. Nonetheless, the actual proportion of emigrants in the population in these countries is low, suggesting that there are many people who want to migrate but who are unable to.

The discrepancy between the large number of people aspiring to emigrate in RW countries and the actual number of emigrants from these countries highlights the importance of the ability to turn aspirations to move abroad into actual migration. Many people from RW countries face financial and other barriers that inhibit them from migrating. In contrast, people aspiring to emigrate in SG countries are more likely to be able to do so because they have experienced a faster rise in income.

Box 4.3. **Empirical analysis of determinants of the decision to migrate**

An empirical study quantifies the mobility transition curve and shows how emigration rates change when people are provided with additional income, building upon the framework developed by Dao et al. (2016). The model estimates the determinants of the proportion of emigrants in the population, allowing for the possibility that the relationship between income in the home country and the emigration rate is quadratic (inverse-U-shaped). In other words, the model assesses whether emigration increases with economic development at origin for a low level of GDP per capita and decreases after a certain level of income. The results described in this section are also presented in Tables 4.A1.2 and 4.A1.3, Annex 4.A1, and a detailed description of the analysis can be found in Aubry (2016b).

In particular, the analysis shows how the mobility transition curve differs for those with a tertiary degree and for those without. People with different educational levels react differently to additional income. The most recent country-level data on the educational attainment of migrants are for the year 2010 and are from the DIOC-E databases. These databases provide comparable information on the education levels of immigrants in OECD countries at two moments in time – in 2000 and 2010. Given the need for information in the year 2000 to build the variable network, only immigration to OECD countries could be studied.

To assess the effect of financial constraints on the proportion of tertiary-educated and non-tertiary-educated migrants, proxies for the income of tertiary-educated and non-tertiary-educated individuals are calculated. The education-specific incomes are computed by adjusting GDP per capita in the origin country by the proportion of tertiary- and non-tertiary-educated individuals as well as by the return to schooling measure computed by the World Bank (Montenegro and Patrinos, 2014).

The following equation is used to estimate the mobility transition curve,

$$\frac{M_{od}}{POP_o} = \beta_0 + \beta_1 (income)_o + \beta_2 (income)_o^2 + \alpha_1 X_{od} + \alpha_2 X_o + A_d + MR_{od} + \varepsilon_{od}$$

where the dependent variable $\left(\frac{M_{od}}{POP_o}\right)$ is the share of emigration from country *o* to country *d*, computed as the number of migrants from country *o* to country *dj* divided by the population of country *o*. Other explanatory variables X_{od} measure the difference between the country of origin and the country of destination, including cultural and geographical distances between countries and other macroeconomic factors that affect the decision to migrate. The explanatory variables X_o are "push" variables, specific to the country of origin o, and include the total population and the proportion of the population aged 15 to 29 in 2010. A_d captures factors in the destination country, such as labour market conditions or migration policies. The error terms ε_{od} are clustered by country of origin to account for specific country characteristics causing the error terms to be correlated across countries of destination. The terms MR_{od} are multilateral resistance terms, as described below.

The multilateral resistance terms control for some of the bias introduced by the relative attractiveness of a destination with respect to other destinations. The absence of multilateral resistance terms requires the assumption that the attractiveness of a particular destination does not vary across origin countries. However, it is unlikely that this assumption holds. Given that only one year of data (the year 2010) is available, the variation in the data across time cannot be exploited as it has been done in the model described in Box 4.1. The distance to other countries and borders shared with other countries are proxies for the relative attractiveness of other destinations. The multilateral resistance terms are computed as follows:

$$MRDIST_{od} = \sum_{k \neq d}^{D} \theta_k \log(Dist_{ok}) + \sum_{m \neq o}^{O} \theta_m \log(Dist_{md}) - \sum_{k \neq d}^{D} \sum_{m \neq o}^{O} \theta_k \theta_m \log(Dist_{mk})$$

$$MRBORDER_{od} = \sum_{k \neq d}^{D} \theta_k Adj_{ok} + \sum_{m \neq o}^{O} \theta_m Adj_{md} - \sum_{k \neq d}^{D} \sum_{m \neq o}^{O} \theta_k \theta_m Adj_{mk}$$

where θ_x represents the proportion of the world population in country *x*, $Dist_{od}$ represents the distance between two countries *o* and *d*, and Adj_{od} is a dummy variable equal to 1 if countries *o* and *d* share a border.

Figure 4.5. **Aspirations to move abroad permanently differ across country categories**

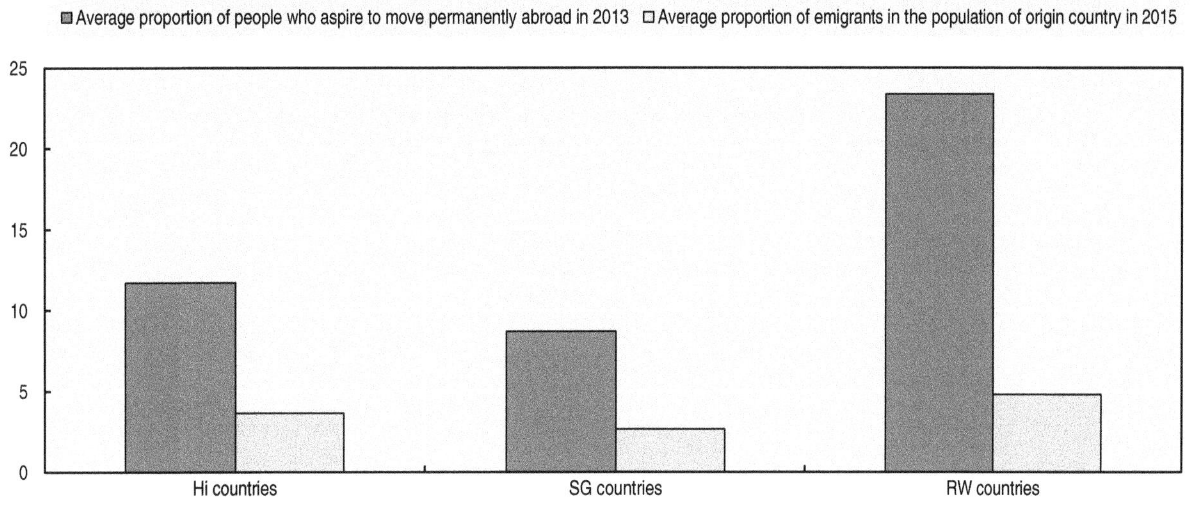

Note: Population-weighted average share of the country's population reporting their aspirations to move permanently abroad in 2013. The country categories are defined in Annex A. Data are missing for Cuba, Eritrea, Gambia, Guinea-Bissau, Libya, Oman and Papua New Guinea.

Source: Authors' calculations based on Gallup (2012), *Worldwide Research Methodology and Codebook* (database).

StatLink http://dx.doi.org/10.1787/888933422398

Economic development eases financial constraints on migration

Economic development stimulates emigration in countries with low GDP per capita by helping people to meet the costs of migration. Additional income provides the opportunity to migrate to people who had been inhibited from leaving by financial constraints (Lopez and Schiff, 1998; Yang, 2006). For countries with high levels of GDP per capita, financial constraints become less relevant as individuals acquire the resources needed to migrate. Furthermore, the aspiration to migrate decreases with development due to increasing domestic opportunities; incremental economic gains no longer stimulate emigration. This relationship between GDP per capita and the emigration rate is referred to as the mobility transition curve (Zelinsky, 1971), based on a pioneering theory that reconciles the trends observed in GDP per capita, aspiration to migrate and the emigration rate.

People in low-income countries generally have high aspirations but low abilities to migrate, while people in high-income countries have low aspirations but high abilities to migrate. The proportion of emigrants in the population is the highest in countries with a GDP per capita close to USD 7 168 (in 2011 PPP), and is lowest both in countries with low GDP per capita and in countries with high GDP per capita (Figure 4.6). More precisely, in 2010, countries with the highest proportion of emigrants in the population had a GDP per capita of around USD 7 168 (in 2011 PPP). The proportion of emigrants in the population of countries with GDP per capita lower than USD 7 168 (in 2011 PPP) is expected to increase with a rise in GDP per capita, while the proportion of emigrants in countries with a GDP per capita above this threshold is expected to decrease.

An increase in GDP per capita can be expected to increase emigration rates in countries that are among the largest sources of emigrants. Fourteen out of the 59 SG countries had a GDP per capita below USD 7 168 (in 2011 PPP). These countries are Armenia, El Salvador, Georgia, Ghana, India, Morocco, the Republic of Moldova, Mongolia, Nigeria, Pakistan, the Philippines, Sudan, Uzbekistan and Viet Nam. For these countries, an increase in GDP per capita increases opportunities to emigrate. India, Pakistan and the Philippines are currently among the countries with the greatest number of emigrants.

Figure 4.6. **The proportion of emigrants from a country relative to the population of the country is related to GDP per capita, 2010**

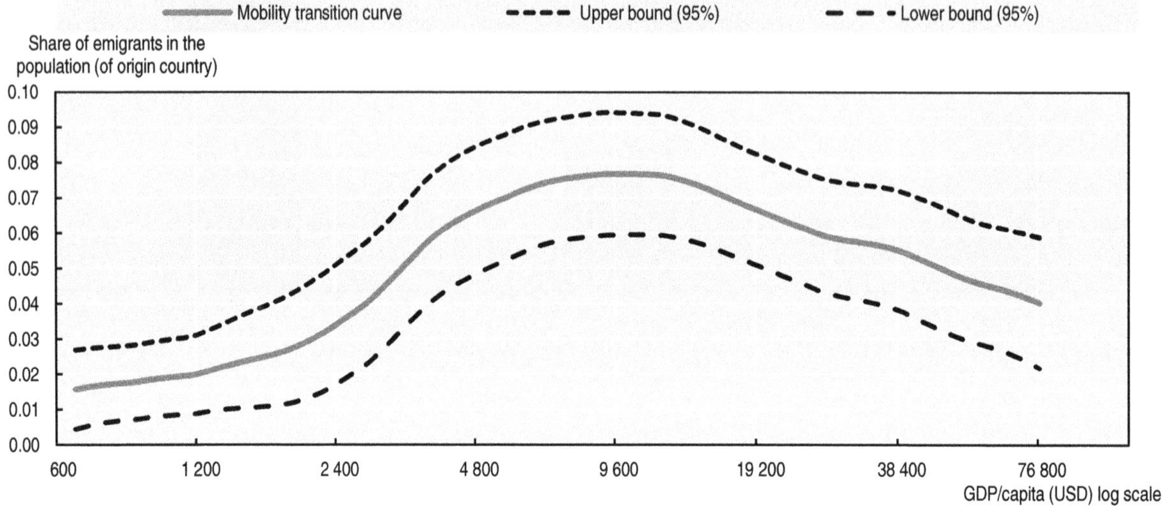

Note: The curve represents the relation between the GDP per capita (logarithmic scale) and the proportion of emigrants in the population of the origin country (specifically, the curve is computed with an Epanechnikov kernel density function from Epanechnikov(1969) that is detailed in Aubry (2016b). The sample includes 143 origin countries and 81 destination countries.

Source: Authors' calculations based on data from OECD (2015), *Connecting with Emigrants: A Global Profile of Diasporas 2015*, *http://dx.doi.org/10.1787/9789264239845-en* and World Bank (2016), *World Development Indicators* (database), *http://data.worldbank.org/indicator*.

StatLink http://dx.doi.org/10.1787/888933422407

Moreover, 45 countries out of the 56 countries classified in the Rest of the World (included in the DIOC and DIOC-E database) have a GDP per capita below USD 7 168 (in 2011 PPP). This suggests that economic progress is likely to increase emigration from these countries.

A priori, higher global income will result in a higher volume of international migration. The implication of the mobility transition curve is that the rate of growth of the number of emigrants for those countries with per capita incomes below USD 7 168 (in 2011 PPP) will be higher than their rates of population increase. Moreover, the mobility transition curve depicted above has been constructed from cross country data for 2010. The relationship between income and emigration rate appears to be changing over time. In addition, there is no consensus on the relationship between economic development and rising income (Clemens, 2014); however, preliminary work with country time series from 1960 to 2000 rather than cross country data at one point in time tends to show a positive relationship (i.e. no hump) for some countries. This would imply that over a time span of 40 years, the growth rate of migrants would tend to grow faster that the rate of population for at least some countries. The relationship between economic development and migration is likely to depend on the levels of development of origin and destination countries and the type of migration. Given the expected future growth of migration, it would be important to undertake more research on the factors that drive the shape of the mobility transition curve (see Dao et al., 2016).[5] Factors include job opportunities, demography, education, networks, migration policies in destination countries and other public policies.

Economic development benefits potential migrants who lack a university degree

Economic development particularly helps people without a university degree to meet migration costs and consequently to emigrate. Those who did not graduate from university generally face greater financial constraints than highly educated people. Emigration rates of people without a university degree increase on average with wages and reach a maximum when wages are around USD 5 011 (in 2011 PPP) (Figure 4.7, and Column 1 in Table 4.A1.3, Annex 4.A1). In other words, an increase in GDP per capita increases emigration by helping people who did not attend university to meet migration costs. In contrast, this effect does not hold for highly educated people (Column 2 in Table 4.A1.3, Annex 4.A1), as individuals who have attended university often already have the opportunity to migrate.

Figure 4.7. **The mobility of those without a university degree depends on income**

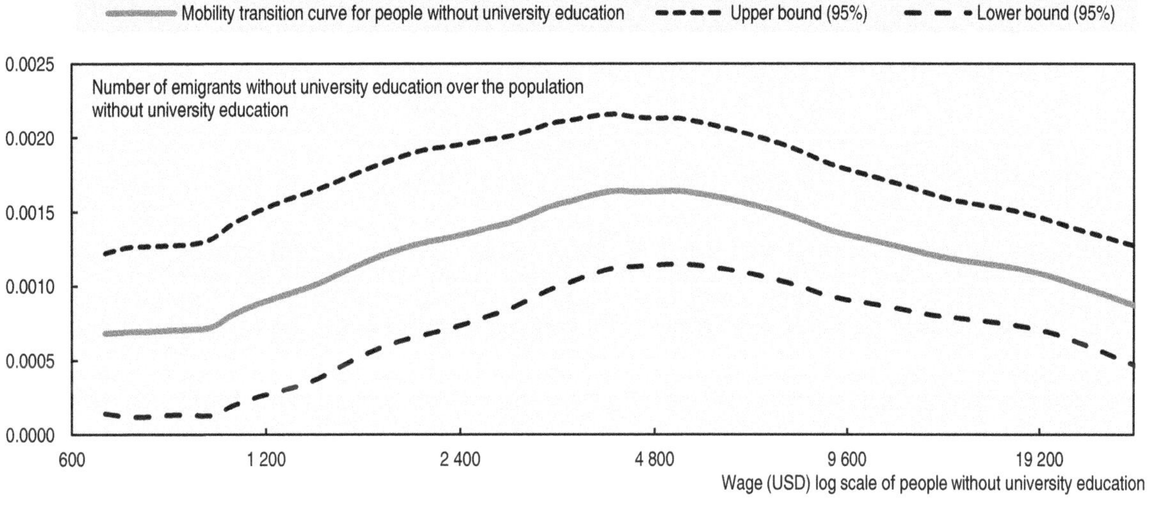

Note: Solid lines represent the relation between wage (expressed in logarithm) and the proportion of emigrants in the population of the origin country (specifically, the curve is computed with an Epanechnikov kernel density function from Epanechnikov(1969) that is detailed in Aubry (2016b). The dotted lines represent the upper and lower bounds of the 95% confidence interval. Observations are country-years 2010 for 76 countries. The level of income for people who did not attend college is proxy by the GDP per capita adjusted by an education premium and the proportion of tertiary individuals in the population.

Source: Authors' calculations based on data from OECD (2015), *Connecting with Emigrants: A Global Profile of Diasporas 2015, http://dx.doi.org/10.1787/9789264239845-en*; World Bank (2016), *World Development Indicators* (database), *http://data.worldbank.org/indicator*; and Montenegro and Patrinos (2014), "Comparable estimates of returns to schooling around the world", *Policy Research Working Paper*, No. 7020, *http://documents.worldbank.org/curated/en/2014/09/20173085/comparable-estimates-returns-schooling-around-world*.

StatLink http://dx.doi.org/10.1787/888933422413

Educational achievement that accompanies economic development facilitates migration

Economic development coincides with an increase in the number of educated migrants. The number of highly educated people in SG countries increased by 99 million from 247 million in 2000 to 346 million highly educated people in 2010. This increase has changed the volume as well as the educational composition of migration flows to OECD countries (most recent comparable data on educational level of migrants are available only for immigrants living in 32 OECD countries). More than 50% of the increase in emigration from poorer countries towards OECD countries results from the change in educational composition in origin countries between 2000 and 2010 (Dao et al., 2016). The number of highly educated immigrants in OECD countries is increasing. However, this is not only the result of the increase in educational achievement in developing countries, but also due to the greater selection of migrants with university education.[6] Here, the selection of highly educated migrants involves two different phenomena. First, migrants select themselves, and educated people may be more likely to aspire to migrate, possibly due to greater access to information. Second, destination countries increasingly select migrants on the basis of their educational achievement.

Three main factors account for the growth in the number of highly educated emigrants: i) the change in overall growth of emigration due to global trends; ii) the change in educational achievement in the population of the country of origin; and iii) the change in the number of highly educated emigrants due to selection (see Annex 4.A2 for a detailed explanation). The contribution of each of these factors by classification of origin countries is presented in Figure 4.8. The growth in the number of migrants with a university degree to OECD countries is greater than the growth of the tertiary-education population in SG countries of origin. Therefore, the mechanical increase in the number of emigrants with university degrees due to the increase in the highly-educated population in countries of origin does not fully explain the growth of highly-educated emigrants (Figure 4.8). Selection explains part of the disproportionate growth of highly educated emigration from SG to OECD countries. The same effect is true for RW countries.

Figure 4.8. **Selection of migrants aged 15 and over explains part of the disproportionate growth rate of emigrants with a university degree to OECD 2000 and 2010**

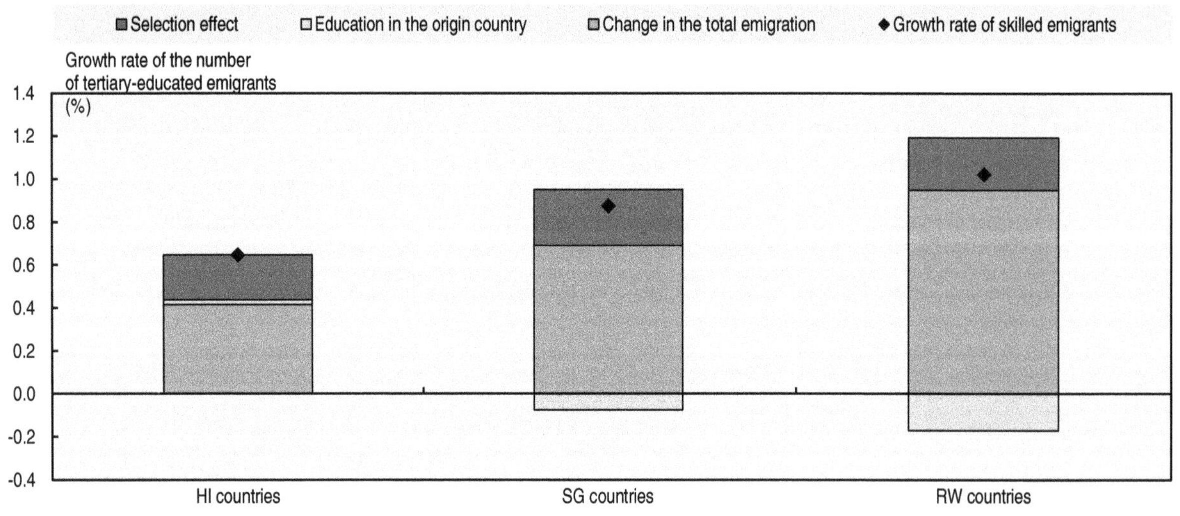

Note: The diamond represents average growth rate of tertiary-educated emigrants between 2000 and 2010 by country category. The bar represents the decomposition of the latter. The shift-share decomposition is described in Annex 4.A2. "Change in the total emigration" represents the part of the growth rate of highly educated emigrants that is explained by the increase in the overall emigration. "Education in the origin country" represents the part of the growth rate of the tertiary-educated emigrants that is explained by the increase in the tertiary-educated population in the country of origin. "Selection effect" represents the growth rate of emigrants with a university degree that is beyond the growth rate of the highly educated population in the origin country. The country categories are described in Annex A.

Source: Authors' calculations based on OECD (2015), *Connecting with Emigrants: A Global Profile of Diasporas 2015*, *http://dx.doi.org/10.1787/9789264239845-en* and UNDESA (2015b), "World Population Prospects: The 2015 Revision, DVD Edition", *Total Population – Both Sexes* (database), Population Division, *https://esa.un.org/unpd/wpp/Download/Standard/Population/*.

StatLink *http://dx.doi.org/10.1787/888933422428*

However, recent data suggest that economic development may eventually decrease the emigration rate of people with university degrees, although better data are needed to determine whether this decrease is statistically significant (Figure 4.9). While an increase in the number of highly educated individuals in origin countries automatically increases the number of emigrants with a university degree, the proportion of highly educated emigrants with a degree relative to the highly educated population is lower in more developed countries. Development may eventually be more likely to retain highly educated individuals by providing better opportunities in the country of origin. This suggests that, in the future, economic development could decrease rather than increase the proportion of emigrants in the population of highly educated individuals in emerging economies.

Figure 4.9. **The mobility of those with a university degree does not change with income**

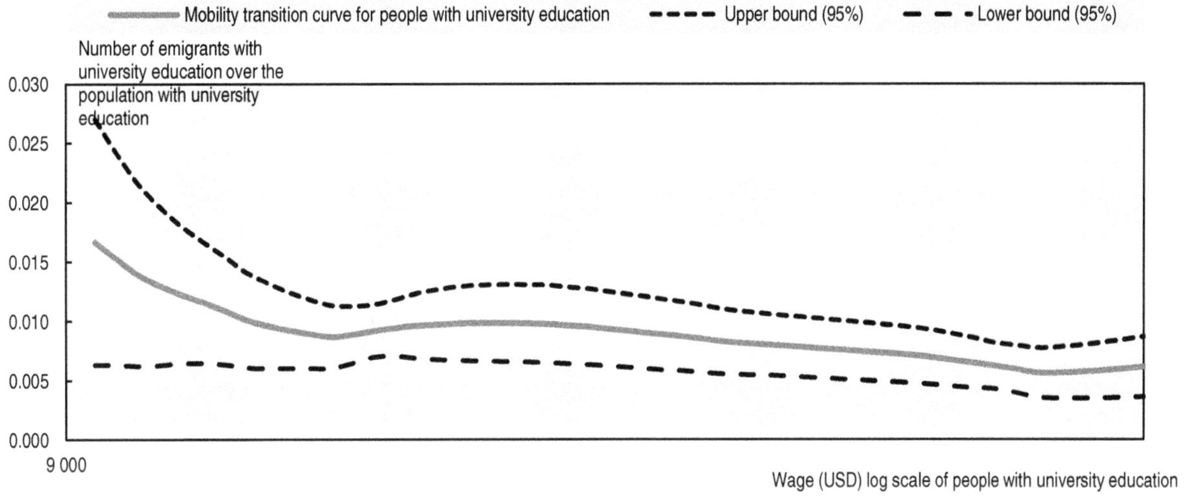

Note: Based on cross country data for 2010. Solid lines represent the relation between wage (expressed in logarithm) and the proportion of emigrants in the population of the origin country (specifically, the curve is computed with an Epanechnikov kernel density function from Epanechnikov (1969) that is detailed in Aubry (2016b). The dotted lines represent the upper and lower bounds of the 95% confidence interval. Observations are country-years 2010 for 76 countries. The level of income for people with a university degree is proxy by the GDP per capita adjusted by an education premium rewarding university education and the proportion of tertiary individuals in the population.

Source: Authors' calculations based on data from OECD (2015), *Connecting with Emigrants: A Global Profile of Diasporas 2015*, *http://dx.doi.org/10.1787/9789264239845-en*; World Bank (2016), *World Development Indicators* (database), *http://data.worldbank.org/indicator*; and Montenegro and Patrinos (2014),"Comparable estimates of returns to schooling around the world", *Policy Research Working Paper*, No. 7020, *http://documents.worldbank.org/curated/en/2014/09/20173085/comparable-estimates-returns-schooling-around-the-world*.

StatLink http://dx.doi.org/10.1787/888933422435

Conclusion

The spatial distribution of migration has significantly changed over the past 20 years. Immigration to HI countries has increased, relative to immigration to SG countries. Migration from SG countries is shifting away from other SG countries and towards HI countries. The proportion of migration from RW countries has remained fairly stable over the past two decades.

The economic transformations in large developing countries undoubtedly explain part of this recent evolution in the worldwide spatial distribution of migration, but in an unexpected way. Rapid and sustained economic growth in SG countries has not yet reduced the income differential between SG and HI countries enough to decrease migration from SG countries to HI countries and to increase migration from RW countries to SG countries. Despite rapid economic growth in SG countries, the economic gains from migrating to HI countries remain extremely large.

Quality of life also plays an important role in explaining the choice of destination countries. Strong economic growth in SG countries does not necessarily translate into large improvements in well-being.

Economic development plays an important role in explaining the change in the spatial distribution of emigration. Economic progress changes the evolution of migration by increasing emigration opportunities. International migration is a costly process that prevents many individuals from developing countries from turning their aspirations to migrate into reality. Economic development in SG countries has increased migration opportunities by boosting educational achievement and allowing potential migrants to amass the financial resources needed to meet the costs of migration. Slow economic progress in countries of the Rest of the World explains the low growth in the proportion of emigrants from these countries, especially when compared to their large population growth.

The growing migration to traditional destination countries is self-perpetuating through the networks that migrants develop in these countries. The presence of past migration lowers information barriers and provides support to incoming migrants in these destinations, effectively limiting the spread of migration towards new strong economic poles.

The economic and non-economic trends discussed in this chapter shed much light on recent trends in global migration. However, migration policies, particularly in destination countries, have become increasingly pro-active in shaping the size and the composition of migration flows. Migration policies have been mostly disregarded in this chapter because of their complexity and multifaceted effects, which deserve to be treated separately and in detail. The migration policies developed by destination countries across the different groups of countries may also explain recent trends, and are examined in Chapter 5. Global analysis must be complemented by analysis of the specific economic and social environments of individuals and their families. Analysis at the individual level places emphasis upon the specific social context of decision making, and incorporates multiple market failures, as explained in Chapter 7.

Notes

1. Figure 4.1 shows the positive correlation between the five-year average relative income differential and the size of five-year bilateral migration flows between 1995 and 2015. The first column in Table 4. A1 shows the results for the estimation of the impact of the relative income differential on migration flows for the whole sample (139 countries of origin and destination over the period 1995-2015). The size of the coefficient of the income differential is similar to the result found by Beine and Parsons (2015) for the period 1960-2000 and Ortega and Peri (2009) for the period 1980-2005.
2. The size of the coefficients shown in Figure 4.2 are similar to the results found by Beine and Parsons (2015) for the period 1960-2000 and Ortega and Peri (2009) for the period 1980-2005, the reference studies for the empirical analysis in this chapter. Different results exist in the literature concerning the effect of a common border, the same official language and colonial ties.
3. The distribution of migration across country-pairs is skewed. Of the country-pair cells in the sample, 66% had zero migration recorded in 2015 (either because of missing data or the absence of migration). Therefore, the average difference between GDP per capita across country-pairs does not precisely reflect the earning opportunities across migration corridors. Here, the difference in the level of GDP per capita is weighted by the number of migrants across each migration corridor.
4. Robustness checks have been conducted concerning the method of constructing the composite indicators and have led to similar results. See OECD (2014) for a detailed description of the composite index and its advantages and limitations.
5. Factors that affect the shape of the curve include credit constraints, migrant networks, demographic transition, inequality and immigration barriers in destination countries, among others. See Clemens (2014) and Dao et al. (2016).

6. Decomposing the growth rate of the emigration of tertiary-educated emigrants involved observation by level of education for at least two points in time. At the global level, the most recent data that can be compared over time between 2000 and 2010 are data on migrants residing in OECD countries at the time of the census. Other comparable data decomposed by the level of education are only available until the year 2000.

References

Aubry A. (2016a), "Recent economic transformations and migration patterns", *Mimeo*.

Aubry, A (2016b), "Education changes migrants' aspiration, prospects and opportunities", Mimeo.

Baudassé, T. and R. Bazillier (2014), "Gender inequality and emigration: Push factor or selection process?", *International Economics*, Vol. 139, pp. 19-47, *http://dx.doi.org/10.1016/j.inteco.2014.03.004*.

Beine, M. (2013), "The Network Effect in International Migration", *CESifo DICE Report*, Vol. 11, pp. 41-47, *https://www.cesifo-group.de/ifoHome/publications/docbase/details.html?docId=19083493*.

Beine, M., S. Bertoli and J. F.-H. Moraga (2015), "A Practitioners' guide to gravity models of international migration", *The World Economy*, Vol. 39(8), pp. 496-512, *http://dx.doi.org/10.1111/twec.12265*.

Beine, M., F. Docquier and Ç. Özden (2011), "Diasporas", *Journal of Development Economics*, Vol. 95(1), pp. 30-41, *http://dx.doi.org/10.1016/j.jdeveco.2009.11.004*.

Beine, M. and C. Parsons (2015), "Climatic Factors as Determinants of International Migration", *Scandinavian Journal of Economics*, *http://dx.doi.org/10.1111/sjoe.12098*.

Chantavanich, S. and P. Vungsiriphisal (2012), "Myanmar migrants to Thailand: Economic analysis and implications to Myanmar development", in *Economic Reforms in Myanmar: Pathways and Prospects, BRC Research Report* No. 10, Bangkok Research Center, IDE-JETRO, Bangkok, *www.ide.go.jp/English/Publish/Download/Brc/pdf/10_06.pdf*.

Clark, X., T. Hatton and J. Williamson (2007), "Explaining US immigration, 1971-1998", *Review of Economics and Statistics*, Vol. 89, pp. 359-373, *http://dx.doi.org/10.1162/rest.89.2.359*.

Clemens, M. (2014), "Does development reduce migration?", in R. E. Lucas (ed.), *International Handbook on Migration and Economic Development*, Edward Elgar Publishing, Washington, DC.

Dao, T. H., F. Docquier, C. Parsons and G. Peri (2016), "Migration and development: Dissecting the anatomy of the mobility transition", *IZA Discussion Papers 10272*, Institute for the Study of Labor (IZA).

Docquier, F., G. Peri and I. Ruyssen (2014), "The cross-country determinants of potential and actual migration", *International Migration Review*, Vol. 48(11), pp. 37-99, *http://onlinelibrary.wiley.com/doi/10.1111/imre.12137/pdf*.

Epanechnikov, V.A. (1969), "Non-Parametric Estimation of a Multivariate Probability Density", *Theory of Probability and its Applications*, Vol. 14(1), pp. 153-158, *http://dx.doi.org/10.1137/1114019*.

Gallup (2012), *Worldwide Research Methodology and Codebook* (database), Washington, DC.

Hausmann, R., L. Pritchett and D. Rodrik (2005), "Growth Accelerations", *Journal of Economic Growth*, 10, pp. 303-329.

Jolly, S. and H. Reeves (2005), *Gender and Migration*, Bridge, Institute of Development Studies, Brighton, UK, *www.bridge.ids.ac.uk/sites/bridge.ids.ac.uk/files/reports/CEP-Mig-OR.pdf*.

Lopez, R. and M. Schiff (1998), "Migration and the skill composition of the labor force: The impact of trade liberalization in LDCs", *Canadian Journal of Economics*, Vol. 31(2), pp. 318-336, *http://dx.doi.org/10.2307/136326*.

Kanaiaupuni, S. (2000), "Reframing the migration question: Analysis of men, women, and gender in Mexico", *Social Forces*, Vol. 78(4), pp. 1311-1347.

Marshall, G., R. Gurr and K. Jaggers (2013), *Polity IV Individual Country Regime Trends, 1946-2013* (database), *Polity IV Project: Political Regime Characteristics and Transitions, 1800-2013* (database), *www.systemicpeace.org/polity/polity4.htm* (accessed on 15 April 2016).

Mayda, A. M. (2010), "International migration: A panel data analysis of the determinants of bilateral flows", *Journal of Population Economics*, Vol. 23(4), pp. 1249-1274, *www.jstor.org/stable/40925859*.

Mayer, T. and S. Zignago (2011), "Notes on CEPII's distances measures: The GeoDist Database", *CEPII Working Paper*, No. 2011-25, *www.cepii.fr/CEPII/en/publications/wp/abstract.asp?NoDoc=3877*.

McKenzie, D.J., C. Theoharides and D. Yang (2014), "Distortions in the international migrant labor market: Evidence from Filipino migration and wage responses to destination country economic shocks", *American Economic Journal: Applied*, Vol. 6, pp. 49-75, *http://dx.doi.org/10.1257/app.6.2.49*.

Montenegro, C. and H. Patrinos (2014),"Comparable estimates of returns to schooling around the world", *Policy Research working paper*, No. 7020, World Bank Group, Washington, DC, *http://documents.worldbank.org/curated/en/2014/09/20173085/comparable-estimates-returns-schooling-around-world*.

OECD (2015), *Connecting with Emigrants: A Global Profile of Diasporas 2015*, OECD Publishing, Paris, *http://dx.doi.org/10.1787/9789264239845-en*.

OECD (2014), "Social Institutions and Gender Index (SIGI) 2014 synthesis report", OECD Development Centre, Paris, *https://www.oecd.org/dev/development-gender/BrochureSIGI2015-web.pdf*.

Ortega, F. and G. Peri (2009), "The Causes and Effects of International Migrations: Evidence from OECD Countries 1980-2005", *Working Paper Series, National Bureau of Economic Research*, No. 14833, *http://dx.doi.org/10.3386/w14833*.

UNDESA (2015a), "Trends in international migrant stock: Migrants by destination and origin", *International Migration* (database), United Nations Department of Economic and Social Affairs, Population Division, New York, *www.un.org/en/development/desa/population/migration/data/estimates2/estimates15.shtml* (accessed 1 February 2016).

UNDESA (2015b), "World Population Prospects: The 2015 Revision, DVD Edition", *Total Population – Both Sexes* (database), United Nations Department of Economic and Social Affairs, Population Division, New York, *https://esa.un.org/unpd/wpp/Download/Standard/Population/* (accessed 1 February 2016).

Van Zanden et al. (eds.) (2014), *How Was Life?: Global Well-being Since 1820*, OECD Publishing, Paris, *http://dx.doi.org/10.1787/9789264214262-en*.

World Bank (2016), *World Development Indicators* (database), World Bank, *http://data.worldbank.org/indicator* (accessed 1 February 2016).

Yang, D. (2006), "Why do migrants return to poor countries? Evidence from Philippine migrants' reponses to exchange rate shocks", *Review of Economics and Statistics*, Vol. 88(4), pp. 715-735, *www.mitpressjournals.org/doi/pdf/10.1162/rest.88.4.715*.

Yeoh, B., T. Lam and L.A. Hoang (2010), "Effects of international migration on families left behind", Background Paper presented at the Experts Meeting, Civil Society Days, GFMD, Mexico City, *https://www.iom.int/files/live/sites/iom/files/What-We-Do/idm/workshops/Migrants-and-Families-2014/IDM-October-2014-Migration-and-Families-Background-paper.pdf*.

Zelinsky, W. (1971), "The hypothesis of the mobility transition", *Geographical Review*, Vol. 61, pp. 219-249, *http://dx.doi.org/10.2307/213996*.

ANNEX 4.A1

Results of the different empirical analyses

Table 4.A1.1. **Determinants of bilateral migration flows, 1995-2015**

	Dependent variable: Log of five-year flows of migration			
	(1)	(2)	(3)	(4)
	World	HI countries	SG countries	RW countries
Ratio of GDP per capita	0.308**	0.178	0.380**	0.530***
	(0.149)	(0.157)	(0.173)	(0.166)
Log of distance	-0.0749***	-0.0186	-0.132***	-0.285***
	(0.028)	(0.027)	(0.033)	(0.047)
Border	-0.347***	-0.341***	-0.264***	-0.464***
	(0.058)	(0.089)	(0.084)	(0.111)
Common language	0.0938***	0.141**	0.114**	0.109
	(0.045)	(0.063)	(0.057)	(0.077)
Colony	0.11	-0.323**	0.153	0.302***
	(0.088)	(0.144)	(0.125)	(0.101)
Network	0.303***	0.244***	0.271***	0.319***
	(0.019)	(0.02)	(0.02)	(0.024)
Constant	-0.894***	-0.265	0.464	0.178
	(0.433)	(0.473)	(0.41)	(0.554)
Observations	94017	16856	36704	34603
R-squared value	0.558	0.499	0.618	0.615
Fixed effects				
Time-origin	Yes	Yes	Yes	Yes
Destination countries	Yes	Yes	Yes	Yes

Note: *** p<0.01, ** p<0.05,* p<0.10. Regression uses the Poisson pseudo-maximum likelihood (PPML) estimator. Regression includes destination and time-origin fixed effects. The full sample consists of 94 018 observations corresponding to bilateral migration flows between 139 origin and destination countries. The migration flows between Chile and Venezuela have been excluded due to negative numbers of migrants in the raw data for the year 2015.

Source: Authors' calculations based on UNDESA (2015a), "Trends in international migrant stock: Migrants by destination and origin", *International Migration* (database), *www.un.org/en/development/desa/population/migration/data/estimates2/estimates15.shtml;* World Bank (2016), *World Development Indicators* (database), *http://data.worldbank.org/indicator;* Mayer and Zignago (2011), "Notes on CEPII's distances measures: The GeoDist Database", *CEPII Working Paper*, No. 2011-25, *www.cepii.fr/CEPII/en/publications/wp/abstract.asp?NoDoc=3877.*

Table 4.A1.2. Determinants of migration rates by country category, 2010

Dependent variable: Proportion of emigrants in the population in 2010				
	(1)	(2)	(3)	(4)
	World	HI countries	SG countries	RW countries
GDP per capita at origin in 2009	6.445***	-61.176***	6.418*	3.166
	(0.918)	(20.345)	(3.732)	(2.216)
GDP per capita at origin in 2009 squared	-0.363***	2.834***	-0.381*	-0.177
	(0.051)	(0.951)	(0.203)	(0.135)
Log of distance	-1.107***	-0.598***	-1.381***	-1.137***
	(0.097)	(0.123)	(0.159)	(0.240)
Border	-0.037	0.152	0.378	0.396
	(0.231)	(0.310)	(0.305)	(0.450)
Common language	0.506***	0.866***	1.000***	0.681***
	(0.173)	(0.262)	(0.310)	(0.257)
Colony	1.314***	0.526*	1.183***	1.370***
	(0.166)	(0.281)	(0.240)	(0.353)
Population at origin	-0.512***	-0.627***	-0.621***	-0.456***
	(0.055)	(0.124)	(0.077)	(0.119)
Network	0.517***	0.512***	0.378***	2.330***
	(0.118)	(0.143)	(0.116)	(0.550)
Proportion of population aged 15 to 29	0.002	-0.124***	0.051	0.059
	(0.023)	(0.046)	(0.033)	(0.049)
MR distance	0.508***	-0.063	1.080***	1.447***
	(0.170)	(0.313)	(0.311)	(0.494)
MR border	-4.409**	-2.616	1.154	-5.292*
	(1.884)	(2.866)	(1.496)	(3.046)
Constant	-23.082***	337.002***	-24.201	-7.501
	(4.296)	(107.239)	(17.400)	(7.315)
Observations	5612	1329	2372	1908
R-squared value	0.595	0.741	0.613	0.786
Fixed effects				
Destination	Yes	Yes	Yes	Yes

Note: *** p<0.01, ** p<0.05,* p<0.10. Regression uses the Poisson pseudo-maximum likelihood (PPML) estimator. Regression include destination and time-origin fixed effects. The full sample consists of 6 378 observations for 143 origin and 71 destination countries. The proportion of emigrants in the population corresponds to the number of emigrants from country *o* to country *d* divided by the population in country *o*. The terms MR are multilateral resistance terms. The multilateral resistance terms control for some of the bias introduced by the relative attractiveness of a destination with respect to other destinations.

Source: Authors' calculations based on OECD (2015), *Connecting with Emigrants: A Global Profile of Diasporas 2015*, *http://dx.doi.org/10.1787/9789264239845-en*; World Bank (2016), *World Development Indicators* (database), *http://data.worldbank.org/indicator*; and Mayer and Zignago (2011), "Notes on CEPII's distances measures: The GeoDist Database", *CEPII Working Paper*, No. 2011-25, *www.cepii.fr/CEPII/en/publications/wp/abstract.asp?NoDoc=3877*.

Table 4.A1.3. **Determinants of migration rates by level of education, 1995-2015**

Dependent variable: Proportion of emigrants in the population by level of education in 2010		
	(1)	(2)
	Unskilled	Skilled
Unskilled wage	4.379**	
	(2.090)	
(Unskilled wage)^2	-0.257**	
	(0.124)	
Skilled wage		-5.286
		(3.602)
(Skilled wage)^2		0.247
		(0.166)
Log of distance	-0.741***	-0.531***
	(0.093)	(0.104)
Border	-0.267	-1.733***
	(0.438)	('0.507)
Common language	0.392	0.989***
	(0.407)	(0.207)
Colony	0.731***	1.343***
	(0.244)	(0.281)
Population at origin	-0.629***	-0.529***
	(0.086)	(0.102)
Network	1.522***	1.636***
	(0.215)	(0.230)
Proportion of population aged 15 to 29	0.063**	0.148***
	(0.030)	(0.035)
MR distance	0.329	-0.217
	(0.286)	(0.144)
MR border	1.442	-1.368
	(1.469)	(1.989)
Constant	-11.048	34.679*
	(8.768)	(18.789)
Observations	3024	3134
R-squared value	0.404	0.376
Fixed effects		
Destination countries	Yes	Yes

Note: *** p<0.01, ** p<0.05,* p<0.10. Regression uses the Poisson pseudo-maximum likelihood (PPML) estimator. Regression includes destination and time-origin fixed effects. The full sample consists of 3 134 observations corresponding to bilateral migration flows between 76 origin and 81 destination countries. The number of observations differs between the two samples due to missing data for the estimation on low-skilled emigrants. The terms MR are multilateral resistance terms. The multilateral resistance terms control for some of the bias introduced by the relative attractiveness of a destination with respect to other destinations.

Source: Authors' calculations based on OECD (2015), *Connecting with Emigrants: A Global Profile of Diasporas 2015, http://dx.doi.org/10.1787/9789264239845-en*, World Bank (2016), *World Development Indicators* (database), *http://data.worldbank.org/indicator*; and Mayer and Zignago (2011), "Notes on CEPII's distances measures: The GeoDist Database", *CEPII Working Paper*, No. 2011-25, *www.cepii.fr/CEPII/en/publications/wp/abstract.asp?NoDoc=3877*.

ANNEX 4.A2

Shift share analysis of the growth rate of tertiary-educated emigrants to OECD countries between 2000 and 2010

A shift share analysis is conducted to disentangle the contribution of different factors to the growth rate of tertiary-educated emigrants to the OECD between 2000 and 2010. The change in the number of tertiary-educated emigrants is affected by the change in the overall emigration. An increase in the number of emigrants is expected to increase the number of tertiary-educated emigrants. An increase in the number of tertiary-educated individuals in the population of the origin country is also expected to affect the number of tertiary-educated emigrants. The growth of the tertiary-educated population in the origin country should mechanically increase the number of tertiary-educated emigrants. However, it may also decrease the incentives to emigrate given that individuals with tertiary education can expect to earn a higher salary at home. Finally, education lowers migration costs by easing access to information and by allowing potential migrants to meet the needs of the labour market in the destination country. It can then increase the actual number of migrants, not only by turning the aspiration to migrate into actual opportunity but also by inducing new migration given the lowered migration cost. This last part of the growth rate in the number of tertiary-educated emigrants reflects the selective nature of migration. The shift share analysis that is conducted is the following:

$$g_{e_s,i} = \underbrace{g_{e,i}}_{(1)} + \underbrace{\left(g_{p_s,i} - g_{e,i}\right)}_{(2)} + \underbrace{\left(g_{e_s,i} - g_{p_s,i}\right)}_{(3)}$$

Where

$g_{e_s,i}$ is the growth rate of tertiary-educated emigrants from country i to OECD countries

$g_{p_s,i}$ is the growth rate of tertiary-educated individuals in the origin country i to OECD countries

$g_{e,i}$ is the growth rate of overall emigration from country i to OECD countries

(1) the effect of the change in overall emigration

(2) the effect of the change in education in the country of origin

(3) the effect of the change in selection of emigration

The most recent data on migration, decomposed by level of education, that are comparable for the years 2000 and 2010 are available only for migrants residing in OECD countries. Consequently, the analysis is limited to emigrants from 131 countries who live in one of the 32 OECD countries available in the data (Korea and Iceland are missing).

Perspectives on Global Development 2017
International Migration in a Shifting World
© OECD 2016

Chapter 5

How public policies affect migration flows

The most evident public policies that can affect patterns of migration are those that explicitly aim to manage the movement of people: border controls, visa requirements, family reunification regulations, etc. Yet other policies, in countries of both destination and origin, can also influence people's decisions to migrate. A country's policies for its labour market, agriculture, education, investment and financial services, and social protection and health all affect the prevailing economic and social climates and, in so doing, influence the incentives to migrate or stay at home. While investigating the impact of public policies on migration, this chapter therefore considers the effect of both explicit migration policies and policies for sectors that are not directly linked to migration.

The previous chapter sought to explain changes in the patterns of international migration observed over the last 20 years by identifying some of the different factors driving migration. Public policies can also play a key role in shaping migration flows and deserve special attention (Box 5.1). This chapter on public policies is divided into two sections. The first focuses on migration policies designed to ease, restrain or regulate the composition of migration flows. Again, the analysis uses a country classification based not only on income level but also on growth performance (a detailed explanation of the precise definition of each group as well as a table listing countries by their classification is provided in Annex A). This classification has three categories:

- **High Income by 1995 (HI)** countries, which were classified as high-income countries by the World Bank in 1995.
- **High and Sustained Growth (SG)** countries, which have experienced a recent period of high and sustained growth. Countries in this group were not classified as high-income countries in 1995 by the World Bank, but many have since attained high-income status.
- **Rest of the World (RW)**, which includes all other countries – those that have not experienced a recent period of high and sustained growth and that remain low- and middle-income countries.

Box 5.1. **Grouping of policies relevant to the migration-development nexus**

Governments implement both direct and indirect policies that influence the volume and composition of migration flows and that harness the benefits of migration. Such policies often reflect the economic needs of a country and respond to voter demands.

Migration policies refer to the "laws, rules, measures and practices implemented by national states with the stated objective to influence the volume, origin and [...] composition of migration flows" (Czaika and de Haas, 2013). In addition to measures aimed at regulating flows, integration and reintegration policies can also be placed in this grouping.

Migration and development policies, in countries both of origin and destination, are those aimed at harnessing migration to advance development outcomes. These policies seek synergies and multiple beneficial situations in areas such as remittances, brain circulation, diaspora engagement and return.

Non-migration sectoral policies with an impact on migration and affected by it are found in various policy domains – such as labour, trade, social protection, health, education and agriculture – that are affected by migration, but that also have an impact on migration flows. Sectoral policies are crucial to implementing national development strategies and can shape the relationship between migration and development. Besides these sectoral policies, this policy grouping includes development co-operation policies that have an indirect impact on the migration-development relationship.

Particular emphasis is placed upon how migration policies vary across the country categories and how migration policies have changed over time. Changes in migration policy are then compared to the changes in migration flows to give an understanding of the link between policies and flows. The overview of general migration policy is complemented by a review of two specific types of policies: those targeting specific skill levels, and those allowing migration through family reunification.

The second section offers evidence on the impact of sectoral policies on the decision to emigrate. It explores in particular the effect on the decision to emigrate of policies in countries of origin relating to the labour market, agriculture, education, and social protection and health. The section concludes by reflecting on how public policies target the very reasons people decide to leave, which are linked to the existence of market failures, financial constraints, risks and skills mismatches.

Changed migration policies are affecting migration patterns

Recent economic transformations (such as increase in openness to trade or in investment) were accompanied with policy changes in many countries, and policy changes have affected migration patterns. This section aims to describe the extent to which migration policies have changed in the last two decades and whether these changes can explain why immigration to HI countries is disproportionately increasing in comparison to immigration to SG countries.

The section analyses emigration and immigration policies over the past two decades designed to influence migration patterns. In particular, it uses data from the UN *World Population Policies* database, collected by the United Nations Department of Economic and Social Affairs (UNDESA) between 1976 and 2013, as well as the *Determinants of International Migration* (DEMIG) database on migration policies, to identify global policy trends and their relationship with migration flows (Box 5.2).

Emigration policies in countries of origin have a limited effect on migration

Emigration policies aim to ease, restrain or control the composition of emigration flows as well as to protect emigrants. The ability of countries of origin to affect migration flows through direct policy is limited compared with that of the countries of destination, which have more instruments to influence the volume and composition of migration flows. This lack of control over emigration is perhaps the reason why most countries do not attempt to intervene to influence emigration patterns.

Indeed, according to UNDESA (2013), most countries do not implement policies designed to influence emigration patterns, although disparities exist across country categories (Figure 5.1). Almost all of the HI countries in the sample stated that they do not intervene to influence emigration patterns. The exceptions are Israel and Saudi Arabia, which reported implementing policy to lower the proportion of people aspiring to emigrate, and Portugal, which stated that it implemented policy designed to maintain the proportion of emigrants in the population. SG countries are most likely to implement emigration policies aimed at lowering the proportion of emigrants in the population. As explained in Chapter 3, these countries face emigration growth because economic development provides individuals with sufficient resources to meet the costs of leaving. However, some top origin countries (that are also SG countries) reported policies aimed at boosting emigration. In 2013, SG countries such as Indonesia, Morocco, Pakistan, Thailand, Tunisia and Viet Nam said they were applying supportive emigration policies in order to increase emigration.

Box 5.2. **Data on migration policies and attitudes of non-migrants towards immigration**

Systematic and comparable cross-country information on migration policies is scarce, and most analyses focus on developed countries, although many gaps in available data are being filled by the *Impala Database* (Beine, Bertoli and Moraga, 2015), DEMIG project (DEMIG, 2015), IMPIC project (Helbling et al., 2016) and the International Migration Outlook series by the OECD (OECD, 2015). This chapter uses two main databases on migration policies across the world, extending the coverage of the analysis of migration policies to SG countries and non-OECD countries.

The UN *World Population Policies* database (UNDESA, 2013), collected by the United Nations Department of Economic and Social Affairs, records data on government attitudes and government policy between 1976 and 2013. This database has wide geographical coverage. The database records information on whether governments implement policies to raise, maintain or lower the overall level of immigration, or rather do not intervene to shape patterns of migration. The chapter uses these data to report the evolution of migration policies over time by the country classification described in Annex A. However, these results must be interpreted with caution, as questions on a government's policy with respect to migration may include complex policy objectives under a single stated objective.

The *DEMIG POLICY* data (DEMIG, 2015) tracks more than 6 500 migration policy changes in 45 countries between 1945 and 2013. Among these 45 countries, 17 are classified as SG countries and 23 are classified as HI countries. This database meticulously records the content, restrictiveness, magnitude and target population of migration policies, providing new ways of observing the evolution of specific types of migration policies.

Unilateral policies designed to facilitate emigration do not appear to be very effective in stimulating emigration. Policies such as pre-departure programmes are generally implemented by the country of origin, or by international institutions such as the International Organization for Migration. Even though such policies are very common, evidence does not show that they foster emigration (Beam, 2014; McKenzie and Yang, 2015).

On the other hand, bilateral policies negotiated between the countries of origin and destination appear to encourage new emigration. Bilateral policies may provide information, administrative support and job opportunities, for example (McKenzie and Yang, 2015). Evidence shows that such bilateral policies have successfully increased the possibility of emigration for individuals who aspired to move abroad but were unable to do so (Gibson and McKenzie, 2014).

Emigration policies are not only designed to influence the number of people aspiring to emigrate but also to protect the migrants. In the Philippines, some emigration policies aim to protect Filipino workers overseas. Over the past 20 years, the Filipino diaspora has more than doubled, reaching approximately 10 million in 2013 (UNDESA, 2015; Commission on Filipinos Overseas, 2013). The government aims to provide Filipinos with better prospects within the Philippines, but at the same time to ensure the well-being of those who decide to leave. Emigration policies in the Philippines are based on human rights: ensuring the dignity and freedom of Filipinos. The government of the Philippines has signed social security agreements with nine countries of destination, most of which are European, in order to provide workers with healthcare while overseas (IOM, 2013). South Asian countries have also undertaken bilateral agreements with countries from the Gulf Co-operation Council that aim to protect migrants living in these countries. Qatar, for instance, signed such bilateral agreements with Bangladesh in 1998 and 2008, with Nepal in 2005 and 2009, with Pakistan in 1978 and 2008, and with India in 1985 and 2007 (GIZ/ILO, 2015). These agreements are designed to protect emigrants before their departure and during the recruitment process, and they also relate to payment of wages, contract requirements or dispute resolution (GIZ/ILO, 2015).

Figure 5.1. **Government policy on emigration levels differs by country category, 2013**

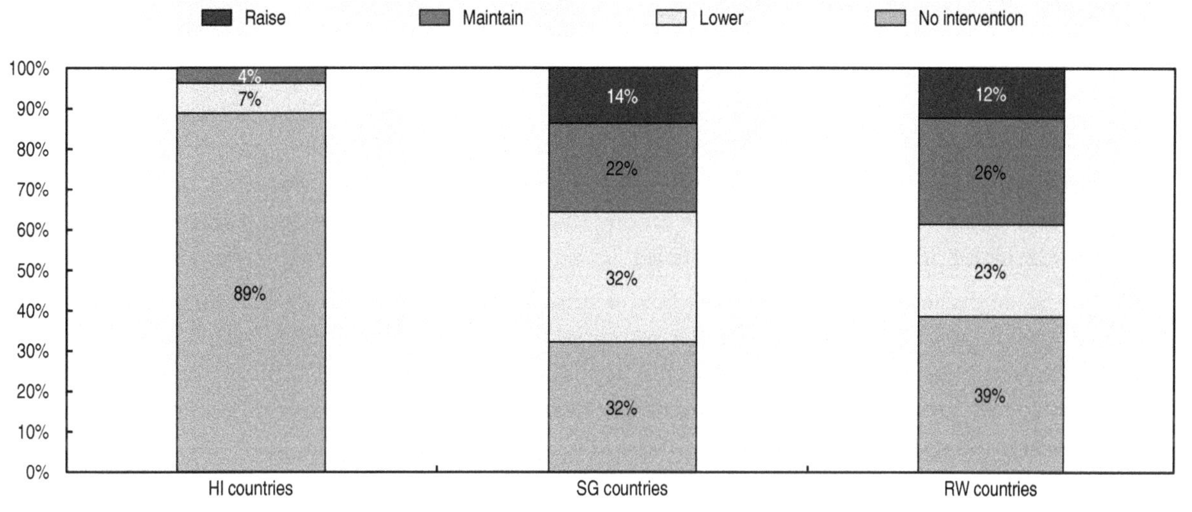

Note: Percentages of countries reporting a particular policy designed to influence the overall level of emigration, by category of countries. The country categories are defined in Annex A. The sample includes data for 27 HI countries, 59 SG countries and 57 RW countries. Hong Kong, China, is omitted due to missing data.

Source: Authors' calculations based on UNDESA (2013), *World Population Policies 2013* (database), *www.un.org/en/development/desa/population/publications/policy/world-population-policies-2013.shtml.*

StatLink http://dx.doi.org/10.1787/888933422447

Immigration policies in destination countries can affect migration levels

Economic transformations and migration policies are interrelated. Changes in the economic environment shape migration policies (see Box 5.3 for the example of a country that encouraged greater immigration). Governments can better accommodate large immigration flows during economic booms than during recessions (Mayda, 2010). Migration policies can also alter the effect of economic factors on migration flows (Mayda, 2010; Ortega and Peri, 2009; Beine, Bertoli and Moraga, 2015). For instance, migration policies such as visa requirements have been found to reduce the responsiveness of migration to economic fluctuations in countries of origin and destination. Such requirements reduce migrant inflows and encourage migrants in the country to stay there, even though economic prospects in the host country may have worsened (Czaika and de Haas, 2016). The economic transformations experienced by countries over the past two decades have affected migration policies. This section presents a global overview of immigration policies in order to help understand the recent evolution of migration policies and their effect.

Box 5.3. **In Botswana, fast economic growth inspired policies to attract foreign workers**

Botswana, rich in natural resources, opened its borders in response to fast economic growth. The country experienced high and sustained economic growth, recording an annual growth rate of at least 7% between 1960 and 2005 (Commission on Growth and Development, 2008). Economic transformations in the country were being inhibited by structural weaknesses such as the size of its population (less than one million in the 1980s). To combat such limitations, the government allowed relatively unrestricted entry to visitors, business people and jobseekers, and actively recruited foreign workers to fill skills gaps in sectors such as education, management and health. The government also provided competitive salaries, subsidised housing and cars, health insurance and free education to expatriate children (Lefko-Everett, 2004).

In 2013, more than two-thirds of governments across the world pursued policies to maintain the level of immigration or not to intervene in shaping the level of immigration, according to UNDESA (2013a). Most HI countries in the sample implemented policies designed to lower or to maintain the level of immigration in 2013 (Figure 5.2). Austria, Finland, Israel, Korea and Sweden are among the HI countries in the sample affirming that they implement pro-immigration policies.

SG countries mostly aim to maintain or raise immigration levels. In the sample, 13 SG countries stated their intention to raise immigration and 10 SG countries stated the intention to lower immigration (Figure 5.2). People's Republic of China (hereafter "China"), Poland, the Russian Federation, Thailand and Uruguay are among the SG countries aiming to increase the level of immigration, while Ecuador, Ghana, the Islamic Republic of Iran, Malaysia, Pakistan and South Africa are among the SG countries aiming to decrease it. RW countries tend either not to intervene or to maintain immigration levels, which may reflect a lack of need for intervention or greater institutional or geographical difficulties in controlling immigration flows. In Africa in 2013, the number of countries that aimed to keep the level of immigration constant (19 out of a sample size of 45) was similar to the number of countries that did not want to intervene in trying to shape migration flows (17). Such results imply satisfaction with the current level of immigration, but they may also illustrate limited faith in a government's ability to affect immigration flows in countries where policy enforcement is challenging.

Immigration policies are becoming less restrictive in many countries

Over time there has been a global trend towards the implementation of policies designed to increase immigration. This trend contradicts the common perception that migration policies are becoming increasingly restrictive. Over the period from 1996 to 2013, immigration policies were tightened by only three of the 27 HI countries and six of the 59 SG countries in the sample, while they were loosened by 14 HI countries and 26 SG countries. The policies became more open over time. In 1996, two SG countries in the sample aimed to raise immigration and 23 to lower the level; in 2013, 13 SG countries aimed to raise immigration and 10 SG countries to decrease the level. Nearly all of the RW countries in the sample maintained or loosened their immigration policies over the period (Figure 5.3).

This trend is also observed using the DEMIG (2015) data on a smaller sample, of 40 countries. The results of this extensive data collection of specific policy changes show that migration policies have become consistently less restrictive since 1945 (Figure 5.4). A possible explanation of the inconsistency between the recorded evolution of migration policies and the perception of increasing restrictiveness of human mobility is confusion between restriction and selection. Migration policies have been less restrictive on average, but have become more sophisticated and more selective through the development of policy instruments targeting particular immigrants groups such as skilled workers (de Haas, Natter and Vezzoli, 2014).

Figure 5.2. **Most governments tried to maintain levels of immigration or did not intervene**

Government policy on immigration levels by country category, 2013

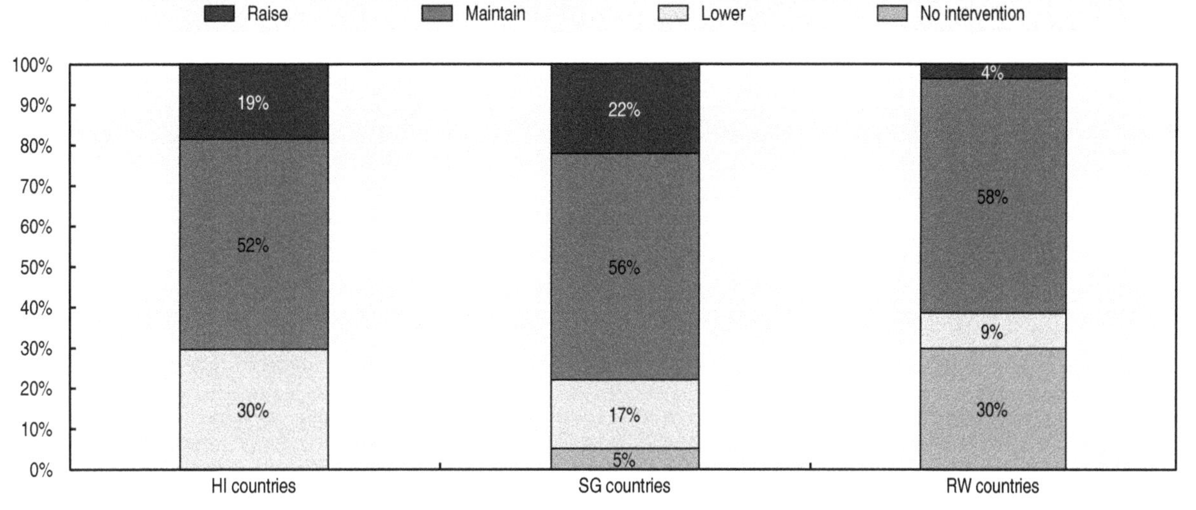

Note: Percentages of countries reporting a particular policy designed to influence the overall level of immigration, by category of countries. The country categories are defined in Annex A. The sample includes data for 27 HI countries, 59 SG countries and 57 RW countries. Hong Kong, China, is omitted due to missing data.

Source: Authors' calculations based on UNDESA (2013), *World Population Policies 2013* (database), *www.un.org/en/development/desa/population/publications/policy/world-population-policies-2013.shtml.*

StatLink http://dx.doi.org/10.1787/888933422453

Figure 5.3. **Globally, policies between 1996 and 2013 aimed to increase migration**

Change in government policies on immigration by country category, 1996-2013

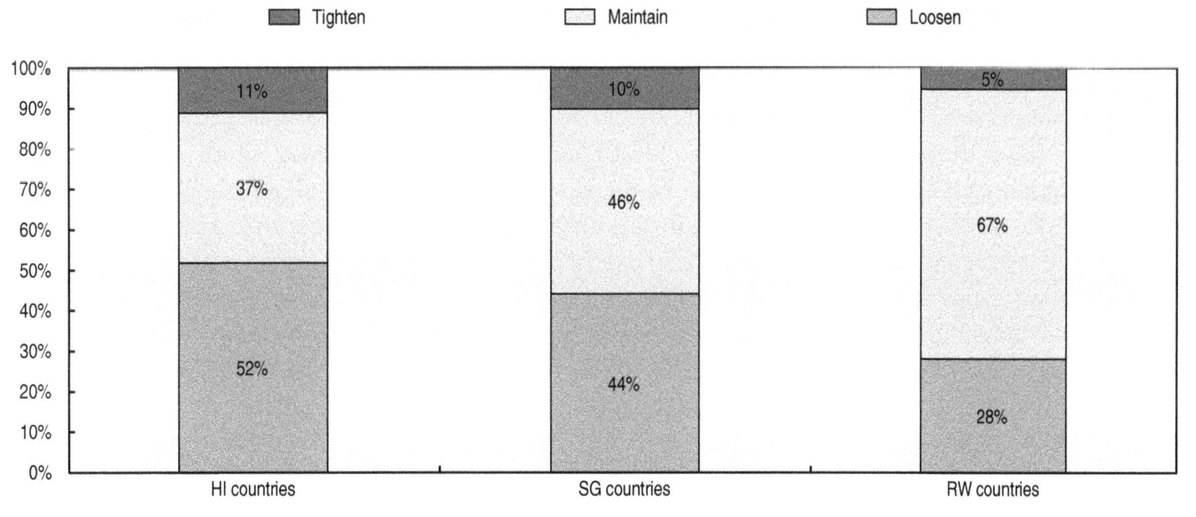

Note: The numbers depicted on the vertical axis indicate the percentage of countries in each category as defined in Annex A. "Tighten" corresponds to the number of countries that changed their immigration policy from raise or maintain/no intervention in 1996 to maintain/no intervention or lower in 2013. "Loosen" corresponds to the number of countries that changed their immigration policy from lower or maintain/no intervention in 1996 to maintain/no intervention or raise in 2013. "Maintain" corresponds to countries reporting the same immigration policy in 1996 as in 2013. Hong Kong, China, is omitted due to missing data.

Source: Authors' calculations based on UNDESA (2013), *World Population Policies 2013* (database), *www.un.org/en/development/desa/population/publications/policy/world-population-policies-2013.shtml.*

StatLink http://dx.doi.org/10.1787/888933422462

Figure 5.4. **Migration policies have become consistently less restrictive since 1945**

Yearly average change in migration restrictiveness, 1900-2013

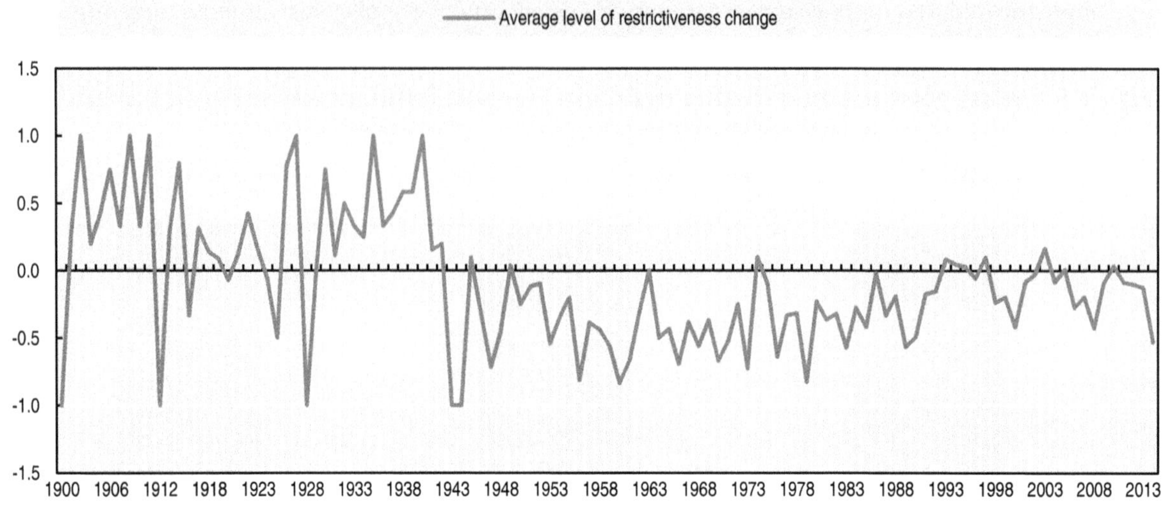

Note: The figure depicts average yearly changes in migration policy restrictiveness for 40 countries from 1900 to 2013. The average is taken across countries and types of policies within a country. A restrictive policy takes the value 1, no change in restrictiveness is coded by the value zero and a less restrictive policy takes the value -1. A score above zero means that the number of restrictive policy changes was larger than the number of less restrictive policy changes. The average should be treated with caution, as for some years the database contains only a small number of recorded policy changes.

Source: Authors' calculation based on DEMIG (2015), *Determinants of International Migration: A Theoretical and Empirical Assessment of Policy, Origin and Destination Effects* (database), *www.imi.ox.ac.uk/data/demig-data/demig-policy-1* and de Haas, Natter and Vezzoli (2014), "Growing restrictiveness or changing selection? The nature and evolution of migration policies", *International Migration Institute Working Papers*.

StatLink http://dx.doi.org/10.1787/888933422474

After the 2008 economic crisis, a number of HI and SG countries tightened migration policies. In HI countries, restrictive policy changes began to outnumber less restrictive policy changes (Figure 5.5). Policies targeting skilled migrants became more restrictive, and foreign investors and entrepreneurs were increasingly scrutinised. Furthermore border controls were strengthened and voluntary returns were encouraged (OECD, 2015). Yet in 2013, migration policies began to ease again in HI countries. While a number of restrictive policy changes were implemented in 2013 in the SG countries included in the sample, less restrictive policies still dominated the overall migration policy changes in these countries. In contrast with other SG countries included in the sample, China and Russia implemented more restrictive policies in 2013 (partially explaining the increased restrictiveness of migration policies in 2013 for SG countries, depicted in Figure 5.5). China reinforced border controls and the fight against irregular immigrants and Russia restricted the conditions of entry to the country. The improving economic situation in OECD countries constituted a favourable context for labour migration over the period 2015-16 explaining why there was no major changes in migration policies in HI countries (OECD, 2016b).The main changes in policies between 2015 and 2016 aimed to favour skilled migration (Japan and Romania for instance set up strategies to target highly qualified professionals) and to ease procedure for labour migration (OECD, 2016b). In Europe, the European Agenda for migration was adopted and implemented in 2015 in response to the unfolding refugee crisis that European countries faced.

Immigration to HI countries is increasing alongside many policy changes facilitating immigration. Yet migration policy changes do not fully explain why immigration to HI countries is disproportionately growing in comparison to immigration to SG countries. Overall, migration policies in SG countries are also loosening, yet immigration towards SG countries has not increased as expected from the strong economic growth in these countries.

Figure 5.5. **Migration policies are on average less restrictive in some SG countries**

Yearly average change in migration policy restrictiveness in HI countries and in some SG countries, 1995-2013

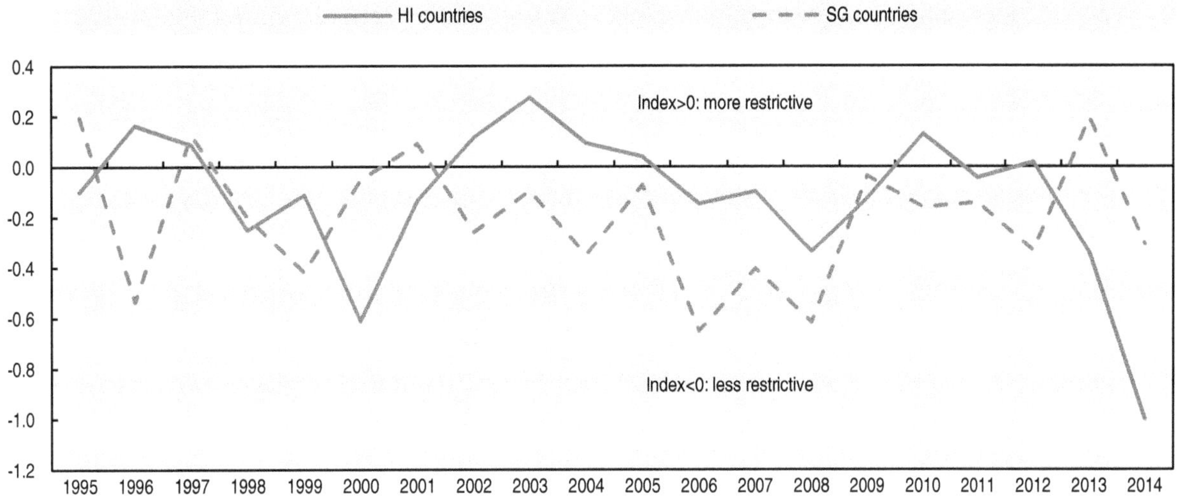

Note: The figure depicts average yearly changes in migration policy restrictiveness for 40 countries from 1995 to 2013. The average is taken across countries and types of policies within a country. A restrictive policy takes the value 1, no change in restrictiveness is coded by the value zero and a less restrictive policy takes the value -1. A score above zero means that the number of restrictive policy changes was larger than the number of less restrictive policy changes. The average should be treated with caution, as for some years the database contains only a small number of recorded policy changes.

Source: Authors' calculations based on DEMIG (2015), *Determinants of International Migration: A Theoretical and Empirical Assessment of Policy, Origin and Destination Effects* (database), *www.imi.ox.ac.uk/data/demig-data/demig-policy-1* and de Haas, Natter and Vezzoli (2014), "Growing restrictiveness or changing selection? The nature and evolution of migration policies", *International Migration Institute Working Papers*.

StatLink http://dx.doi.org/10.1787/888933422485

Comparison of migration policies with the evolution of migration flows yields useful information

Comparing policies reported by governments with the evolution of migration flows in the destination countries provides imprecise but useful information on the relation between migration policies and migration flows. Observing this relationship shows that countries implementing policies designed to increase immigration can successfully increase the proportion of immigrants in the population. Nevertheless, countries implementing policies designed to decrease immigration do not necessarily see a reduction in immigration flows. For better understanding of the relation between changes in migration policies and migration flows, the year 2005 was chosen: it provides the opportunity to review migration flows over the ten years before and after the policy changes. In this analysis, migration flows correspond to the difference between the numbers of migrants across five-year periods, as only the number of migrants by country of destination and by country of origin are available at the global level. The limitations of this method are described in Box 4.1 in Chapter 4.

Regardless of governmental policies, the proportion of immigrants in the population of HI countries increased over the last 20 years (Figure 5.6). In 2005, 15 of the 27 HI countries in the sample reported policies designed to maintain immigration. However, the proportion of immigrants in the population of these countries *increased* by 2 percentage points on average from 2005 to 2015 (from 10% to 12%). Among the HI countries aiming to increase immigration in 2005, the proportion of immigrants in the population increased on average from 13% to 17% over the ten-year period. Most surprisingly, the proportion of immigrants in the population of HI countries implementing policies in 2005 to *reduce* immigration also increased – from 14% to 19% on average over the period.

The growing share immigration in HI countries aiming at maintaining the level of immigration in 2005 is partly explained by the expansion of the free mobility zones in Europe since 1995. The implementation of the Schengen Agreement (abolishing any border control between its members) and the expansion of the European Union (guaranteeing free mobility of individuals among its members) fostered intra-migration between members of these agreements. However, such type of agreements do not explain why countries aiming at lowering immigration such as Saudi Arabia and Kuwait have also experienced large increases in the share of immigration.

The same effect can be observed in those SG countries aiming to reduce immigration. Despite policies intended to lower immigration in 2005, the proportion of immigrants in the population grew from 2.6% to 3.4% between 2005 and 2015. Among SG countries implementing policies to maintain or raise immigration in 2005, the proportion of immigrants in the population remained stable, at around 1% and 8% respectively, on average, between 2005 and 2015. Nevertheless, the proportion of immigrants in the population of SG countries remains less than half of that in HI countries.

Figure 5.6. **The proportion of immigrants in HI countries increased in the last 20 years, regardless of policies**

Proportion of immigrants in 1995, 2005 and 2015 viewed against immigration policy of destination countries in 2005

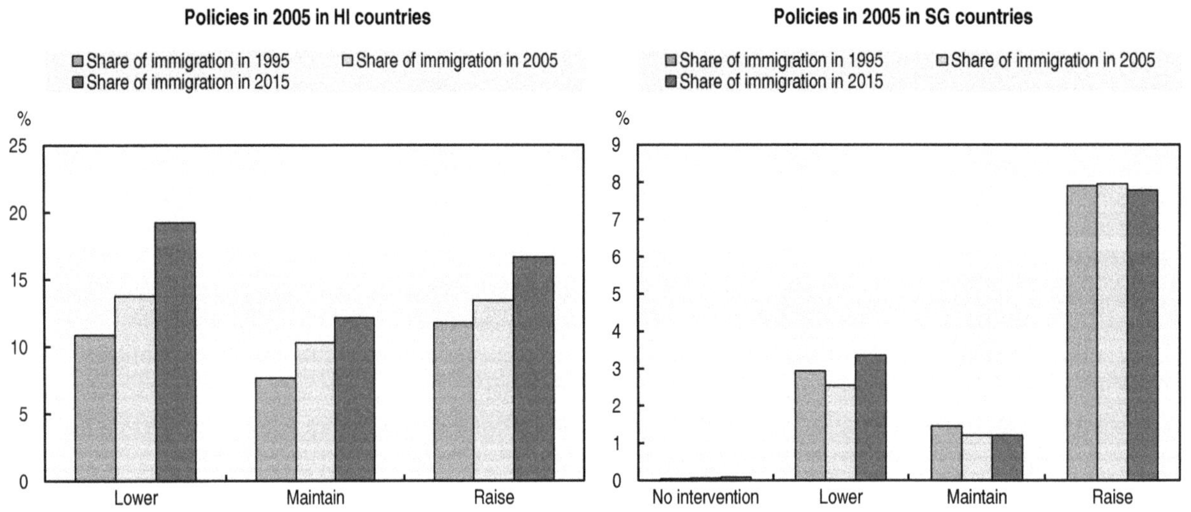

Note: The average proportion of immigrants in the population is a population-weighted average. The sample includes all countries classified in Table A.2 in Annex A, except for Hong Kong, China, due to missing data on migration policies.

Source: Authors' calculations based on UNDESA (2013), *World Population Policies 2013* (database), *www.un.org/en/development/desa/population/publications/policy/world-population-policies-2013.shtml* and UNDESA (2015), "Trends in International Migrant Stock: Migrants by Destination and Origin", *International Migration* (database), *www.un.org/en/development/desa/population/migration/data/estimates2/estimates15.shtml.*

StatLink http://dx.doi.org/10.1787/888933422496

These trends show the asymmetric effects of policy on migration flows. Inflows may decrease only gradually after more restrictive policy changes, whereas they increase almost immediately after the lifting of some restrictions. The quick response after a relaxation of migration policies may result from fear of a future re-introduction of restrictions (Czaika and de Haas, 2016). This asymmetrical effect should be further investigated when additional detailed data on migration policies become available.

Targeting of skills and family reunification are two key policies in shaping migration

Migration policies include varying types of measures targeting different groups of individuals based on income, ethnicity, skills and other factors. There is a contradiction between the evolution of immigration flows in SG countries, their stated policies reported in UN data and the common perception of increasing restrictiveness. This results in part from the process of forming migration policy and the diversity of migration policies. Migration policies are partially the result of a bargaining process between groups and individuals with varied interests. Furthermore, migration policies are diverse and defined at different levels of governance (e.g. by national or local governments) with multiple and sometimes contradictory objectives (de Haas, Natter and Vezzoli, 2014).

To say that a country aims to increase, decrease or maintain the volume of migration is often an oversimplification of a diverse range of policies. This helps explain the discrepancies that can appear between a government's stated objectives and the changes in migration flows. This section illustrates two types of policy that have played an important role in shaping migration in recent decades: policies targeting particular skills, on the one hand, and policies allowing family reunification, on the other.

Policies for selecting migrants based upon their skills have become less restrictive

Migration policies based on selection of skills have become less restrictive since 1995 (Figure 5.7). In HI and SG countries present in DEMIG (2015), policies targeting high-skilled immigrants have been loosened more than policies affecting low-skilled workers. The number of migrants to OECD countries possessing a university degree increased disproportionately (by 65%) between 2000 and 2010, according to the *Database on Immigrants in OECD Countries* (OECD, 2016a). Chapter 3 shows that economic transformations partially explain the growing number of migrants with a university degree, who are often recruited for high-skilled jobs. Moreover, the selection of countries by migrants based on their skills and educational achievement also explains the growing proportion of skilled migrants in OECD countries. Migration policies targeting high- or low-skilled workers for high- or low-skilled jobs depend on the labour market needs of the country of destination. Malaysia, for instance, has recruited low-skilled migrants to ease labour shortages in its economy (Box 5.4).

China is actively trying to attract foreign talent. The working-age population is declining in China (OECD, 2014). In particular, skilled workers are increasingly in short supply in China, as in many Asian countries. China may face a skills gap of more than 20 million tertiary-educated workers by 2030 (INSEAD, 2013). Scarce vocational skills are also an obstacle to innovation in the country (INSEAD, 2015). The Chinese government is actively promoting the immigration of skilled workers by various policy reforms. As part of a process of increasing economic openness, the country increasingly opened its labour market to high-skilled migrant workers after 1996, and offered permanent residency for high-skilled foreigners starting in 2004. The Thousand Talents Plan, launched in 2008, was a programme designed to attract 2 000 highly talented migrants within a few years; it provided selected individuals with a residence permit and access to various subsidies and grants. The talent visa, called the R-visa, came into force in July 2013 with the Exit and Entry Administration Law, and provided a series of rights to highly qualified workers or much-needed talent (European Commission, 2016). The Chinese government is also actively trying to attract foreign students. In recent years, the ministry of education has signed agreements with foreign governments on the mutual recognition of degrees. Between 2002 and 2007, the total number of international students enrolled in Chinese universities increased by 56% to around 200 000 (Bhandari and Blumenthal, 2011).

Figure 5.7. **Policies targeting skilled migrants are becoming less restrictive than policies targeting low-skilled migrants, 1995-2014**

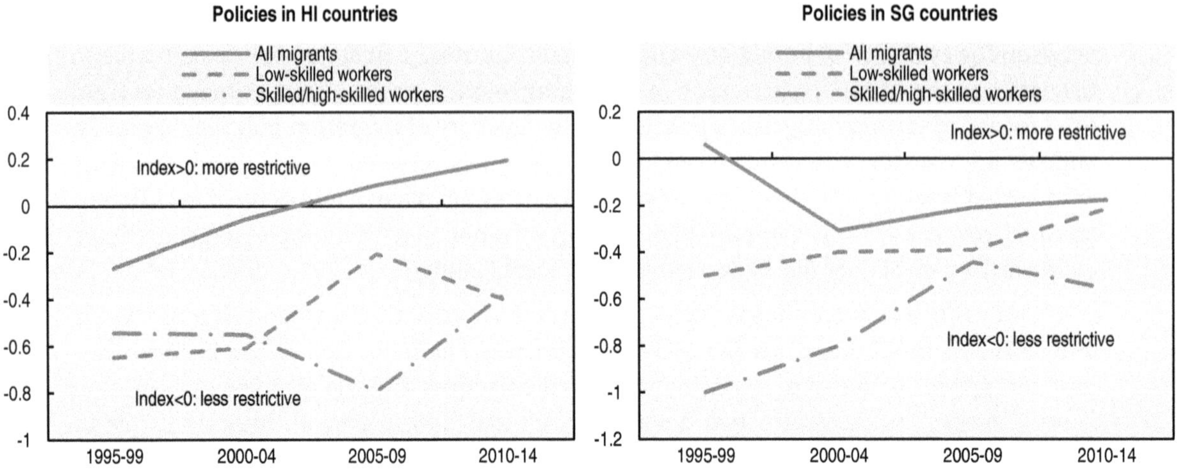

Note: The vertical axis is an indicator of policy restrictiveness. A more restrictive policy change takes the value 1 and a less restrictive policy change takes the value -1. If restrictive policies are more numerous within the time frame, then the average will be positive. If less restrictive policies are more frequent, then the average will be negative. Based on 553 policy changes between 1995 and 2014 in 23 HI countries and on 209 policy changes between 1995 and 2014 in 17 SG countries.

Source: Authors' calculations based on DEMIG (2015), *Determinants of International Migration: A Theoretical and Empirical Assessment of Policy, Origin and Destination Effects* (database), *www.imi.ox.ac.uk/data/demig-data/demig-policy-1*.

StatLink http://dx.doi.org/10.1787/888933422506

Box 5.4. **Immigration policies in Malaysia**

Foreign labour became a part of the Malaysian development model from the 1970s, when the country began to rely on low- to medium-skilled foreign workers to fuel growth and facilitate a deep economic transformation. Labour flows to Malaysia have continued ever since, but the policy stance has reacted to changes in the country's economic performance and the political climate (Kanapathy, 2006).

Unlike many OECD countries, Malaysia does not prioritise skilled and educated immigrants. Migrant labour in Malaysia is largely concentrated in physically demanding sectors. About 32% of the migrant population work in the agriculture sector and 14% in the construction sector (World Bank, 2013).

The large proportion of low-skilled immigrants is a result of government strategies in the 1970s and 1980s to support growth. In the 1990s, formal guidelines for recruitment were introduced to meet the demand for low-skilled workers. This plan was part of the country's strategy to modernise the economy and expand the supply of skilled workers. Increased education among the Malaysian population, the relatively small population size, as well as massive urbanisation and internal migration towards urban areas, led to a labour shortage in agriculture. The government then supported immigration in this sector, followed by the construction and service sectors. It has been estimated that the immigrant population grew from 380 000 in 1990 to 2.1 million in 2010 – around 9% of the country's population. This large inflow of low-skilled workers resulted not only from internal factors, but also from external factors such as political instability and slower economic growth in neighbouring countries (World Bank, 2013).

Family reunification is an important channel of entry

Family reunification remains an important channel of entry to OECD countries. Migration for the purpose of family reunification principally involves the migration of family members considered dependants. These are usually the spouse and young children, emigrating to join another member of the family who is already living in a different country in a regular situation (OHCHR, 2005). Since the 1980s, family reunification has become an important source of immigration. It has been the main source of legal entry for migrants to member countries of the European Union and traditional immigration countries (Australia, Canada and the United States), accounting for a third of permanent migration to OECD countries in 2013.

Many SG countries, such as China, Latvia, the Philippines and Poland, aimed to raise the level of immigration for the purpose of family reunification in 2011 (UNDESA, 2013). While migration policies concerning family members of migrants are tightening in HI countries, such policies are becoming less restrictive in SG countries (de Haas, Natter and Vezzoli, 2014). Despite the more restrictive family reunification policies in HI countries and a decrease in the volume of migration for familial reasons, it continues to be one of the major sources of regular migration.

Family reunification policies allow migrants to provide security for elderly relatives in the country of destination and to provide children with access to foreign education. For example, Chinese emigrants tend to be young and take into account the future prospects of their children. Many Chinese migrants have used the opportunity that family reunification policies provide to bring their relatives to the country to which they emigrate. In 2013-14, Chinese nationals accounted for the largest source of immigrants entering through the family reunification channel in Australia, amounting to 17% of all family visas granted (DIBP, 2014). However, the criteria for accessing family reunification programmes have been tightened. At the end of 1970, family reunification was the major channel of entry for Chinese emigrants, while currently it mostly concerns the families of investors and high-skilled Chinese migrants (Xiang, 2016).

Policies not directly related to migration can also affect flows

Besides migration policies focused on regulation and border management, non-migration policies also have repercussions on migration flows. In the 1980s and 1990s, when developing countries were encouraged to liberalise their economies and reduce public intervention, most social and labour safety nets tended to disappear. In many countries, especially in Latin America, this translated into a significant increase in emigration (Khoudour-Castéras, 2010). The pendulum is now moving in the other direction and there is a growing awareness of the importance of policies aiming to reduce poverty and improve social conditions (OECD, 2011). With the adoption of the 2030 Agenda for Sustainable Development and focus on distributional concerns, there could be an orientation shift in public policies towards social objectives, which could help reduce poverty-driven migration outflows.

Despite the role played by non-migration sectoral policies, their indirect effects on migration are poorly identified and rarely appear on the policy-making dashboard. This section highlights the way sectoral policies can affect migration flows.

Sectoral policies affect the decision to migrate in both origin and destination countries

The analysis and results presented here on the impact of non-migration policies build on the IPPMD project (OECD, forthcoming) – covering ten countries (see Box 5.5). The project especially focused on five sectoral policies: labour markets, agriculture, education, investment and financial services, and social protection and health.

Box 5.5. **Identifying and measuring the interrelation between sectoral public policies and migration**

In January 2013, the European Union and the OECD Development Centre launched a new project: **Interrelations between public policies, migration and development: Case studies and policy recommendations** (IPPMD). This project – carried out in ten low- and middle-income countries between 2013 and 2017 – sought to provide policy makers with evidence of the importance of integrating migration into development strategies and fostering coherence across sectoral policies.

A balanced mix of ten developing countries was chosen to participate in the project: Armenia, Burkina Faso, Cambodia, Costa Rica, Côte d'Ivoire, Dominican Republic, Georgia, Haiti, Morocco and the Philippines.

The IPPMD project aimed to provide empirical evidence about the interrelations between migration and public policies based on quantitative and qualitative fieldwork. The methodological framework was developed by the OECD Development Centre and the data were collected by its local research institutions in each partner country. Three main tools were used in compiling the data underpinning the empirical analysis:

1. **Household surveys:** In each country, around 2 000 households were interviewed, with an oversampling of migrant households to obtain a near 50/50 share with non-migrant households. Questions ranged from those about the very basic demographic and personal characteristics of each member of the household, to household-level characteristics and specific modules on key sectors (employment, education, agricultural and business activities and social protection) and specific migration experience (emigration, remittances, return migration and immigration).

2. **Community surveys:** These were carried out in the same localities as the household surveys to complement them and provide more information about the communities in which the households reside. Close to 700 local authorities and community leaders were interviewed. The questionnaire included around 75 questions to gather demographic, social and economic information on the communities, as well as specific questions on policies and programmes implemented in the localities.

3. **Qualitative stakeholder interviews:** In addition to the quantitative data collected, an average of 40 in-depth stakeholder interviews were carried out across the ten partner countries. The semi-structured interviews were intended to collect qualitative information on perceptions, trends and policies related to the various aspects of migration in partner countries. The respondents were representatives from ministries and other public institutions, both at the national and local levels; civil society organisations; trade unions and private companies; academia; and international organisations.

The main findings of the IPPMD project are presented below. These findings reflect the experience of the ten IPPMD partner countries and do not profess to cover all the potential effects of sectoral policies on migration flows. Yet the geographic, economic, socio-cultural and institutional diversity of the selected countries may help provide some important lessons for policy makers from other developing countries.

Labour market policies have an impact on migration

Because most migrants decide to migrate for job-related reasons, migration flows are directly influenced by employment conditions in countries both of origin and destination. These conditions depend not only on the population and economic dynamics, but also on a large set of public policies. Industrial policies, for instance, stimulate the productive transformation of the economy and therefore affect labour demand in the country. Likewise, education policies can contribute to reducing skills mismatches, and hence unemployment. Most countries also use more direct labour market policies to stimulate employment and help create jobs. Policy instruments that improve labour market conditions may therefore reduce the incentive to migrate.

Effective labour market policies can have an indirect impact on households' decisions on whether to migrate. On the one hand, aspects of the labour market, such as minimum wages, unemployment benefits and employment protection legislation, influence employment outcomes. On the other, active labour market policies (ALMPs) target specific groups particularly affected by unemployment. Such policies can be implemented through several channels and with different objectives:

- Expanding government employment agencies can enhance labour market efficiency.
- Enlarging the scope of technical and vocational education and training (TVET) can contribute to reducing skills mismatches.
- Introducing public employment programmes can increase labour demand.

Government employment agencies can reduce intentions to migrate by helping people find jobs

Government employment agencies aim to improve the functioning of the labour market by providing information on the economy and the local labour market. If job seekers can find employment in the domestic labour market through job centres, they may choose to stay rather than to move abroad in search of better job opportunities. The IPPMD data confirm that those who found jobs through government agencies had less intention to move abroad than those who found jobs without using the government agencies.

Technical and vocational education and training (TVET) may solidify plans to migrate

Vocational training has become a fundamental instrument of labour market strategies in many developing countries. With growing global economic integration and rapid technological change, the acquisition of new skills across all sectors is important in adapting to market demand. Vocational training programmes can therefore play a crucial role in building a labour force with skills that match the changing needs of the economy. At the same time, TVET programmes can also affect the decision to migrate. By improving their skills, people may find better jobs in the domestic labour market, thereby reducing the incentive to emigrate. On the other hand, vocational training can be a means to make would-be migrants more employable overseas. Figure 5.8 compares the migration intentions of employed and unemployed individuals who benefited from vocational training with those who did not. In most countries (except Armenia and Cambodia), the proportion of individuals planning to migrate appears to be higher among those who participated in a vocational training programme than for those who did not.

Public employment programmes can affect migration decisions

Public employment programmes (PEPs) are in place in many countries, with many aims and varying priorities. Some governments introduce PEPs to increase overall labour demand and complement job creation in the private sector. In other contexts, PEPs act as a social safety net, especially for the poorest and most vulnerable. For instance, cash-for-work or food-for-work programmes often target households close to the poverty line in order to provide a minimum income in return for temporary work. In some cases, governments use public employment programmes following a disaster or as emergency mechanisms.

Figure 5.8. **Plans to migrate are largely correlated with participation in vocational training programmes**

Ratio of participants in vocational training programmes to non-participants among people with plans to migrate

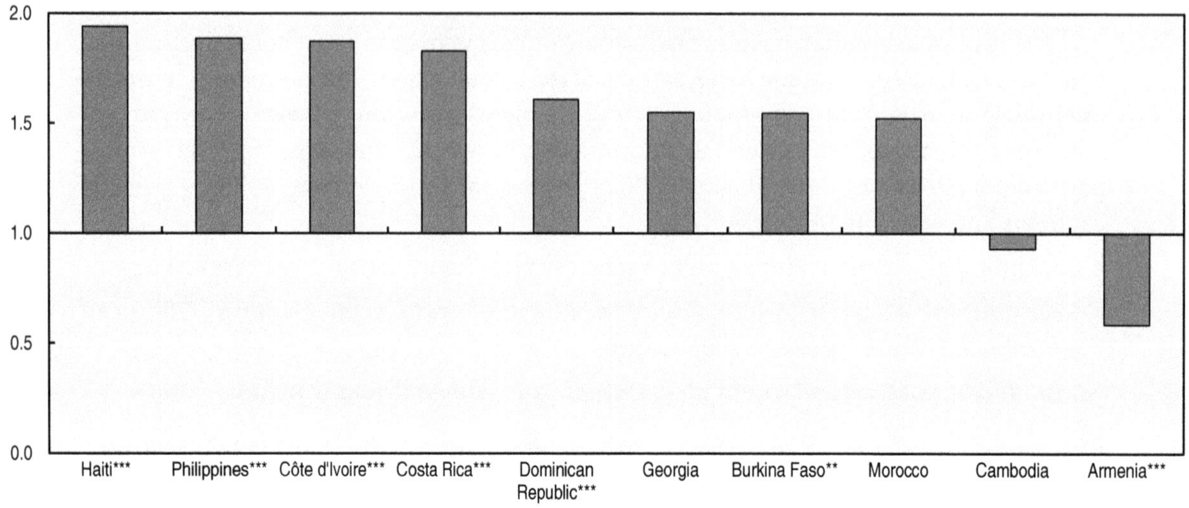

Note: If the ratio is above 1, the share of people who plan to emigrate is higher among the group who participated in vocational training programmes than those who did not; the opposite is true for a ratio below. Statistical significance calculated using a chi-squared test is indicated as follows: ***: 99%, **: 95%, *: 90%.

Source: OECD (forthcoming), *Interrelations between Public Policies, Migration and Development.*

StatLink http://dx.doi.org/10.1787/888933422512

Public employment programmes can affect incentives to migrate, depending on households' response to the additional income received. Where public employment programmes improve local employment opportunities, the incentives to migrate may diminish as the opportunity cost of migration increases. In rural areas in particular, public works programmes to support agricultural workers during the farming off-season can provide an alternative to seasonal migration.

Labour market policies resulting in better outcomes in terms of employment and higher wages tend to affect migration decisions. By making it easier for job seekers to find employment, government employment agencies are liable to reduce emigration. The impact of job centres on migration depends, however, on the way they operate. If their main objective is to help job seekers find employment abroad or if they only provide job opportunities at the local level, employment agencies will probably contribute to increasing outflows. By contrast, if job seekers can find opportunities on the domestic labour market and the coverage is national, such active labour market policies will likely curb emigration. In the same way, it seems that the main reason why TVET programmes may encourage emigration is related to the fact that there is a mismatch between the needs of the domestic labour market and the skills provided by TVET. It is therefore necessary that ALMPs be oriented towards the needs of the domestic labour market, so that migration becomes really an individual choice and not a decision by default.

Education policies can accelerate or brake decisions to migrate

Education policies can affect migration patterns in various ways. In the countries of destination, the quality of the education system can act as a magnet for students from other countries. Many developing countries that have invested in improving their education system over the last decades have thus become attractive for students from neighbouring countries seeking to benefit from a better education than is available in their own countries, but at a lower cost than in most high-income countries. Visas are often also easier to get in these countries, above all if they are part of regions with human mobility conventions.

In countries of origin, a curriculum that does not match the needs of domestic labour markets can be a source of emigration pressure. This can occur either when the supply of those with a tertiary education, for instance in social sciences, exceeds the demand, or when certain important skills that are in high demand, for instance agronomy, are not covered by the education system.

The education of children is a driver of emigration in many countries. Adults may decide to emigrate if educational conditions are not of a high enough standard for their children in the home country. If there are not enough schools where they live, families may decide to send their children to school in other parts of the country or abroad. Thus, education policies aiming to improve the education system may increase the incentives to return to the country of origin, especially for migrants with children of school age.

Parents also emigrate to finance the schooling of children in the country of origin. Education programmes aimed at supporting attendance and enrolment rates may decrease the incentive to emigrate if the motivation for emigration is to finance children's education. The link between education programmes and migration is, however, not straightforward, as households that benefit from such programmes, especially if they are cash-based, may enjoy reduced credit constraints, allowing them to finance the emigration of a household member. The IPPMD project focused on three different groups of programmes to analyse how various education programmes that provide support for schooling affect migration decisions (OECD, 2016c):

- **cash-based programmes** such as conditional cash transfer (CCT) programmes and educational scholarships
- **in-kind distribution programmes** such as the distribution of school textbooks, uniforms and free school meals
- **other types of educational support programmes** such as school transport programmes, literacy programmes and support programmes to allow young parents to stay in school.

Conditional Cash Transfers (CCTs) have mixed effects on migration

The strongest relation between emigration and education policies is found with the analysis of CCTs, which are implemented in four of the IPPMD partner countries. CCTs provide cash payments to households to send their children to school. They often also require members of the household to be present physically to benefit from the transfer, which may deter migration outflows (Stecklov et al., 2005). Previous literature on the link between CCTs and emigration finds mixed results. A review of five different CCT programmes in Latin America showed both increased and decreased propensities to emigrate for households receiving a transfer. Factors that might explain these opposing results include the size of the transfer (households may decide to emigrate if the transfer is not large enough to satisfy the need of the household) and variation in conditionality that makes it possible for some members to emigrate and still receive the transfer (Hangen-Zanker and Himmelstine, 2013).

The IPPMD data indicate that CCTs for education tend to reduce emigration. As shown in Figure 5.9, households that received conditional cash transfers are less likely to have a member who emigrated abroad in the past five years in all countries but Haiti. In Costa Rica, none of the households receiving CCTs had an emigrant.

Figure 5.9. **Conditional cash transfers tend to be negatively linked with emigration**

Share of households receiving conditional cash transfers for education purposes, by emigration status

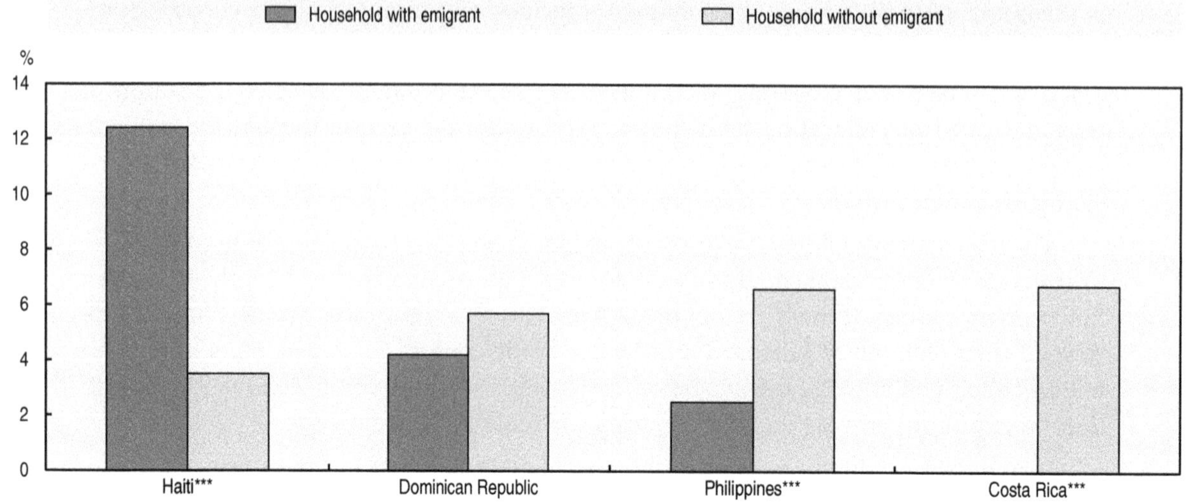

Note: Statistical significance calculated using a chi-squared test is indicated as follows: ***: 99%, **: 95%, *: 90%. The figure shows households with emigrants who left in the five past years prior to the survey (households with emigrants who left at an earlier stage are excluded from the sample). No households with emigrants received CCTs in Costa Rica. The sample of emigrant households that left in the past five years is, however, very limited in Costa Rica (only 28 households) but the pattern is the same when looking at the link between intentions to emigrate and CCT beneficiaries: only very few households that receive CCTs have members planning to emigrate in the future (2 out of 108 households, or less than 2%).

Source: OECD (forthcoming), *Interrelations between Public Policies, Migration and Development.*

StatLink http://dx.doi.org/10.1787/888933422521

Education policies that address the quality of the education system and support child schooling can affect emigration patterns by altering the incentives to emigrate or loosening credit constraints. Programmes with less binding conditionality requirements and an uncertain funding basis, such as the CCT programme in Haiti, are thus linked to a greater tendency to emigrate, while longer-term and better managed programmes are linked to a lower tendency. Policy makers should therefore consider such effects when designing and implementing CCT programmes in areas with high emigration rates in order to avoid unintended outcomes on migration flows.

Social protection and health policies have a limited effect on migration

There is a debate as to whether immigrants are more likely to move to countries with generous welfare systems, the so-called welfare magnet hypothesis. Individuals are not only attracted by economic opportunities, although this is often the main factor, but also by their own well-being, which increases when social safety nets are in place. Although a review of the literature concludes mixed evidence, and is partly determined by the type of migration regime in place (Giulietti and Wahba, 2013), some studies point to the fact that immigrants sometimes do choose the destination country based on such criteria (De Giorgi and Pellizzari, 2006). The extent of generosity of the welfare state, in particular, seems to attract workers with lower skills, thus affecting not only the volume of migration, but also its composition (Boeri, 2010 and 2011). However, this effect seems relatively small compared to the effect of wage differences as a pull factor for migration. Despite the widespread view in a number of OECD countries that migrants are net beneficiaries of the social system, estimates of the fiscal impact of immigration show that it is in reality around zero on average (OECD, 2013). In fact, in most countries, immigrants contribute more to the system through the taxes they pay than they cost through the social services they receive.

The lack of social protection can also push people to look for better benefits in other countries. Emigration is often a response to shocks, uncertainty and vulnerability in the home country (Hagen-Zanker and Himmelstine, 2013; Sabates-Wheeler and Waite, 2003). By decreasing the vulnerability of households and individuals, social protection programmes can keep them from emigrating from necessity rather than by choice. On the other hand, households may accumulate savings as an insurance mechanism, and use them when times are lean. A reduction in risk may free up such savings or loosen assets that are then used to finance emigration.

A review of the links between social protection and emigration shows that an increase in social insurance coverage in the home country, through programmes such as unemployment insurance, disability pay, free medical care, day-care of children and old-age pensions, is linked to a decrease in emigration (Hagen-Zanker and Himmelstine, 2013). The breadth and reach of such programmes is a function of the money the government invests, and basic evidence suggests that such expenditures are negatively correlated with the rate of planned emigration. In this respect, the proportion of individuals planning to emigrate in each country derived from the IPPMD data is negatively correlated with public social expenditures in the eight countries for which data are available (Figure 5.10).

Figure 5.10. **Public social expenditures reduce the rate of emigration**

Share of individuals planning to emigrate and public social expenditures

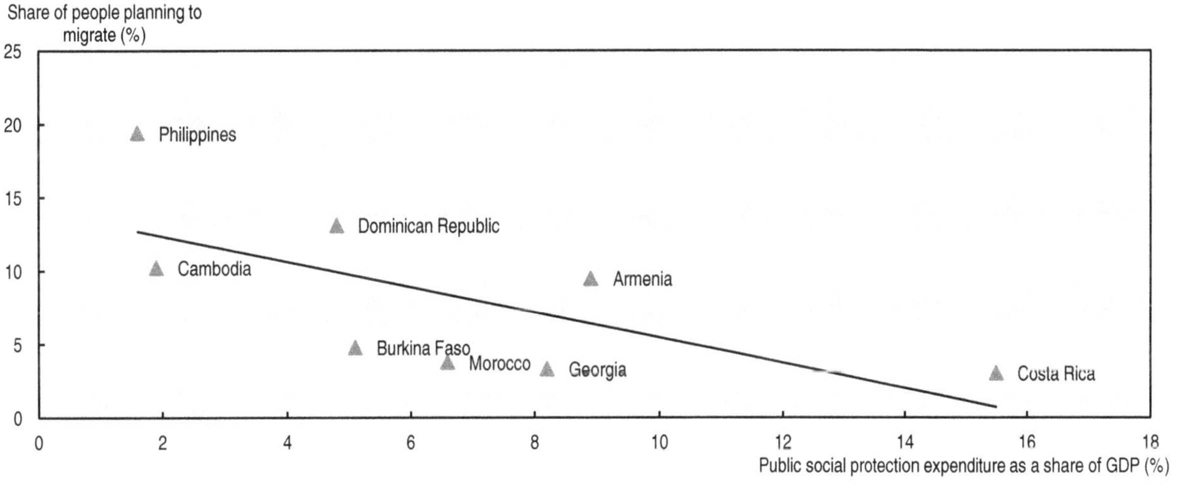

Note: Data on public social expenditures taken from the last year available, from 2010 to 2012. Proportion of individuals planning to emigrate is from the IPPMD project survey calculated as a proportion of adults who have plans to emigrate in the future among the total population aged 15 and above.

Source: Public social protection expenditures are from ILO (2016), *ILOSTAT* (database), International Labour Organization, *www.ilo.org/ilostat/faces/oracle/webcenter/portalapp/pagehierarchy/Page137.jspx?_afrLoop=4507540746758&clean=true#!%40%40%3F_afrLoop%3D4507540746758%26clean%3Dtrue%26_adf.ctrl-state%3D115ef6bvvr_9*; and OECD (forthcoming), *Interrelations between Public Policies, Migration and Development*.

StatLink http://dx.doi.org/10.1787/888933422534

One way for individuals to have access to minimal social protection is through formal labour contracts, which minimise the likelihood of working under precarious conditions and increase the probability of obtaining work-related benefits and insurance. Formal labour contracts often ensure that workers use legal systems if problems arise between the worker and the employer (Jütting and de Laiglesia, 2009). Not having a formal labour contract significantly reduces individual well-being and may push workers to seek work elsewhere. The IPPMD data show that plans to emigrate increase among workers lacking a formal labour contract (Figure 5.11).

Figure 5.11. **The lack of a formal labour contract increases the rate of emigration**

Share of non-agricultural workers planning to emigrate and those that do not have a formal labour contract

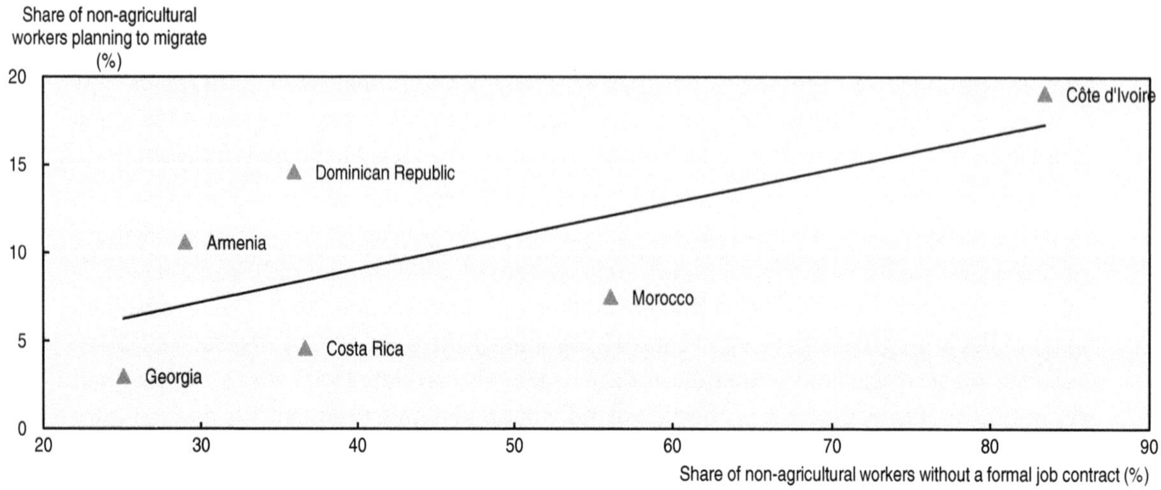

Note: Figure only includes non-agricultural workers. Burkina Faso, Cambodia, Haiti and the Philippines are not included as the question on type of labour contract was not asked in those countries. Share of individuals planning to emigrate is calculated as a share of adults who have plans to emigrate in the future among the total population aged 15 and above.

Source: OECD (forthcoming), *Interrelations between Public Policies, Migration and Development.*

StatLink http://dx.doi.org/10.1787/888933422540

Figure 5.12. **Socially marginalised individuals are less likely to plan to emigrate**

Share of individuals who either were denied or do not have access to a health facility

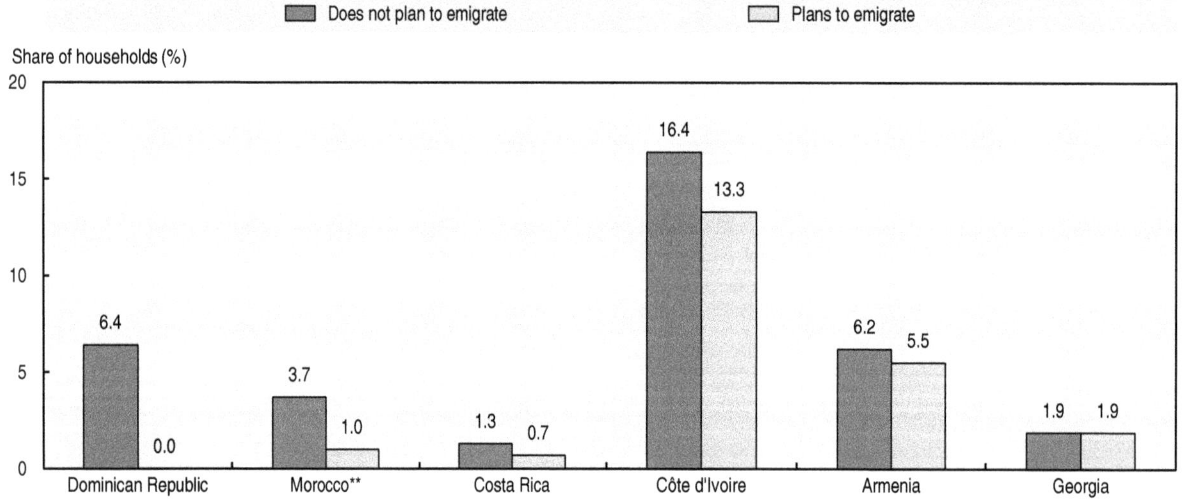

Note: The figure is based on the proportion of individuals who answered that they did not visit a health facility because they did not have access to one. Statistical significance calculated using a chi-squared test is indicated as follows: ***: 99%, **: 95%, *: 90%. It is indicative of the difference in rates between those not planning to emigrate and those planning to. Order of countries is based on the ratio of individuals not planning to emigrate over those planning to do so. Proportion of individuals planning to emigrate is from the IPPMD project survey calculated as a proportion of adults who have plans to emigrate in the future among the total population aged 15 and above.

Source: OECD (forthcoming), *Interrelations between Public Policies, Migration and Development.*

StatLink http://dx.doi.org/10.1787/888933422559

However, in many cases, the proportion of people planning to emigrate increases with social protection coverage (OECD, forthcoming). The IPPMD data show that in some countries, namely Armenia and Costa Rica, the probability of plans to emigrate increases among people who belong to a labour union or have access to health care. Having an open-ended contract in Costa Rica also seems to be correlated with people emigrating. This could indicate that individuals with decent jobs in their home may also have good job prospects abroad, and suggests that individuals may have access to outside options through their aptitude and social standing. In contrast, marginalised groups, in particular those without access to health care, are less likely to plan to emigrate (Figure 5.12).

Conclusion

This chapter has sought to review the degree to which migration and non-migration policies have an impact on international migration.

Contrary to common perceptions, most countries do not aim to decrease immigration. In reality, most SG countries and HI countries state the intention to maintain or to increase immigration. Whether migration policies are open or restrictive is partly determined by individual attitudes towards migrants, as individuals can influence political decisions through voting in elections. These attitudes are, in turn, driven by both economic and non-economic factors. The skills composition of immigrants relative to the native population is a major determinant of attitudes.

Furthermore, there is significant evidence demonstrating that migration policies in SG countries and in HI countries have in fact loosened over the past 20 years. Key countries of destination have been more likely to remove various legal and administrative constraints than to put in place further barriers. Immigration policies do not fully explain the recent evolution of migration. Despite increasingly open immigration policies in many SG countries, immigration to SG countries has not increased to the same extent as immigration to HI countries.

Regardless of migration policies, the proportion of immigrants in the population of SG countries and of OECD countries increased on average between 2005 and 2015. This is not to say that migration policies did not affect migration flows. Countries that loosened migration policies were more likely to observe an increase in migration flows than countries that did not. In contrast, countries that tightened migration policies were no more likely to observe a decrease in migration flows than countries that did not.

The impression that migration policies are tightening is possibly due to the fact that these policies are increasingly targeting workers with complementary skills in order to fulfil labour market needs. Such policies can have a significant impact on the skills composition of migration flows. On the other hand, family reunification policies are tightening in HI countries, but continue to loosen in SG countries.

Beyond migration policies, non-migration policies also have impacts on migration flows. The indirect effects of sectoral policies on migration are often poorly identified and seldom taken into account by policy makers. Yet sectoral policies, in both origin and destination countries, play a key role in migration decisions. In areas such as the labour market, education and the social sector, these policies affect market efficiency, financial constraints and skills development, and therefore contribute to encouraging or deterring migration flows.

The effect of sectoral policies on migration is not always straightforward, however. Similar programmes can generate different effects in different countries. It is the combination of several policies that is more likely to influence the decision to migrate. Targeting a single policy will in most cases not be enough to influence emigration if a market inefficiency in another domain remains.

The main challenge is that sectoral policies are generally not targeted towards migration, but have their own sector-related objectives. But this is precisely why it is so important for policy makers to integrate migration into their development strategies. Beyond specific objectives in terms of sustainable development, such as spurring economic growth, investing in human capital, creating jobs, reducing poverty and inequalities, or protecting the environment, different ministries need to take into account the repercussions of their policies in terms of migration. A lack of coherence across policies might indeed represent an obstacle to the successful attainment of government objectives.

References

Beam, E. (2014), "Incomplete information in job search: Evidence from a field experiment in the Philippines", *Working Paper*, National University of Singapore, *www-personal.umich.edu/~ebeam/jmp_incompleteinfo_BeamEmily.pdf*.

Beine, M., S. Bertoli and J. F.-H. Moraga (2015), "A Practitioners' guide to gravity models of international migration", *The World Economy*, Vol. 39(8), pp. 496-512, *http://dx.doi.org/10.1111/twec.12265*.

Beine, M. et al. (2015), "Comparing immigration policies: An overview from the IMPALA database", *International Migration Review*, pp. 1747-7379, *http://dx.doi.org/10.1111/imre.12169*.

Bhandari, R. and P. Blumenthal (eds.) (2011), "International students and global mobility in higher education: national trends and new directions", *International and Development Education*, Palgrave Macmillan, *http://dx.doi.org/10.1057/9780230117143*.

Boeri, T. (2011), "Migration and welfare state", Fondazione Rodolfo De Benedetti, Workshop on basic income and income redistribution, Luxembourg, 1 April.

Boeri, T. (2010), "Immigration to the land of redistribution", *Economica*, Vol. 778(308), pp. 651-687, *http://dx.doi.org/10.1111/j.1468-0335.2010.00859.x*.

Commission on Filipinos Overseas (2013), *Stock Estimate of Overseas Filipinos* (database), *http://beta.cfo.gov.ph/downloads/statistics/stock-estimates.html* (accessed 12 July 2016).

Commission on Growth and Development (2008), *The Growth Report: Strategies for Sustained Growth and Inclusive Development*, World Bank, Washington, DC. *https://openknowledge.worldbank.org/bitstream/handle/10986/6507/449860PUB0Box3101OFFICIAL0USE0ONLY1.pdf*.

Czaika, M. and H. de Haas (2016), "The effect of visas on migration processes", *International Migration Review*, *http://dx.doi.org/10.1111/imre.12261*.

Czaika, M. and H. de Haas (2013), "The effectiveness of immigration policies", *Population and Development Review*, Vol. 39(3), pp. 487-508, *http://dx.doi.org/10.1111/j.1728-4457.2013.00613.x*.

De Giorgi, G. and M. Pellizzari (2006), "Welfare migration in Europe and the cost of a harmonised social assistance", *IZA Discussion Paper*, No. 2094, IZA, Bonn, *http://repec.iza.org/dp2094.pdf*.

De Haas, H., K. Natter and S. Vezzoli (2014), "Growing restrictiveness or changing selection? The nature and evolution of migration policies", *International Migration Institute Working Papers*, No. 96, International Migration Institute, Oxford, *www.imi.ox.ac.uk/publications/wp-96-14*.

DEMIG (2015), *Determinants of International Migration: A Theoretical and Empirical Assessment of Policy, Origin and Destination Effects* (database), International Migration Institute, University of Oxford, *www.imi.ox.ac.uk/data/demig-data/demig-policy-1* (accessed 17 June 2016).

DIBP (2014), "Australia's Migration Trends 2013-14", Department of Immigration and Border Protection, Commonwealth of Australia, *www.border.gov.au/ReportsandPublications/Documents/statistics/migration-trends13-14.pdf*.

European Commission (2016), "Proposal for a Directive of the European Parliament and of the Council on the conditions of entry and residence of third-country nationals for the purposes of highly skilled employment", *Commission Staff Working Document*, Strasbourg, *http://ec.europa.eu/dgs/home-affairs/what-we-do/policies/european-agenda-migration/proposal-implementation-package/docs/20160607/directive_conditions_entry_residence_third-country_nationals_highly_skilled_employment_en.pdf*.

Gibson, J. and D. McKenzie (2014), "The development impact of a best practice seasonal worker policy", *The Review of Economics and Statistics*, Vol. 96(2), pp. 229-243, *http://dx.doi.org/10.1162/REST_a_00383*.

GIZ/ILO (2015), *Labour Market Trends Analysis and Labour Migration from South Asia to Gulf Cooperation Council Countries, India and Malaysia*, Deutsche Gesellschaft für Internationale Zusammenarbeit (GIZ) and International Labour Organization, Kathmandu, *www.ilo.org/wcmsp5/groups/public/---asia/---ro-bangkok/---ilo-kathmandu/documents/publication/wcms_377416.pdf.*

Commission on Growth and Development (2008), *The Growth Report: Strategies for Sustained Growth and Inclusive Development*, World Bank, Washington, DC, *https://openknowledge.worldbank.org/bitstream/handle/10986/6507/449860PUB0Box3101OFFICIAL0USE0ONLY1.pdf.*

Giulietti, C and J. Wahba (2013), "Welfare Migration", published in: Amelie F. Constant and Klaus F. Zimmermann (eds.), *International Handbook on the Economics of Migration*, Edward Elgar, Cheltenham, and Northampton, US, Chapter 26, 489-504.

Hagen-Zanker, J. and C.L. Himmelstine (2013), "What do we know about the impact of social protection programmes on the decision to migrate?", *Migration and Development*, Vol. 2(1), pp. 117-131.

Helbling, M., L. Bjerre, F. Römer and Z. Malisa (2016), "Measuring immigration policies: The IMPIC database", *European Political Science*, pp. 1747-7379, *http://dx.doi.org/10.1057/eps.2016.4.*

ILO (2016), *ILOSTAT* (database), International Labour Organization, *http://www.ilo.org/ilostat/faces/oracle/webcenter/portalapp/pagehierarchy/Page137.jspx?_afrLoop=4507540746758&clean=true#!%40%40%3F_afrLoop%3D4507540746758%26clean%3Dtrue%26_adf.ctrl-state%3D115ef6bvvr_9 (accessed 1 June 2016).*

INSEAD (2015), *The Global Talent Competitiveness Index 2015-2016*, Fontainebleau, *http://global-indices.insead.edu/gtci/documents/INSEAD_2015-16_Full_Book_Ebook.pdf.*

INSEAD (2013), *The Global Talent Competitiveness Index 2013*, Fontainebleau, *http://global-indices.insead.edu/gtci/documents/INSEADGTCI2013REPORT.pdf.*

IOM (2013), *Country Migration Report: The Philippines 2013*, International Organization for Migration, Geneva, *www.iom.int/files/live/sites/iom/files/Country/docs/CMReport-Philipines-2013.pdf.*

Jütting, J. and J. de Laiglesia (2009), *Is Informal Normal?: Towards More and Better Jobs in Developing Countries*, OECD Publishing, Paris, *http://dx.doi.org/10.1787/9789264059245-en.*

Kanapathy, V. (2006), "Migrant workers in Malaysia: An overview", *Workshop on an East Asian Cooperation Framework for Migrant Labour*, Kuala Lumpur.

Khoudour-Castéras, D. (2010), "Unexpected effects of the Washington Consensus: Trade liberalization and migration flows in Latin America", *International Trade Journal*, Vol. 24(4), pp. 440-476.

Lefko-Everett, K. (2004), "Botswana's changing migration patterns", *The Online Journal of the Migration Policy Institute, www.migrationpolicy.org/article/botswanas-changing-migration-patterns.*

Mayda, A. M. (2010), "International migration: A panel data analysis of the determinants of bilateral flows", *Journal of Population Economics*, Vol. 23(4), pp. 1249-1274, *www.jstor.org/stable/40925859.*

Mayda, A. M. (2006), "Who is against immigration? A cross-country investigation of individual attitudes towards immigrants", *Review of Economics and Statistics*, Vol. 88(3), pp. 510-530, *www.mitpressjournals.org/doi/pdf/10.1162/rest.88.3.510.*

McKenzie, D. and D. Yang (2015), "Evidence on policies to increase the development impacts of international migration", *World Bank Research Observer*, Vol. 30(2), pp. 155-192, *http://documents.worldbank.org/curated/en/2014/10/20272192/evidence-policies-increase-development-impacts-international-migration.*

OECD (2016a), *Database on Immigrants in OECD and Non-OECD Countries*, *www.oecd.org/els/mig/dioc.htm* (accessed 1 February 2016).

OECD (2016b), *International Migration Outlook 2016*, OECD Publishing, Paris, *http://dx.doi.org/10.1787/migr_outlook-2016-en.*

OECD (forthcoming), *Interrelations between Public Policies, Migration and Development*, OECD Publishing, Paris.

OECD (2015), *International Migration Outlook 2015*, OECD Publishing, Paris, *http://dx.doi.org/10.1787/migr_outlook-2015-en.*

OECD (2014), *Perspectives on Global Development 2014: Boosting Productivity to Meet the Middle-Income Challenge*, OECD Publishing, Paris, *http://dx.doi.org/10.1787/persp_glob_dev-2014-en.*

OECD (2013), *International Migration Outlook 2013*, OECD Publishing, Paris, *http://dx.doi.org/10.1787/migr_outlook-2013-en.*

OECD (2011), *Perspectives on Global Development 2012: Social Cohesion in a Shifting World*, OECD Publishing, Paris, *http://dx.doi.org/10.1787/persp_glob_dev-2012-en*.

OHCHR (2005), "Annual Report", Geneva, *http://www.ohchr.org/Documents/AboutUs/annualreport2005.pdf*.

Ortega, F. and G. Peri (2009), "The causes and effects of international migrations: Evidence from OECD countries 1980-2005", *NBER Working Paper*, No. 14833, *www.nber.org/papers/w14833*.

Sabates-Wheeler, R. and M. Waite (2003), "Migration and social protection: A concept paper", *Development Research Centre on Migration, Globalisation and Poverty Working Paper*, T2, University of Essex, Brighton, *www.migrationdrc.org/publications/working_papers/WP-T2.pdf*.

Stecklov, G. et al. (2005), "Do conditional cash transfers influence migration? A study using experimental data from the Mexican Progresa program", *Demography*, Vol. 42(4), pp. 769-790, *www.jstor.org/stable/4147339*.

UNDESA (2015), "Trends in international migrant stock: Migrants by destination and origin", *International Migration* (database), Population Division, *www.un.org/en/development/desa/population/migration/data/estimates2/estimates15.shtml* (accessed 1 February 2016).

UNDESA (2013), *World Population Policies 2013* (database), United Nations, New York, *www.un.org/en/development/desa/population/publications/policy/world-population-policies-2013.shtml*.

World Bank (2013), "Immigration in Malaysia: Assessment of its economic effects and a review of the policy and system", *Mimeo*, World Bank.

Xiang, B. (2016), "Emigration Trends and Policies in China: Movement of the Wealthy and Highly Skilled", Migration Policy Institute, Washington, DC.

Perspectives on Global Development 2017
International Migration in a Shifting World
© OECD 2016

Chapter 6

A new refugee era

Migrants leave their home countries for many reasons: usually to seek a better life elsewhere for themselves and their families. But for many – the statistics suggest it is the case of 1 in 14 migrants – the choice is dictated by fear of persecution, violence and insecurity. The world appears to be entering a new era of refugees, some 20 years after the waves of refugees who in the 1990s fled the Balkans, Liberia, Iraq and Afghanistan. In 2015 most refugees came from three countries: the Syrian Arab Republic, Afghanistan and Somalia. Most find shelter in neighbouring countries, even if patterns of origin and desired destination have been changing in recent years. This new surge represents an immense challenge to the international community, which needs to profit from the skills of the refugees and do all it can to resolve the problems that caused flight in the first place.

Armed conflicts are dramatically changing the patterns of refugee flows. The number of refugees resulting from the current humanitarian crisis in the Syrian Arab Republic (hereafter "Syria") and other countries experiencing instability are at levels not seen since the mid-1990s. While the refugee flows to Europe have drawn much attention from the media and European policy makers, acute and protracted refugee crises exist around the world and managing arrivals and accommodating refugees is a challenge for policy makers in many developing countries.

Chapter 3 showed that an increasing share of international migration is from developing to developed countries, yet refugee flows do not follow this pattern: 87% of refugees are hosted in low- and middle-income countries. With refugee situations tending to last longer, refugees need to be included more explicitly in discussions and analyses of the impacts of migration on development. Managing refugee situations increasingly requires a shift from a humanitarian response logic to thinking about longer-term development concerns, including the integration of refugees into host country societies and economies.

This chapter begins by examining trends in the numbers of refugees as well as whence and where people are fleeing (and in some cases, via), before exploring potential explanations for these patterns and proposing policy responses.

Refugee flows need to be seen distinctly from other types of international migration as it is the push factors – fear of violence, insecurity and persecution – which dominate people's decisions to leave their homes, although a number of factors play a role in terms of where displaced people choose to seek refuge. Refugees, like other international migrants, are not passive, but rather active agents making decisions whether to move or stay, and where to go. Furthermore, the nature of refugee flows differs from international labour migration. Changes in labour migration generally tend to happen gradually over time and are therefore easier to analyse and manage. By contrast, flows of refugees are usually sudden and unexpected making them more difficult to anticipate, manage and respond to. Forced migration as a result of environmental reasons (whether disasters or slower onset events) may have similar dynamics and impacts to conflict-induced migration, but is beyond the scope of this chapter. The concept of "environmental refugees" or "climate refugees", while much debated, is not recognised currently under international law.

The figures reported in this chapter were correct at the time of writing in June 2016. Because the situation is evolving rapidly, numbers may change quickly. This chapter draws primarily on United Nations High Commissioner for Refugees (UNHCR) data from 1960 to 2015, which are the most widely-used sources of data on refugees and asylum applications and yet have some limitations. The UNHCR data make possible comparison across countries and over time, but it should be noted that some countries dispute the official figures. Jordan, for example, reports that it hosts 1.3 million refugees based on a recent census, whereas UNHCR reports that over 664 000 refugees have registered with them in the country. Furthermore, whereas the UNHCR data on the country of origin and country of destination of refugees cover all countries, their data on asylum applications record applications to 44 industrialised countries and so present only a partial picture of asylum applications worldwide.

The terminology used to discuss refugees and migration can be confusing. In line with the UNHCR definition, the term refugee is used in this chapter to refer to refugees as recognised under the 1951 United Nations Convention, as well as people in refugee-like situations, which include people who are outside their country or territory of origin and who face risks similar to those of refugees, but to whom refugee status has, for practical or other reasons, not been attributed (Box 6.1). When referring to refugee numbers, the figures presented in this chapter do not include asylum seekers, defined as persons whose application for asylum or refugee status is pending at any stage in the asylum procedure. Data on asylum seekers are presented separately.

Box 6.1. **Understanding migration terminology: Definitions of key terms**

Refugee: A person who, "owing to a well-founded fear of persecution for reasons of race, religion, nationality, membership of a particular social group or political opinions, is outside the country of his nationality and is unable or, owing to such fear, is unwilling to avail himself of the protection of that country."

Source: UNHCR (1967), *Convention Relating to the Status of Refugees*, Art. 1A(2), 1951 as modified by the 1967 Protocol.

This chapter uses UNHCR figures on the total numbers of refugees which include people recognised as refugees under the 1951 UN Convention/1967 Protocol, the 1969 Organisation of African Unity (OAU) Convention, in accordance with the UNHCR Statute, persons granted a complementary form of protection and those granted temporary protection as well as **people in refugee-like situations** (a term which is descriptive in nature and includes groups of persons who are outside their country or territory of origin and who face protection risks similar to those of refugees, but for whom refugee status has, for practical or other reasons, not been ascertained).

Refugee status determination: A process (conducted by states and/or UNHCR) to determine whether an individual should be recognised as a refugee in accordance with applicable national and international law.

Source: IOM (2011), *Glossary on Migration, 2nd edition.*

Asylum seeker: A person who seeks safety from persecution or serious harm in a country other than his or her own and awaits a decision on the application for refugee status under relevant international and national instruments. In case of a negative decision, the person must leave the country and may be expelled, as may any non-national in an irregular or unlawful situation, unless permission to stay is provided on humanitarian or other related grounds.

Source: IOM (2011), *Glossary on Migration, 2nd edition.*

Internally displaced persons (IDPs): Persons or groups of persons who have been obliged to flee or leave their homes or places of habitual residence, in particular as a result of, or in order to avoid, the effects of armed conflict, situations of generalised violence, violations of human rights or natural or human-made disasters, and who have not crossed an internationally recognised state border.

Source: United Nations (2004), "Guiding principles on internal displacement", UN Doc E/CN.4/1998/53/Add.2.

Recent trends in refugee movements

This section examines trends in the number of refugees from 1960 to 2015 as well as their origin and destination countries.

A new era of high numbers of refugees is opening

A new era of high refugee numbers is opening. Refugee numbers have been rising sharply over the last four years and by the end of 2015 totalled 16.1 million (UNHCR, 2016a). There are a further 3.2 million asylum seekers. These numbers do not include the 5.2 million Palestinian refugees under the UNRWA's mandate (UNRWA, 2015).[1] The recent rise in refugee numbers has been largely driven by the continuing conflict in Syria, which started in 2011. By the end of 2015, Syrian refugees accounted for 30% of all refugees. These numbers do not reveal the true scale of displacement, as many people are displaced by war within their own countries. Because of this report's focus on *international* migration, the analysis focuses on refugee flows, not internally displaced persons (IDPs). This is not to minimise the quantity of IDPs. IDPs – numbering 37.5 million people – significantly outnumber refugees and the ratio of IDPs to refugees has been increasing over time.

These levels are not, however, unprecedented. Refugee numbers peaked at nearly 18 million in 1992 because of the conflict in the Balkans, as well as significant increases in refugees from Liberia, Afghanistan and Iraq in the early 1990s. This peak came at the end of a decade of steadily rising refugee numbers that began in the late 1970s and early 1980s, a product of several conflicts including the Soviet invasion of Afghanistan, conflicts in Iraq, the Mozambican civil war, and wars involving Viet Nam, People's Republic of China (hereafter "China") and Cambodia (Figure 6.1). After the peak in 1992, the number of refugees fell steadily and reached a low of 8.7 million in 2005. As a share of total international migrants, refugees accounted for 7% in 2015 (Figure 6.2), a decrease since 1990 when refugees made up 12% of the total.

Figure 6.1. **Refugee numbers have increased sharply in the last three years**

Total refugee numbers, 1960-2015

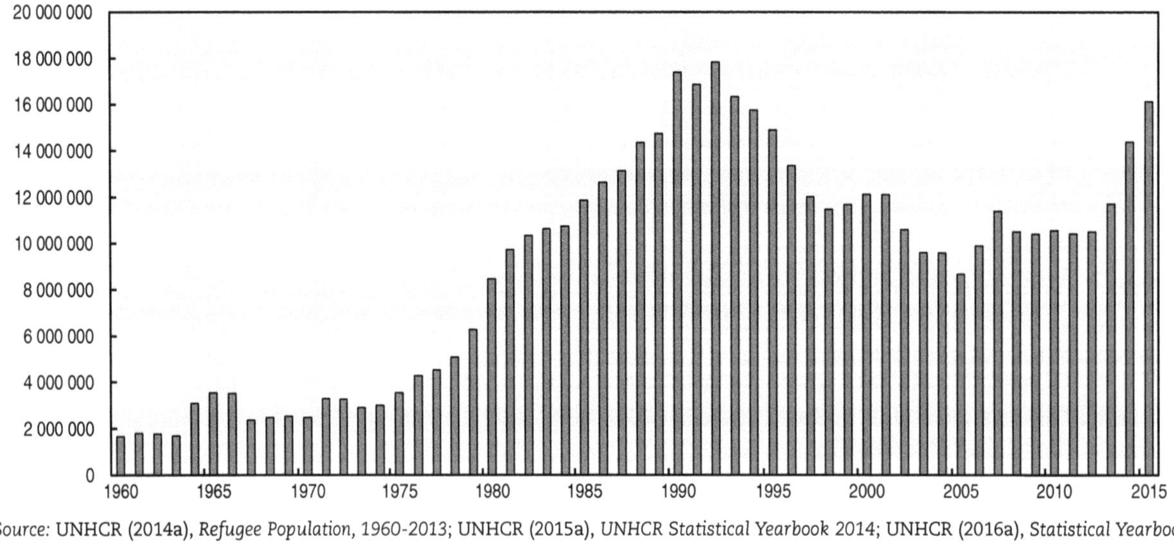

Source: UNHCR (2014a), *Refugee Population, 1960-2013*; UNHCR (2015a), *UNHCR Statistical Yearbook 2014*; UNHCR (2016a), *Statistical Yearbook 2015* (database).

StatLink http://dx.doi.org/10.1787/888933422562

Figure 6.2. **Refugees represent a small share of all international migrants**

Percentage of refugee stocks in total international migration stocks, 2015

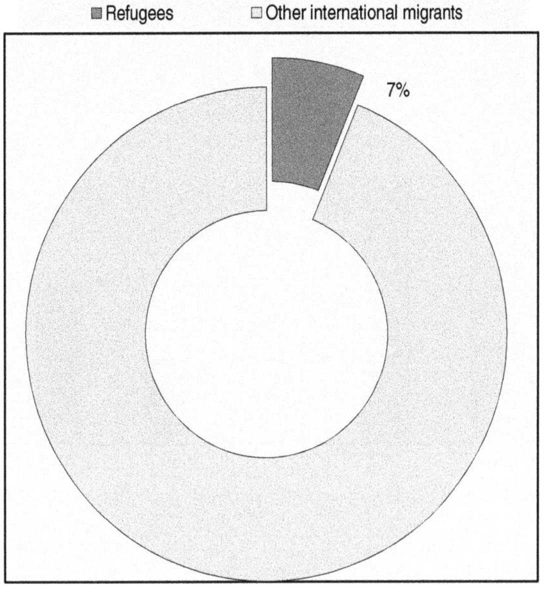

Source: Authors' calculations based on UNHCR (2016a), *Statistical Yearbook 2015* (database) and United Nations (2015), *Trends in International Migrant Stock: The 2015 Revision* (United Nations database, POP/DB/MIG/Stock/Rev.2015).

StatLink http://dx.doi.org/10.1787/888933422576

The number of refugees has increased rapidly over the last three years, although still not at the rate of the early 1990s. In 2014 annual flows reached a peak of over 2.9 million people. Again, the size of the yearly refugee flows in the early 1990s was even greater than the flows that have been seen in recent years (Figure 6.3). Absolute flows of refugees in 1990 were a little over 3 million, and slightly higher still in 1992 at 3.2 million.

It is the geographical concentration of recent refugee flows that makes the current situation more challenging to manage than the refugee movements of the 1990s. Whereas refugee flows of a similar magnitude were seen in the early 1990s, there were a number of major source countries and flows were more geographically dispersed. The largest refugee flow in 1990, at over 700 000, was from Liberia. This can be compared with the 1.7 million people who fled Syria in 2013 and the further 1.4 million Syrian refugees the next year. In 2012 Syrians made up 60% of all refugee flows, rising to 84% in 2013. In 2014 the proportion dropped somewhat but remained high at 50%.

A small number of countries account for most of the world's refugees

A handful of countries account for the majority of the world's refugees. Over 50% of refugees are from just three countries: Syria, Afghanistan and Somalia (Figure 6.4). These figures show numbers of refugees accumulated over time. Afghanistan was the largest source country of refugees from 1981 to 2014, although the annual refugee flows from the country fluctuated considerably. Similarly, other countries such as Myanmar have featured among the top source countries of refugee numbers for many years. Syria, by contrast, did not feature in the top 30 countries of origin in 2011, but by 2015 had become the largest source country of refugees.

Figure 6.3. **Annual refugee flows were larger in the early 1990s than in recent years**

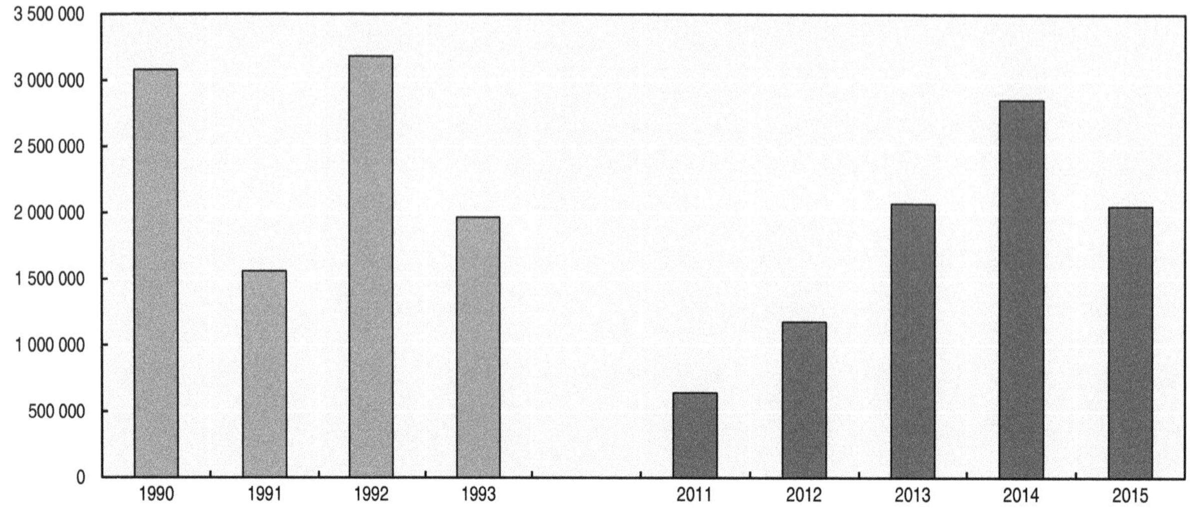

Source: Authors' calculations based on UNHCR (2016a), *Statistical Yearbook 2015* (database) and UNHCR (2014a), *Refugee population, 1960-2013*.

StatLink http://dx.doi.org/10.1787/888933422588

Figure 6.4. **Over 50% of refugees are from just three countries**

Refugee numbers by top ten countries of origin, 2015

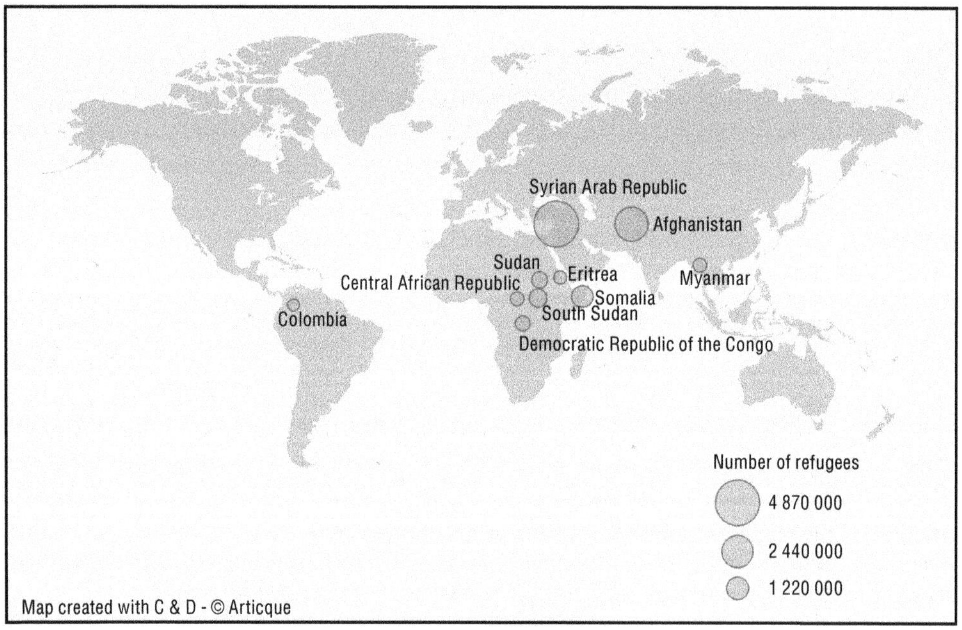

	Country of origin	Total refugees and people in refugee-like situations	% of world's refugees
1	Syrian Arab Republic	4 872 585	30.2
2	Afghanistan	2 666 254	16.5
3	Somalia	1 123 052	7.0
4	South Sudan	778 697	4.8
5	Sudan	628 770	3.9
6	Democratic Republic of the Congo	541 499	3.4
7	Central African Republic	471 104	2.9
8	Myanmar	451 807	2.8
9	Eritrea	411 342	2.6
10	Colombia	340 240	2.1

Source: UNHCR (2016a), *Statistical Yearbook 2015* (database).

Recent changes in the refugee population show a somewhat different composition than the global numbers of refugees, although Syrian refugees and asylum seekers still far exceed those from other countries. Combined with the number of asylum applications, refugee numbers indicate the magnitude of the flows from different countries in 2015. During this period, the largest increases have been from Syria. Other significant increases have been from Burundi, Afghanistan, Iraq, South Sudan and Ukraine (Table 6.1, Table 6.2).

Table 6.1. **Increases in refugee populations by country of origin, 2015**

Increases in refugee populations by top ten countries of origin, 2015

	Country of origin	Increase in refugee population in 2015	Share of total change in refugee population (%)
1	Syrian Arab Republic	1 229 151	53
2	Burundi	231 056	10
3	South Sudan	163 491	7
4	Ukraine	153 057	7
5	Central African Republic	94 020	4
6	Eritrea	76 673	3
7	Nigeria	73 532	3
8	Iraq	43 754	2
9	Democratic Republic of the Congo	38 744	2
10	Somalia	31 395	1

Source: UNHCR (2016a), *Statistical Yearbook 2015* (database).

Table 6.2. **Asylum applications by place of origin, 2015**

Asylum applications by top ten places of origin, 2015

	Place of origin	No. of applications during 2015	Share of all asylum applications in 2015 (%)
1	Syrian Arab Republic	782 290	25
2	Afghanistan	486 708	16
3	Iraq	300 556	10
4	Ukraine	177 736	6
5	Serbia and Kosovo*	133 645	4
6	Pakistan	92 822	3
7	Albania	71 238	2
8	Democratic Republic of the Congo	66 316	2
9	Eritrea	62 899	2
10	Iran	60 472	2

Note: *This classification is used by UNHCR in its *Statistical Yearbook 2015*.
Source: UNHCR (2016a), *Statistical Yearbook 2015* (database).

Developing countries act as hosts to most of the world's refugees

While Chapter 3 showed that an increasing share of international migration is from developing to developed countries, refugee movements do not follow this pattern. Overall, low- and middle-income countries accommodate 87% of refugees, up from 70% ten years ago.[2] Turkey, Pakistan and Lebanon act as hosts to the largest number of refugees, and the top ten countries of asylum or residence are all either low- or middle-income countries (Figure 6.5). Low- and middle-income countries also receive the largest number of asylum applications (Figure 6.6).

Figure 6.5. **Low- and middle-income countries act as hosts to the majority of refugees**

Refugees by top ten host countries, 2015

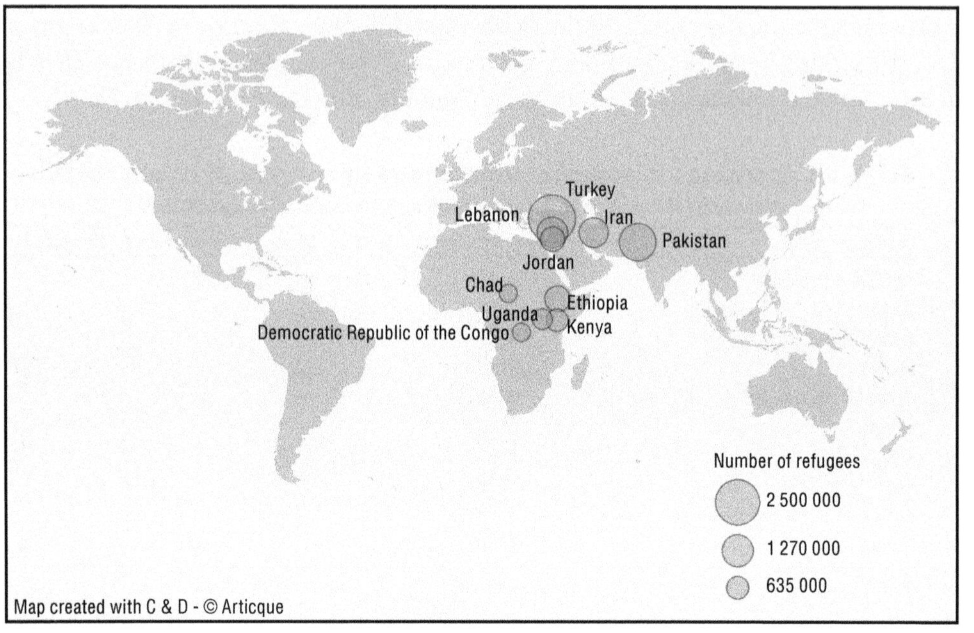

	Country or territory of asylum/residence	Total refugees and people in refugee-like situations	% of world's refugees	Income category
1	Turkey	2 541 352	16	Upper middle-income
2	Pakistan	1 561 162	10	Lower middle-income
3	Lebanon	1 070 854	7	Upper middle-income
4	Iran	979 437	6	Upper middle-income
5	Ethiopia	736 086	5	Low-income
6	Jordan	664 118	4	Upper middle-income
7	Kenya	553 912	3	Lower middle-income
8	Uganda	477 187	3	Low-income
9	Democratic Republic of the Congo	383 095	2	Low-income
10	Chad	369 540	2	Low-income

Source: UNHCR (2016a), *Statistical Yearbook 2015* (database) and World Bank (2016), *World Development Indicators* (database), *http://data.worldbank.org/indicator.*

The degree of solidarity that developing countries show towards refugees can also be seen by measures other than absolute numbers, in particular the number of refugees relative to population, and relative to their income level. Lebanon and Jordan have the highest numbers of refugees per capita (Table 6.3). In Lebanon, there are 183 refugees for every 1 000 inhabitants. This would be the equivalent to France taking in 12 million refugees. Ethiopia hosts the largest population of refugees relative to its level of income.

The conflicts in the Middle East are changing the landscape in terms of which countries act as hosts to the most refugees. For many years, Pakistan acted as host to the largest number of refugees, a large proportion of whom were from Afghanistan. Since the outbreak of fighting in Syria, however, its neighbouring countries have received millions of refugees. Turkey has received the largest number of Syrian refugees in absolute numbers, while Lebanon and Jordan have the highest numbers of refugees per capita. Similarly, Yemen received many Syrian refugees, as well as significant numbers of refugees from the Horn of

Africa countries, but the civil war that started in the country in 2015 means that thousands of people are now fleeing Yemen (Box 6.2).

Figure 6.6. **Low- and middle-income countries host more refugees and receive more asylum applications**

Share of refugees and asylum applications by income category

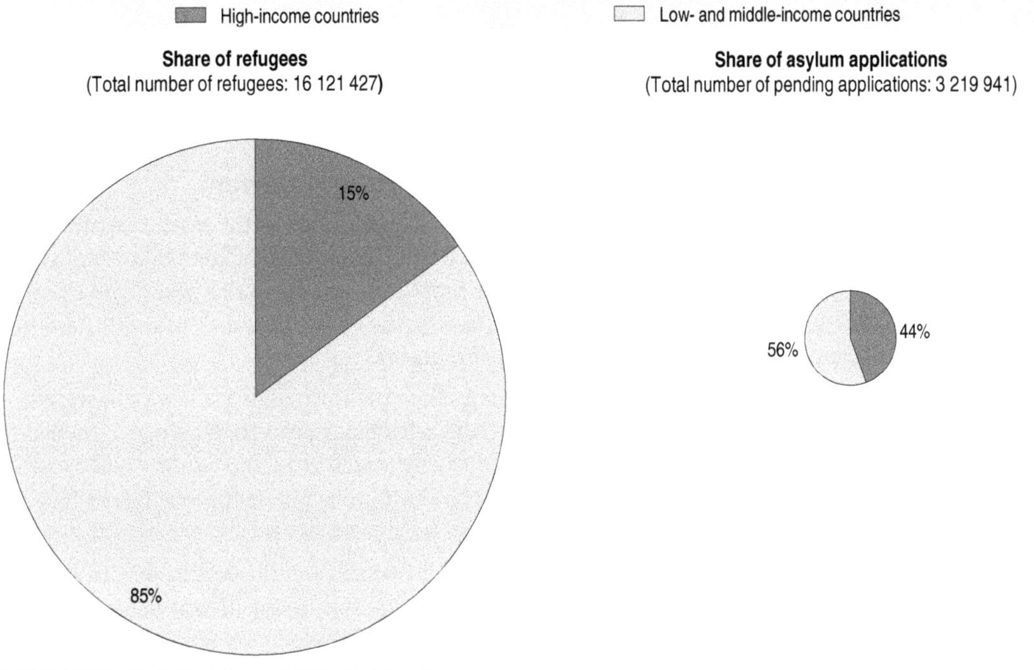

Source: UNHCR (2016a), *Statistical Yearbook 2015* (database).

StatLink http://dx.doi.org/10.1787/888933422599

Table 6.3. **Lebanon hosts the most refugees relative to its population**

Refugees relative to host country population, top ten countries

	Country or territory of asylum	Refugees per 1 000 inhabitants
1	Lebanon	183
2	Jordan	87
3	Nauru	50
4	Turkey	32
5	Chad	26
6	Djibouti	22
7	South Sudan	21
8	Mauritania	19
9	Sweden	17
10	Malta	17

Source: UNHCR (2016a), *Statistical Yearbook 2015* (database).

Major bilateral refugee corridors often run between neighbouring countries

When the major refugee corridors over the last few years are examined, most refugee corridors are seen to run between neighbouring countries. Refugees from Burundi in 2015 found refuge in neighbouring Tanzania. People fleeing South Sudan in 2012 found refuge in

Ethiopia. At the end of 2014 three-quarters of the world's refugees were resident in a country bordering their own (UNHCR, 2015a).

Syria features frequently in the major bilateral refugee corridors in the last four years (Table 6.4). The country was the origin of the largest refugee corridor every year from 2012 to 2015, and in 2013 the five largest refugee corridors all originated in Syria. In that year Lebanon received the largest number of refugees fleeing the country. The data for 2015 show that the Syria-to-Germany corridor was the fourth largest bilateral refugee corridor that year, reflecting the changing geography of refugee movements from Syria which are now reaching beyond its neighbouring countries.

Box 6.2. **Yemen: Country of refuge, country of war**

For years Yemen has been a country of refuge for people fleeing countries in the Horn of Africa (Djibouti, Ethiopia, Somalia and Sudan) and more recently, Syria. Latest UNHCR estimates indicate that Yemen is host to 264 615 refugees, of whom 250 260 are Somali. In one of the most complex dynamics of refugee movements, Yemen has now become a country of origin of refugees fleeing the civil war which started there in 2015, while remaining a country of destination for thousands of refugees.

Since 2015, people in Yemen – including refugees originally from the Horn of Africa – have been fleeing the country because of civil war. The current crisis began in 2011 with mass protests leading to the overthrow of the Saleh government which had been in power since 1990. By March 2015, the conflict had evolved into a civil war between Houthi forces allied with forces loyal to the former president and forces loyal to the new government. Al-Qaeda in the Arabian Peninsula and the Islamic State are also active in the country.

As of April 2016, over 177 000 people had fled Yemen to other countries in the region (Figure 6.7). Among them were Yemeni nationals (61 000) but most were other nationalities, many of whom were refugees in Yemen. Nearly 28 000 Somalis have returned to Somalia; over 8 000 Ethiopians have returned to Ethiopia. Most Yemeni nationals have fled to Saudi Arabia (30 000) but thousands have also gone to countries which had typically been the origin countries of refugees in Yemen, including nearly 20 000 to Djibouti and 4 000 to Somalia. An estimated 5 000 Yemeni nationals have also sought refuge in Oman (Figure 6.8).

Figure 6.7. **The number of people fleeing Yemen surged in 2015**

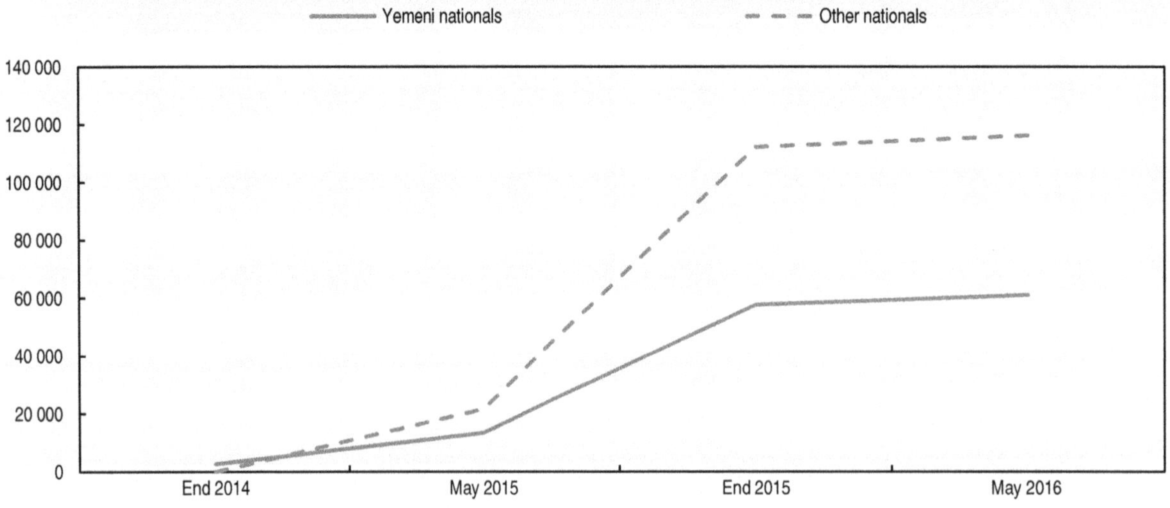

Source: UNHCR (2015a), *UNHCR Statistical Yearbook 2014*, *www.unhcr.org/56655f4b3.html*; UNHCR (2016b), *Yemen Regional Refugee and Migrant Response Plan* (portal), *http://data.unhcr.org/yemen/regional.php*.

StatLink http://dx.doi.org/10.1787/888933422608

Box 6.2. **Yemen: Country of refuge, country of war** *(cont.)*

Figure 6.8. **Yemenis and other nationalities are fleeing Yemen for other countries in the region**

Refugee population by nationality and country of asylum

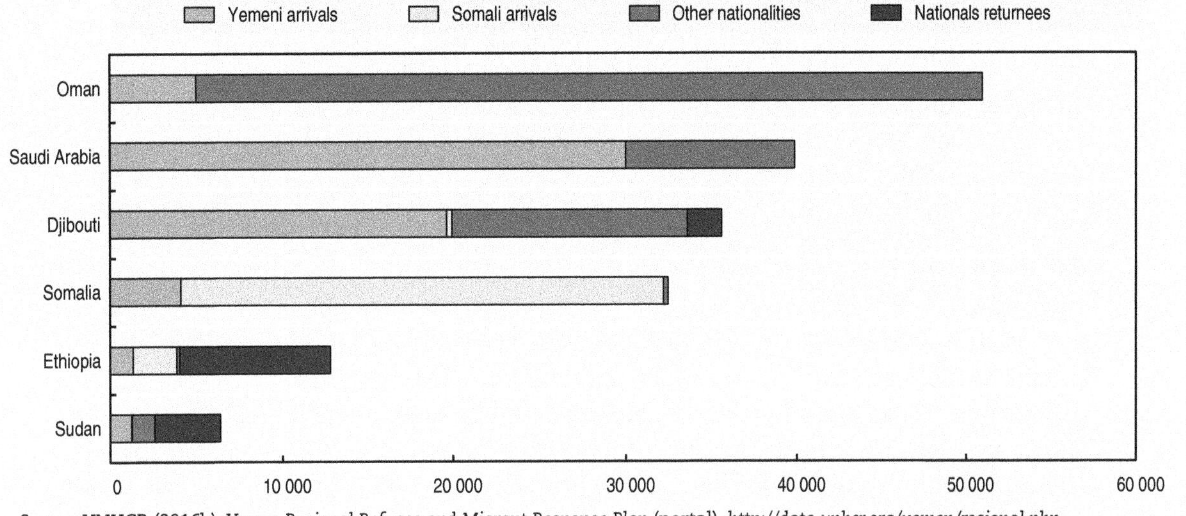

Source: UNHCR (2016b), *Yemen Regional Refugee and Migrant Response Plan* (portal), *http://data.unhcr.org/yemen/regional.php.*

StatLink http://dx.doi.org/10.1787/888933422612

Despite this exodus, refugees from other countries continue to arrive in Yemen. Data on sea arrivals in Yemen show that over 90 000 people arrived in Yemen by boat in 2015, two-thirds of whom arrived after the start of the conflict in March 2015. This is one of the highest annual totals of the past decade.

Source: Pettersson and Wallensteen (2016), *Armed Conflicts, 1946-2015, http://dx.doi.org/10.1177/0022343315595927;UNHCR* (2016b), *Yemen Regional Refugee and Migrant Response Plan* (portal), *http://data.unhcr.org/yemen/regional.php;* United Nations (2015), *Trends in International Migrant Stock: The 2015 Revision*,(database).

Table 6.4. **Top five bilateral refugee corridors: Annual refugee flows, 2012-15**

	2012		2013		2014		2015	
1	Syrian Arab Republic → Turkey	317 000	Syrian Arab Republic → Lebanon	740 000	Syrian Arab Republic → Turkey	1 000 000	Syrian Arab Republic → Turkey	946 790
2	Syrian Arab Republic → Jordan	251 000	Syrian Arab Republic → Jordan	670 000	Syrian Arab Republic → Lebanon	361 000	Ukraine → Russia	148 463
3	Syrian Arab Republic → Lebanon	132 000	Syrian Arab Republic → Turkey	478 000	Pakistan → Afghanistan	280 000	Burundi → Tanzania	122 855
4	Sudan → South Sudan	100 000	Syrian Arab Republic → Iraq	176 000	Ukraine → Russia	248 000	Syrian Arab Republic → Germany	101 661
5	South Sudan → Ethiopia	63 266	Syrian Arab Republic → Egypt	122 000	South Sudan → Ethiopia	188 000	South Sudan → Sudan	79 009

Source: UNHCR (2016a), *Statistical Yearbook 2015* (database).

Other significant refugee corridors are found in sub-Saharan Africa, in particular South Sudan to Ethiopia and Sudan, and more recently, from Burundi to Tanzania.

Given the rapid changes in the nature of the Middle East-to-Europe corridor, the new distribution of refugees was still emerging in mid-2016. Among the new asylum applications received in 2015, Serbia and Kosovo, Germany and Hungary received the largest number (Table 6.5).

Table 6.5. **New asylum applications in 2015**

Number of asylum applications received in 2015, by top ten destinations

	Place of asylum	Asylum applications	% of total new applications
1	Serbia and Kosovo*	578 065	18.7
2	Germany	476 649	15.4
3	Hungary	351 565	11.4
4	Sweden	173 845	5.6
5	Russia	152 489	4.9
6	United States	135 964	4.4
7	Turkey	134 826	4.4
8	South Africa	120 531	3.9
9	France	118 469	3.8
10	Austria	89 900	2.9

Note: *This classification is used by UNHCR in its *Statistical Yearbook 2015*.
Source: UNHCR (2016a), *Statistical Yearbook 2015* (database).

In particular, European countries have seen increasing numbers of people arriving and claiming asylum over the last two years, often undertaking dangerous journeys to reach their destination. Migration routes to Europe across the Mediterranean and through the Balkans have seen much higher volumes of people (OECD, 2015a). For example, on the Eastern Mediterranean route, more than one million people, mostly refugees from Syria, Iraq and Afghanistan, crossed into Greece since the start of 2015 (UNHCR, 2016c). European entities[3] received 935 000 asylum applications from Syrians between April 2011 and January 2016, equivalent to 0.2% of the European population. The emerging refugee corridors into Europe are among the migratory routes with the highest death tolls in the world: in 2015, 3 770 people died while attempting to cross the Mediterranean to safety in Europe (Box 6.3).

Box 6.3. **Dying for safety: Migrant and refugee deaths on dangerous migratory routes**

Refugees often undertake gruelling journeys to reach countries of safety, risking their lives in the process. Many do not make it. In 2015, 5 417 people died while migrating. The IOM's *Missing Migrants Project* (2016) tracks deaths of migrants and those who have disappeared along migratory routes worldwide. Their figures capture refugees, people in refugee-like situations and irregular migrants, reflecting the mixed flows along the migratory routes. Many deaths are simply never recorded. The reported numbers therefore represent the lowest estimates of the total number of deaths.

The migratory routes across the Mediterranean witness by far the largest number of deaths: 3 770 of all deaths recorded in 2015 – nearly 70% – occurred on the sea crossings in the Western Mediterranean route from Morocco to Spain; the Eastern route from Turkey to Greece; and especially the Central Mediterranean route from Libya to Italy. This trend continued into 2016. By the beginning of May 2016, already 1 343 people who attempted the Mediterranean crossings were dead or missing, out of a total of 1 624 dead and missing worldwide.

Southeast Asia and the US-Mexico border are other areas which have seen high numbers of deaths on migratory routes. Last year over 780 migrants and refugees died while attempting to reach safety in Southeast Asia, while over 300 died along the US-Mexico border.

Expanding safe, legal procedures for people to claim asylum without them needing to make dangerous journeys should be a priority for policy makers.

Source: IOM (2016), *Missing Migrants Project* (portal), *http://missingmigrants.iom.int/*.

Refugee situations are tending to last longer

A greater percentage of the world's refugees are in protracted exile than before and these stalemates are lasting longer. Protracted refugee situations are defined as situations in which refugees have lived in exile for five years or more and where there is a low likelihood of resolving their situation in the near future. In 2015 there were 32 protracted refugee situations worldwide, accounting for 41% of the refugee population under UNHCR's mandate, or 6.7 million people (UNHCR, 2016d). The average length of stay in these states of virtual limbo is now 26 years, up from an average of nine years in the early 1990s.

The reasons that refugee situations are tending to last longer relate to slowdowns or lack of progress in the three sustainable solutions to refugee situations: return, resettlement and integration.

Return, or "voluntary repatriation", where refugees choose to return to their home countries is becoming less common. The past decade has witnessed a significantly lower number of refugee returns (5.2 million) than the preceding decade (13 million). In 2015, 201 400 refugees returned home (UNHCR, 2016a). This was a slight increase on the previous year. In 2014, 126 800 refugees returned to their country of origin. This was the lowest number recorded since 1983, when 103 000 refugees returned during the year (UNHCR, 2015a).

Resettlement is another route out of refugee status, but only a very small proportion of refugees are resettled from an asylum country to a third country. Fewer than 1% of refugees are resettled each year, and since 1990 the trend has been for lower numbers of refugees to be resettled, although numbers have been increasing again in the last five years. In the last ten years, a total of 879 800 refugees have arrived in industrialised countries through resettlement programmes[4] (UNHCR, 2016e). The number of countries participating in the UNHCR resettlement scheme increased from 12 in 1990 to 26 in 2014. Despite this, over 90% of resettlement places are consistently provided by just three countries: the United States, Canada and Australia.

Integration into host communities is the third lasting solution for refugees. Over the past decade, 1.1 million refugees around the world have become citizens in their country of asylum (UNHCR, 2016f). Many refugees, however, remain economically, socially and politically isolated within their host countries. The most extreme expression of this is the refugee camp. In host countries, some 40% of all refugees live in camps, most often because they have no alternatives, although this figure varies considerably by country (UNHCR, 2014b). Only 10% of Syrian refugees, for example, (490 000 people) live in camps. While camps may be perceived as an efficient, centralised way of delivering services to refugees, they very often limit refugees' rights and freedoms, such as freedom of movement, and seriously curtail refugees' ability to contribute to society and the local economy, and reach their potential. Prolonged refugee situations have implications for human rights and the livelihoods of refugees. In camps, levels of sexual and physical violence are causes for concern, as is the violation of rights including freedom of movement and the right to seek wage-earning employment. Without documentation, refugees in urban areas face discrimination, inadequate housing and lack of employment and access to social services (Loescher and Milner, 2009).

Displacement often denies refugee children access to education. Refugee children are five times less likely to attend school than other children: only 50% are in primary school and fewer than 25% are receiving secondary education (ODI, 2016). Instead, many find themselves forced into child labour and early marriage. The lack of education risks creating lost generations whose prospects will be permanently diminished, entailing massive human, social and economic costs.

The unrealised potential of refugees is enormous. As the next section will show, refugees tend to be young and with the potential to bring knowledge, skills and an entrepreneurial spirit to their destination countries.

Demographic and skills profiles of refugee populations

This section examines the demographic and skills characteristics of refugee populations.

Refugees tend to be young, with roughly equal numbers of men and women at the global level

Overall, refugees tend to be young, and numbers are fairly balanced in terms of men and women. Just over half (51%) of refugees are under 18 years of age and 46% are of working age, between 18 and 59 – with roughly equal numbers of men (51%) and women (49%). Among Syrian refugees – the largest refugee population – there are roughly equal numbers of men (53%) and women (47%) (UNHCR, 2016a). There can, however, be significant variations within specific refugee movements. The current flows to Europe, for example, appear to have a different demographic make-up with variations by country of origin and over time (Box 6.4).

Box 6.4. **Recent refugee arrivals in Europe**

Snapshots from different flows at different times can give an insight into the demographic composition of refugee flows, although it is difficult to get an accurate global picture.

Recent arrivals in Europe tend to be very young with higher numbers of men than women.

- In Sweden, over 70% of asylum applications in 2015 were from men, with significant variations by nationality: over 90% of applications from Algerians and Moroccans were by men; 82% for Afghans, and 64% for Syrians (Statistics Sweden, 2016).
- A survey of Afghan arrivals on Greek islands in January 2016 showed that 60% were men, 17% were women and 23% were children. Arrivals were overwhelmingly young: 36% were men aged 19-24, 22% were boys aged 15-18, and 16% were boys aged 10-14. Only 3% of all arrivals (men and women) were aged over 25 (UNHCR, 2016c).
- The demographic profiles of Syrian arrivals on Greek islands in January 2016 were somewhat different, with a higher proportion of women and children among the flows: 49% were men, 32% were women and 19% were children. They also tended to be on average older than Afghan arrivals: 57% were aged 25-59, and only 21% were aged 19-24 and 8% aged 15-18.

However, over time, the demographics of the flows arriving in Europe are changing, with greater proportions of women and children arriving in 2016.

- In Serbia, the demographics of the flows shifted significantly between June 2015 and February 2016. Whereas in June 2015, 66% of arrivals were men, 11% were women and 23% were children, these proportions changed steadily over the months so that by February 2016 only 38% of arrivals were men, whereas 22% were women and 40% were children (UNHCR/Serbia MOI, 2016).
- A similar pattern over a shorter time period can be seen in new arrivals to Croatia: while 45% of arrivals in January 2016 were men, this had dropped to 33% by March 2016. In that month, children represented the largest group (41%) and 26% of arrivals were women (UNHCR/MOI Croatia, 2016).
- In flows to Greece in early 2016, women and children made up nearly 60% of sea arrivals, compared to less than 30% in June 2015 (UNHCR, 2016c).

A particular feature of recent flows has been the high numbers of unaccompanied children. This has become a growing concern, both in flows to Europe and in flows from Central America to the United States.

There are large and increasing numbers of unaccompanied children in the current flows to Europe. Nearly 90 000 unaccompanied children sought asylum in the European Union in 2015, four times more than the numbers in 2014. Sweden, Germany, Hungary and Austria were the main destination countries. Half of the children came from Afghanistan, while 16% – the second largest group – were from Syria.

The high number of unaccompanied minors is different from previous refugee flows and has implications for the type of policy response needed. For example, labour market access may not be the immediate issue, but rather provision of education and specialised social services. Child protection measures also become fundamental given the number of children reported missing. In January 2016 Europol estimated that at least 10 000 child refugees have disappeared since arriving in Europe. It is feared many have become victims of exploitation by criminal gangs and human traffickers, forced into prostitution, child labour and the drugs trade. The volume of unaccompanied minors in current flows could also have consequences for family reunification policies.

This is a challenge that is also being encountered in other regions beyond Europe, particularly in the Central America to United States migration corridor. Between 2013 and 2014, the number of unaccompanied minors crossing the US-Mexico border increased by 90%, attracting the increased attention of the US government, media and public. In 2014, 68 600 unaccompanied children were apprehended at the US-Mexico border. More than half of those apprehended were from El Salvador, Guatemala and Honduras, countries severely affected by gang violence and insecurity linked to drug-trafficking and organised crime. As with the flows to Europe, the vast majority (75%) were teenage boys (Pew Research Center, 2016). The numbers fell in 2015 as border enforcement efforts were increased – particularly on Mexico's southern border – but 2016 has seen a resurgence in the numbers of unaccompanied children attempting this journey. As long as the underlying conditions of violence, poverty and political instability continue in Central America, the flows can be expected to continue (Rosenblum and Ball, 2016).

Refugees bring with them knowledge and skills

Refugees bring with them knowledge and skills that they could contribute to their host country as well as the potential to learn new skills. In many cases, this human potential remains untapped as refugees face a series of barriers to entry into the labour market. In many countries, refugees are not legally allowed to work, and may end up in informal, precarious jobs as a consequence. Even in places where refugees are legally allowed to work, they may face other obstacles to contributing their skills, such as language barriers, or reluctance on the part of employers to hire refugees with a lack of host country work experience.

There is a paucity of data on the educational levels and skills of refugees. Samples and surveys provide snapshots of different refugee populations but systematic data collection does not exist, rendering it difficult to get a complete picture. The following section draws on the findings from various surveys of recent refugee populations, largely but not only Syrians, on different migratory routes or based in different host countries to give an indication of the skills of the refugees in the recent flows.

As would be expected, there are differences in the educational and skills levels of refugees from different places of origin. For example, evidence from surveys of arrivals to Greek islands suggests that refugees from Syria tend to have higher levels of education than arrivals from Afghanistan (Figure 6.9). The two refugee populations also have different previous professional experiences. Of those who were over 18 years old, 24% of Afghans did not have professional activities back in their country of origin, compared to 19% of Syrian refugees. In both groups, the figures were much higher for women. For Afghans, the most common occupation in their country of origin was construction (18%) followed by service sector work (11%) and manufacturing (10%). Among Syrian respondents, 18% had worked in the service sector in Syria, 13% were students, 9% worked in manufacturing and 8% in education.

Figure 6.9. **Education levels of refugees differ by nationality**
Reported education level of Afghan and Syrian arrivals in Greek Islands, 2016

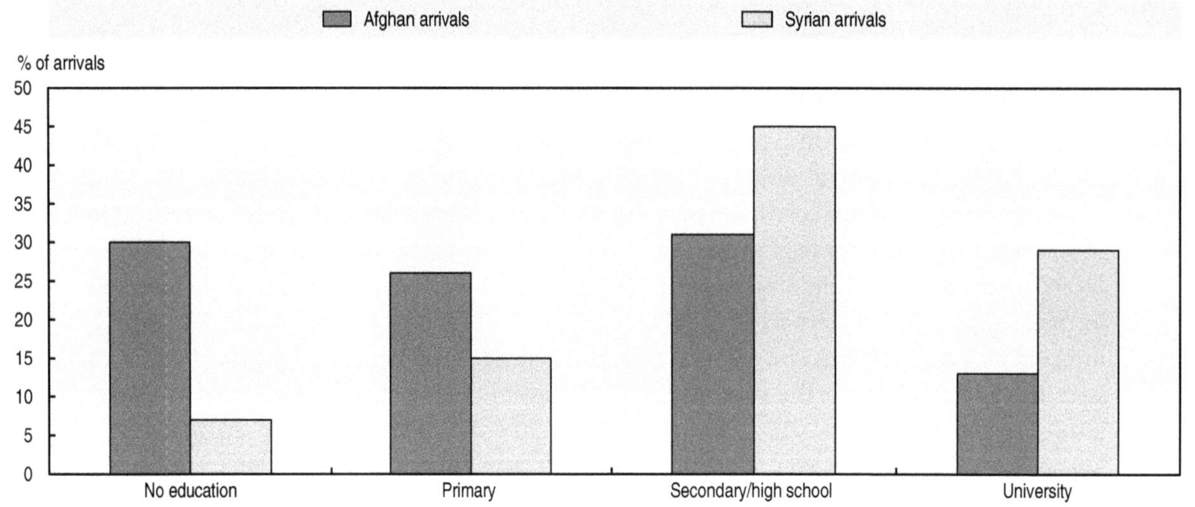

Source: UNHCR (2016c), *Profiling of Afghan arrivals on Greek islands – January 2016, www.refworld.org/docid/56cd6f7f4.html* and *Profiling of Syrian arrivals on Greek islands – January 2016, http://data.unhcr.org/syrianrefugees/regional.php.*

StatLink http://dx.doi.org/10.1787/888933422622

Explaining the patterns of refugee flows

This section examines potential explanations for the patterns of refugee flows and asylum applications that were described in the previous section. It starts by looking at the factors which drive people from their home countries before turning to the factors which may affect the choice of destination country.

Different types of conflict affect the likelihood and magnitude of refugee flows from source countries

Armed conflict and the associated threat of violence are overwhelming drivers of displacement. People move to protect themselves and their children. Previous instances of displacement demonstrate that armed conflict and in particular genocide and politicide (defined as the killing or extermination of a particular group because of its political or ideological beliefs) drive refugee flows (Schmeidl, 1997; Davenport, Moore and Poe, 2003; Moore and Shellman, 2004; Hatton and Moloney, 2015). Studies focusing on individuals' decisions to move confirm that physical threat to life – either actual physical assault or threat of violence – is an important cause of displacement (Adhikari, 2013). In some cases, the loss of economic opportunity in the place of origin is an additional important factor taken into account by individuals when they make their decision on whether to leave. For example, in the case of forced migration in Nepal, displacement was significantly less likely when there were employment opportunities created by the presence of industry (Adhikari, 2013).

The type of armed conflict can affect the likelihood and volume of refugee flows. Intrastate[5] (civil) rather than interstate[6] wars tend to be associated with significant refugee movements (Schmeidl, 1997; 2001) and foreign intervention in civil wars[7] is associated with larger proportions of refugees as opposed to internally displaced people (IDPs) (Schmeidl, 1997; Moore and Shellman, 2007). Furthermore, foreign intervention in intrastate wars tends to prolong displacement (Schmeidl, 1997). Similarly, dissident terror and government violence have been seen to increase the number of refugees relative to the number of IDPs (Moore and Shellman, 2007). In recent years there has been an increase in the number of intrastate conflicts that are internationalised – that is, that have another state supporting one side or another (UCDP, 2014a) which could explain increasing refugee flows.

The scope rather than the intensity of fighting influences the magnitude of refugee flows. The more widespread geographically the scope of fighting, the bigger the refugee flows, especially if the fighting takes place in urban areas (Melander and Öberg, 2007). Perhaps surprisingly, the intensity of fighting, measured by the number of battle deaths, does not appear to have an impact on the magnitude of refugee flows (Melander and Öberg, 2007) or asylum applications (Hatton and Moloney, 2015). This suggests that the threat perceived by potential forced migrants is more related to where the fighting is taking place than to the overall intensity of the fighting.

Human rights abuses are the most powerful drivers of asylum applications from source countries to industrialised countries (Hatton and Moloney, 2015). Using UNHCR data on asylum applications to industrialised countries, it can be seen that state-inflicted political terror (as measured by the Political Terror Index[8] which includes acts such as extrajudicial killings, torture, disappearances and political imprisonment) and lack of civil liberties (measured by the Freedom House civil liberties index which captures freedoms of expression, assembly, association, education and religion) are associated with increased asylum applications from source countries.

The sharp increase in refugee flows in recent years has been primarily the result of the conflict in Syria (Box 6.5). Surveys of refugees from Syria report fear of violence and threat to life as the principal reasons for leaving. Of the Syrians arriving in Greece in January 2016 94% cited escaping conflict and violence in Syria as the main reason they left their country (UNHCR, 2016c).[9] In a survey of refugees located in the Kurdistan Region of northern Iraq respondents gave varying reasons for their flight from Syria, including: the fear of physical violence (25%); the fear of being used as a human shield (25%); the fear of rape (24%); the fear of forced military service (22%). Only 3% stated that the economic situation was a reason for fleeing from Syria (Salman, 2012). A survey of Syrian refugees in Germany found that nearly 70% left Syria because of the imminent threat to their life or their family's life (from armed conflict, kidnapping, siege, lack of food or killing), 13% cited economic reasons, 8% cited avoiding military conscription and 7% said it was to reunite with family (Berlin Social Science Center, 2015).

Box 6.5. **Syria's exodus**

The Syrian civil war is an extremely complex conflict affecting huge swathes of the country and causing displacement on a massive scale.

Up to 1 200 armed opposition groups are involved in the fighting in addition to government forces and their allied militia groups (UCDP, 2014b). There have been reports of war crimes and crimes against humanity – such as the use of barrel bombs to kill civilians – committed by the regime and by rebel groups (Amnesty International, 2015). Violence is spread throughout the country and the areas affected by conflict include major urban centres including the capital Damascus as well as Aleppo, Homs and Hama.

The scale of the Syrian exodus is enormous. Of Syria's pre-war population of nearly 21 million, 60% have been displaced, 7.6 million internally and over 4.8 million as refugees (UNHCR, 2016g). Up to 470 000 people have been killed in the fighting (Syrian Center for Policy Research, 2016). By way of contrast, in Afghanistan, the second largest refugee-origin country, 11% of the population are displaced, 8% as refugees and 3% as IDPs.

Infographic: Syria's exodus

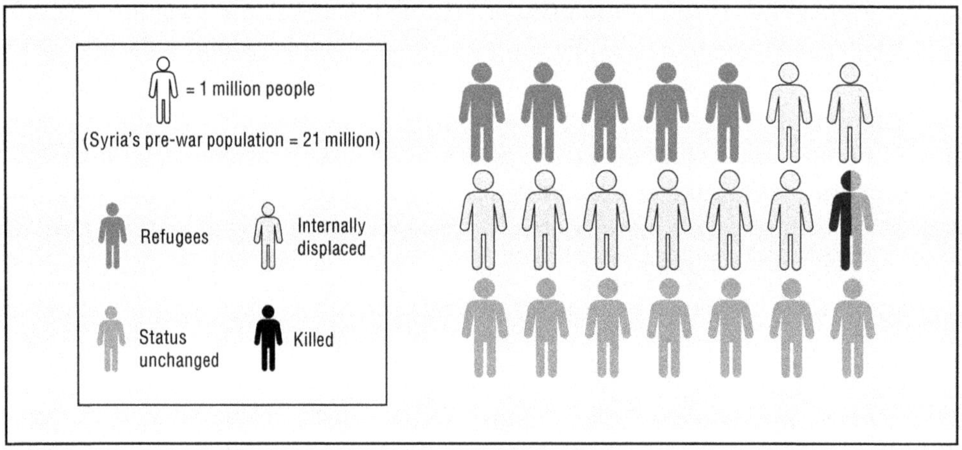

Most Syrian refugees have sought refuge in neighbouring countries, in particular Turkey, Lebanon, Jordan and Iraq. Slightly more than 10% of those who have fled the conflict in Syria have sought safety in Europe (UNHCR, 2016g).

Source: UCDP (2014b), "Complexities of Coding Syria", UCDP note online, *www.ucdp.uu.se/gpdatabase/info/Complexities%20of%20coding%20Syria.pdf*; Amnesty International (2015), *Death Everywhere: War Crimes and Human Rights Abuses in Aleppo, Syria*, *www.amnesty.org/en/documents/mde24/1370/2015/en/*; Syrian Center for Policy Research (2016), website, *http://scpr-syria.org/*; UNHCR (2016g), *Syria Regional Refugee Response* (data portal), *http://data.unhcr.org/syrianrefugees/regional.php*.

Many factors affect which countries people decide to flee to

While the factors leading people to leave their homes in episodes of forced migration are relatively clear, once people have taken the decision to leave, understanding the reasons behind where people decide to flee to is more complex. In the cases where people flee across international borders, flight direction is influenced by spatial, temporal and cultural factors. Their journeys may also involve them transiting through countries – and perhaps staying there for extended periods of time – before reaching their final destination.

Refugees overwhelmingly move to neighbouring countries. Many studies have shown that geographical proximity is the most important factor determining where refugees flee to (Iqbal, 2007; Melander and Öberg, 2007; Schmeidl, 1997; Rüegger and Bohnet, 2015). The case of Syria provides a striking example of this. Of the 4.8 million Syrian refugees, 4.4 million are registered in neighbouring countries (2.7 million in Turkey, 1.1 million in Lebanon and 640 000 in Jordan).[10] At the global level, three-quarters of the world's refugees reside in a country neighbouring their own (UNHCR, 2016d). Neighbouring countries may simply be the first safe country that people reach, and in doing so have the right to claim asylum or some form of temporary protection. In this respect, refugees' "choice" of country is relatively limited at this stage of the migration process.

After refugees reach the first safe country, their ability to continue their journey to a third country may be limited by several factors. As with other forms of migration, financial constraints may prevent refugees from being able to travel further than to a neighbouring country. Similarly, the border controls of potential host countries beyond neighbouring states may prevent people from being able to enter their territory, as has been seen in a number of European countries during the 2015-16 refugee crisis. Refugees may consider the journey to reach another host country to be too dangerous, in particular if formal, legal channels to reach the country are not available. Journeys may also be physically strenuous, preventing elderly people, those in poor health or those with disabilities from attempting them. The emotional toll should also not be underestimated. It is important to note that these same factors also affect people's initial decisions about whether or not to leave their home country in the first place.

Cultural pull factors can also play a role. Refugees tend to choose to flee to neighbouring countries where they have ethnic ties. This factor becomes even stronger if the refugees' kin group in the host country has a history of accepting co-ethnic refugees and is relatively large, as they have better capacities to absorb any influx (Rüegger and Bohnet, 2015).

Refugees often follow previous migration flows, whether forced or voluntary. Reasons for this could include established transportation networks, aid facilities and the presence of support networks in the destination country.

The evidence is less conclusive in respect of economic pull factors. Some studies have shown that refugees tend to be drawn to democratic and wealthy states where incomes are higher (Moore and Shellman, 2007) even if they remain highly affected by distance and previous migration flows. Other studies have found no such connection when looking at refugee movements.

Social and economic factors influence the choice of country in which to apply for asylum. The choice of asylum country seems to be strongly influenced by existing social networks or other bilateral links. These include: the presence of friends and family in the destination country, the number of migrants from the source country in the country of asylum application, colonial links and common language (Neumayer, 2004; Day and White, 2001). Labour market conditions, in particular the unemployment rate, also appear to influence the choice of asylum country, with lower asylum applications to countries with higher rates of unemployment (Thielemann, 2006; Hatton, 2004; Hatton and Moloney, 2015). Other economic factors are less clear-cut. Relative income and the level and growth rate of GDP in the destination have sometimes been shown to have an important influence (Hatton, 2004; Neumayer 2004), whereas the effect of destination GDP per capita has been shown to be weak (Neumayer, 2004).

Asylum policy can also have an effect, although these effects are likely to differ across countries and between types of policy (Hatton and Moloney, 2015). Stricter destination country asylum policies have been shown to have a negative effect on the number of asylum applications received (Hatton, 2004). When the different types of asylum policy are categorised, it appears that policies restricting access to the territory and stricter processing/ refugee status determination policies may have a negative deterrent effect (Thielemann, 2006; Hatton, 2009). Other policies, such as refugee integration policies, living conditions of asylum seekers or what can be described more broadly as welfare policies towards asylum seekers, have only a weak impact on the number of asylum applications countries receive (Hatton and Moloney, 2015; Thielemann, 2006; Hatton, 2009).

Explaining the flight direction of refugees from the current refugee crisis is challenging for several reasons. The situation has changed over the course of the Syrian conflict. As was shown earlier in the chapter, the vast majority of refugees (from the conflict but also more generally worldwide) are accommodated in low- and middle-income countries – often neighbouring countries – but the recent flows to Europe show a slight shift towards high-income countries. The patterns of refugee flows also respond and adapt to changes in border policies. For example, flows along the so-called "Balkan route" through the Former Yugoslav Republic of Macedonia, Serbia, Hungary, Croatia and Slovenia dropped when those countries closed their borders to refugees in early 2016, leaving people stranded in Greece. The EU-Turkey deal on refugees which came into force in April 2016 was expected to have an impact on flows, refusing passage to Europe for many, potentially acting as a deterrent to attempting the journey for others, or diverting some refugees to other routes (Collett, 2016). The volume of flows to Europe also varies according to the season, with higher numbers of people arriving to Europe in the warmer months when overland travel is easier and sea conditions less dangerous.

Furthermore, for large numbers of Syrian refugees, migration has been a two-step process. Neighbouring Turkey, Lebanon or Jordan may have been the first port of call and refuge from war, but the difficulty of life and lack of prospects have led many refugees to decide to continue their journeys and attempt to seek refuge in European countries. A survey of Syrian refugees arriving in the Greek islands in January 2016 revealed that 34% had been living in a country other than Syria (mainly Turkey, Lebanon or Jordan) for an average of two and a half years before travelling to Greece across the Mediterranean.

Conditions in the initial destination countries have become untenable for many refugees. A UNHCR survey of the Syrian refugees arriving in Greece found that the principal reasons for leaving were a lack of jobs which matched their skills or could meet basic living expenses, or to avoid exploitation (41%); followed by discrimination (14%) (UNHCR, 2016c). Refugees face several barriers to being able to work legally in their initial countries of destination, forcing many into informal, precarious employment (Box 6.6). In Turkey, over half of refugees living outside camps earn below the minimum wage. Life is extremely difficult, with families living in overcrowded conditions and children out of school (ILO, 2015). Assessments of the livelihoods of Syrian refugees in Lebanon paint a similarly bleak picture (Oxfam/BRIC, 2013). With monthly expenditures at more than double the average monthly incomes, refugees quickly exhaust personal savings, often within the first six months of their stay in the country, and get into debt. Aid from international organisations and NGOs supports less than 20% of their expenditure. Most have few resources left, and 75% of refugee families struggle to secure their food needs (ILO, 2015). Increasing numbers of refugees have no viable alternative for survival other than situations that could be defined as exploitation and trafficking in national and international law (ICMPD, 2015).

Box 6.6. **Refugees and asylum seekers often lack access to labour markets in host countries**

Refugees' work rights, including the right to engage in wage-earning employment and self-employment, are explicitly provided for in Chapter III of the 1951 UN Convention on the Status of Refugees (Refugee Convention). However, many of the countries which accommodate most Syrian refugees have not signed the convention, and domestic laws effectively block access to legal work.

Jordan has not signed the Refugee Convention. Syrians entering the country as asylum seekers or who are registered as refugees were not given residency, which seriously limited their ability to seek lawful employment, as Jordanian companies are prohibited from employing foreigners without a residence permit. In 2016, however, a regularisation mechanism was introduced and Jordan committed to granting work access in the future, although the mechanism is still to be designed. Furthermore, the process to obtain work permits is convoluted, and permits are only granted provided the positions they are applying for do not involve competition with Jordanians, which in many cases they do. Also, employers are required to pay for a worker's permit under the law, but workers often end up paying for them. At USD 240 to USD 550 for a permit, the cost is prohibitively expensive for many. As a result, many refugees engage in paid work without a permit.

Existing domestic laws in Jordan allow certain refugees to participate in the labour force, including skilled workers from Arab countries with which it has previous agreements. For over a decade, Jordan had a labour co-operation agreement with Syria, which allowed Syrians to participate in the labour market as migrant workers. Foreign entrepreneurs can also obtain a residence permit if they are in Jordan to invest in commercial or industrial ventures. The Jordanian government recently allowed Syrian manufacturers to operate in several industrial zones and gave permission for 30% to 60% of the workforce to be made up of Syrian workers in certain remote areas.

Source: ILO (2015), "Access to work for Syrian refugees in Jordan: A discussion paper on labour and refugee laws and policies".

Lebanon: Before the Syrian civil war, an estimated 300 000 Syrians were working in Lebanon, most of whom were employed in construction, agriculture and services, sometimes on a seasonal basis. Unlike other nationalities, Syrians did not need a visa to enter the country. Registered Syrians can live and work in Lebanon indefinitely, although in theory they need a work permit. Syrians can apply for a work permit from inside Lebanon and do not need to pay a deposit. The cost of work permits varies depending on work category and Syrian workers pay only 25% of the normal fee. In reality, few Syrians have applied for a work permit as most work in informal sectors, with unregistered enterprises or without a written contract. Lebanon is lenient towards those who are in Lebanon irregularly and those working without permits.

Source: ILO (2015), "Access to work for Syrian refugees in Jordan: A discussion paper on labour and refugee laws and policies".

Turkey has ratified the Refugee Convention, but has a geographical limitation meaning that only those fleeing as a consequence of "events occurring in Europe" can be granted refugee status (ILO, 2015). Syrians are hosted in Turkey under a "temporary protection regime". Since January 2016, a new law has given Syrians access to legal employment. To qualify for a work permit, a Syrian needs to have held a certain kind of ID card, known as a *kimlik*, for six months and an applicant's employer must give the Syrian a contract. However, in practice employers may be unwilling to offer a contract and prefer to hire Syrians informally, often paying less than the minimum wage and requiring working hours longer than the legal daily limit.

Source: Kingsley, P. (2016), "Fewer than 0.1% of Syrians in Turkey in line for work permits", *The Guardian*.

A similar multi-staged migration can be seen for Afghan arrivals, some of whom have in fact never lived in Afghanistan. Of Afghan arrivals in Europe (the Greek islands) 19% have never lived in Afghanistan, but were in Iran or Pakistan. An additional 26% lived in another country (not Afghanistan) for six months or more before starting the journey to Europe, where the average stay in the country of residence was two and half years. Fear of expulsion led 25% to leave that country of residence, while 17% left for reasons including not having a job matching their skills, inability to meet basic living expenses and to avoid exploitation (UNHCR, 2016c).

A variety of reasons influence refugees' preferred choice of destination country in the current flows to Europe. Family reunification is an often-cited factor in recent flows: 43% of Syrians surveyed in the Greek islands in January 2016 cited family reunification as the reason for their choice of destination country (the highest percentage of all of the reasons given). Education (22%) was the next most popular response, followed by presence of a community of their culture (15%), and economic reasons (14%). With Afghan arrivals, the reasons were somewhat different: 47% stated that education was the reason for their choice of destination country, 26% cited respect of human rights and 23% cited family reunification.

The importance of cultural factors discussed above can also be seen in other refugee flows from Syria. Significant numbers of Syrians of Kurdish ethnicity have sought refuge in the Kurdish region in northern Iraq: 94% of Syrian refugees in this region are Kurdish (Salman, 2012). Surveys indicate that after safety, cultural and linguistic ties were important reasons that refugees chose the region. The top three reasons reported were: the security and stability of the region (21%); the shared ethnic, religious and linguistic affinities (17%); and the presence of better livelihood opportunities (16%) (Salman, 2012). The livelihood opportunities are relevant as, unlike in other neighbouring countries, Syrian Kurds can legally work in Kurdistan.

Managing refugee crises

Effectively managing refugee crises requires action on all levels, from the international level so that the responsibility for supporting refugees is shared between nations, to the local authorities who are at the forefront of reception and integration efforts. One of the most challenging aspects of managing refugee crises is their often sudden onset. Any mechanisms for response and co-ordination therefore need to be designed precisely to work under conditions of sudden peaks in refugee flows, and policy making needs to shift from reactionary to anticipatory mode.

Responsibility for hosting refugees needs to be shared among countries

This chapter has shown that the majority of refugees are hosted in countries neighbouring their own. While it may be natural that countries of first arrival are usually neighbouring countries – they are very often simply the closest safe place when fighting breaks out – there is no reason why neighbouring countries should continue to host the majority of refugees for the longer term. As Peter Sutherland, United Nations Special Representative of the Secretary-General for International Migration and Development stated, "we cannot allow responsibility to be defined merely by proximity to a crisis" (Sutherland, 2016). This is particularly true for large-scale refugee influxes which strain the capacity of host countries which, as this chapter also showed, tend to be low- and middle-income countries. Effective international co-operation and shared responsibility is vital to avoid any one country being stretched beyond capacity with the negative effects this can have on socio-economic conditions and on refugees themselves.

International solidarity can be expressed primarily in two ways. First, through adequate financial support, both to the governments of low- and middle-income countries that host large refugee populations to enable them to expand public service provision to refugee groups (beyond immediate humanitarian needs), and to international organisations and NGOs delivering key services to refugees in these countries. To give an indication of the current shortfall, UNHCR's Syria Regional Refugee Response was only 30% funded as of June 2016 (UNHCR, 2016g). Second, wealthier countries could increase the number of people fleeing conflict that they accept – both through humanitarian channels and through other migration channels – to alleviate the pressure in poorer countries bordering conflict zones.

The financial cost of managing refugee situations should not fall solely or largely on the low- and middle-income countries that host the majority of the world's refugees. New and innovative forms of financing are needed. The "Education Cannot Wait" fund for education in emergencies[11] that was launched at the World Humanitarian Summit in May 2016 is one positive development that has been catalysed by the current refugee crisis, but a more comprehensive approach is needed.

Financing for forced displacement is a major challenge: how to ensure enough quality finance for not just humanitarian, but also comprehensive solutions to preventing, addressing and ending forced displacement situations? The solution lies in three parts: making sure there are enough resources, that these resources are the right type to deliver the expected results, and increasing efficiency – making those resources go further.

There is scope for increasing the financing for forced displacement programming: maintaining, and potentially increasing funds from traditional donors, alongside efforts to grow newer funding sources such as new donors, private giving, social finance and the private sector. In response to the Syria refugee crisis, for example, funding sources could include new donors from the Gulf states, Islamic social finance as well as private actors. Other types of financial instruments, such as loans provided on a concessional basis, risk financing and seed funding for innovations, may also be useful new additions to the financing pool. Properly targeted development funds – aligned with development objectives – may also be useful in different forced displacement situations, recognising, however, that using this type of funding may require a recalibration of the humanitarian delivery model. Finally, the domestic resources of refugee hosting countries are also an essential part of financing an effective response – although asking these host countries to continue to bear what is often an enormous burden is, of course, unsustainable: compensation options should be considered.

Financial flows also need to be properly layered – matching the particular needs and risks of different forced displacement situations to the right type of finance: not just more money, but the right money in the right place at the right time. As part of this, the push towards multi-annual funding based on true multi-annual plans has been suggested as a key means to provide better and more useful finance for forced displacement situations. Further, a proper solution for financing forced displacement in middle-income countries is still to be found.

Finally, there is also the need to reduce the cost of responses, and recognise that the current financing model is most likely unsustainable. Shifting to greater conflict prevention and preparedness could go some way to reducing the costs – both economic and human – of forced displacement situations. New ways of responding – cash transfer programming, delivering through national social safety nets, and using economic modelling to determine what type of response represents the best value for money, can also play a key role in driving down costs (and increasing effectiveness). Reducing transaction costs and administration requirements – by setting out a better model for funding headquarters costs and streamlining grant reporting requirements, for example, may also help improve cost-effectiveness. Finally, funding for results – rather than funding activities – has the potential to deliver significant benefits by encouraging operational agencies to use the most cost effective programming solution, no matter how the situation evolves.

Beyond financing, ensuring safe and legal channels for people to escape from violence and conflict in their home countries must be a priority. First, allowing people to apply for asylum in a third country from their country of first arrival would address several of the negative consequences that have been seen in the recent refugee crisis. Opening up this possibility would reduce the incentive for people to make dangerous journeys to a third country irregularly, deny human traffickers the opportunity to exploit and profit from people's desperation, and in the process decrease the likelihood of mixed flows of economic migrants and refugees arriving in third countries. Of course, some people may still attempt to make these dangerous and irregular journeys. In these cases, international solidarity can be expressed through the assurance of search and rescue at sea operations. Indeed, many countries have made significant efforts to rescue refugees in the Mediterranean.

Second, international resettlement programmes need to be scaled up. As this chapter has reported, very few refugees are resettled to third countries through the UNHCR resettlement programme. While it is encouraging that increasing numbers of countries are taking part in the programme, the total numbers of refugees who are resettled has not changed significantly in the last few years and the proportion of refugees who are resettled has actually declined. More countries could follow the lead of the United States, Canada and Australia – the three countries which offer the most resettlement places – and substantially expand the number of refugees that they accept through this channel. Furthermore, resettlement programmes usually only provide places for the most vulnerable groups of refugees. One additional option could therefore be to include quotas for groups that are not necessarily the most vulnerable within resettlement programmes (OECD, 2016a).

Third, alternative pathways through which people escaping conflict can migrate could complement resettlement programmes (OECD, 2016a). There are two kinds of alternative pathways – general mobility and humanitarian. Alternative general mobility pathways include labour migration, international study and family migration visas. Alternative humanitarian channels refer to humanitarian visas and private sponsorship schemes. While these alternative pathways were not designed for international protection, they can contribute to the goal of increasing the number of people able to escape conflict and violence. The alternative pathways should be open to those who have been granted temporary protection and those who have conventional refugee status, but would exclude those who are not yet registered in a country of first asylum (OECD, 2016a). These pathways are already available, so the challenge is to reduce the barriers that prevent displaced people from availing of them.

- ***Labour migration*** could be encouraged by helping refugees to access existing labour immigration channels, by creating incentives for employers to recruit people under international protection from abroad (e.g. ease labour market tests and shortage occupation lists) or by introducing new labour migration programmes specifically for refugees.
- ***Student visas*** enable refugees to pursue higher education in a third country. Obstacles include securing financing that covers tuition fees and living costs and complying with entrance requirements, especially as documentation and proof of qualifications may have been left behind or lost while fleeing.
- ***Family reunification*** brings together refugees with close relatives who are citizens or permanent residents in other countries. A range of measures could lower barriers to family reunification, including: widening eligibility to include non-core family members;

expediting procedures; and relaxing conditions of admissions. To avoid family reunification becoming a "pull factor" for migration, temporary family reunification programmes could be exclusively for refugees who arrived over a specified period of time.

- ***Humanitarian visas*** are used to enable people to lawfully enter a destination country to file a formal asylum application. The non-discretionary use of humanitarian visas is, however, a very unlikely prospect, and the number of visas granted is more likely to increase extensively (as more countries use them) than intensively (as countries that already use them issue more).
- ***Private sponsorship programmes*** take a variety of different forms and cover costs ranging from, for example, the transportation of refugees, medical expenses, housing, support with finding employment and accessing education after resettlement.

These two acts of international solidarity – providing finance and taking in people – are interrelated. More generous financial support would improve the living conditions and prospects of refugees if it ensures access to vital public services such as healthcare, education, infrastructure and sanitation. Improved living conditions reduces the likelihood that refugees will look to move on to another country for asylum (although better living conditions alone may not be sufficient if other determinants of future prospects – such as access to labour markets – are not available). Reducing the numbers of refugees in the countries of first arrival by opening up safe and legal channels to third countries would take some of the strain off, reducing the need for increased financial support to extend public services.

What has been clear from the recent Middle East to Europe flows is that if the level of action on these two fronts combined is inadequate, refugees will vote with their feet. This secondary migration is often irregular, involves dangerous journeys that put lives at risk, and gives the impression to citizens in the second receiving countries that the situation is not managed. This can give space to extremist and xenophobic parties and movements to exploit these fears, undermining social cohesion and public support for helping refugees and for immigration in general. It also opens up opportunities for human smuggling and trafficking gangs. Unaccompanied children are particularly exposed to the dangers of human trafficking. Corruption is one of the primary facilitators of refugee smuggling (OECD, 2015b). The international community must understand the connections between corruption and refugee smuggling in order to address this crime and help refugees safely realise their rights.

A shift from a humanitarian response logic to thinking about longer-term development concerns is needed

After the initial humanitarian and emergency phase, policy responses are needed that address the medium- and long-term implications of hosting refugee populations. This chapter has shown that protracted refugee situations are becoming more common and lasting longer. Many of the shortcomings of existing policy responses can be attributed to the extension of a humanitarian response logic to what is a longer-term development concern. An overarching goal needs to be to minimise the economic, social and geographic marginalisation of refugee populations in their host countries. Integration instruments should be made available quickly after the arrival of refugees in destination countries. This requires fast administrative procedures, for example, to clarify the status of refugees.

Local authorities are often at the forefront of reception and integration efforts. For the recommendations below to be successfully implemented, building their capacity to respond to the increases in service demand by culturally different populations will require education and training activities (OECD/LEED, 2016).

- ***Support refugees' integration through access to the labour market.*** One of the most powerful tools of integration is giving refugees the right to work legally. Access to the labour market may even be granted before a formal decision about the status of the refugee has been taken. Institutional arrangements can facilitate labour market access. For example, in Germany, the agency dealing with asylum applications and integration issues has been linked more closely to the federal job agency (OECD, 2016b).
- ***Provide training and recognise existing skills and qualifications to support economic and social integration.*** Labour market integration can also be supported through training for refugees that is targeted to local labour market conditions. The level and types of skills of refugees will determine the appropriate policy responses in host countries. In some cases, skills training may need to include language training. Language training, including for children below primary school age, is key for successful integration. In other cases, refugees may already have the skills that are needed in local labour market. Here, policies that ensure that refugees' skills and qualifications are recognised will be especially important. Offering courses on local cultural and social norms can also facilitate social integration.
- ***Take into account refugee populations in development planning processes.*** Uganda's new National Development Plan II is a good example of such an approach. The plan contains objectives and interventions related to managing the country's refugee situation and refugees are also identified as specific user groups within the plan's other objectives, for example the objective to expand access to safe water supply in rural areas.
- ***Avoid the establishment of camps.*** Camps can be important in the initial phase of responding to a refugee situation. They can help organisations ensure the delivery of essential services and identify people who are in need of specialised protection services, such as unaccompanied children or disabled people. Yet in practice camps often remain after the emergency phase. As this chapter has shown, camps can have negative consequences on refugees and host communities. Ultimately, camps reduce the capacity of refugees to be resilient and self-reliant and perpetuate a state of dependence.
- ***Mainstream public service delivery to refugee populations into existing national and local systems.*** For example, the inclusion of refugee children in national schools in Jordan, Lebanon, Pakistan and other host countries are examples of good practice. Financing the expansion of public service provision is one area in which support from the international community will be essential. Public service delivery systems are very often already constrained in many low- and middle-income countries. Expanding access to services, especially in the cases of very large refugee populations, will not be feasible without sufficient external financing.

Conclusion

Armed conflict and the accompanying threat of violence have driven millions of people from their homes and across international borders in search of safety. Contrary to other forms of international migration, most refugees are accommodated in developing countries. A new era is opening of high refugee numbers, levels of which have not been seen since the early 1990s. This is being driven largely by the conflict in Syria, although refugee crises are by no means limited to the Middle East-to-Europe corridor that is currently dominating the headlines.

The changing nature of conflicts globally suggests that refugee situations could increase in the future. Despite a general trend towards fewer armed conflicts since the 1990s, some observers argue that the nature of conflict seems to be changing (SIPRI, 2014). In recent years there has been an increase in the number of intrastate conflicts that are internationalised – that is, that have another state supporting one side or another. This could be significant in terms of migration flows as intrastate rather than interstate wars tend to be associated with significant refugee movements (Schmeidl, 1997) and foreign intervention in intrastate wars is associated with larger proportions of refugees (as opposed to IDPs) and tends to prolong displacement.

People fleeing conflict and violence overwhelmingly seek refuge in neighbouring countries, often following the route of previous migration flows. Beyond their search for safety, their decisions about where to flee are influenced by a number of social, cultural, and to a lesser extent, economic factors. Sometimes, refugees' flight can take place in two or more stages, especially if lack of opportunity in the initial host country drives them to leave again in search of better prospects.

Refugee situations demand policy responses at local, national and international levels that ultimately lead to the three sustainable solutions for refugees depending on the context: return, resettlement and integration.

For many refugees, the dream of returning home remains elusive while conflicts, violence and instability persist in their countries. Where national solutions are failing or unviable, the international community needs to prioritise and redouble its efforts in supporting conflict resolution, peacebuilding and providing continuing support to post-conflict countries. Only then will return become a realistic prospect and a durable solution to refugee situations.

Sudden peaks in refugee flows, as were seen in the early 1990s and now with the Syrian war, can challenge the international community's capacity and resolve to meet its obligations to international protection as enshrined in the UN Refugee Convention. Mechanisms for global co-operation on refugee issues need to be robust enough and designed specifically to cope with sudden peaks in numbers. Furthermore, international resettlement programmes need to be enlarged to respond to the scale of the number of refugees and provide durable solutions. Expanding alternative pathways – such as labour migration, student visas and family reunification – could also be explored.

Beyond the challenges of processing large numbers of asylum applications and attending to the immediate humanitarian needs of refugees, policy responses are also needed to ensure that refugees' full potential can be realised for the benefit of the refugees themselves and their countries of destination. Refugees represent a potentially enormous source of skills and expertise, yet they are often marginalised economically, socially, politically and even geographically within host countries. Policies that promote the integration of refugees can unlock this potential.

Notes

1. This chapter only considers trends in refugee numbers of UNHCR-registered refugees. Data presented in figures do not include Palestinian refugees under UNRWA's mandate as annual data is not available for the period 1960-2015.
2. Figures reported for stocks of refugees do not capture people who previously had refugee status in host countries and who have since been naturalised (i.e. granted citizenship in their host country). For example, in 2014, Tanzania granted citizenship to over 160 000 Burundi refugees who had been in the country since 1972. These people are therefore no longer counted in refugee stocks for Tanzania. A number of countries have established pathways to naturalisation (e.g. in the United States refugees can apply after (usually) five years of permanent residence in the country; in Europe

the time requirement ranges from three to 12 years depending on the country) whereas in many other countries the naturalisation of refugees is extremely rare.

3. European entities include EU member states, Norway, Switzerland, Serbia and Kosovo.
4. As a consequence, these people are not included in refugee statistics as they have found a durable solution.
5. A conflict between a government and a non-governmental party, with no interference from other countries.
6. A conflict between two or more governments.
7. An armed conflict between a government and a non-government party where the government side, the opposing side, or both sides, receive military support from other governments that actively participate in the conflict.
8. See *www.politicalterrorscale.org/*.
9. Similarly, 71% of the Afghans surveyed cited conflict and violence as the main reason they left their country.
10. Figures correct at time of writing (March 2016). Due to the rapidly evolving situation, numbers may change quickly.
11. The fund aims to raise nearly USD 4 billion over the next five years to reach 13.6 million children whose education has been disrupted by conflict and humanitarian emergencies.

References

Adhikari, P. (2013), "Conflict-induced displacement, Understanding the causes of flight", *American Journal of Political Science*, Vol. 57, No. 1, January, pp. 82-89.

Amnesty International (2015), *Death Everywhere: War Crimes and Human Rights Abuses in Aleppo, Syria*, *www.amnesty.org/en/documents/mde24/1370/2015/en/*.

Berlin Social Science Center (2015), *Survey of Syrian Refugees in Germany*, *https://docs.google.com/spreadsheets/d/1WYn4N7STdP2eW3EYdX86Gsb6lxE4VrcNvZ4aEczsFwI/edit#gid=833561282*.

Collett, E. (2016), "The paradox of the EU-Turkey refugee deal", *MPI Commentary*, March, Migration Policy Institute, *www.migrationpolicy.org/news/paradox-eu-turkey-refugee-deal*.

Davenport, C., W. Moore and S. Poe (2003), "Sometimes you just have to leave: Domestic threats and forced migration, 1964-1989", *International Interactions*, No. 29, pp. 27-55.

Day, K. and P. White (2001), "Choice or circumstance: The UK as the location of asylum applications by Bosnian and Somali refugees", *Geo Journal* No 55, pp. 15-26.

Hatton, T. (2009), "The rise and fall of asylum: What happened and why", *Economic Journal*, No. 119, pp. F183-F213.

Hatton, T. (2004), "Seeking asylum in Europe", *Economic Policy*, No. 38, pp. 5-62.

Hatton, T. and J. Moloney (2015), "Applications for asylum in the developed world: Modelling asylum claims by origin and destination", *Centre for Economic Policy Research Discussion Paper* No. 10678, June.

ICMPD (2015), *Targeting Vulnerabilities: The Impact of the Syrian War and Refugee Situation on Trafficking in Persons – A Study of Syria, Turkey, Lebanon, Jordan and Iraq*, International Centre for Migration Policy Development, Vienna, *www.icmpd.org/fileadmin/ICMPD-Website/Anti-Trafficking/Targeting_Vulnerabilities_EN__SOFT_.pdf*.

ILO (2015), "Access to work for Syrian refugees in Jordan: A discussion paper on labour and refugee laws and policies", International Labour Organization, Regional Office for Arab States, Beirut.

IOM (2016), *Missing Migrants Project* (portal), International Organization for Migration, Geneva, *http://missingmigrants.iom.int/*.

IOM (2011), *Glossary on Migration*, 2nd edition, International Organization for Migration, Geneva.

Iqbal, Z. (2007), "The geo-politics of forced migration in Africa, 1992-2001", *Conflict Management and Peace Science*, Vol. 24(2), pp.105-119.

Kingsley, P. (2016), "Fewer than 0.1% of Syrians in Turkey in line for work permits", *The Guardian*, 11 April, *https://www.theguardian.com/world/2016/apr/11/fewer-than-01-of-syrians-in-turkey-in-line-for-work-permits*.

Loescher, G. and J. Milner (2009), "Understanding the challenge", *Forced Migration Review* No. 33, September, *www.fmreview.org/sites/fmr/files/FMRdownloads/en/FMRpdfs/FMR33/FMR33.pdf.*

Melander, E. and M. Öberg (2007), "The threat of violence and forced migration: Geographical scope trumps intensity of fighting", *Civil Wars 9(2)*, pp, 156-173.

Moore, W. and S. Shellman (2007), "Whither will they go? A global study of refugees' destinations, 1965-1995", *International Studies Quarterly*, Vol.51, pp. 811-834.

Moore, W. and S. Shellman, (2004), "Fear of persecution: Forced migration, 1952-1995", *Journal of Conflict Resolution*, Vol. 40, pp. 727-753.

Neumayer, E. (2004), "Asylum destination choice: What makes some West European countries more attractive than others?", *European Union Politics*, Vol. 5, pp. 155-180.

ODI (2016), *Education Cannot Wait: Proposing a Fund for Education in Emergencies*, Overseas Development Institute, London, *www.odi.org/sites/odi.org.uk/files/resource-documents/10497.pdf.*

OECD (2016a), *International Migration Outlook 2016*, OECD Publishing, Paris, *http://dx.doi.org/10.1787/migr_outlook-2016-en.*

OECD (2016b), *OECD Economic Surveys: Germany 2016*, OECD Publishing, Paris, *http://dx.doi.org/10.1787/eco_surveys-deu-2016-en.*

OECD (2015a), "Is this humanitarian migration crisis different?", *Migration Policy Debates* No. 7 September, OECD Publishing, Paris, *www.oecd.org/migration/Is-this-refugee-crisis-different.pdf.*

OECD (2015b), "Responses to the refugee crisis: Corruption and the smuggling of refugees", October, Paris, *www.oecd.org/corruption/Corruption-and-the-smuggling-of-refugees.pdf.*

OECD/LEED (2016), *Local Responses to Welcoming Refugees* (website), *www.refugeelocalwelcome.wordpress.com/.*

Oxfam/BRIC (2013), "Survey on the livelihoods of Syrian refugees in Lebanon", *Research Report*, November, Oxfam and Beirut Research and Innovation Center, *www.oxfam.org/sites/www.oxfam.org/files/file_attachments/rr-bric-livelihoods-syrian-refugees-lebanon-211113-en_0.pdf.*

Pettersson, T. and P. Wallensteen (2016), "Armed Conflicts, 1946-2015", *Journal of Peace Research*, Vol. 53, n° 5, *http://dx.doi.org/10.1177/0022343315595927.*

Pew Research Center (2016), "Europe sees rise in unaccompanied minors seeking asylum, with almost half from Afghanistan", Pew Research Center, Washington, DC, *www.pewresearch.org/fact-tank/2016/05/10/eu-unaccompanied-minors.*

Rosenblum, M.R. and I. Ball (2016) "Trends in unaccompanied child and family migration from Central America", Migration Policy Institute, Washington, DC, *www.migrationpolicy.org/research/trends-unaccompanied-child-and-family-migration-central-america*

Rüegger, S. and H. Bohnet (2015), "The ethnicity of refugees (ER): A new dataset for understanding flight patterns", *Conflict Management and Peace Science* 1-24, *http://dx.doi.org/10.1177/0738894215611865.*

Rüegger, S. and H. Bohnet (2012), *No Undifferentiated Mass: Introducing a Quantitative Data Set on the Ethnic Composition of Refugee Movements*, *http://file.prio.no/files/projects/RueggerBohnet_RefugeeDataPaper.pdf.*

Salman, M. (2012), *Assessment of the Situation of the Syrian Refugees in Kurdistan Region – Iraq*, MPC RR 2012/15, Robert Schuman Centre for Advanced Studies, San Domenico di Fiesole (FI): European University Institute, *www.migrationpolicycentre.eu/docs/MPC%202012%2015.pdf.*

Schmeidl, S. (2001), "Conflict and forced migration: A quantitative review", in A.R. Zolberg and P.M. Benda (ed.), *Global Migrants, Global Refugees: Problems and Solutions*, Berghahn Books, New York, Oxford, pp. 62-94, *www.berghahnbooks.com/title.php?rowtag=ZolbergGlobal.*

Schmeidl, S. (1997), "Exploring the causes of forced migration: A pooled time series analysis, 1971-1990", *Social Science Quarterly* 78(2), pp. 284-308.

SIPRI (2014), *SIPRI Yearbook 2014*, Stockholm International Peace Research Institute, *www.sipri.org/yearbook/2014.*

Statistics Sweden (2016), *Applications for asylum received, 2015*, Statistical database, *www.statistikdatabasen.scb.se/pxweb/en/ssd/START__BE__BE0101__BE0101P/Asylsokande/?rxid=0b678338-87f7-4f74-9606-2837f032c0c1.*

Sutherland, P. (2016), "Helping refugees together", *Project Syndicate*, 4 April, *www.project-syndicate.org/commentary/fixing-the-migration-and-asylum-system-by-peter-sutherland-2016-04.*

Syrian Center for Policy Research (2016), website, *http://scpr-syria.org/*.

Thielemann, E. (2006), "The effectiveness of governments' attempts to control unwanted migration", in C. A. Parsons and T. M. Smeeding (eds.), *Immigration and the Transformation of Europe*, Cambridge University Press, Cambridge.

UCDP (2014a), *UCDP/PRIO Armed Conflict* (dataset), Uppsala Conflict Data Program, Sweden, *www.prio.org/Data/Armed-Conflict/UCDP-PRIO*.

UCDP (2014b), "Complexities of Coding Syria", UCDP note online, *www.ucdp.uu.se/gpdatabase/info/Complexities%20of%20coding%20Syria.pdf*.

UCDP/PRIO (2016), *Yemen Regional Refugee and Migrant Response Plan*, Uppsala Conflict Data Program/Peace Research Institute, Oslo, *http://data.unhcr.org/yemen/regional.php*.

UNHCR (2016a), *Statistical Yearbook 2015* (database), United Nations High Commissioner for Refugees, *http://popstats.unhcr.org/en/overview#_ga=1.261217871.393378321.1447865158* (accessed 20 June 2016).

UNHCR (2016b), *Yemen Regional Refugee and Migrant Response Plan* (portal), *http://data.unhcr.org/yemen/regional.php* (accessed 20 June 2016).

UNHCR (2016c), *Profiling of Afghan Arrivals on Greek Islands – January 2016, www.refworld.org/docid/56cd6f7f4.html* and *Profiling of Syrian Arrivals on Greek Islands – January 2016, http://data.unhcr.org/syrianrefugees/regional.php*.

UNHCR (2016d), *Global Trends in Forced Displacement 2015*, *www.unhcr.org/statistics/country/576408cd7/unhcr-global-trends-2015.html*.

UNHCR (2016e), UNHCR website on resettlement, *www.unrefugees.org/what-we-do/*.

UNHCR (2016f), UNHCR website on integration *www.unrefugees.org/what-we-do/*.

UNHCR (2016g) *Syria Regional Refugee Response* (data portal), *http://data.unhcr.org/syrianrefugees/regional.php* (accessed 18 March 2016).

UNHCR (2015a), *UNHCR Statistical Yearbook 2014*, *www.unhcr.org/56655f4b3.html*.

UNHCR (2015b), *Yemen*, United Nations High Commissioner for Refugees, *www.unhcr.org/pages/49e486ba6.html*.

UNHCR (2014a), *Refugee Population, 1960-2013*, *http://popstats.unhcr.org/en/persons_of_concern* (accessed 4 September 2014).

UNHCR (2014b), "UNHCR policy on alternatives to camps", 22 July, UNHCR/HCP/2014/9, *www.refworld.org/docid/5423ded84.html*.

UNHCR (1967), *Convention Relating to the Status of Refugees*, Art. 1A(2), 1951 as modified by the 1967 Protocol), United Nations High Commissioner for Refugees.

UNHCR/MOI Croatia (2016), *Croatia Snapshot YTD 2016*, *http://data.unhcr.org/mediterranean/regional.php*.

UNHCR/Serbia MOI (2016), *Serbia: Weekly Registration Statistics of Population on the Move*, 13 March, *http://data.unhcr.org/mediterranean/regional.php*.

United Nations (2015), *Trends in International Migrant Stock: The 2015 Revision* (database), POP/DB/MIG/Stock/Rev.2015, United Nations Department of Economic and Social Affairs, Population Division.

United Nations (2004), "Guiding principles on internal displacement", UN Doc E/CN.4/1998/53/Add.2, United Nations Office for the Co-ordination of Humanitarian Affairs.

UNRWA (2015), *UNRWA in Figures*, Communications Division, June, United Nations Relief and Works Agency, Jerusalem, *www.unrwa.org/sites/default/files/unrwa_in_figures_2015.pdf*.

World Bank (2016), *World Development Indicators* (database), World Bank, *http://data.worldbank.org/indicator*.

Perspectives on Global Development 2017
International Migration in a Shifting World
© OECD 2016

Chapter 7

The development impact of migration in origin countries

Emigration can have both positive and negative effects on the countries of migrant origin. Migration is not an absolute necessity for those countries' development but it does bring benefits in terms not only of tangible form in the shape of the money and goods that the migrants send home but also in less tangible forms: the expertise, skills and knowledge acquired abroad and a wider view of the world that can help transform the societies they have left. But there is a price. Families are split. There may be adverse consequences for households that lose working family members. The departure of the brightest and best diminishes the country's stock of human capital. Countries that see large numbers of their citizens emigrate have every interest in encouraging their return and discouraging some departures in the first place, and some have instituted relevant policies with this goal.

Chapter 3 concluded that low- and middle-income countries were the origin of 80% of all migrants in 2015, up from 79% in 1995. Moreover, using the new typology of countries proposed by this report (see Chapter 2), it also showed that the biggest change in the stocks of migrants from 1995 to 2015 has been from High and Sustained Growth (SG) and Rest of the World (RW) countries to countries that were high-income by 1995. This has implications for development.

Different countries at similar development levels show very different migration patterns. Emigrants make up about 11% of the population in Mexico and the Philippines, but only 1% in Brazil and Indonesia. These differences are the result of many factors, including the geographical, linguistic and cultural distance to the main countries of destination, the existence of former colonial links and the presence of a large community of emigrants already living abroad. But often different emigration patterns are related to different development strategies. Countries investing in skills systems able to meet labour market needs and in fair social protection mechanisms register lower emigration rates on average than their neighbours. The quality of institutions also has an impact on the decision to migrate and it is not a coincidence if countries with high levels of corruption tend to register higher emigration rates.

In this sense, emigration is often the result of failed development policies. The incapacity of some governments to implement adequate economic and social reforms leads part of the population to leave their countries of birth in search of better opportunities abroad. On the other hand, it is also when the country reaches a certain level of economic wealth that its citizens start emigrating more massively. Migration is costly, which explains why it is not the poorest countries that have the highest emigration rates.

Even though emigration is not an indispensable condition, it nevertheless can contribute significantly to the development of countries of origin. To be sure, emigration entails a series of costs for the migrants themselves, for those left behind, especially children, and for the countries of origin. But, it also brings positive effects not only by relieving pressures on the labour market, but also by generating new sources of financial, human and social capital.

The first section of this chapter highlights the benefits of emigration to countries of origin, in particular through the joint action of taking pressure off the domestic labour market, remittances, diasporas and return migration. The second focuses on the potential negative effects of emigration in the countries of origin. The third highlights the role that public policies, both those targeted directly at migration and sectoral development, play in minimising the costs of migration and maximising its benefits. The chapter builds on previous literature but also on data from the OECD project on the *Interrelations between Public Policies, Migration and Development* (OECD, forthcoming).[1]

Emigrants bring many benefits to their home countries

Emigration can benefit countries of origin through several channels: by taking pressure off the domestic labour market, through remittances, diasporas and return migration. Emigration can play a key role in relieving the pressure on the labour market, helping increase wages and reduce unemployment in countries of origin. Remittances are a stable source of finance that reduces poverty and may add to investment opportunities. Active diasporas sending collective remittances, or being part of knowledge networks, also represent an important asset for the development of the countries of origin. Finally, return migrants bring back with them financial, human and social capital that feeds the socio-economic development of their home countries.

Emigration may take pressure off the domestic market

Emigration acts as a safety valve on the labour market. In the short term, emigration can be of direct benefit to the origin country's labour market. While losing labour can damage an economy, in certain cases the loss relieves pressure in an over-crowded market. Emigration becomes a safety valve where there is low demand for labour. By decreasing the labour pool in the sending country, emigration may help alleviate unemployment and increase the incomes of the remaining workers (Asch, 1994). If emigrants were unemployed before moving or if those who stayed took the jobs previously held by employed emigrants, emigration might have efficiently relieved countries with excess labour, and contributed to lowering unemployment and enhancing wage growth (Zaiceva, 2014).

According to Figure 7.1, unemployment rates decreased and hourly labour costs increased in Lithuania, Poland and Romania as emigration to the European Union's (EU) 15 countries (as they then were) increased. However, if emigrants were not working before, the direct impact they may have on the labour markets in the countries of origin may be minimal. Empirical evidence confirms the upward effect of emigration on wages, at least in the short term, when waves of emigrants leave (Aydemir and Borjas, 2007; Gagnon, 2011; Hanson, 2007; Mishra, 2007).

Figure 7.1. **Unemployment rates decreased and hourly labour costs increased following emigration from new EU member states**

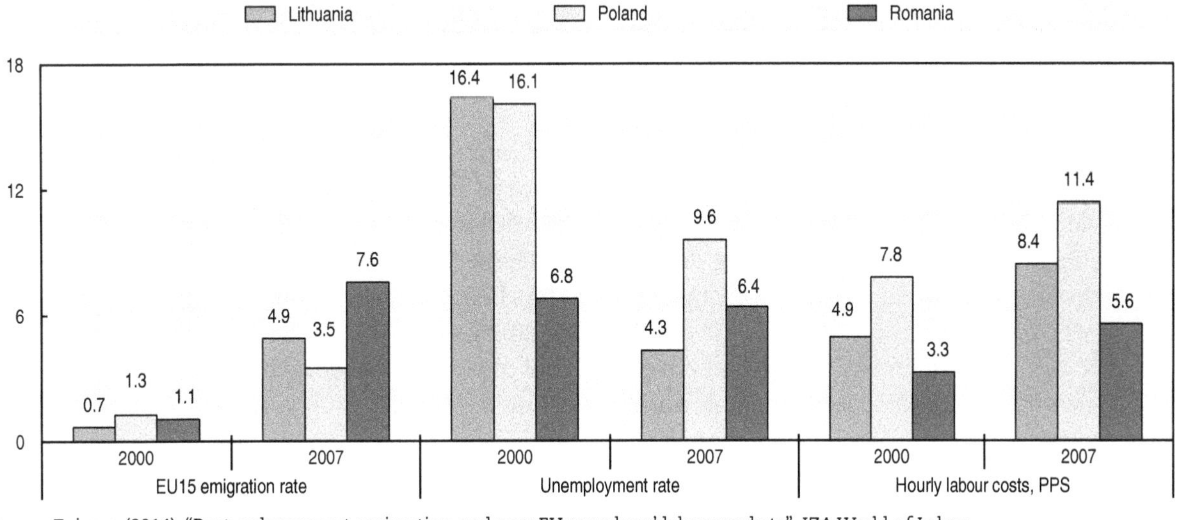

Source: Zaiceva (2014), "Post-enlargement emigration and new EU members' labor markets", IZA World of Labor.

StatLink http://dx.doi.org/10.1787/888933422637

The effects of migration are often felt more strongly at the local level. That is because in many developing countries, markets are not well integrated across the country. If emigration leads to shortages or skills mismatches, the upskilling and internal migration of workers needed to fill those shortages would require time. As an example Figure 7.2 displays data collected at the local level in four countries, showing that the share of individuals claiming they want to emigrate because job prospects are better elsewhere is lower in communities where the emigration rate is higher (11% or more of households with at least one member abroad). One plausible explanation is that if there are fewer competitors for jobs in the community, the motivation to emigrate for work-related reasons decreases.

Figure 7.2. **Emigrating for labour-related reasons is less common in communities where emigration rates are higher**

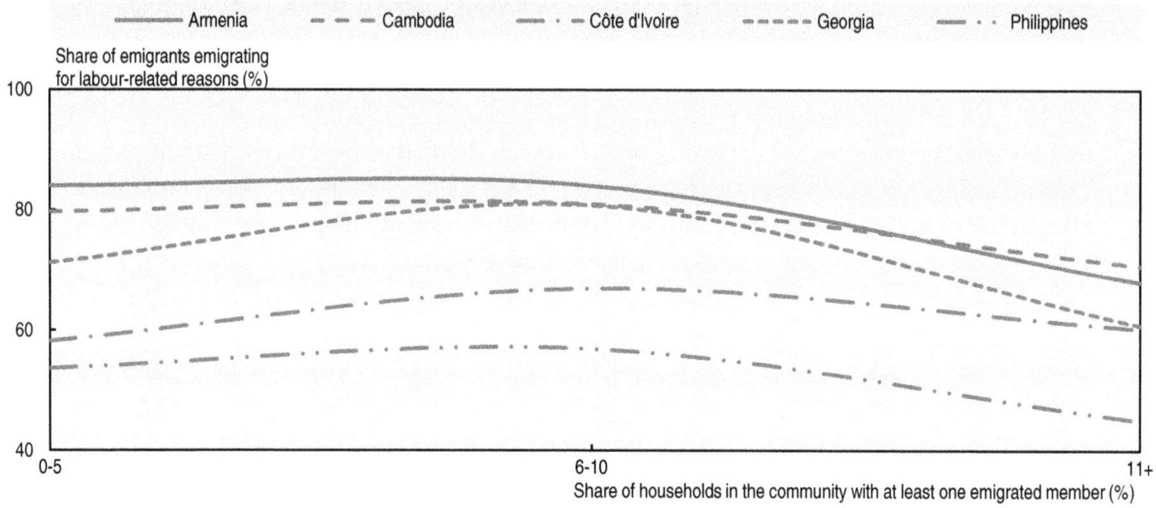

Note: The rate of community-level emigration was estimated by asking a community leader the share of households with at least one member living in another country. Respondents were given the chance to provide several reasons for emigrating, but only the first reason was taken into account.

Source: OECD (forthcoming), *Interrelations between Public Policies, Migration and Development*.

StatLink http://dx.doi.org/10.1787/888933422641

Remittances represent an important and stable source of capital for developing countries

The development potential of remittance flows into low- and middle-income countries has generated interest among policy makers in the past decades. More recently, the Addis Ababa Action Agenda and the Sustainable Development Goals acknowledged the role of remittances in harnessing development. These financial flows far exceed official development assistance, and remittances have often been shown to be more stable in times of economic turmoil compared with other foreign capital flows. Money sent by migrants has the potential to lift individuals and households out of poverty, and contribute to economic growth and human development in countries of origin.

Financial remittances help reduce poverty and spur investment

Remittances to developing countries have increased rapidly in recent years and are estimated to have reached USD 441 billion in 2015 (Figure 7.3). With 37% of total remittance flows, transfers from high-income to low- and middle-income countries make up the largest share, which is consistent with the fact that most migrants move from low- and middle-income to high-income countries. However, remittances between developing economies still represent 34% of all transfers (World Bank, 2016a).

Figure 7.3. **Remittances to developing countries far exceed official development assistance (ODA)**

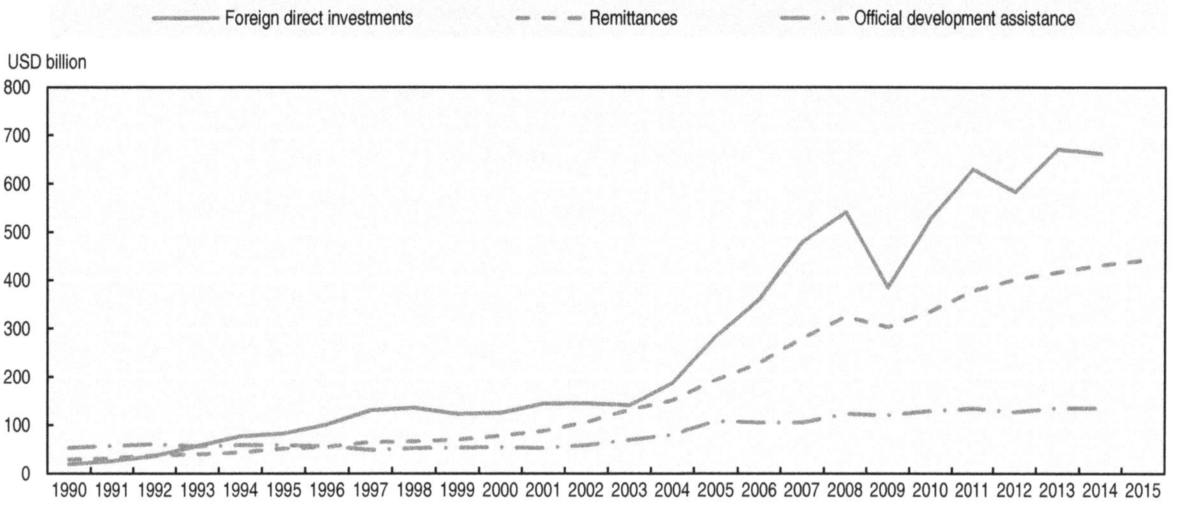

Source: World Bank (2016a), *Migration and Remittances Factbook 2016: Third Edition* and OECD (2016), *DAC International Development Statistics* (database), *www.oecd.org/dac/stats/idsonline.htm.*

StatLink http://dx.doi.org/10.1787/888933422652

Remittances can affect countries of origin both at the household and macroeconomic levels. From a macroeconomic perspective, remittances can increase a country's creditworthiness and thereby increase access to international capital markets,[2] which in turn can finance local development projects. The inflow of international remittances can also lead to more stable consumption and production levels (Ratha, 2007). These factors can benefit short- and long-term GDP growth.

At the household level, remittances have been shown to have positive effects on poverty reduction among households receiving them in the migrant's country of origin (Acosta et al., 2008; Adams and Page, 2005). Remittances reduce poverty by increasing household income, and can also help smooth household consumption and act as protection against the risks caused by weather-related shocks. In addition, remittances can have a positive impact on other economic and social development outcomes, such as investments in productive activities, human capital and health. The evidence regarding the impact of remittances on inequality is more mixed. If remittances are disproportionately received by better-off households, they might lead to an increase in inequality. Evidence from empirical studies suggests that the effects of remittances on inequality vary over time, leading to a decrease in inequality in the short term, but that the effect is limited in the long run (World Bank, 2006).

The effects of remittances on household expenditures and investments have been subject to some debate. While some studies show that households are more inclined to spend their remittances on daily consumption and consumption goods (Adams and Cuecuecha, 2010a; Chami, Fullenkamp and Jahjah, 2003), others argue that remittances lead to productive investments, such as investment in housing and business creation (Adams and Cuecuecha, 2010b; Woodruff and Zenteno, 2007; Yang, 2008). Studies from different regions have also shown that a substantial part of remittances is spent on the purchase of land. A World Bank study found that a significant proportion of remittances received by households in a number of African countries were spent on land purchases, investment in building a house and farm investments (Mohapatra and Ratha, 2011).

Data collected in the framework of the Interrelations between Public Policy, Migration and Development (IPPMD) project show that real-estate ownership is in general higher among households that receive remittances compared with households that do not (Figure 7.4).

Figure 7.4. **Share of households owning real estate is higher among households with remittances than households without remittances**

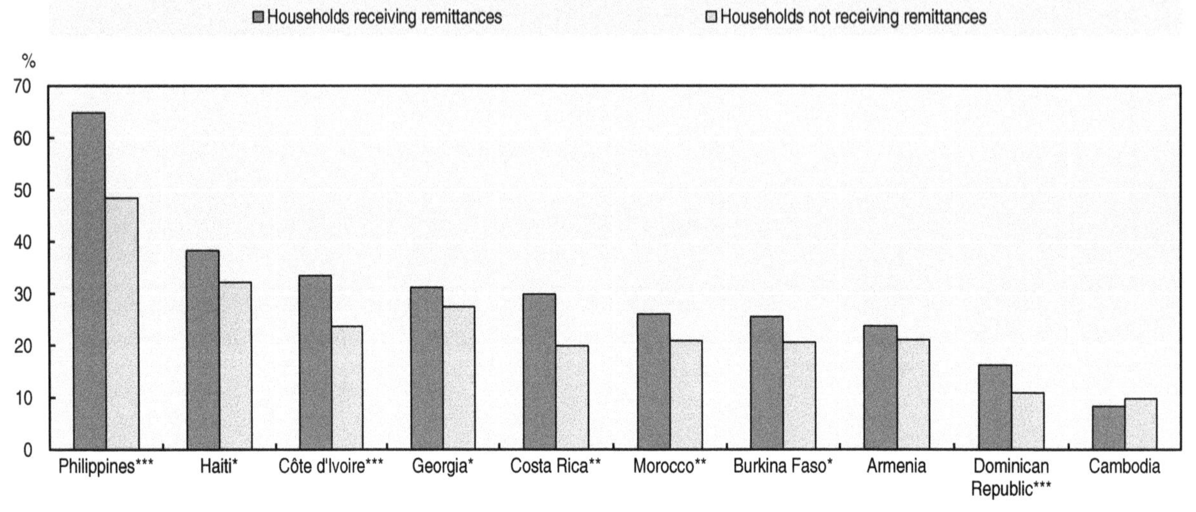

Note: Real estate includes non-agricultural land and/or housing other than housing used as accommodation by the household. Statistical significance calculated using a chi-squared test is indicated as follows: ***: 99%, **: 95%, *: 90%.

Source: OECD (forthcoming), *Interrelations between Public Policies, Migration and Development.*

StatLink http://dx.doi.org/10.1787/888933422667

Remittances may also affect investment in education and the educational outcomes of children in the countries from which migrants originate. Studies generally find that remittances reduce school dropout rates and increase the years of schooling of children in households that receive them (Adams, 2006; Cox-Edwards and Ureta 2003; Hanson and Woodruff, 2003; Yang, 2008).

IPPMD data show that households receiving remittances spend more on education than households not receiving remittances in five out of nine partner countries (Figure 7.5).

Migrants send not only money, but also social remittances

The term **"social remittances"** refers to the circulation of "ideas, behaviours, identities, and social capital that flow from receiving country to sending country community" (Levitt, 1998). Migrants are indeed exposed in their host country to different socio-political norms and values and to alternative media and institutional contexts. The new set of norms and values adopted by migrants can be transmitted directly (through returnees) and/or indirectly (through diaspora networks) to the country of origin. Social remittances can generate positive spillover effects, for instance through calls to halt corruption and participation in pacification processes, but also negative ones, as when they involve sending money to insurgent groups or reinforcing discriminatory social norms. One interesting case of social remittances is the indirect contribution of emigrants to changing demographic trends. Emigrants also play a role in bringing political changes through mitigation of corruption, lobbying and conflict resolution.

Figure 7.5. **Households receiving remittances spend more on education in a majority of the IPPMD countries**

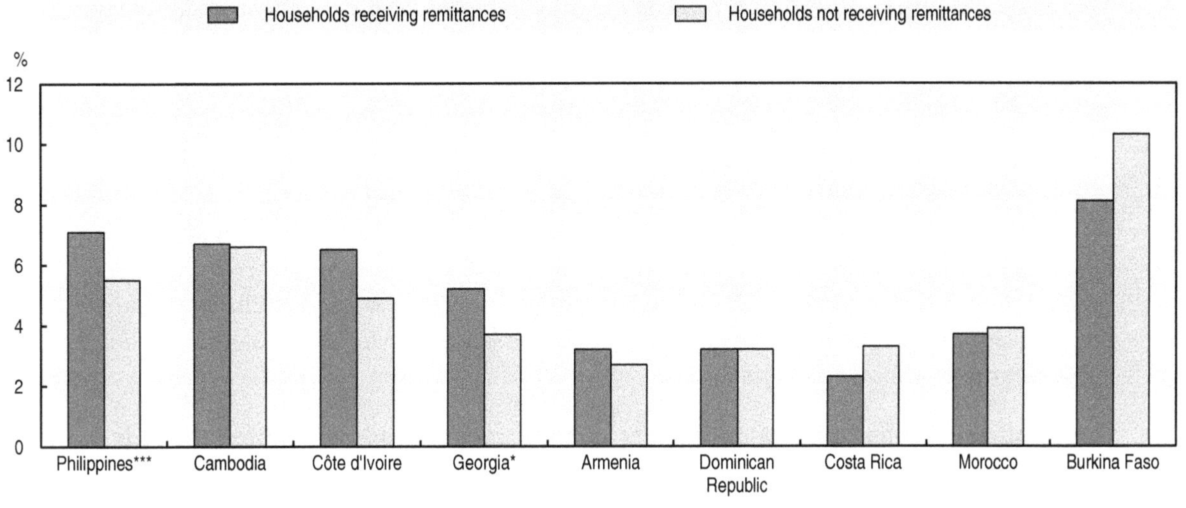

Note: The sample includes households with children of primary and secondary school age. Haiti is not included as the response rate was low for the expenditure questions. Statistical significance calculated using a chi-squared test is indicated as follows: ***: 99%, **: 95%, *: 90%.

Source: OECD (forthcoming), *Interrelations between Public Policies, Migration and Development.*

StatLink http://dx.doi.org/10.1787/888933422672

Changes in demographic behaviours. Pioneering work on social remittances focused on the impact of emigration on the fertility rates of the countries of origin. A comparison of birth rates in Egypt and Morocco shows that emigrants contribute to transferring the demographic behaviour from their receiving to their home country (Fargues, 1993, 1997). When migrants go to countries with low fertility rates, especially in Europe, families back home tend to adopt the same patterns, which translates into lower birth rates. By contrast, when migrants move to countries with high fertility rates, in particular Gulf countries, birth rates at home tend to increase. Such transfer of norms happens when migrants travel, or communicate with their families back home. Even though migrants' households are the first to be concerned, the circulation of foreign values and ideas also affects the rest of the community and has a direct impact on fertility as well as on marriage habits.

Lobbying and institutional changes. Social remittances can also refer to the implication of emigrants in the political situation of their home countries and their contribution to changing political behaviours. Their role is particularly important, even though sometimes ambiguous, in countries affected by conflicts.

The combined effects of financial and social remittances give migrants' families a voice at the negotiation table, hence fostering the integration of the families that have stayed behind into the national political community. Thus, political participation seems to be positively correlated with remittances (Tyburski, 2012). In particular, remittances tend to encourage family members back home to vote more frequently for opposition parties (Kurtz, 2004). It also appears that the higher the political participation of migrants in their host-states, the higher their involvement in home-state politics (Chaudary, 2016).

Diasporas have an ambivalent role in conflict zones. They can act in favour of democratisation and conflict resolution (Mohamoud, 2005) as much as they can support rebels, thereby contributing to perpetuating the conflict in the region. In terms of conflict resolution, emigrants are considered as having more legitimacy to intervene in the domestic policies of their nation states compared with other international actors (Cochrane, 2007). For conflict countries in Africa, it has been highlighted that diasporas play a great role not only in the pacification process, but also in post-conflict reconstruction (Turner 2008; Turner and Mossin, 2010). In some cases, however, emigrants may also be involved in conflicts by providing substantial resources to separatists' movements allowing insurgencies as it is the case for the Sikh and Tamil diasporas (Fair, 2005) through illegal fundraising (Wayland, 2004) or money extortion (La, 2004).

The transfer of social remittances, however, is not automatic. It depends on many factors, such as migrants' interactions with the host society and origin country society, migrants' status and influence in home country, return migrants' connections with former host country networks and access to host country's media, and their situation on return (e.g. voluntary or forced return).

Emigration can have a brain-gain effect by encouraging those left behind to study longer, hence increasing the stock of human capital

While many people see the international migration of the tertiary-educated as a brain drain, emigration may actually translate into a rise in education levels. Known as the "brain gain", such a phenomenon is the consequence of people in the home country wanting to emigrate. Individuals left in the home country may seek to increase their education and skills levels to increase their chances of emigrating as well. However, as not all individuals will do so, the general education level in the home country will increase. Evidence using a cross section of countries shows that the "brain gain" hypothesis holds for countries with low levels of emigration and education (Beine, Docquier and Rapoport, 2008). Micro-evidence suggests that such a mechanism is indeed possible. Following the change in the educational requirement for recruitment to the British Gurkha military forces in Nepal in 1993, which contributed to increasing that group's emigration rate, the general investment in human capital of the Gurkha community increased despite a limit in the number of job opportunities with the army (Shrestha, 2011).

Diasporas represent a huge development potential for the countries of origin

The term diaspora can bear different meanings, depending on the angle from which the subject is approached. In policy circles, diaspora often refers to groups of migrants and their ongoing relationship with their community of origin – normally the home country (Sharma et al., 2011). The relationship with the home country can be material (e.g. remittances), as well as taking the form of professional, sociocultural and identity ties maintained over the distance (Ratha and Plaza, 2011). Different diasporas display different degrees of organisation, be it in the host country or the country of origin. They can take the form of cultural associations, hometown associations, professional or interest networks that are often transnational in nature and therefore cut across the host/home country divide.

Diasporas can also organise themselves through the use of information and communication technologies and activate their political, social, cultural and knowledge capital in this way (Brinkerhoff, 2009). Their engagement and contribution towards development in the communities or countries of origin has been at the forefront of current policy thinking and the effort of establishing practical guides of action for diaspora-focused policies and programmes (Agunias and Newland, 2012).

In this respect, diaspora strategies are designed to win support from expatriates and extend networks, especially in the field of science and technology where networks are of vital importance. The local component is particularly important, as it allows the diaspora to focus on projects that are closer to home.

Migrants' philanthropy contributes to financing local development projects or rebuilding countries

Collective remittances refer to migrant communities' channelling remittances to their hometowns from their places of settlement places. In this case, hometown associations (HTAs) maintain bonds of solidarity between group members (Levitt, 2001). They have been qualified in the literature as transnational communities forging transnational networks and spaces. Their activities consist in, among other things, paving roads and improving housing and village electrification.

Nepal is a good instance of how diasporas can play a key role in helping the countries of origin. After the April 2015 earthquake, diaspora organisations rapidly channelled funds to Nepal. This financial and human contribution was made possible by a diaspora that was already well organised and by the quick implementation of fund-raising campaigns in host countries. Following the earthquake, a new diaspora organisation named NEVRHA (Nepal Earthquake Victims Research and Help Association) sponsored by the Nepali embassy was created in Japan, with the goal of combining organisations' resources. However, data confirm that funds were mainly channelled by the organisations themselves. This example suggests a complementarity between grassroots and governmental initiatives and it recalls how migrants like to control the way their money is being used.

Diaspora investments in origin countries increasingly rely on innovative financing mechanisms

Diasporas can contribute to their home-country development through different innovative financing mechanisms, such as microfinance, long-distance entrepreneurship and diaspora bonds.

Microfinance: the case of the Philippines. Created in 1994 on the return of two overseas Filipino workers, the New Rural Bank of San Leonardo (NRSBL) is a finance institution that provides loans to overseas Filipinos and their relatives (Opiniano and Rispens-Noel, 2015). To develop micro-finance, NRBSL calculates the loan with regard to the client's economic and social situation to reduce the risk of payment default. In exchange, borrowers commit themselves to maintain their businesses within the locality. Another way for NRBSL to assure repayment is to select loan candidates based on the merits of the loan application. Other criteria are also taken into account: the regularity of the remittances, their borrower's wealth and their administrative status overseas: when migrants do not have a regular status in respect of the host-country administration, the bank does not lend money to their families. This procedure reflects the hardening of conditions of entry and residence in most developed countries. It limits the investment capacity of undocumented workers and probably postpones their project of return.

Long-distance entrepreneurship. Diaspora investments result from transnational social networks (of migrants). As non-pecuniary interests are assumed to lead to these investments, it is claimed that diaspora investments are lasting and independent from the national political and economic context. In this sense they differ from foreign direct investment (FDI).

Diaspora-owned firms represent a significant weight of FDI. A recent study showed that 17% of foreign-owned firms in Georgia belong to diaspora members (Graham, 2014). Nonetheless, diaspora-owned firms are not only driven by non-pecuniary motivations: "diaspora-owned firms are more likely than other foreign firms to report keeping their total labour costs as low as possible" and are slightly less likely to "report devoting resources to socially responsible employment practices". But they do prioritise local labour.

Many countries (for instance, Armenia, China, Lebanon and South Korea) are involved in leveraging development through diaspora business networks (Kitchin and Boyle 2011). Thus, the World Korean Business Convention promotes South Korea's exports by creating business linkages with its diaspora. Likewise, in Armenia, the National Competitiveness Foundation and the Enterprise Incubator Foundation, a joint initiative of the World Bank and the Armenian government, count on diaspora organisations such as *Armenia 2020* to encourage investments (Chen et al., 2015).

Diaspora bonds. Diaspora bonds are not new. Israel has raised them almost since its creation. They consist of a debt instrument to raise funds from the overseas diaspora (Chander, 2001; Ratha and Ketkar, 2010). They enable developing countries to borrow from their citizens and diaspora communities abroad at a very attractive rate for the borrower, thanks to loans form the diaspora that are driven by feelings of altruism. In this way Israel has benefited to the tune of USD 25 billion to develop basic infrastructure projects such as transport, water supply, energy, and so on.

Diaspora bonds have been issued by many countries, mostly in Israel (raising over USD 25 billion since 1951) and India (raising over USD 11 billion through the State Bank of India), but also in other developing countries such as Eritrea, Ethiopia, Ghana, Lebanon, Nepal (which developed an infrastructure development bond), Pakistan, the Philippines and Sri Lanka (Akkoyunlu and Stern 2012). Not much is known, however, about how governments use these bonds.

Critics make two points questioning the bonds. In the first place, financial expertise is limited and high political risks can act as a deterrent to the issuance of bonds of this nature. In Ethiopia, for instance, they did not manage to attract diaspora investors because of the perception of high political risk (Ratha and Plaza 2011). Secondly, the risk of issuing bonds beyond the ability of the state to reimburse is high, as no means of control exist. One potential option to remedy this problem would be to adopt "growth-indexed bonds" (Ratha and Ketkar, 2009).

Return migrants bring financial, human and social capital back to their countries of origin

The financial, human and social resources that return migrants accumulated in destination countries can help spur development in countries of origin.

Returnees are more likely to engage in entrepreneurial activities than those who stay behind

Return migrants can invest in business start-ups and self-employment on their return. Savings accumulated abroad can eliminate credit problems and be used as a resource for establishing businesses. Returnees intending to engage in own-account work and entrepreneurial activities in their country of origin are also more likely to acquire higher savings abroad. Entrepreneurship and self-employment upon return might be integral parts of any employment strategies building on migration.

On the other hand, such activities may also represent the last resort, especially for those unprepared to return, or those whose skills do not match the labour market needs of the country (Mezger Kveder and Flahaux, 2013). Employment in the country of destination, as well as that before actual emigration, (in particular experience in business investment, or with status as an employer) make it more likely that migrants will start entrepreneurial activities upon return (Gubert and Nordman, 2011; Hamdouch and Wahba, 2012).

There is growing evidence suggesting that return migrants are more likely to engage in entrepreneurial activities or own-account work (Ammassari, 2004; De Vreyer, Gubert and Robilliard, 2010). IPPMD data point in the same direction, as illustrated in Figure 7.6. Although no causal relationship can be established, the figure shows that households with returnees are more likely to run businesses than households without return migrants, with the exceptions of Cambodia, Costa Rica and Côte d'Ivoire. Most businesses, however, employ only family members or close relatives because of limitations arising from the scale and sectors of business established.

Figure 7.6. **Business ownership is higher in households with return migrants than households without return migrants in a majority of the countries**

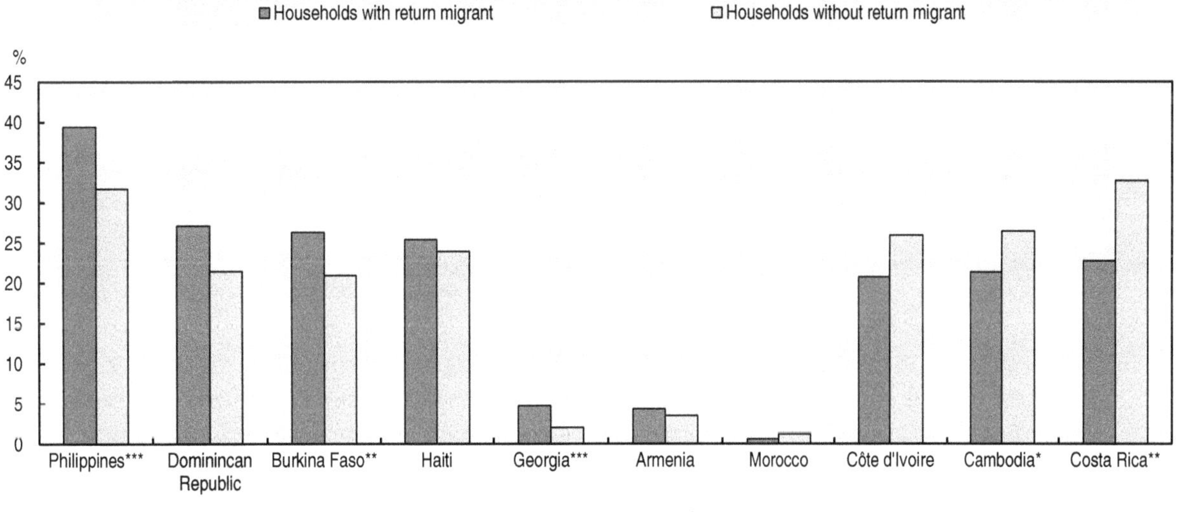

Note: Statistical significance calculated using a chi-squared test is indicated as follows: ***: 99%, **: 95%, *: 90%.

Source: OECD (forthcoming), *Interrelations between Public Policies, Migration and Development.*

StatLink http://dx.doi.org/10.1787/888933422682

Social norms also play a role in entrepreneurial activities that are undertaken by return migrants, in particular when it comes to female returnees. The prevailing notion that entrepreneurship is an activity for men, and the cultural constraints that accompany it, mean that a low proportion of women returnees are involved in entrepreneurial activities (Chitsike, 2000, Kilic et al., 2009). Furthermore, female entrepreneurs usually operate in a narrow range of sectors, mostly traditional ones, and tend to be the "invisible entrepreneurs" (Liedholm, 2002). This factor may have only a limited impact on the labour market with the creation of fewer jobs.

The skills and knowledge accumulated abroad by return migrants help increase the stock of human capital in countries of origin

Better educated return migrants contribute to human capital gains in the countries of origin and reduce the potential negative loss in terms of human capital caused by emigration (OECD, 2008). In this respect, migration experience abroad contributes to the improvement in educational levels and skills. Figure 7.7 shows that return migrants tend to be better educated than non-migrants, with the exception of Burkina Faso, Cambodia and Morocco where education levels in general are significantly lower than in the other countries. Return migrants' higher level of educational attainment might be due to the initial positive emigration selection, or to multiple educational or training enrolments abroad, or a combination of both.

Figure 7.7. **Return migrants tend to be better educated in most countries**

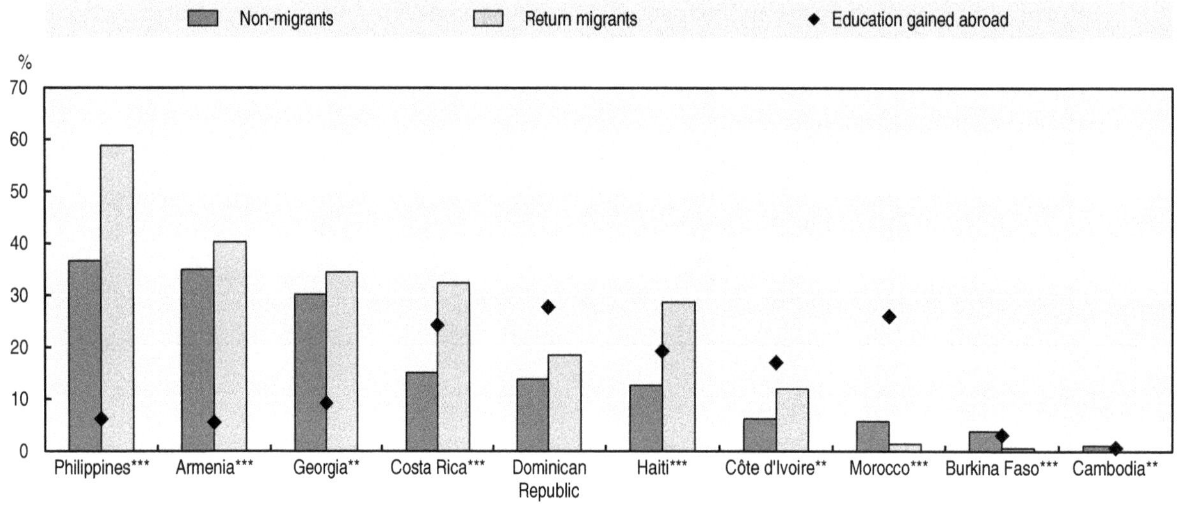

Source: OECD (forthcoming), *Interrelations between Public Policies, Migration and Development.*

StatLink http://dx.doi.org/10.1787/888933422695

Returning professionals equipped with technological, managerial, marketing or scientific competencies often create new companies, transfer knowledge and increase the human capital stock. In the Chinese private sector, return migrants have applied their international experience to make businesses more competitive and innovative. More than 20 000 returnees worked in over 8 000 start-ups established in China within the National Returnee Entrepreneurial Parks and a high share of the Chinese companies listed on the NASDAQ are founded or managed by returnees (Wang, 2012).

To harness fully the returnees' sets of skills and knowledge acquired abroad, the portability of skills (that is, skills that can be productively used across jobs, occupations and industries) plays an important role. It influences the employment status and the wage premium of return migrants. If skills are not portable from the destination country to the country of origin, that non-portability might lead to unemployment, whether registered or unregistered, or to the sole possibility of part-time employment (Calenda, 2014; CODEV-EPFL et al., 2013). Skills mismatch or over-qualification might mean that return migrants would have to wait before rejoining the labour market.

Return migrants also help transform social norms in their home communities

One of the effects of migration, and particularly of return migration, resulting from the physical presence of migrants back in the country of origin is the transformation of norms. Return migrants help shape the public discourse, transform the local environment and question traditional approaches. However, their actual influence is based on their individual characteristics, migration experience and the size of the return migrants' community in the local area.

Return migrants tend to have an influence on electoral behaviour and engagement at the local political level as well as an effect on the political engagement of non-migrants. Migration experience might influence political attitudes and the behaviour of return migrants both positively and negatively, when the values of return migrants before their actual emigration and after return are compared. Within the complex group of return migrants, students studying abroad may form an influential group, transferring democratic values upon return, but only if they spent their studies in a democratic country (Spilimbergo, 2009). Furthermore, a spillover effect appears towards non-migrants; in other words, the presence of return migrants tends to increase the electoral participation of non-migrants (Waddell and Fontenla, 2015) as well as to alter electoral behaviour within communities (Chauvet and Mercier, 2014). Furthermore, experience abroad leading to a higher exposure to different religious, social or political norms helps enhance tolerance towards diversity by comparison with non-migrants (Pérez-Armendáriz and Crow, 2009).

The contribution of return migration to development in the countries of origin is largely subject to the portability of the resources that returnees acquire in the country of destination. This implies that development potential can be limited if return migration occurs as a consequence of failed migration where accumulation of any sort of capital might have been obstructed. The resources brought back by returnees have to be applicable in the countries of origin. If countries of origin have less favourable environments for the resources to be transferred and used, the possible contribution of return migration may be diminished.

Return in the contexts of the aftermaths of conflicts can be understood in this context. The development potential of return migration may be more ambiguous in post-conflict environments, as migrants do not automatically contribute to development and peacebuilding when they are challenged to re-establish their lives in the post-conflict areas (van Houte, 2014). There can be several reasons. Refugees who return to their country of origin need to reintegrate into a context that may be very different from the country they left behind. There may be resentment and hostility towards them from the people who stayed. Countries may not have the capacity to absorb large numbers of returnees, especially to integrate them into the labour market, and local communities may have limited resources and a lack of experience for the reintegration of those returned.

On the other hand, returning refugees may consist of the most educated people, with potential to rebuild education systems in the countries affected by conflicts (IBRD and World Bank, 2005). Whether migrants are willing and able to contribute to development can depend on whether they remain "mobile" after their return (i.e. whether they have a legal status in the country of destination that gives them the option to leave their country of origin again). In spite of the complexity of human factors influencing the development potential of returnees, voluntary return and sustainable reintegration have to be supported at the national level. Commitment to the sustainability of return of Afghan refugees at the governmental level translated into higher numbers of Afghans returning from abroad in the first half of 2015 compared with 2014, strengthening the core of returnees able to help enhance both financial and human capital.

But emigration can come with economic, human and social costs

The effects of emigration are very ambiguous and sometimes difficult to identify. For instance, it might be the consequence of sustained economic growth rates, which mean people are wealthier and can afford to move abroad. But the correlation between economic growth and the increase in emigration might be interpreted in a different way; that is, the increase in emigration rates is the *cause* of the economic growth. Similarly, problems of productivity in the agricultural sector might be seen as the consequence of emigration, while they might actually be the cause. This is why it is important to be careful when analysing the potential costs or benefits of emigration. Yet, the empirical evidence makes it possible to draw some lessons on the effects of migration in the countries of origin. The main costs are related to the labour shortages, the negative impact in terms of human capital and the social repercussions of emigration, especially for those left behind.

Emigration and remittances can generate labour shortages

While most migrants go abroad to find better job opportunities, their absence can have mixed effects on the labour market of their home countries. Certainly, emigration can help relieve pressures on the labour market and translate into higher wages and more employment opportunities for those who stay behind. Yet it is not always possible to replace the departed labour force, partly because emigrants might have skills that are not easily replaced and partly because labour market institutions do not work in an efficient way, in particular in rural areas. In addition, the households that receive remittances might have fewer incentives to work, especially when the amounts received are high compared to local current salaries.

Emigrant households may face a problem of "lost labour", especially in rural areas

The immediate effect of emigration on the labour market is manifested at the household level. The subtraction of what is typically a working-age contributing member usually alters the behaviour of the household, at least in the short term. The extent to which the household is affected by this "lost labour" depends on who leaves and what the migrant was doing before leaving. The departed member could have been contributing to the household's well-being in a number of ways by, for example, working many hours, taking care of children, managing the family business or doing heavy manual labour tasks, all of which must be compensated for in different ways.

In the poorest countries, where economic decisions are typically pooled, the loss of a contributing member implies either a reduction in output or an increase in labour supply to maintain the same levels of output. The drop in production and income from the household may also push its members towards jobs they would normally not accept. Members remaining in the household may thus be obliged to spend more time in unpaid work, as there are fewer adults in the household (Carletto and Mendola, 2009), in particular taking over the household duties of the departed members (Görlich, Toman and Trebesch, 2007) including child-rearing (Acosta, 2006; Sadiqi and Ennaji, 2004). In extreme cases, the loss of labour in the household may force households to make their children work, at the expense of their education, when mothers (Sarma and Parinduri, 2016) and fathers (Antman, 2011) leave. The lost-labour effect is reinforced by the fact that emigrants leave during the most productive years of their life.

The extent of the lost-labour effect depends on both the levels of income and skills of the emigrant households. In most cases, it is the poorest households, those with members with lower or mid-education levels that suffer the labour loss the hardest. In these households, contributing household members typically work in labour-intensive jobs, often informally, and the income they bring back to the household constitutes its lifeline.

Whether the household lies in a rural or urban region will also affect the impact of the departed member, particularly for agricultural households, where production and consumption are tightly linked (Benjamin, 1992). In such households, the loss of a contributing member is even stronger, since a change in production will equate to a change in consumption. Such a change can push households at subsistence levels further into poverty.

Women in agricultural households are particularly affected by the loss of labour. Evidence from internal migration in China reveals that there is a lost-labour effect manifested through increased farm labour by women when men leave, but not when women depart. This suggests that Chinese men are likely to be the ones working in the fields when they are home, but that women take over those tasks when men are away working elsewhere in the country (Mu and van de Walle, 2011; Démurger and Shi, 2012).

There is also evidence that women in emigrant households have moved to take over tasks traditionally held by men, after the men leave to work in other countries (Sadiqi and Ennaji, 2004; Wouterse, 2010). Where there are children or elderly people in the household, child-rearing and help for the old can be factors in how households reorganise their labour. In a household with a high dependency ratio (the ratio of children and elderly to those of working age living in the household) household members must spend time tending to their needs as opposed to working for an income. Tasks may be specific to skills or genders. Agricultural households may need to change the type of crop they grow or the livestock they raise, as a function of the skills and labour intensity required.

The effect of a loss of labour because of emigration is probably more visible in rural areas, where the ablest workers move to work elsewhere and the elderly and young stay behind. Such a situation can lead to a food shortage in countries where productivity in rural areas is a factor in the country's primary food source. When many young workers leave, there may be fewer workers left behind to tend to the fields, leading to a drop in output. In areas that are poor, badly connected or without working credit markets, the drop in agricultural labour force can directly affect the available food and resources in the community (Cissé and Daum, 2010; Wouterse, 2010).

The problem of food security is a good illustration of the fact that the labour market impact of emigration reaches much further than the household. If large numbers emigrate there are repercussions for the country and for the communities which they leave. This implies generalised changes for the social and economic climate of the country, including for households without any direct link to migration. In this respect, the effect of emigration on a country extends far beyond losing its best and brightest. Emigration reduces the factors of production of the country, thus altering its economic potential to grow.

Remittances tend to reduce labour supply

While remittances provide financial support to their recipients, they also contribute to reducing labour supply. Remittances can indeed act as a substitute for labour income and therefore increase the "reservation wage" – the minimum wage at which individuals are willing to accept to work in a given job – of the members of a beneficiary household, thus reducing their incentives to work. In this respect, the empirical evidence tends to identify a negative impact of remittances on the labour supply (Acosta, 2007; Airola, 2008; Jadotte, 2009; Mora, 2010).

This phenomenon can be amplified by the asymmetry of information between the household members that send remittances and those who receive them. While remitters cannot control the way remittances are used, receivers have an interest in making remittance flows as permanent as possible. By working less, remittance recipients remain eligible to benefit from future transfers. Such effect has been found in the Kayes region of Mali, where the decrease in labour supply also translated into a drop in agricultural productivity (Azam and Gubert, 2005).

However, the decrease in labour supply arising from remittances can also be related to the positive impact of financial transfers in terms of poverty reduction (OECD, 2011):

- Remittances may encourage household members to create their own businesses. But since self-employment and micro-enterprises are often considered as informal, the transition from formal (but badly remunerated) to informal (but with relatively higher benefits) activities appears in surveys as a decrease in labour supply.
- Remittances can contribute to increasing productivity and efficiency in small companies, thus allowing households to reduce the number of hours worked.
- Remittances are often used to invest in education. Some members of the household can thus make the transition from work to school. This is the case of children who were forced to go to work to help the family, but also of adults who decided to go back to school and improve their skills.

Overall, the downward effect of remittances on labour supply is not always negative for the country. First, the decision of opting out of the labour market is an individual choice based on personal or household preferences. Remittance recipients should not be blamed for that. Then, the decrease in labour supply often reflects changes in household behaviours and patterns: from formal to informal, from low- to high-productive or from labour to educational activities. That does not mean that policy makers should not care about these effects, above all when they are coupled with problems of lost labour. Agricultural activities, in particular, might suffer from labour shortages, thus affecting the productivity of the sector and even raising food security concerns.

The emigration of the tertiary-educated can have adverse effects on human capital

The migration of highly educated individuals towards countries offering better opportunities to the detriment of the countries of origin, in particular those that are developing, is often called the brain drain. Such terminology, however, is subject to a number of criticisms, especially for the negative implications it infers. This does not change the reality that several countries, especially the poorest, register high emigration rates for their tertiary-educated citizens and that this phenomenon might be damaging to their human capital.

For several decades now, debate has raged on whether emigration is fair for developing economies that are unable to compete with the good and stable high paying jobs in richer countries. The argument backing unfairness is that developing countries spend their already scarce resources to pay for the education of their citizens, but do not benefit directly from their investment.

Figure 7.8 presents the emigration rate of the tertiary-educated for the top 15 countries in 2010 (Arslan et al., 2014). With three out of four tertiary-educated students going abroad, Haiti is the country with the highest emigration rate of the tertiary-educated (75.1%). Zimbabwe (43.6%) and Congo (37.4%) also record very high emigration rates of the tertiary-educated. They are followed by Sierra Leone (32.7%), Honduras (32.2%) and Albania (31.3%).

Figure 7.8. **Small and poor countries have the highest emigration rate of tertiary-educated people (2010-11)**

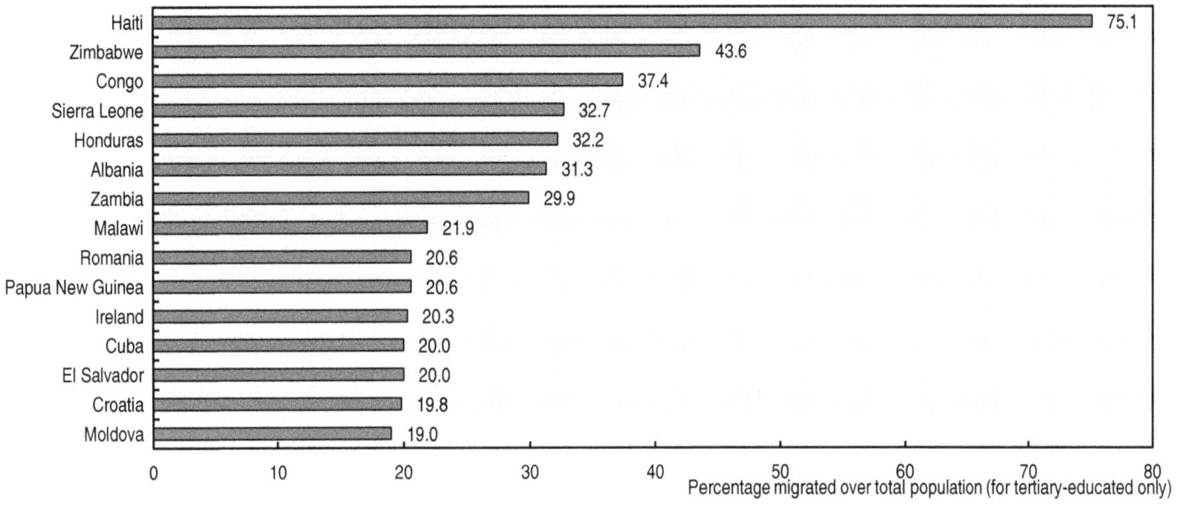

Note: The emigration rate of tertiary-educated is the proportion the tertiary-educated who emigrated to OECD countries as a percentage of the total population of the tertiary-educated in their native country.

Source: Arslan et al. (2014), "A new profile of migrants in the aftermath of the recent economic crisis", *OECD Social, Employment and Migration Working Papers*, No. 160, *http://dx.doi.org/10.1787/5jxt2t3nnjr5-en*.

StatLink http://dx.doi.org/10.1787/888933422700

Only two out of the top 15 countries are high-income countries: Croatia and Ireland. Five countries belong to the low-income category: The Republic of Congo, Haiti, Malawi, Sierra Leone and Zimbabwe; five others to the lower-middle-income group: El Salvador, Honduras, Moldova, Papua New Guinea and Zambia; and three are upper-middle-income countries: Albania, Cuba and Romania. With five countries in the list, Africa is overrepresented among the top 15 countries with high emigration rates of the tertiary-educated. This reflects the fact that this continent registers the highest emigration rates of the highly educated (9.6%), followed by Latin America (7.6%), Europe (5.8%), Oceania (5.2%) and Asia (3.4%). Overall, low-income countries recorded in 2010/11 the highest emigration rates of the tertiary-educated: 7.1%, compared to 5.6% and 4.5%, respectively, in lower-middle-income and upper-middle-income countries.

The emigration of the tertiary-educated can have a negative impact on origin countries, especially the smallest and poorest, where the size of the educated base is small. The effect is most visible for key skills linked with well-being, such as those in the medical field. In 2006, the World Health Organization defined a medical sector as being in critical shortage where there were fewer than 22.8 health professionals per 10 000 people and where fewer than 80% of childbirths were attended by skilled professionals. The number of countries that were deemed to be in critical shortage fell only slightly between 2000/01 and 2010/11, from 57 to 54, 31 of them in Africa (OECD, 2015). The shortage is equivalent to 2.8 million health workers.

In the long term, the emigration of the tertiary-educated could lead governments to reduce their investment in education, especially at the tertiary level. The incentives to invest in human capital tend indeed to decrease as educated people leave their countries and go to work in countries with higher incomes. The long-term negative effect induced by high rates of tertiary-educated emigration is likely to affect more particularly the poorest countries, where budget constraints increase the opportunity cost of investing in tertiary education. In practice though, there is no direct evidence of any causal relationship between the emigration rates of the highly skilled and government spending on tertiary education.

Emigration can also generate social costs

Beyond the potential economic costs in terms of labour shortages and human capital, emigration also affects social behaviours and can represent a social cost not only for the migrants themselves, either in the destination country or when they return home, but also the families left behind.

The absence of a family member has a cost for those left-behind, especially children

Emigration can affect the social dimensions of the household. The loss of a family member imposes a psychological cost on it, commonly referred to as family disintegration. Spouses, children and siblings are separated, adding to the stress of emigrating to a new country. According to the data shown in Figure 7.9, the proportion of emigrants with children left in the country of origin varies widely from 17% in Georgia to 82% in Burkina Faso, but this is correlated with the level of development in the country. The three countries with the highest rates of emigrants with children left in the country of origin are also the three countries with the lowest Human Development Index (HDI). The exception is the Philippines, with a relatively high HDI but also a high rate of emigrants with children in the home country, where the issue of left-behind children is particularly acute (Reyes, 2007). In 2005, approximately 10% to 20% of all children in the Philippines had a parent overseas, compared to 2% to 3% in Indonesia and Thailand (Bryant, 2005).

Figure 7.9. **The proportion of emigrants with children left in the country of origin is highest in poor countries**

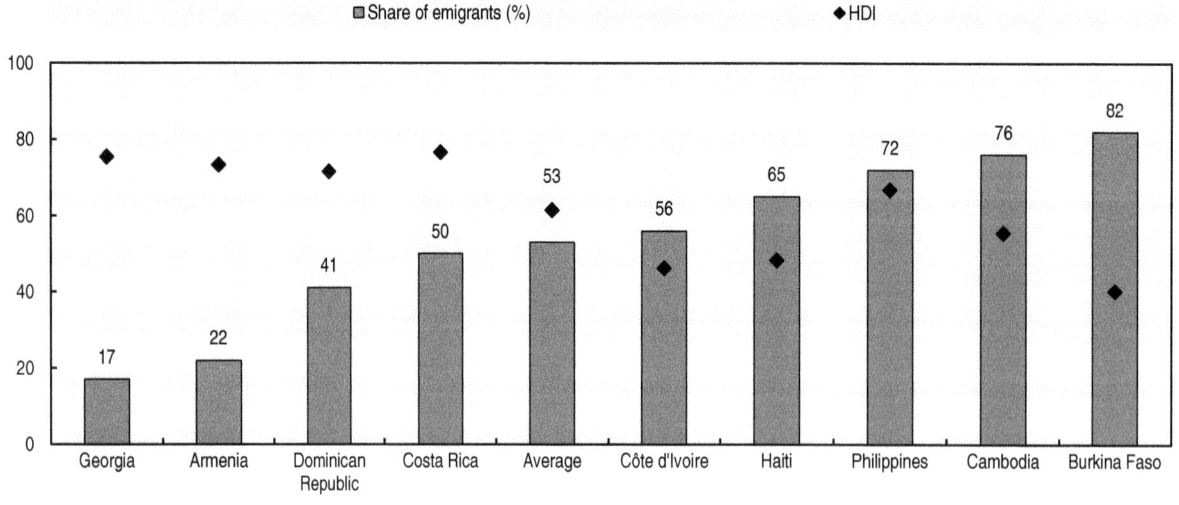

Note: Because of data limitations, the sample only includes emigrants who are heads of their households and their spouses. Emigrants that are children of household heads, for instance, are not included even though they may have children of their own. They should therefore not be interpreted as actual rates of children left behind by migrant parents.

Source: OECD (forthcoming), *Interrelations between Public Policies, Migration and Development.*

StatLink http://dx.doi.org/10.1787/888933422714

The literature on transnational families tends to regard children as a vulnerable group (Mazzucato, Siegel and Vanore, 2014). Even though there is no consensus on this issue, recent research shows that the absence of a parent can damage a child's social and psychological development (Yanovich, 2015). Children living in households with pressures on labour because of emigration may be sent out to work, at the expense of irreversible lost time at school. The loss of labour income in the household, in the short term, may make schooling unaffordable. Evidence also points to children left behind by emigrant parents being more likely to experience deteriorating academic performance, declining attendance and a lack of motivation (Castañeda and Buck, 2011). In Moldova, 22% of children whose parents are emigrants do not attend school, and many develop health concerns including drug use, as they may not seek help when it is needed (Yanovich, 2015).

Reintegration is more challenging when return is a consequence of failed migration

The contribution of return migrants to development in their countries of origin is largely a function of the portability of the resources that returnees acquired in the country of destination. This implies that development potential can be limited if return migration occurs as a consequence of failed migration where accumulation of any sort of capital might have been obstructed. Once the resources are brought home with returnees, they have to be applicable in the countries of origin. If countries of origin have less favourable environments for the resources to be transferred and used, the possible contribution of return migration may be diminished.

The development potential of return migration may be particularly ambiguous in post-conflict environments, as migrants face a number of challenges to re-establish their lives in post-conflict areas (van Houte, 2014). This could be for several reasons:

- Refugees who return to their country of origin need to reintegrate into a dynamic context that may be very different from that in the country they left behind.
- There may be resentment and hostility towards them from people who stayed.
- Countries may not have the capacity to absorb large numbers of returnees, especially to integrate them into the labour market.
- Local communities may have limited resources and a lack of experience for the re-integration of returnees.

Finally, return migrants could also have social costs to the community level through a negative process of transfer of norms. As such a transfer is influenced both by the country of origin and destination, there is a risk that returnees bring back with them discriminatory patterns of behaviour to the household and more widely to countries with lower levels of discriminatory measures. For instance, returnees to Jordan from more conservative Arab countries tend to display a higher degree of tolerance of gender inequalities, thereby increasing discriminatory practices in respect of women (Tuccio and Wahba, 2015).

The impact of migration on development depends upon the policies in place

Even though migration can have some negative effects for the countries of origin, most empirical studies show that the benefits of emigration are usually higher than the costs. However, the positive contribution of international migration to the development of the countries of origin can also turn into a poverty trap. While the departure of a significant proportion of the workforce helps relieve the pressure on the labour market, remittances provide an informal social safety net to beneficiary households. As a result, governments in emigration countries do not always have the incentives to reform labour markets and social welfare systems. This poverty trap phenomenon can explain why some countries prefer to develop policies that encourage part of the labour force to work abroad instead of instituting active labour policies in their own countries. The strong dependence of some developing economies on remittances also represents a problem when these financial flows drop sharply as was the case during the 2008/09 global economic crisis.

Yet the emigration poverty trap is not inevitable. Many developing countries have managed to capitalise on migration and remittance flows and turn them into an important development tool. To do so, it is important that policy makers in origin countries adopt policies that help the families of those left behind as well as migrants' communities and the country itself to make the most of emigration. In this perspective, governments need not only to adopt migration-related development policies, but also to take into account the different effects of sectoral development policies on migration, by integrating better the different dimensions of migration into their strategies.

Origin countries need to adopt targeted policies to minimise the costs of emigration and maximise its benefits

Most countries of origin trying to build a strategy based on migration tend to focus on the positive effects of emigration and remittances, but forget the negative side. One reason is probably that it is easier to target the migrants themselves as well as recipients of remittances than those negatively affected by emigration, in particular rural households suffering from lost labour and children left behind.

To reduce the negative effects of emigration, it is important to have a strategy oriented towards those who stay behind

Policy makers in origin countries need to understand who is particularly affected by the emigration process and adjust their policies according to their needs:

- **Potential migrants** need better to understand the risks of migrating without documents, of being victims of human trafficking and of leaving their children with other people. National and local authorities can carry out information campaigns in the media as well as in schools to make people aware of such risks.
- **Family members staying behind and those in charge of migrants' children** also deserve special attention. Policy makers can provide legal, social and financial assistance to households with absent parents, as it is the case with the Philippines and Sri Lanka, and psychological support can be offered to help those who stay behind and suffer from mental health issues and depression.

Countries of origin have developed many tools aimed at lowering the costs of remittances and channelling them towards productive investment

Policy makers can play an important role in enhancing the positive impacts of remittances by making these transactions less costly and enabling remittances to be used in more productive ways. An important step towards maximising the benefits of remittances was taken with the adoption of the 2015 Addis Ababa Action Agenda. The agenda includes commitments to ensure that adequate and affordable financial services are available to migrants and their families in countries of origin and destination, and that they can benefit from financial literacy and inclusion.

Certainly remittances are private sources of funding, and policy makers cannot decide how individuals and households spend their money. However, public policies can play an important role in creating an enabling environment that helps migrants and recipients of remittances to maximise the sending and the use of remittances. Such policy action can go through three main channels:

- the **decision to send remittances** or not
- the **amount and frequency** of remittances sent
- the **use of remittances**.

Policy efforts to promote and enhance the development potential of remittances mainly focus on lowering the costs of remittances though increased competition among service providers and changes in regulatory frameworks, expanding financial literacy, fostering financial inclusion among migrants and remittance-recipients, and expanding service provision to make services more available.

The high costs of sending remittances have been one of the main areas of policy intervention. Initiatives to lower these costs, such as technology improvements through on-line and mobile money transfer systems, have been adopted in both sending and receiving countries. As a result, the average global costs of sending remittances decreased by about 2.2 percentage points between 2009 and 2015 (Figure 7.10). The cost of sending USD 200 was about 7.4% in the third quarter of 2015. Costs vary largely across regions, however. Certain regions and remittance corridors still experience very high costs, in particular sub-Saharan Africa. The average cost in the region is about 10%, with certain corridors, such as South Africa to Zambia and Botswana, and Tanzania to Rwanda and Uganda, facing costs above 17% (World Bank, 2016b).

Figure 7.10. **Overall remittance costs have fallen by approximately 2 percentage points since 2009, but costs vary greatly across regions**

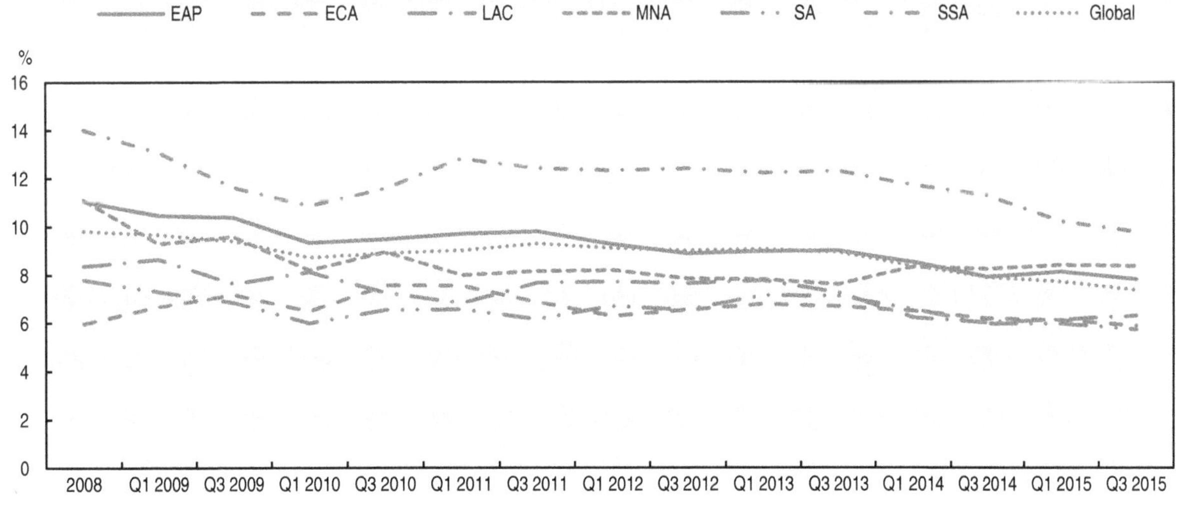

Note: The regions in the figure include: East Asia and Pacific (EAP), Eastern and Central Asia (ECA), Latin American and the Caribbean (LAC), Middle East and North Africa (MNA), Southeast Asia (SA), Sub-Saharan Africa (SSA).

Source: The World Bank (2016b), *Remittance Prices Worldwide* (dataset), *http://remittanceprices.worldbank.org*.

StatLink *http://dx.doi.org/10.1787/888933422720*

Besides increasing remittance flows, policies usually also aim to channel remittances towards productive investments. Such policies include tax exemptions for remittance income, creating incentives to attract diaspora investments, and matching grants schemes targeting the diaspora, as shown by the experience of Mexico and El Salvador.

Mexico

The government chose to involve migrant hometown associations (HTAs) in local economic development. To do so, the government set up in 2000 a programme where every dollar a HTA remits is to be matched with one dollar from the municipality, one from the federal government and one from the state, known as the "Tres por Uno" programme (Orozco, 2005; Orozco and Garcia-Zanello, 2009; Valenzuela and Lanly, 2004). In 2010, the total investment was of 1.7 billion (446.3 million coming from 881 HTAs).

Projects range from water and electricity amenities, to schools, health clinics building and scholarships to study in the United States. Between 2001 and 2008, 67% of the projects were public works and 26% were social infrastructure (Burgess, 2012). The latest evaluation of the programme by the Ministry of Social Development (SEDESOL) shows a constant increase in investments and in HTAs involved (from 20 HTAs involved in 2002 to 881 in 2010). The evaluation also reports a positive impact in terms of social inclusion (SEDESOL, 2012).

Critics of the "Tres por Uno" programme point to issues of transparency and resources management, and suggest that economic structures are too weak to secure long-term development and new jobs (Garcia Zamora, 2007). Others emphasise an unequal participation between municipalities, as the poorest are not taken into account because of a "self-selection bias"[3] (Burgess, 2006 and 2012; De Graauw, 2005) benefiting primarily emigrants' villages (particularly in the states of Michoacán, Zacatecas and Oaxaca where migrants' clubs are well organised) and "partisan bias" as municipalities with strong Partido de Acción Nacional (PAN) political support are more likely to receive projects (Aparicio and Meseguer 2012; Burgess 2012).

Some critics also question the ability of the programme to increase money transfers from HTAs and whether HTA initiatives should continue to be funded given the lack of evidence that investing in the "Tres por Uno programme is more productive than any other investment.

El Salvador

El Salvador counts on well-structured HTAs abroad. Since the late 1990s the government has been actively trying to reach migrant communities in the United States and channel remittances to foster development. In 2002, El Salvador established a co-financing programme managed by the Fund for Local Development (FISDL) (Gammage, 2005; Terry and Wilson, 2005) named *Unidos por la Solidaridad*. This programme aimed to channel collective remittances of HTAs. It did so by promoting joint participation of municipalities, non-governmental organisations (NGOs), ministries and the private sector.

The programme was created for the building of small infrastructures. The major part of the investment comes from the FISDL and municipalities and to a lesser extent from HTAs (10-15%). Nonetheless, from 2002 to 2004, 45 projects in 27 municipalities contributed to "financing and building small infrastructure for schools, communal recreation facilities and health centres" (Gammage, 2005).

Critics highlight the fact that collective remittances do not have the impact some would like to believe (Orozco, 2000) especially since they represent only 1% of the total amount of financial remittances. Another criticism made is that HTAs challenge governance, letting public officials "off the hook" in the provision of basic services and infrastructure (Burgess, 2012).

Policy makers can also enhance the contribution of emigrants by actively engaging diasporas in development projects

Diaspora networks can spur investment in origin countries, but also become major drivers of scientific and economic development. In developing countries, scientific diasporas are expected to engage actively in science and technology development back home through an increased participation in knowledge networks. This participation represents a way to compensate for the main negative effects of high-skilled migration without requiring the physical return of the migrant. The different national experiences presented below show how different developing countries have built such knowledge networks.

Moldova

Forms of transnational collaboration adopted by the Moldovan government include knowledge sharing, co-publications, joint research, temporary visits for conferences or lectures and co-mentoring. Since 2008 the government has sought co-operation with Moldovan scientists abroad through the Academy of Sciences of Moldova (ASM).

The Council of Scientists and Personalities of Culture Born in the Republic of Moldova, created in 2010, aims to connect its scientific diaspora with the economic and scientific development of the country of origin. This programme is part of a broader policy agenda (PARE 1+1 Programme), which includes assisting Moldovans abroad and promoting productive investments through official financial transfer and entrepreneurship support.

Colombia

Colombia has been reaching out to its diaspora for more than 25 years now. Since the implementation of the Red Caldas in the early 1990s the state has been actively involved in diaspora building. The Red Caldas initiative was then replaced by two different policies aiming to foster circulation of knowledge between Colombia and the diaspora:

- The first one, ColombiaNosUne, has been designed to build skilled migrant organisations abroad. But users have reported a series of dysfunctions in the network.
- The second policy aims to review certain coercive measures. Commonly, and not only in Colombia, a way to prevent the negative effects of the emigration of the tertiary-educated is contractually to oblige students to return to their home country for a period fixed by the contract as soon as their studies abroad are finished. In 2010, Colciencias implemented a new policy giving students the possibility to remain abroad in exchange for long-distance contributions in research and development activities (Caplan, 2014).

Argentina

Programa Raíces is dedicated in Argentina to the return of skilled nationals and to the creation of knowledge networks. It does so through mechanisms of scientific co-operation and the development of researcher networks. In respect of scientific co-operation, it aims to foster knowledge coproduction between a research team in Argentina and one or more Argentine researcher(s) abroad. This mechanism is called "Scientific and Technological Research Projects" (PICT).

... and fostering brain circulation by promoting the temporary or permanent return of high-skilled migrants

Return migration can hold great potential for development in origin countries. While policies regarding migrant return have been addressed as a key issue in the management of migration flows in many destination countries (OECD, 2008), return migration has emerged as an important policy issue in the countries of origin as well. Return policies in developing countries can focus on two main objectives (Figure 7.11):

- Policies can aim to attract back their nationals abroad to the country of origin. Attraction policies may include direct and/or indirect incentives for return.
- Policies can support the adjustment and resettlement of return migrants in their countries of origin. Reintegration policies may provide measures for productive use of returnees' financial, human and social capital acquired abroad.

Figure 7.11. **Typology of return policies in countries of origin**

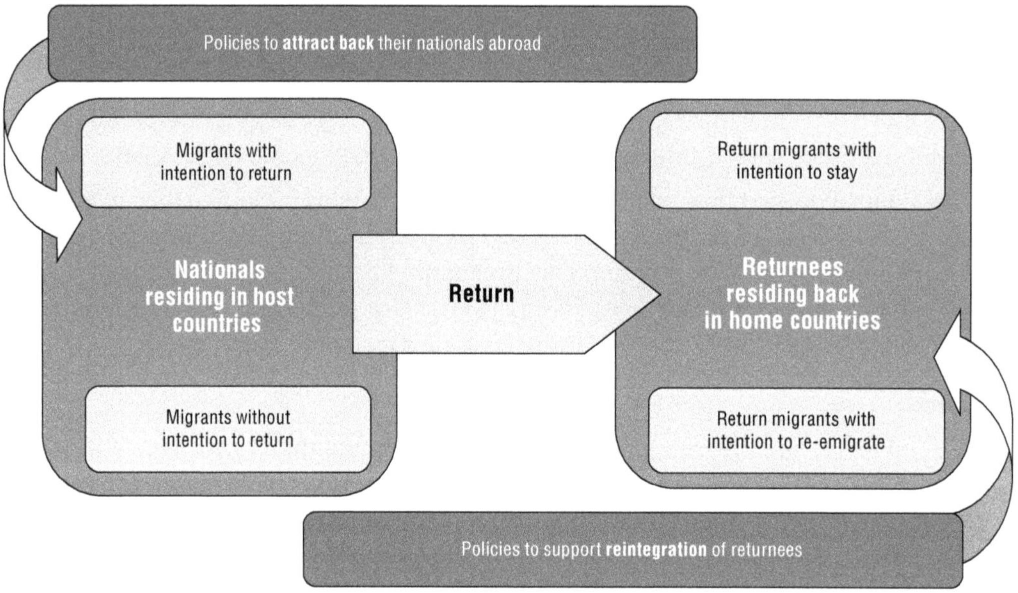

Countries of origin can adopt policies specifically targeting citizens residing abroad regardless of their intentions to come back. Likewise, those actual returnees with or without reasons to stay permanently can be targeted for re-integration. More general sectoral development policies can also have an indirect impact on return migration, in particular on successful reintegration of the returnees (see below).

A better understanding of the reasons why migrants decide to return to their countries of origin is important for developing policies to attract them. The IPPMD data report why returnees in eight developing countries decided to come back. While there are some variances across different countries (Figure 7.12), some general patterns appear. The decision to return is strongly correlated with personal preferences, for instance to reunite with family or to live in the countries of origin after retirement. Experiences in countries of destination can encourage migrants to return. A substantial number of return migrants came back because they failed to obtain relevant legal status for work or residency in destination countries. Difficulties in economic and social integration in destination countries represent another factor. Some groups of migrants decided to return when they recognised there were better employment and investment opportunities in their countries of origin.

Figure 7.12. **Most return migrants surveyed came home because they prefer their country of origin**

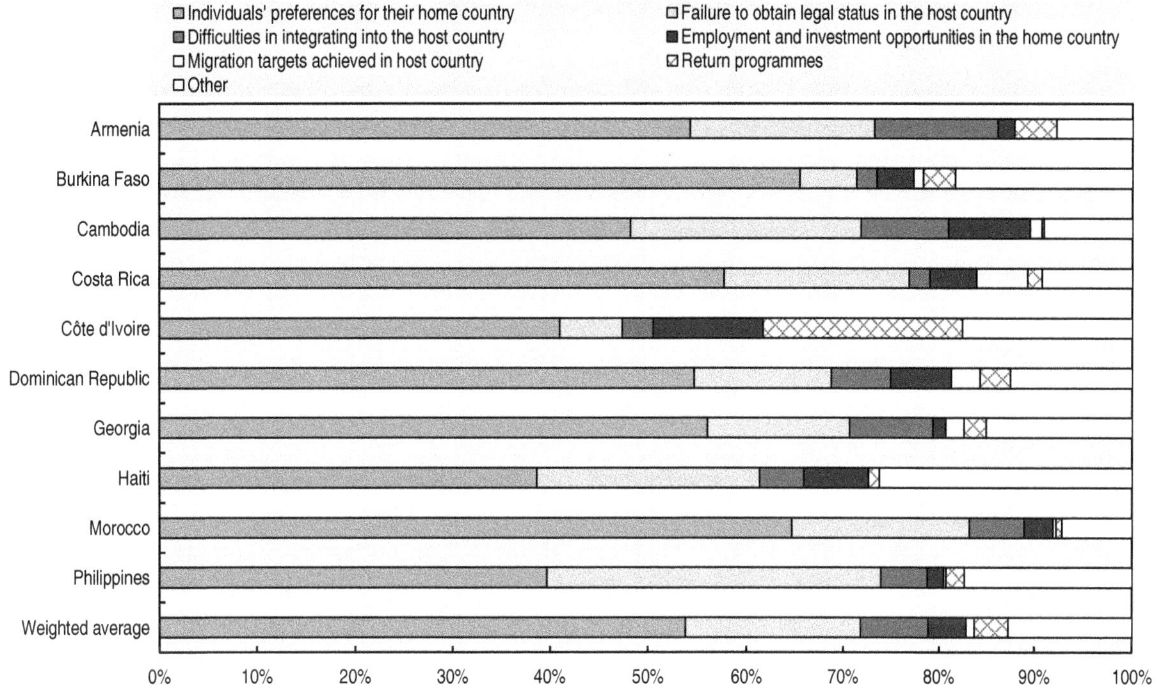

Source: OECD (forthcoming), *Interrelations between Public Policies, Migration and Development.*

StatLink http://dx.doi.org/10.1787/888933422732

Armenia provides a good example of a country willing to promote return migration by strengthening information channels. It organises job fairs in countries where it has strong ties with diaspora networks to present vacancies for various job positions in the Armenian labour market suitable for potential return migrants. Armenia also runs a bilingual website with comprehensive information on return-related issues. Both measures help potential return migrants overcome the lack of information about the local context.

Financial and non-financial benefits provided to returnees increase the incentives to go home. This includes benefits ranging from tax and duty exemptions related to the transport of personal belongings (offered in, among other countries, Jamaica and Malaysia) to salary subsidies (Thailand) or capital provided for the start of micro businesses (Cabo Verde, Georgia and the Philippines).

Targeted return policies, such as those implemented by Malaysia, combining these incentives and offering additional benefits to high-skilled migrants might have a more direct impact on return.

Malaysia

The Malaysian Return Expert Programme (REP) was introduced in 2001. In 2011, its administration was entrusted to the newly created agency TalentCorp, under the prime minister's department. The programme focuses on successful Malaysian migrants residing and employed abroad. The applicants must hold at least a diploma or degree and have

12 years of accumulated working experience abroad. The obligatory number of years of working experience decreases according to the level of the qualification. Another criterion to be eligible is based on the salary earned abroad. Beneficiaries of the programme are eligible for a 15% flat tax rate for two consecutive years, tax exemption for personal effects as well as a vehicle (special conditions apply) and for receiving permanent resident status for closest family members (spouse and children).

Evaluation of the programme on the sample of 1 656 applicants processed between 2011 and 2014 showed positive results derived from the fiscal cost-benefit analysis (Del Carpio, Özden and Testaverde, 2016). The programme increases the likelihood of a return to Malaysia once the applicant is selected and the tax gains from the return migrants are higher than the costs in form of the flat tax rate offered by the programme. Although the study does not evaluate other aspects and potential benefits and costs of the programme, it introduces positive returns to the economy of the country from return migration.

Programmes aimed at promoting reintegration can contribute to more sustainable return

To help return migrants settle permanently in their home countries, and thus make return sustainable, targeted reintegration programmes should be available. Some programmes focus on immediate support to migrants whose return is forced. Jamaica provides a good example of this with its Rehabilitation and Reintegration Programme. The programme supports return migrants who came back against their will by providing assistance related to transport and short-term accommodation and legal support for those needing new identity documents. Reintegration programmes may also provide financial support in the form of loans for self-employment assistance and business start-ups as seen in Cabo Verde and the Philippines. They can also focus on return migrants' skills, through qualification recognition and training, such as financial literacy and small business management.

Policies and programmes with a high impact on the sustainability of return are not necessarily limited to the phase when return has already taken place. Maximising the impact of return on the country of origin might be constantly supported even before emigration occurs (financial literacy courses for potential overseas workers to acquaint them with benefits of bank accounts, remittances transfers and saving possibilities), during the emigration phase (job advertisings and requalification training, loans for investment in the country of origin accessible from abroad and targeted return programmes) and after return to the country of origin.

One of the major difficulties with policies targeting return migrants is the lack of systematically gathered information about nationals residing abroad as well as return migrants. Therefore it proves to be hard to design custom-made policies to attract migrants to return. Only scattered evidence exists related to return migrants, covered by country surveys or census data. Lack of, or a difference in, information on nationals residing abroad limits the possibilities of introducing policies targeting the needs of potential return migrants.

Sectoral policies also play a key role in turning emigration into development

Chapter 5 highlights the role that sectoral policies can play in the decision to migrate. Labour market, agriculture, education and social protection policies can thus influence migration rates, both in countries of origin and destination (OECD, forthcoming). Beyond the decision to migrate, sectoral policies can also affect other migration outcomes, such as the use of remittances and the sustainability of return migration.

Non-migration policies help create an enabling environment for a more productive use of remittances

Sectoral development policies can have an indirect effect on remittances by affecting the incentives to emigrate, but also a direct impact on the volumes and use of remittances. Economic and social policies may create incentives for migrants and diasporas to invest more in the country of origin and channel remittances towards productive investments.

First, sectoral development policies can affect the decision to send remittances, and the volume of remittances sent. Benefiting from a policy programme, such as a formal social protection programme, could mean less pressure for migrants to send remittances. However, access to social protection programmes and other types of government support could potentially also increase the incentives for the migrant to send remittances when the basic needs of the household are fulfilled and remittances can be spent more productively. In the same way, sectoral development policies can have an impact on the use of remittances. Receiving government support can enable the household to redirect remittances and use them for productive investments. Evidence from a number of country studies show that social security transfers tend to lower household private transfers in general (Cox, Eser and Jimenez, 1998, for Peru) and household remittances in particular (Jensen, 2004, for South Africa; Murrugarra, 2002, for Armenia).

As discussed above, public policies can also alter the way remittances are sent and used. Financial systems in developing countries often serve a very small proportion of the population. Policies to make the financial sector more accessible to all parts of the population can encourage more remittances to be sent via the formal financial system. Remittances sent through formal channels are not only more secure for the sender and the receiver, but can also contribute to developing the financial sector and create multiplier effects when resources are made available to finance economic activities, which in turn can encourage more productive investments.

Evidence from the OECD IPPMD project shows that remittance-receiving households with access to the formal financial market through a bank account receive more remittances on average than those without a bank account in all countries but Georgia (Figure 7.13), and that they are more likely to receive remittances through formal channels (OECD, forthcoming). Remittances sent through informal channels also limit the ability of households to save and borrow money in the formal financial system. In addition, households without bank accounts are often subject to higher costs when accessing basic financial services.

Sectoral policies can facilitate the re-integration of return migrants and increase their contribution to the development of their home countries

Sectoral development policies can have indirect impacts on migrants' decision to return to their country of origin and on the successful reintegration of return migrants:

- Labour market policies to enhance market efficiency and increase human capital through, for instance, vocational training, can further support return migrants' participation in the local labour market.
- Education policies aiming at improving the education system can also play a role in the incentives to return, especially for return migrants with children of school age.
- Investment policies can have indirect effects on the use of the financial resources that return migrants bring back with them.

Figure 7.13. **Remittance-receiving households with bank accounts receive more remittances on average**

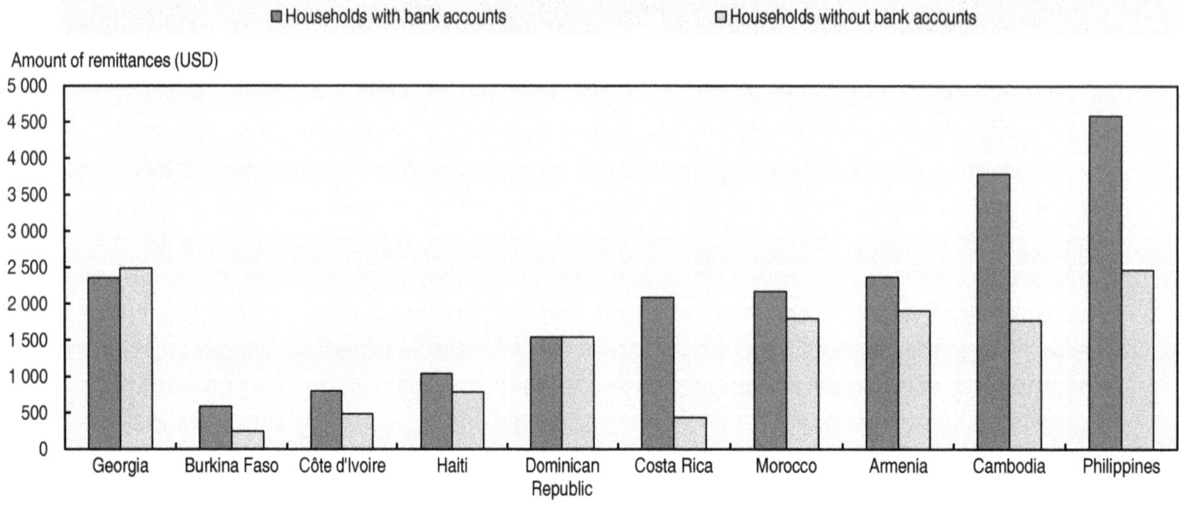

Note: Remittances are defined as the average amount of money (in USD) received from anyone living abroad by the households in the 12 months prior to the survey. The sample only includes households that receive remittances.

Source: OECD (forthcoming), *Interrelations between Public Policies, Migration and Development.*

StatLink http://dx.doi.org/10.1787/888933422749

To ensure the sustainability of return, the conditions in the country of origin need to be favourable, including demographic, socio-economic as well as political and security aspects (Black et al., 2004). Otherwise a non-supportive environment in the country of origin might be a push factor for returnees to re-emigrate (Cantore and Cali, 2015).

Conclusion

Emigration of part of the population represents a great opportunity for countries of origin, as acknowledged by the *2030 Agenda for Sustainable Development*. However, the contribution of migration to development depends, to a great extent, on the policies in place. The problem is that, in many cases, policy makers do not sufficiently understand the potential implications of migration in their area of work. This can happen, for example, when a government, through its ministry of education, spends millions of dollars to develop specific skills, but most of the qualified people then decide to migrate to other countries where there is a high – and better remunerated – demand for this type of skills. A better understanding of the domestic labour market's needs, but also of the migration context, would help public authorities to design policies in line with the needs of the population and the economy.

For this reason development strategies should take into account the impact of sectoral policies on people's decision to migrate, on the use of remittances and on the sustainability of return. This does not mean that emigration should be considered as a development strategy by itself. Many countries have developed without registering massive population outflows and, by contrast, many countries with high emigration rates have not managed to break away from the risk of a poverty trap generated by emigration. In fact, the notion of development itself should imply that inhabitants of a country have the option to migrate if they wish to do so, but that emigration is not seen as the only alternative to move forward in life. At the same time, countries of origin can make the best of the migration process and manage to overcome the risk of a poverty trap generated in particular by remittances.

This entails the adoption of suitable and coherent policies that allow migration to be a true engine for development.

Notes

1. The IPPMD project features ten partner countries. The following partner countries are part of the SG group of countries: Armenia, Costa Rica, the Dominican Republic, Georgia, Morocco and the Philippines. The following are part of the RW countries: Burkina Faso, Cambodia, Côte d'Ivoire and Haiti. For more details on the IPPMD project, see Box 5.5 in Chapter 5.
2. Banks in a number of countries, including Brazil, Egypt, Mexico and Turkey, have used future remittance flows as collateral to obtain cheaper and longer-term financing from international capital markets (Ratha, 2007).
3. HTAs are not necessarily coming from the poorest villages, and are not very likely to come from the poorest areas. In the same way, it is well known that HTAs are prevalent among migrants coming from Zacatecas, Michoacán, Oaxaca, Guanajuato and Jalisco (see Fox and Rivera-Salgado, 2004).

References

Acosta, P. (2007), "Entrepreneurship, labor markets and international remittances: Evidence from El Salvador", *International Migration Policy and Economic Development: Studies Across the Globe*, World Bank and Palgrave Macmillan, Washington, DC.

Acosta, P. (2006), "Labor supply, school attendance, and remittances from international migration: The case of El Salvador", *World Bank Working Paper No. 3903*, World Bank.

Acosta, P. et al. (2008), "What is the impact of international remittances on poverty and inequality in Latin America?", *World Development*, Elsevier, Vol. 36(1), pp. 89-114.

Adams, R.H., Jr. and A. Cuecuecha (2010a), "The economic impact of international remittances on poverty and household consumption and investment in Indonesia", *World Bank Working Paper* 5433, World Bank.

Adams, R. H., Jr. (2006), "Remittances, poverty and investment in Guatemala", in C. Özden and Schiff (ed.), *International Migration, Remittances and the Brain Drain*, World Bank and Palgrave Macmillan, Washington, DC, pp. 53-80.

Adams, R.H., Jr. and A. Cuecuecha (2010b), "Expenditure and investment in Guatemala", *World Development*, 38 (11), pp. 1626-1641,Washington, DC.

Adams, R.H. and J. Page (2005), "Do International migration and remittances reduce poverty in developing countries", *World Development*, Elsevier, Vol. 33(10), pp. 1645-1669.

Airola, J. (2008), "Labor supply in response to remittance income: The case of Mexico", *The Journal of Developing Areas*, Vol. 41(2), pp.69-78.

Akkoyunlu, S. and M. Stern (2012), "An empirical analysis of diaspora bonds", *Global Migration Research Paper No. 3*, Programme for the Study of Global Migration, Geneva.

Ammassari, S. (2004), "From nation-building to entrepreneurship: The impact of élite return migrants in Côte d'Ivoire and Ghana", *Population Space Place*, 10, pp. 133-154, *http://dx.doi.org/10.1002/psp.319*.

Antman, A.M. (2011), "The intergenerational effects of paternal migration on schooling and work: What can we learn from children's time allocations?", *Journal of Development Economics*, 96, pp. 200-208.

Aparicio, F. J. and C. Meseguer (2011), "Collective Remittances and the State: The 31 Program in Mexican Municipalities, World Development", *http://dx.doi.org/10.1016/j.worlddev.2011.05.016*.

Arslan, C. et al. (2014), "A new profile of migrants in the aftermath of the recent economic crisis", *OECD Social, Employment and Migration Working Papers*, No. 160, OECD Publishing, Paris, *http://dx.doi.org/10.1787/5jxt2t3nnjr5-en*.

Asch, B. eds. (1994), "Emigration and its effects on the sending country", Center for Research on Immigration Policy, Rand Corporation, Santa Monica.

Aydemir, A.B. and G. Borjas (2007), "A comparative analysis of the labor market impact of international migration: Canada, Mexico and the United States", *Journal of the European Economic Association*, Vol. 5, No. 4, pp. 663-708.

Azam, J. P. and F. Gubert (2005), "Those in Kayes. The impact of remittances on their recipients in Africa", *Revue économique*, Presses de Sciences-Po, Vol. 56(6), pp. 1331-1358.

Beine, M., F. Docquier and H. Rapoport (2008), "Brain drain and human capital formation in developing countries: Winners and losers", *The Economic Journal*, Vol. 118(528), pp. 631-652, *http://dx.doi.org/10.1111/j.1468-0297.2008.02135.x.*

Benjamin, D. (1992), "Household composition, labor markets, and labor demand: Testing for separation in agricultural household models", *Econometrica* 60(2), pp. 287-322.

Black, R. et al. (2004),"Understanding voluntary return", *Technical Report*, Home Office, London.

Borjas, G. (2008), "Labor outflows and labor inflows in Puerto Rico", *Journal of Human Capital*, University of Chicago Press, Vol. 2, No. 1, pp.32-68.

Brinkerhoff, J.M. (2009), *Digital Diasporas: Identity and Transnational Engagement*, Cambridge University Press.

Bryant, J. (2005), "Children of international migrants in Indonesia, Thailand and the Philippines: A review of evidence and policies", *Innocenti Working Paper* 2005-05, UNICEF.

Burgess, K. (2012), "Collective remittances and migrant-state collaboration", *Latin American Politics and Society*, Miami University, pp. 119-146.

Burgess, K. (2006), "Migrant philanthropy and local governance in Mexico", in Metz B. (ed.), *New Patterns for Mexico: Remittances, Philanthropic Giving and Equitable Development*, Harvard University Press.

Calenda, D. (2014), "Return Migrants' Employment Trajectories", in J.-P. Cassarino, *Reintegration and Development*, European University Institute.

Cantore, N. and M. Calì (2015), "The Impact of temporary migration on source countries", *International Migration Review*, *http://dx.doi.org/10.1111/imre.12178*.

Caplan C. (2014), "Les réseaux transnationaux et diasporiques de la migration qualifiée andine en Europe", *Géographie d'un partage*, Université Paul Valéry, p. 525.

Carletto G. and M. Mendola (2009), "International migration and gender differentials in the home labor market: Evidence from Albania", *Policy Research Working Paper* 4900, World Bank, Washington, DC.

Castañeda, E. and L. Buck (2011), "Remittances, transnational parenting, and the children left behind: Economic and psychological implications", *Latin Americanist*, 55(4), pp. 85-110.

Chami, R., C. Fullenkamp and S. Jahjah (2003), "Are immigrant remittance flows a source of capital for development", *IMF Working Paper 03/189*, International Monetary Fund, Washington, DC.

Chander A. (2001), "Diaspora bonds", *New York University Law Review*, Vol. 76.

Chaudary A. (2016), "Transnational politics and immigrant political participation in Europe", *IMI Working Papers*.

Chauvet, L. and M. Mercier (2014), "Do return migrants transfer political norms to their origin country? Evidence from Mali", *Journal of Comparative Economics*, Elsevier, Vol. 42/3, pp. 630-651.

Chen, Y-W., E. Racine and N. Collins (2015), "Gone but not forgotten: The (re-)making of diaspora strategies", *Asian Ethnicity*, 16(3), pp.371-379.

Chitsike, C. (2000), "Culture as a barrier to rural women's entrepreneurship: Experience from Zimbabwe", *Gender and Development* 8(1), pp. 71-77.

Cissé, P. et C. Daum (2010), "Migrations internationales maliennes, recomposition des territoires migratoires et impacts sur les sociétés d'origine", in *Dynamique migratoire, migration de retour et impacts sur les sociétés d'origine au Maghreb et en Afrique de l'Ouest*, Université Mohammed V-Agdal, Rabat, Morocco, 22-23 November.

Cochrane, F. (2007), "Irish America, the end of the IRA's armed struggle and the utility of soft power", *Journal of Peace Research*, Vol. 44, n° 2, pp. 215-231.

CODEV-EPFL/IDSK/JNU/ILO (2013), "Migration, scientific diasporas and development: Impact of skilled return migration on development in India", *Final Research Report, Cahier de la Coopération* No. 8, CODEV-EPFL, Lausanne.

Cox, D., E. Eser and E. Jimenez (1998), "Motives for private transfers over the life cycle: An analytical framework and evidence for Peru", *Journal of Development Economics*, 55(1), pp. 57-80.

Cox-Edwards, A. and M. Ureta (2003), "International migration, remittances and schooling: evidence from El Salvador", *Journal of Development Economics*, 72(2), pp. 429-461.

De Vreyer, P., F. Gubert and A. S. Robilliard (2010), "Are there returns to migration experience? An empirical analysis using data on return migrants and non-migrants in West Africa", *Annals of Economics and Statistics*, Vol. 97/98, pp. 307-328, *www.jstor.org/stable/41219120*.

Del Carpio, X., C. Özden and M. Testaverde (2016), "The global migration of talent and tax incentives: Evidence from Malaysia's returning expert programme", unpublished working paper.

De Graauw, E. (2005), "Government Courtship of Migradollars: International Migrants' Remittances and Policy Intervention in the Case of Contemporary Mexico", 2nd Annual Political Science Graduate Student Conference, University of California at Berkeley.

Démurger, S. and L. Shi (2012), "Migration, remittances and rural employment patterns: Evidence from China", *Mimeo*.

Fair C. (2005), "Diaspora Involvement in Insurgencies: Insights from the Khalistan and Tamil Ealam Movements", *Nationalism and Ethnic Politics*, 11, pp. 125-156.

Fargues, P. (1997), "State policies and the birth rate in Egypt: From socialism to liberalism, *Population and Development Review*, 23 (1), pp. 115-138.

Fargues, P. (1993), "Demographic explosion or social upheaval?", in *Democracy without Democrats?* London, pp. 155-181.

Fox, J. and G. Rivera-Salgado (2004), "Building Civil Society Among Indigenous Migrants", in Fox, J and G. Rivera-Salgado (eds.), *Indigenous Mexican Migrants in the United States*, pp. 1-65.

Gagnon, J. (2011), "Stay with us? The impact of emigration on wages in Honduras", *Development Centre Working Paper* No. 300, OECD Publishing, Paris, *http://dx.doi.org/10.1787/5kg9xf23zfbt-en*.

Gammage, S. (2005), "Exporting people and recruiting remittances: A development strategy for El Salvador", *Latin American Perspectives*, Vol. 33, N°6, pp.75-100.

Garcia Zamora, R. (2007), "El programa Tres por Uno de remesas colectivas en México: Lecciones y desafíos", *Migraciones internacionales*, Vol. 4 (1).

Graham, B. (2014), "Diaspora-owned firms and social responsibility", *Review of International Political Economy*, 21(2), pp. 432-466.

Görlich D., M. Toman, and C. Trebesch (2007), "Explaining labour market inactivity in migrant-sending families: Housework, hammock, or higher education?", *Working Paper* 1391, Kiel Institute for the Working Economy, Kiel, Germany.

Hamdouch, B. and J. Wahba (2012), "Return migration and entrepreneurship in Morocco", *Economic Research Forum*.

Hanson, G. (2007), "Emigration, labor supply, and earnings in Mexico", NBER chapters in *Mexican Immigration to the United States*, National Bureau of Economic Research Inc., Cambridge, MA, pp.289-328.

Hanson, G.H. and C. Woodruff (2003), "Emigration and educational attainment in Mexico", University of California, San Diego, *Mimeo*.

IBRD and World Bank (2005), "Reshaping the Future Education and Postconflict Reconstruction", World Bank, Washington, DC, *http://siteresources.worldbank.org/INTCPR/Resources/Reshaping_the_Future.pdf*.

Jadotte, E. (2009), "International migration, remittances and labour supply: The case of the Republic of Haiti," *UN-Wider Research Paper* No. 2009/28, *https://www.wider.unu.edu/sites/default/files/rp2009-28.pdf*.

Jensen, R. (2004), "Do private transfers displace the benefits of public transfers? Evidence from South Africa", *Journal of Public Economics*, 88(1-2), pp. 89-112.

Kilic, T., G.Calogero, B.Davis and A.Zezza (2009), "Investing back home: return migration and business ownership in Albania", *Economics of Transition*, Vol. 17/3, pp. 587-623.

Kitchin R. and M. Boyle (2011), *Diaspora Strategies in Transition States: Prospects and Opportunities for Armenia*, National University of Ireland, Maynooth.

Kurtz M. J. (2004), *Free Market Democracy and the Chilean and Mexican Countryside*, Cambridge University Press.

La, J. (2004), "Forced Remittances in Canada's Tamil Enclaves", *Peace Review*, 16(3), pp. 379-385.

Levitt P. (2001), *The Transnational Villagers*, University of California Press.

Levitt P. (1998), "Social remittances: A local-level, migration-driven form of cultural diffusion", *International Migration Review*, Vol. 32, pp. 926-949.

Liedholm C. (2002), "Small firm dynamics: evidence from Africa and Latin America", *Small Business Economics* Vol. 18/1-3, pp. 227-242.

Mazzucato, V., M. Siegel and M. Vanore (2014), "'Left behind' but not left alone: Parental migration and the psychosocial health of children in Moldova", *Social Science & Medicine*, 08/2014; p. 132.

Mezger Kveder, C. and M. L. Flahaux (2013), "Returning to Dakar: A mixed methods analysis of the role of migration experience for occupational status", *World Development*, Vol. 45, pp. 223-238.

Mishra, P. (2007), "Emigration and wages in source countries: Evidence from Mexico", *Journal of Development Economics*, No. 82, pp. 180-199.

Mohamoud A. (2005), "Diasporas: Untapped potential for peacebuilding in the homeland", in P. van Tongeren et al., *People Building Peace II: Successful Stories of Civil Society*, Lynne Rienner Publishers, pp. 339-353.

Mohapatra, S. and D. Ratha (2011), *Remittance Markets in Africa*, World Bank, Washington DC.

Mora, J. J. (2010), "Remittances and labor participation in Colombia," Department of Economics at Universidad Icesi, *Mimeo*.

Mu, R. and D. van de Walle (2011), "Left behind to farm? Women's labor re-allocation in rural China", *Labour Economics*, Elsevier, Vol. 18(S1), pp. S83-S97.

Murrugarra, E. (2002), "Public transfers and migrants' remittances: Evidence from the recent Armenian experience', *World Bank Economists' Forum*, 2, pp. 25-47.

OECD (forthcoming), *Interrelations between Public Policies, Migration and Development*, OECD Publishing, Paris.

OECD (2016), *DAC International Development Statistics* (database), *www.oecd.org/dac/stats/idsonline.htm* (accessed 7 September 2016).

OECD (2015), *International Migration Outlook 2015*, OECD Publishing, Paris, *http://dx.doi.org/10.1787/migr_outlook-2015-en*.

OECD (2011), *Tackling the Policy Challenges of Migration: Regulation, Integration, Development*, OECD Publishing, Paris, *http://dx.doi.org/10.1787/9789264126398-en*.

OECD (2008), "Return migration: A new perspective", in *International Migration Outlook 2008*, OECD Publishing, Paris, *http://dx.doi.org/10.1787/migr_outlook-2008-en*.

Opiniano, J. and L. Rispens-Noel (2015), "Development-friendly investments and entrepreneurship by overseas migrants and their outcomes: Lessons for migrants and development actors", in E. Fornalé et al. (eds) (2015), *The Palgrave Handbook of International Labour Migration*, Palgrave MacMillan.

Orozco, M. (2005), *Transnational Engagement, Remittances and their Relationship to Development in Latin America and the Caribbean*, Institute for the Study of International Migration, Georgetown University, *https://monroecollege.edu/uploadedFiles/_Site_Assets/PDF/Remittances-and-Development-in-Latin-A-and-CA.pdf*.

Orozco, M. (2000), "Latino hometown associations as agents of development in Latin America", *Inter-American Dialogue*, Tomás Rivera Policy Institute, Washington, *www.focal.ca/pdf/remit_IAD_Orozco%20Latino%20HTAs%20as%20Development%20Agents%202000.pdf*.

Orozco, M. and E. Garcia-Zanello (2009), "Hometown associations: Transnationalism, philanthropy, and development", *Brown Journal of World Affairs*, 14(2).

Pérez-Armendáriz, C. and D. Crow (2009), "Do migrants remit democracy? International migration, political beliefs, and behavior in Mexico", *Comparative political studies*, Vol. 43/1, pp. 119-148.

Ratha, D. (2007), "Leveraging Remittances for Development", *Policy Brief*, Migration Policy Institute, Washington DC, June.

Ratha, D. and S. Ketkar (2010), "Diaspora bonds: Tapping the diaspora during difficult times", *Journal of International Commerce, Economics and Policy*, Vol. 1(2), pp. 251-263.

Ratha D. and S. Ketkar (2009), *Innovative Financing for Development*, World Bank, Washington DC.

Ratha D. and S. Plaza (2011), "Harnessing diasporas", *Finance and Development*, Vol. 48(3).

Reyes, M.M. (2007), "Migration and Filipino children left-behind: A literature review", UNICEF background paper.

Sadiqi, F. and M. Ennaji (2004), "The impact of male migration from Morocco to Europe on women: A gender approach", *Finisterra* 39(77), pp. 59-76.

Sarma V.J. and R.A Parinduri (2016), "What happens to children's education when their parents emigrate? Evidence from Sri Lanka", *International Journal of Educational Development*, 46, pp. 94-102.

SEDESOL (2012), "Informe final", Programa 3x1 para Migrantes, Meta Evaluación 2007-2012, *www.2006-2012.sedesol.gob.mx/work/models/SEDESOL/EvaluacionProgramasSociales/2012/META_EV_2012/3x1_MetaEvaluacion1.pdf*.

Sharma, K., A. Kashyap, M.F. Montes and P. Ladd (2011), "Realizing the development potential of diasporas", United Nations University, New York.

Shrestha, S.A. (2011), "Human capital investment responses to skilled migration prospects: Evidence from a natural experiment in Nepal", University of Michigan, *Mimeo*, *www-personal.umich.edu/~slesh/jobmarketpaper.pdf*.

Spilimbergo, A. (2009), "Democracy and foreign education," *American Economic Review*, 99(1), pp. 528-543.

Terry D. and S. Wilson (2005), *Beyond Small Change: Making Migrant Remittances Count*, Inter-American Development Bank, Washington, DC.

Tuccio, M. and J. Wahba (2015), "Can I have permission to leave the house? Return migration and the transfer of gender norms", *IZA Discussion Paper* No. 9216, *http://ftp.iza.org/dp9216.pdf*.

Turner S. (2008), "The waxing and waning of the political field in Burundi and its diaspora", *Ethnic and Racial Studies*, 31(4), pp. 742-765.

Turner S. and B. Mossin (2010), "From watch-dogs to nation-builders: The dilemmas of diaspora engagement in post-conflict Burundi", *DIIS Working Paper Series*, 10.

Tyburski M. (2012), "The resource curse reversed? Remittances and corruption in Mexico", *International Studies Quarterly*, 56, pp. 339-350

Valenzuela B.V. and G. Lanly (2004), *Clubes de migrantes oriundos mexicanos en los Estados Unidos. La política transnacional de la nueva sociedad civil migrante*, Centro Universitario de Ciencias Económico-Administrativas, Guadalajara.

Van Houte, M. (2014), *Moving Back or Moving Forward? Return Migration after Conflict*, PhD dissertation, Maastricht University/United Nations University, *www.merit.unu.edu/training/theses/vanhoute.pdf*.

Waddell, B. J. and M. Fontenla (2015), "The Mexican dream? The effect of return migrants on hometown development", *The Social Science Journal*.

Wang, H. (2012), *Globalizing China: The influence, strategies and successes of Chinese returnee entrepreneurs*, Emerald Group Publishing, Bingley.

Wayland, S. (2004), "Ethnonationalist networks and transnational opportunities: The Sri Lankan Tamil diaspora", *Review of International Studies*, 30, pp. 405-426.

Woodruff, C and R. Zenteno (2007), "Migration Networks and Microenterprises in Mexico", *Journal of Development Economics*, 82 (2), pp. 509–28.

World Bank (2016a), *Migration and Remittances Factbook 2016: Third Edition*, World Bank, Washington, DC.

World Bank (2016b), *Remittance Prices Worldwide* (dataset), *http://remittanceprices.worldbank.org* (accessed 1 July 2016).

World Bank (2006), *Global Economic Prospects 2006: Economic Implications of Remittances and Migration*, World Bank, Washington DC.

Wouterse, F. (2010), "Migration and technical efficiency in cereal production: Evidence from Burkina Faso", *Agricultural Economics*, Vol. 41(5), pp. 385-398,

Yang, D. (2008), "International Migration, Remittances and Household Investment: Evidence from Philippine Migrants' Exchange Rate Shocks", *The Economic Journal*, 118(528), pp. 591-630.

Yanovich, L. (2015), "Children left behind: The impact of labor migration in Moldova and Ukraine", Migration Policy Institute, *www.migrationpolicy.org/article/children-left-behind-impact-labor-migration-moldova-and-ukraine*.

Zaiceva, A. (2014), "Post-enlargement emigration and new EU members' labor markets", *IZA World of Labor*: 40.

Perspectives on Global Development 2017
International Migration in a Shifting World
© OECD 2016

Chapter 8

Impacts of immigration to developing countries

About 35% of international migrants live at present in low- or middle-income countries and their presence has effects on the host economies, social structures and the environment. Developing countries, as countries of destination, face limits to their ability fully to benefit from immigration because the informal economy is so widespread and there is a lack of access to markets and resources for the development of public goods. Everything is made more complicated by a shortage of in-depth analyses and active policy debates on immigration. This chapter identifies the impacts of immigration in developing countries on their economic and socio-cultural dimensions and discusses how policies shape these impacts.

Developing countries are not only countries of origin. They are also countries of destination. About 35% of international migrants live at present in low- or middle-income countries. In 22 countries with at least one million inhabitants in this category, more than 5% of the population are immigrants (World Bank, 2011). For many developing countries, immigration plays a role equal to, or even greater than, emigration. For example, immigration to Brazil increased by 87% between the 1995-2000 and 2005-10 census periods (International Organization for Migration, 2013); and Côte d'Ivoire, Eritrea, Jordan, Lebanon, Thailand and Zimbabwe recently became net immigration countries after periods where more people left than arrived. These immigration flows inevitably have economic and social consequences.

Immigration can represent an opportunity for development, but its benefits do not occur automatically. As countries of destination developing countries have a limited ability fully to benefit from immigration. They have less access to markets for capital and goods and a shortage of fiscal resources to adapt to change. On the positive side, immigration can bring an opportunity for developing countries to expand their skills base, advance their technological development and increase their trade and investment connections with the rest of the world. Policy adjustments are needed, but in spite of active public debates on immigration in these countries, there is a shortage of in-depth analyses of immigration, and in particular of policies seeking to integrate the newcomers. These shortcomings cloud an understanding of the contribution of immigration to development. More dramatically, they prevent positive impacts from being maximised and negative impacts from being minimised.

As discussed in Chapter 2, economic activity is shifting globally and pushing the economic point of gravity towards the Global South, albeit at a slower pace than in previous years. This shift is also visible in an average wage growth rate that has been markedly higher in developing than in developed countries. Furthermore, as described in Chapter 4, social ties and geographic proximity do not cease to play an important role in the migration decision and above all the choice of destination. These two factors imply that not only emigration but also immigration will gain in importance as a topic for policy makers in developing countries.

This chapter discusses the impacts of immigration in developing countries and the policies that shape these impacts. The chapter is divided into three sections which will focus first and second on the economic and socio-cultural effects of immigration and third on the shaping role of policy. Since few studies of this topic focus on developing countries (see Box 8.1), the analysis relies on the experience of OECD countries while describing how and why effects may differ elsewhere. Empirical data are sparse and based on diverse country examples, hence the heterogeneity of countries chosen for empirical illustrations.

Box 8.1. **Assessing the economic contribution of labour immigration in developing countries**

The project Assessing the Economic Contribution of Labour Migration in Developing Countries as Countries of Destination is co-funded by the European Commission and jointly implemented by the OECD Development Centre and the International Labour Organization. The aim of the project is to assess the economic importance of labour immigration in a number of developing countries where immigrants represent a large part of the workforce. Given that immigrants have an influence on their host countries' economies not only as workers, but also as consumers, investors, entrepreneurs, taxpayers and users of public services, the project:

- looks closely at the contribution of immigration to economic growth
- studies its impact on the labour market and the productive sector
- reviews the implications of immigration for public finances and public services.

The project addresses the economic contribution of labour migration in developing countries, an issue which has received little attention compared with the impact of immigration in developed countries. The project will evaluate this impact across ten countries. Four are in Africa (Côte d'Ivoire, Ghana, Rwanda and South Africa), three in Asia (Kyrgyzstan, Nepal and Thailand) and three in Latin America (Argentina, Costa Rica and the Dominican Republic).

The project will produce results relevant to low- and middle-income countries that experience similar migration inflows. To ensure high-quality data collection and analysis of results, the project will encourage deeper collaboration between public institutions in partner countries, including national statistical offices, as well as with worker and employer organisations, academia and civil society actors. The project runs from August 2014 to January 2018.

Understanding the economic impacts of immigration

Immigration can affect different aspects of an economy. The effects include the impact on wages, employment, education and skills, entrepreneurship, trade, inflation, economic growth, and public finances. There may be trade-offs between positive and negative effects of immigration across different outcomes or time frames. For example, immigrant inflows may boost long-term economic growth but may come at the cost of short-term reductions in wages.

Because of the structural differences between developing and developed countries as well as the different compositions of migrant populations, it is not obvious that the research results reported for OECD countries also apply to developing countries. While in OECD countries negative impacts tend to be limited (OECD, 2013a; OECD, 2014), in developing countries, theoretically, the scope for positive impacts on growth, but also for negative short-term effects, may be larger.

Labour market effects of immigration are limited in developed countries

Migrants, at least economic migrants, cross borders because they are searching for better opportunities. Sometimes this is the opportunity to live in an environmentally or culturally rich and safe region, or close to family. But usually it is the opportunity to improve the standard of living through better educational and professional outcomes. That is why the impact of immigration is mostly discussed in the context of receiving countries' labour markets.

An increase in the number of workers of a particular skill level can improve the prospects for native workers with skills that are different, but complementary. Such an increase can adversely affect the prospects of native workers with the same skills, but this negative phenomenon may be offset by other positive effects. For example, when immigration eases skills shortages in bottleneck areas, production can increase. That may translate into more jobs locally. Immigration might also make the labour market more flexible and lessen negative shocks if immigrants are quicker to move away from areas experiencing an economic downturn than the native population.

In high-income economies, the estimated average effects on wages and unemployment tend to be relatively small. For example, to take the United States, the average impact appears to be at most a 3% to 4% reduction in wages for a 10% increase in the number of immigrants (Kerr and Kerr, 2011). However, certain population groups such as unskilled workers and immigrants who arrived in earlier years, may be negatively affected. In developing countries, the labour market competition might increase but the overall effect on wages will be highly context-specific.

Subject to two conditions, labour market outcomes in developing countries may also remain unaffected by immigration. The presence of immigrant workers may have no negative effects on native workers if, first, they complement the native labour force and, second, if employers can adjust flexibly. The first condition may be met in countries of any income level, while the second is more likely to be met in middle-income and, above all, in high-income countries.

Immigrants *complement* the native labour force if they have levels of education that are scarce in the receiving economy or if they specialise in occupations or sectors that native workers are less likely to work in or are seeking to leave. Many developing economies simultaneously have high levels of under-employment or unemployment, unmet skills demand and high emigration rates. If immigrants fill skills gaps that come about through an insufficient match of education and training opportunities with the needs of the labour market or the emigration of individuals with key skills, the employment rates and wages of the native population may actually improve.

The characteristics of labour markets in low- and middle-income countries are different from those of high-income countries. One important difference is the sector allocation. For example, more than two thirds of workers in low-income economies are employed in low-productivity agricultural activities, while the proportion working in this sector in middle-income countries is on average less than a third. In high-income economies, unemployment is lowest among those with the highest levels of education; in low-income economies, the opposite is often true (ILO, 2015).

The sector allocation of immigrant labour is not dependent on the level of development, but rather on the specific economic structure of each country. As can be observed in Figure 8.1, a small number of OECD and non-OECD countries, such as Costa Rica, the Dominican Republic and the United States, immigrant workers are more likely to work in the agricultural sector. They are over-represented in private household services in all the sampled countries except the Dominican Republic. The same is true for the construction sector, except for Ireland and Kyrgyzstan, as well as the hotels and restaurants sector, where the Dominican Republic and Ghana are exceptions. Immigrants are under-represented in education, financial services, and public administration and defence in almost all of these countries.

Figure 8.1. **The allocation of immigrant workers depends on the economic structure**

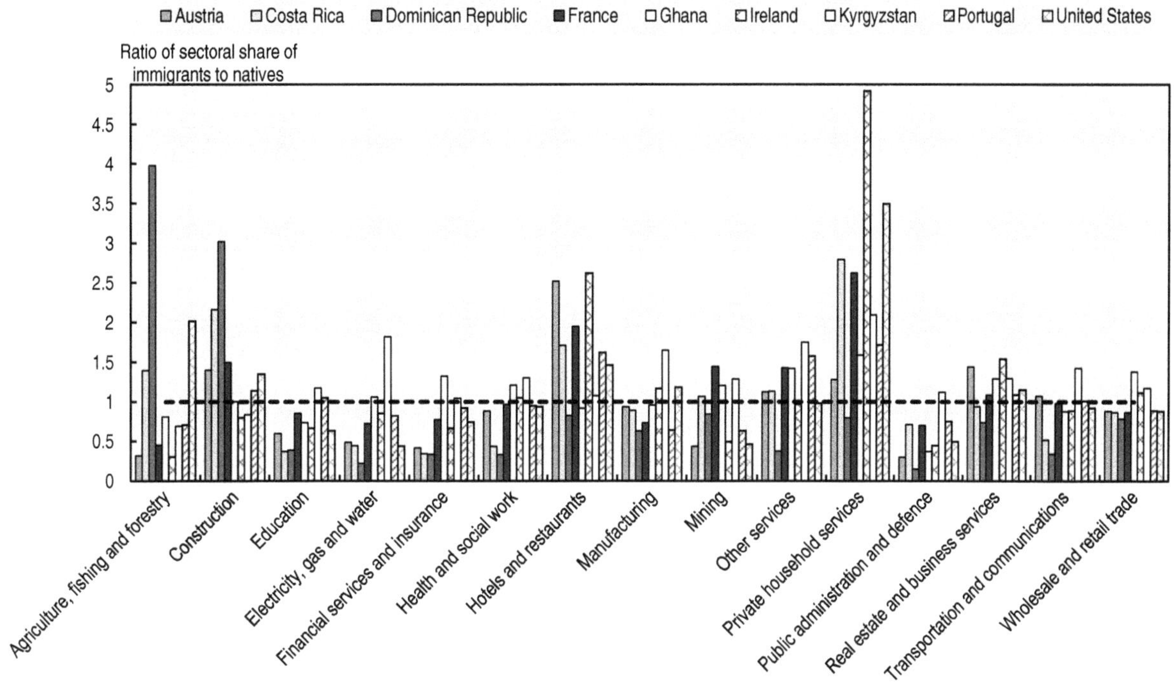

Source: IPUMS, using countries with data after 2005 (Minnesota Population Center, 2014).

StatLink http://dx.doi.org/10.1787/888933422755

The scope for firms to adjust to immigration inflows also affects how much wages change. Here, in particular, developing countries that did not experience high sustained growth in the 50 years following 1955 may be at a disadvantage. When capital markets are less developed, fewer firms will invest, even when their products are in more demand and when their choice of employees is larger. Therefore, there is less additional demand for workers, which would otherwise counter the negative impact of a larger labour force on wages and employment rates. Credit constraints and other barriers to investment are more common in non-OECD than in OECD countries. In a number of countries with high immigration levels, including Costa Rica, Kazakhstan and the Russian Federation, a high proportion of enterprises identify capital as the main constraint (Figure 8.2.).

Hiring practices in developing countries might also follow different dynamics, altering the impact of immigration. A recent study in West Africa showed that the hiring of internal migrants was influenced by kinship ties. Enterprise owners seemed to show a tendency to hire family members and members of close social groups more often than their businesses really needed and thereby limited the profitability of their activities (Grimm, Knorringa and Lay, 2012). Although it is not easy to draw general conclusions from the results from this study, they point to an important aspect of international migration. Since kinship ties can also be transnational, solidarity enforced by social pressures within the extended family might hamper economic activity in countries that are receiving international migrants.

The proportion of informal employment and the informal sector are larger in many developing countries than in OECD countries (Figure 8.3). It remains a matter of dispute whether the informal sector is a last resort for workers who cannot access the formal sector or whether workers and enterprises choose the informal sector voluntarily because there are fewer restrictions. In either case, the dynamics may be different from countries of immigration where the informal sector is smaller.

Figure 8.2. **Credit constraints are more common in developing countries, including some with large immigrant populations**

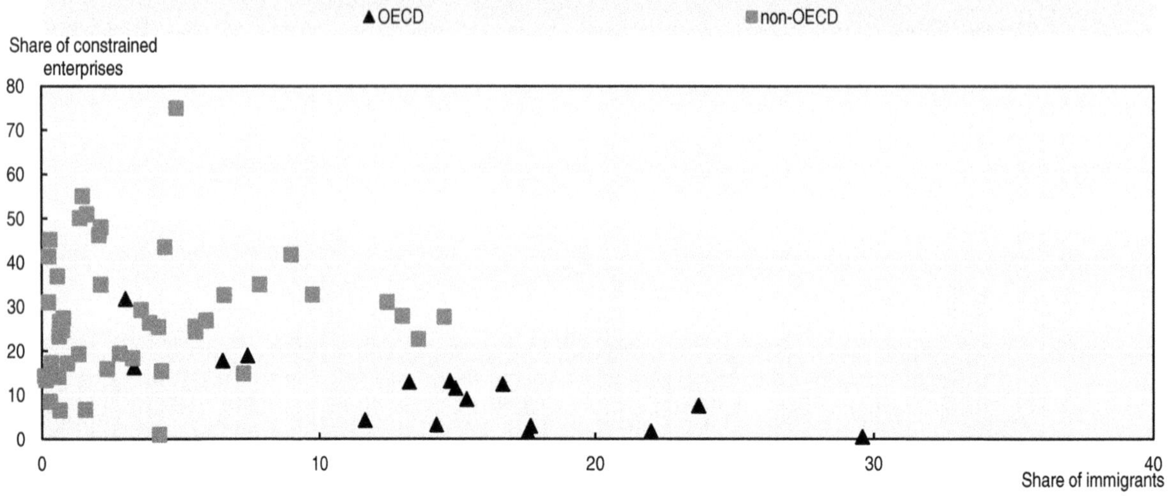

Source: World Bank (undated A), *Enterprise Surveys* (database), *www.enterprisesurveys.org/data*, most recent result for "Firms Identifying Capital as Biggest Constraint", and OECD (2015), *Database on Immigrants in OECD and non-OECD Countries, www.oecd.org/els/mig/dioc.htm.*

StatLink http://dx.doi.org/10.1787/888933422769

Figure 8.3. **The informal sector is large in most developing countries**

Persons employed in the informal sector as % of non-agricultural employment

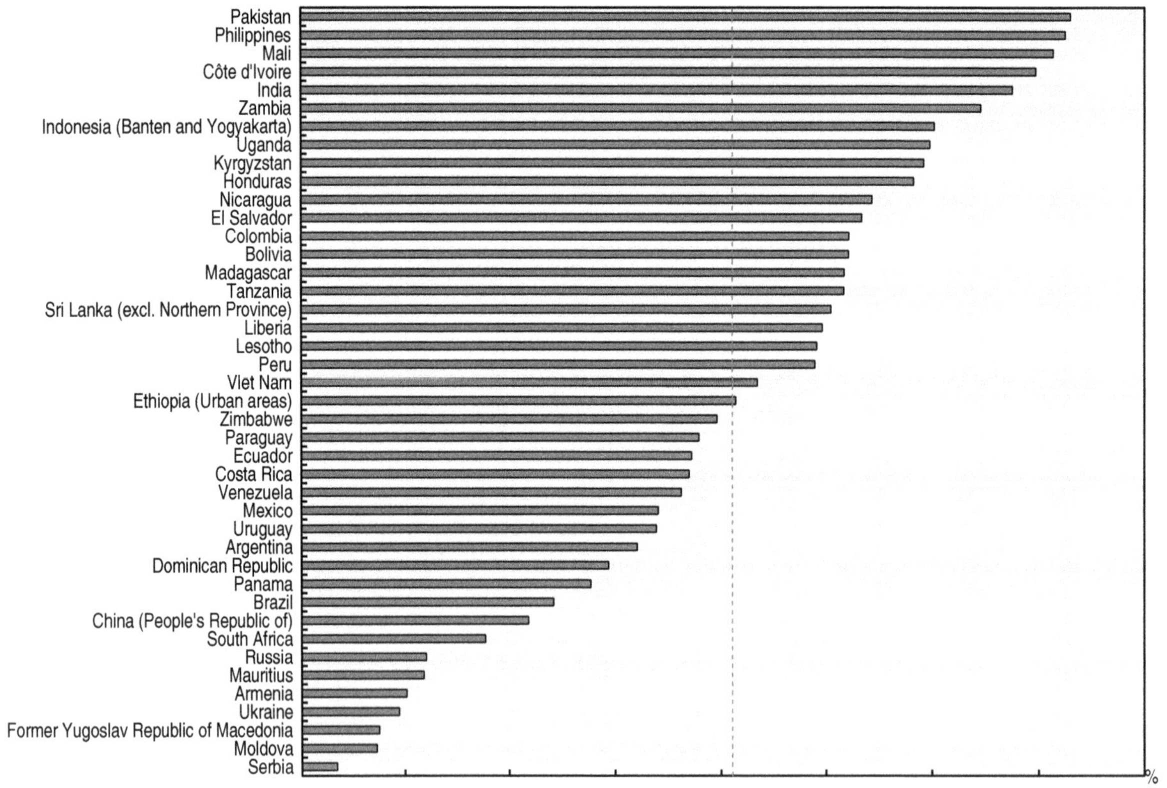

Note: The dashed line indicates the overall average.

Source: ILO (2012), *Women and men in the informal economy - Statistical picture* (database) *http://laborsta.ilo.org/*.

StatLink http://dx.doi.org/10.1787/888933422772

The effects of immigration on wages and employment in developing countries have no clear pattern. In South Africa, immigration is associated with decreases in native employment at the local but not at the national level. Moreover, income decreases at the national but not at the local level. The discrepancy arises from internal migration: as international migrants arrive, local-born workers move elsewhere (Facchini, Mayda and Mendola, 2013). In Malaysia, more immigrant workers are associated with more hiring of native workers and higher male wages (Özden and Wagner, 2014). In Costa Rica, immigration from Nicaragua is not associated with changes in the average wages of men or women (Gindling, 2009). The arrival of Rwandan and Burundian refugees had an overall positive impact on the local economy in Tanzania. The implications for native workers depended on their human capital endowment and position in the labour market.

Differences in the educational characteristics of immigrants may be one explanation for these different outcomes. In Malaysia, immigrants are on average less well educated than the native population; in Costa Rica, the distribution is similar between native and foreign-born individuals; and in South Africa, the proportion of immigrants with a completed university degree is higher than the share of native individuals with a comparable education. Therefore, economic theory suggests that lower-educated individuals are hurt by, and higher-educated individuals benefit from, immigration in Malaysia, and vice versa for South Africa. Since changes at the upper end of the wage distribution most probably translate into larger average changes, these discrepancies could explain the different outcomes.

Labour market effects of immigration seem more pronounced among female workers

Female immigration can allow native-born women to increase their engagement in the labour market. The share of immigrants working in the household services sector has been found repeatedly to be positively correlated with the labour supply of native-born women. That is, among native-born women, skilled female workers work more hours while more unskilled female workers take up work because of those immigrants. As an example, in Malaysia the female labour force participation rate increased by at least 13 percentage points as a result of foreign-born, primarily Indonesian, housekeepers (Tan and Gibson, 2013). Not all effects are positive, however. In Costa Rica, for instance, foreign-born workers seem to have a slightly negative effect on the wages of native-born female workers with low educational attainment (Gindling, 2009).

The level of female labour force participation in a source country can also be associated with immigrant women's labour market activity in the destination country. Highly skilled female immigrant workers may also find themselves decoupling from traditional gender roles, or being able to re-educate themselves in order to enter the labour market in the destination country. However, female immigrants are most likely to be over-qualified, compared to male immigrants and native-born women, at least in the OECD countries (OECD, 2007).

In some countries, immigrants are responsible for a higher level of job turnover among native-born women than native-born men. This is probably the result of women's labour force characteristics. In the case of Spain, women have a higher educational attainment, shorter job tenures and lower job relocation costs. This leads to a greater competition from foreign-born workers than is the case for native men (Amuedo-Dorantes and de la Rica, 2011).

Refugees can also contribute to their host country's labour market and development

As was seen in Chapter 6, developing countries, including Iran, Lebanon and Pakistan, acted as hosts to more than 86% of the world's refugees in 2014. Over 40% of refugees resided in countries where the per capita GDP was below USD 5 000. About half of refugees were under 18 years old. In general, less than 1% of refugees per year are resettled (UNHCR, 2014).

Refugees can contribute positively to their host economies in several ways. Refugee populations can hold significant economic potential in terms of the skills and human capital that they can bring to their host countries and create trade and new job opportunities. Recent research carried out in Uganda, for example, challenges the assumption that refugee populations are passive recipients of aid (Betts et al., 2014). Refugees make positive contributions to the Ugandan economy, for example through the trade in goods and services with Ugandan nationals and through creating job opportunities for Ugandans. In Tanzania, the presence of temporary refugee populations from Burundi and Rwanda in the mid-1990s was found to have had a persistent and positive impact on the welfare of the population in the host region of Kagera (Maystadt and Duranton, 2015). The positive impact can be attributed to lower trade costs following road construction to serve refugee camps. The effects may not be uniform across the population. For example, while the presence of Syrian refugees in the Turkish labour market has displaced low-educated female Turkish workers in the informal sector, it has also created higher-wage formal jobs and enabled occupational upgrading of Turkish workers who now enjoy higher average wages (Del Carpio and Wagner, 2015).

Immigration can lead to increased innovation and entrepreneurship

Immigration can be associated with overall growth in productivity and the economy. On the positive side, an inflow of highly motivated and skilled workers may prompt innovations through knowledge transfers and a larger diversity of approaches. More native workers may decide to become entrepreneurs as workers with previously scarce skills become available. Similarly, entrepreneurial ventures by immigrants may increase innovation, provide job opportunities and introduce new products into the market.

Immigration may foster innovation in the form of introducing new goods. Estimates suggest that a twofold increase in the migration stock is associated with a 60% increase in the likelihood of exporting a new product within ten years after the arrival of the migrants (Bahar and Rapoport, 2014). The economic value of an immigrant is therefore estimated to be around USD 90 000 with highly skilled immigrants being "worth" even more.

On the negative side, firms may find it harder to innovate if their employees find it harder to communicate among themselves because, for example, they speak different languages. Moreover, if immigrants choose self-employment because they are marginalised in the formal labour market, they will face the same problems as small and medium-sized enterprises run by native workers, such as a lack of capital, suboptimal technology adoption and regulatory burdens. Their companies may be characterised by little growth potential and positive effects might then be limited.

Box 8.2. **Chinese immigration in Africa**

In recent years, there has been an increase in Chinese immigration in Africa. The exact numbers are not known. An estimate for 2005-07 put their number at 585 000 – 820 000 while in 2001, there were possibly fewer than 130 000 living in African countries (Park, 2009). In 2013, their number might have reached 1 million according to the Chinese Academy of Social Sciences (Wang, 2014). A number of estimates suggest that Madagascar, Nigeria and South Africa host some of the largest Chinese diasporas on the African continent (Sautman and Hairong, 2007).

Chinese immigrants are not a monolithic group. A small proportion, such as doctors and agricultural advisors, are sent by the Chinese government in the context of development aid projects. A much larger group is recruited by private employment agencies and works on large-scale construction and mining projects that are sometimes carried out by Chinese state companies (Tang, 2010). A third important group arrived independently. Some work in agriculture and many are small- or large-scale entrepreneurs who work in retail and wholesale trade (Park, 2009).

The impacts of these immigrants on the economy are manifold, but the relationships with investment, trade, and the labour market are particularly noteworthy.

Chinese immigration in Africa is associated with a rise in investment. First, many Chinese immigrants either arrive in the context of a big investment project or they come with the necessary capital to launch their own businesses. Second, contract workers may save up their salaries and set up a business once their contract expires. The increase in investment is large. For example, between 2003 and 2007, Chinese foreign direct investment (FDI) to African countries increased by a factor of more than 20, which translates into a yearly growth rate of 114% (Tang, 2010). While this increase can of course not be causally attributed to immigration, it shows that Chinese immigration in these countries is probably not associated with a decrease in the amount of capital available per worker, but rather an increase.

Similarly, trade between China and many African countries has risen since the turn of the century. As an example, China was not among the top five import partners of South Africa as late as 2006, and not among the top five export partners as late as 2001. By 2009, it was its top import and export partner, and this state of affairs persists to this day (World Bank, undated B). As with investment, both the projects by Chinese state companies and the activities of independent entrepreneurs contribute to this increase. State companies sometimes have to import capital goods from China in order to implement their projects, and if the projects are in mining some of the primary goods excavated thanks to the project are exported to China. Both retailers and wholesalers often import the goods they sell directly from producers in China, thereby further increasing imports to African countries. Because middlemen are eliminated these Chinese retailers are often able to offer goods at lower prices, benefitting local consumers, but naturally creating more competition for native entrepreneurs.

A commonly levelled criticism at Chinese investment projects is that they are mostly staffed by Chinese workers. If true, Chinese investment and immigration would at best be associated with no impacts on the employment prospects and wages of native-born individuals. At worst, there would even be a negative impact as native entrepreneurs are driven out of business.

However, these worries may in many cases be exaggerated. First, many of the framework agreements as well as investment laws stipulate that a minimum percentage of jobs created by investment projects needs to be filled by native workers. This minimum threshold is 70% in Angola, although it does not include managers and technical workers (Tang, 2010). Second, private investors often invest in African countries because of competitively low labour costs. Field research suggests that in the manufacturing sector, one Chinese immigrant is associated with the hiring of 15 local workers (Shen, 2013). Third, new companies may initially find it difficult to recruit locally. Once they have time to train local employees, the share of Chinese workers typically declines (Tang, 2010).

Taken together, the overall impact of Chinese immigration in Africa seems positive, but there may be winners and losers. In order to ensure that the largest possible long-term benefits can be drawn from this immigration and that negatively affected groups are compensated, the respective governments could consider developing policies that further encourage skills development and technology transfers.

The prevalence of self-employment often differs between immigrant and native workers. In OECD countries, self-employment rates tend to be higher among immigrant than native workers (OECD, 2011a). Among countries that have made a sample of their 2000 or 2010 censuses available for public use (Minnesota Population Center, 2014), there are more where the male self-employment rate is higher among native-born than foreign-born individuals. It is only among upper-middle-income countries that the self-employment rate is higher among the foreign-born than the native-born males. For women, the opposite is true: the self-employment rate among foreign-born women is higher in all low- and middle-income economies (Figure 8.4). A possible explanation is that a higher proportion of women in OECD countries arrive in the context of family reunification.

The quality of self-employment also influences how much it contributes to the economy. One possible measure of quality is the rate of business ownership. Based on the most recently available census data for more than 50 countries, only male immigrants in high-income countries have a lower business ownership rate than their native counterparts. Elsewhere, and for women, it is the other way around.

Figure 8.4. **Self-employment rates among immigrants vary by national income and gender**

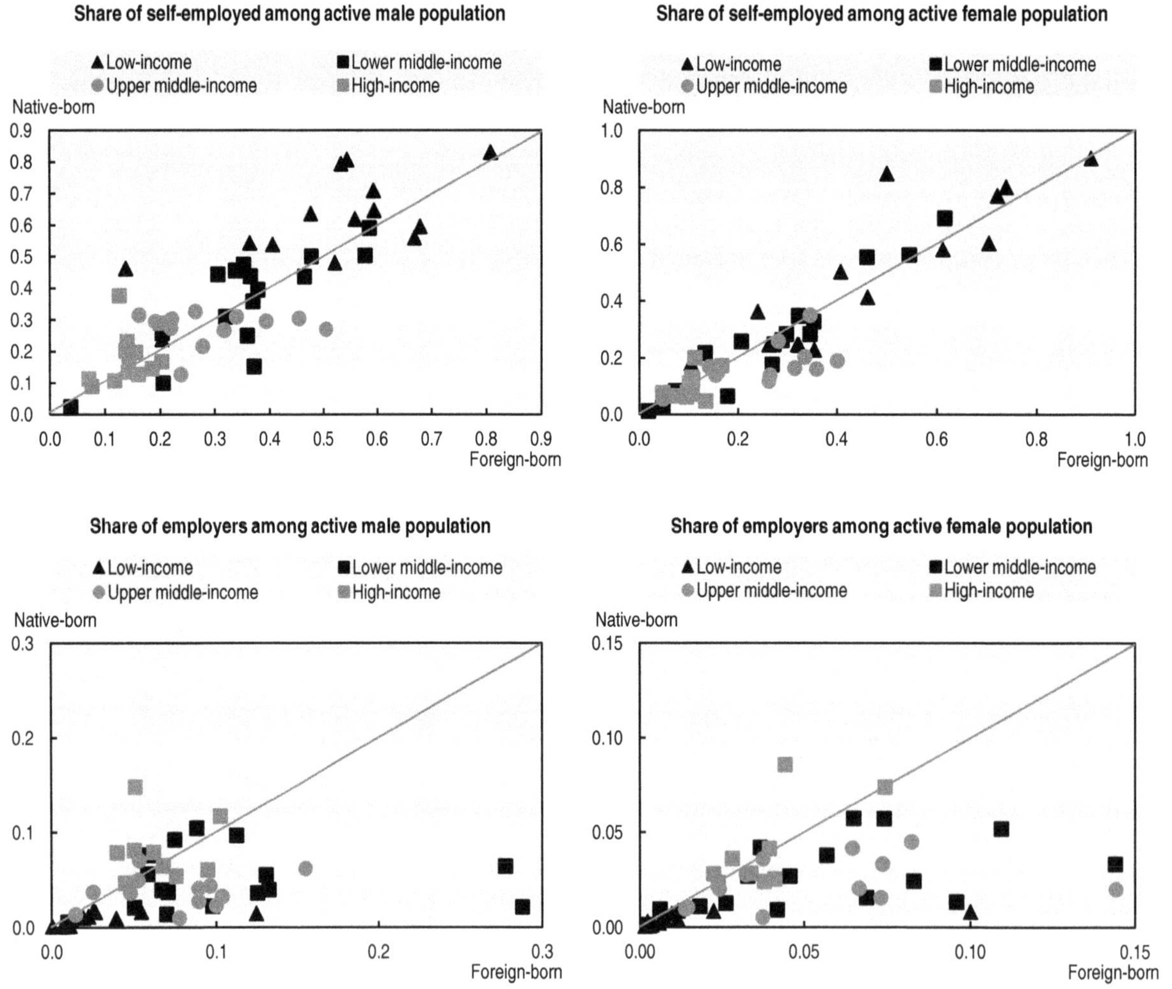

Source: Authors' calculations based on Minnesota Population Center (2014), *Integrated Public Use Microdata Series, International: Version 6.3.*
StatLink http://dx.doi.org/10.1787/888933422782

Immigration enhances trade and investment flows

Immigration can increase trade and investment flows thanks to lower transaction costs, increased demand for foreign goods and higher income levels. Transaction costs fall for many reasons when people move across borders. Migrants may bring knowledge about their home countries that can be used for commercial ventures and may be able to identify investment opportunities in their new country of residence more readily while living there than from abroad. Moreover, migrant networks can enforce contracts even in situations where legal enforcement possibilities are patchy. In addition, imports may rise when immigrants prefer goods from their home countries. Finally, if immigration boosts per capita income, this may enhance the demand for imported and domestically produced goods and services as well as for foreign investment.

The positive relationship between immigration, investment and trade appears to be quite strong (Hatzigeorgiou, 2010). In low-income countries, the effect may be stronger if immigrant networks can effectively substitute for weak legal institutions. Other factors may weaken the effect. For example, falls in unobserved trading costs may not be enough to offset prohibitively high observed transaction costs such as those related to transport and duties. Moreover, the effect of immigration on trade is larger between culturally distant country pairs. Since many immigrants in developing regions come from neighbouring countries, the effect may be smaller.

Immigration does not have a uniform impact on receiving countries' fiscal balances

There is no *a priori* reason to believe that the average immigrant household always pays more taxes than it "takes out" of the system in terms of the cost of public goods and transfers, or vice versa. In fact, many factors determine whether the impact is positive or negative. Among these are the age and education of immigrants, their propensity to stay and have children, their integration into the host society and labour market, and the structure of the tax and benefits system. For example, employed individuals tend to pay more taxes and use fewer benefits and public services than children, teenagers, retirees and the unemployed.

The average estimated current fiscal effects for OECD countries tend to be small (OECD, 2013a). These estimates typically neglect spill-over as well as long-term effects. The spill-over effects are changes in the tax payments and benefit usage of the native population that are due to overall changes in the economy in response to immigration. For example, if wages of high-skilled individuals rise, but more low-skilled individuals lose their job, the overall effect is ambiguous. Higher tax payments by the well-off may be offset by the costs created by unemployment benefits for laid-off low-skilled workers. Much therefore depends on the design of the country's fiscal system. Long-term effects are that working-age immigrants gain rights to pension and health care benefits later and that their children and grandchildren typically stay, pay taxes and use public services. Several estimates for OECD countries suggest that the effects are positive even when taking long-term costs into account (e.g. Auerbach and Oreopolous, 1999; Collado, Iturbe-Ormaetxe and Valera, 2004).

Evidence on the fiscal effects of immigration in developing countries is not readily available. As among OECD countries, the effects probably vary. Fiscal benefits are likely to be larger in countries where immigrants are over-represented in the formal sector and/or among the working-age population. In the short run, fiscal costs may also be lower if immigrants are excluded from certain social programmes or services. There is evidence of such exclusions, even for services that immigrants have access to by law, for example in

Mexico (Carte, 2014). In the long run, such exclusion may, however, have negative impacts on the integration of immigrants and on their potential economic and fiscal contribution. Moreover, depending on the service in question it may be at odds with the preservation of the human and civil rights of immigrants.

Box 8.3. The fiscal contribution of immigrants in the Dominican Republic

The Dominican Republic has an immigrant population that makes up around 4% of its total population (World Bank, 2011). Most of these immigrants are from Haiti.

The existence of a household income and expenditure survey, the National Study on Household Income and Expenditures, makes it possible to estimate the difference in the average net direct fiscal contribution between households where the household head (and their potential partner) were both born in the Dominican Republic and those where both were born abroad. The counted direct contributions comprise income taxes, social security contributions and estimated value-added tax (VAT) payments. The counted transfers include pension and assistance payments received from the government. Indirect and longitudinal effects are not taken into account, nor are other government expenditures or taxes.

The analysis reveals that foreign-born households make a higher average net direct fiscal contribution than native households. Immigrants do not pay higher taxes or contributions, but instead, they generate fewer public costs. In particular, they receive fewer pension payments or other transfers, are less likely to have used public health facilities recently and less frequently have children in public primary or secondary schools.

Table 8.1. Immigrants have a higher direct average net fiscal contribution than the native-born

Average net direct fiscal contribution of households by migration status of the household head and partner, in 2007 euros

Average	Native-born	Foreign-born
Taxes and social security contributions	1 299	1 224
Transfers, health and education expenditures	663	277
Net contribution	**636**	**947**
Average household size	3.7	3.0

Source: Authors' calculations based on the 2006-07 data in Oficina Nacional de Estadísticas (undated), *Encuesta Nacional de Ingresos y Gastos de los Hogares*, *http://enigh.one.gob.do/*.

The economic growth effect of immigration in developing countries is uncertain

While an increase in the working population is almost always associated with an increase in total output, it is far from certain that native per capita income always increases when labour immigrants arrive. Everything else being equal, immigration may initially lower the amount of capital available per worker. This lowers per capita income until these rates are restored to their previous levels.

However, immigration can also drive growth. For example, an immigrant labour force that complements the skills of the native labour force or allows local workers to specialise in occupations that are more remunerative can lead to increases in the incomes of native workers. As mentioned above, native-born women may enter the labour force thanks to an increased pool of domestic workers. Increased demand from immigrants allows local firms to produce on a more efficient scale. Immigrants may also transfer technology from their home countries and a more diverse workforce may spur innovation, thereby raising economic growth rates in the long term. Finally, immigrants might bring capital or encourage investments by others. If so, the capital-labour ratio could be quickly restored to its original or even reach a higher level.

There is no empirical consensus on whether immigration increases economic growth. In developing countries, the initial effects may be more negative if firms cannot make investments because they cannot obtain credits. However, the long-term effects may be positive if immigrants have skills that are complementary to the native-born population and if immigrants transfer capital or technology.

The effect of immigration is even more ambiguous for transit migration countries

Developing countries are often subject to transit migration, with uncertain economic effects. Definitions differ, but a transit migrant is usually understood to be someone who stays in the country for a defined period of time with the intention to moving to a third country. Inevitably, intent may be difficult to define. For example, a migrant may originally plan to stay but then change his mind and continue on to a further destination. Other migrants may become transit migrants by accident, after being abandoned by human traffickers who had promised to take them to the intended destination. Other cases are clearer: for example, in southern and eastern Europe where many migrants from North Africa and the Middle East have plainly expressed intentions to move on to destination countries such as Sweden or the United Kingdom. Even clearer are cases when migrants are granted legal status as transit migrants. Moreover, the duration of stay creates a definitional problem. There is no clear delineation between being a transit or temporary migrant or a resident.

Many transit migrants are not registered. A result of this lack of legal status may be that transit migrants cannot find stable and regular employment. In these cases, the economic contribution can be negative as the immigrant may take advantage of social services, the transit country may have to set up temporary shelters and civil society actors may contribute financial and material assistance. However, in many developing countries transit migrants are unlikely to benefit from such social services.

An example of a transit country is Morocco, which receives migrants from many sub-Saharan African countries, especially from West Africa. Many of these migrants travel to Morocco on study or work visas. Transit migrants come into the country from Algeria east of Oujda, after crossing the Saharan desert from Niger. Their goal is to enter Europe through the Spanish enclaves of Ceuta or Melilla, two ports located on the North African coast. Many who enter Spain by this route are allowed to continue their journey, as Spain has few repatriation agreements with origin countries in sub-Saharan Africa. Migrants who fail to enter Europe often choose to settle temporarily in cities such as Casablanca, Rabat and Fes. A 2007 survey of 1 000 migrants showed that sub-Saharan transit migrants in Morocco are from many different African countries (Figure 8.5). Of these migrants 76% are irregular and 73% intend to migrate to a third country (AMERM, 2008). Females made up 20% and the average age was 28 years. Only 2.3% have regular work. Most were young, male, single and they had stayed in Morocco on average for two-and-a-half years.

Figure 8.5. **Transit migrants in Morocco by country of origin**

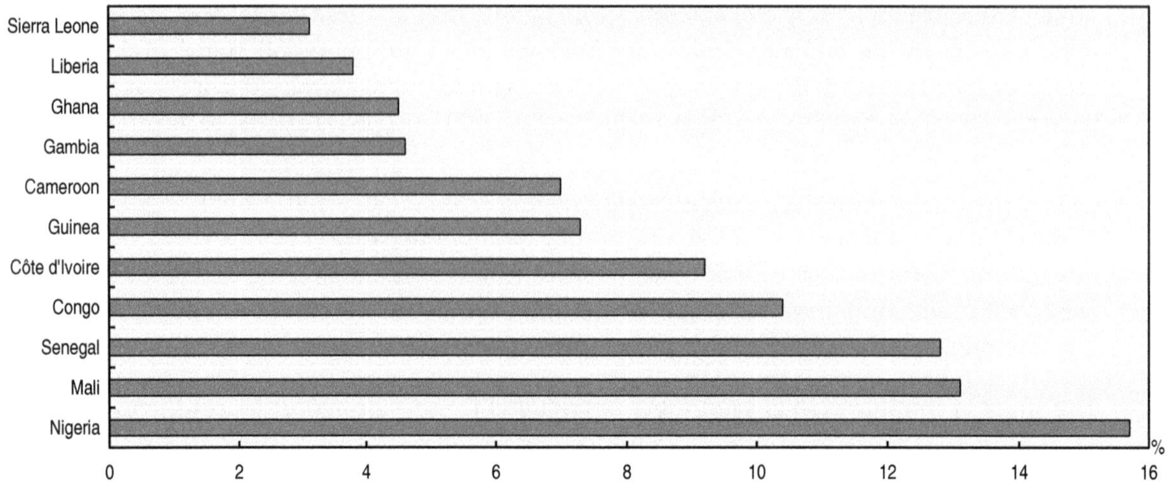

Source: AMERM (2008), "L'immigration subsaharienne au Maroc, analyse socio-économique".

StatLink http://dx.doi.org/10.1787/888933422799

Analysing the socio-cultural and environmental impacts of immigration

Just as immigration can have an economic impact, it can also have a socio-cultural impact. Immigrants bring different cultures, traditions, languages and values as well as a different demand for goods and services. These additions and changes to the destination country can result in socio-cultural impacts, such as changes in social cohesion, poverty and income inequality, human capital and education, and the quality of public goods. Many of these impacts – and others, such as on the environment – are difficult to analyse. Whether these impacts are positive or negative may depend on the number and characteristics of immigrants, but also on the perception of the native population in respect of those immigrants.

Socio-cultural impacts can also appear through the change of local socio-cultural institutions and norms. For example, new languages, dietary preferences and artistic forms of expression can be introduced through the presence of migrants. One economic manifestation of socio-cultural impacts is so-called ethnic occupational niches: entrepreneurs who cater directly to the needs of new ethnic or socio-cultural groups (e.g. Foner, 2012).

Since institutions change slowly, it is hard to assess in which form and to which extent immigration will have an impact. One historical example is the adoption of compulsory education in the United States that was used to homogenise the civic values of migrants in the 19th century. The evidence seems to suggest that immigration played an important role for the establishment of this fundamental institution (Bandiera et al. 2016).

The overall effect of immigration will depend on three major factors: first, the number of immigrants and the size of the country; second, the duration of the movement as not all migration movements are permanent; and lastly, the composition of migrant inflows and the social structure of the host country.

Since the potential socio-cultural impacts are numerous, we will focus on the following selected aspects. We will discuss first diversity and social cohesion, and thereafter poverty and inequality, education, and public goods. The focus on poverty, education and public goods is due to the fact that they can be measured and that their development has strong socio-economic repercussions.

Immigration increases cultural diversity, for better or worse

Increased cultural diversity arising from immigration may be or may not be valued by the native population, depending on personal experience, preferences and socio-economic background. If cultural diversity is positively valued, it can lead to both positive economic and social impacts including new sources of ideas, goods and services. If it is negatively valued, it can lead to negative impacts such as social unrest and a decline in social cohesion. However, it is important to distinguish public opinions on perceived impacts from the actual impacts. Actual measurements of the social and cultural impacts of immigration are rare, and often the public opinion of immigration is considered to be an indirect measurement of these impacts.

Cultural diversity can be a great strength for a society. However, some believe that if immigration exceeds a certain threshold and diversity becomes overwhelming, a society's capacity to integrate immigrants successfully and to benefit from that cultural diversity could decrease until social cohesion is at stake and public opinion massively opposes immigrants (Collier, 2013). Although research on this aspect is rare, one possible measure for whether diversity is valued is the willingness of individuals to pay more to live in cities that are diverse, as they do in the United States (Ottaviano and Peri, 2006).

Even though a society can benefit from cultural diversity, individuals can still fear an increase in immigration. For example, people may enjoy the widespread availability and better quality of foreign food, but can still have fears about a diluted national identity. In fact, more than a quarter of individuals who stated that immigration undermines the culture of the country also agreed that immigrants brought new ideas and cultures (2013 survey on national identity by ISSP Research Group (2013), Figure 8.6). Two interpretations of this result are possible. First, respondents might agree that immigrants bring new ideas and cultures, but see this as a negative, undermining force. Second, they might believe that some groups of immigrants benefit the country while others do not.

Figure 8.6. **People believe that immigrants change the culture for the better or for worse**

Percentage of respondents agreeing that immigrants bring new ideas or undermine culture

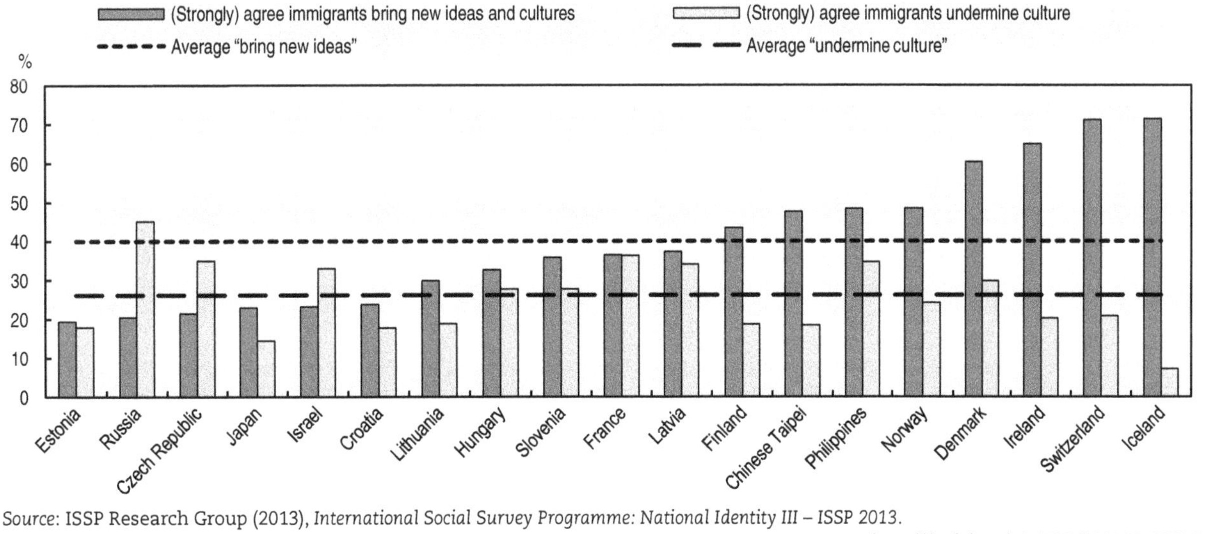

Source: ISSP Research Group (2013), *International Social Survey Programme: National Identity III – ISSP 2013.*

StatLink http://dx.doi.org/10.1787/888933422808

Limited data do not suggest that diversity is only valued above a certain wealth level. For example, the share of respondents in the Philippines to the above-mentioned survey who agreed that immigrants bring new ideas and cultures was as high as it was in Norway, a country more than eight times richer in per capita terms.

Immigration can create fears of a decline in social cohesion

There are different definitions of social cohesion. Some define it as common values and a common national identity. To others, a socially cohesive society has a high degree of internal solidarity and its members feel a sense of belonging and actively participate in community life. Features such as trust, co-operation and civic engagement are also sometimes defined as "social capital", and seen as an important determinant of economic development (OECD, 2011b).

People may have different feelings about the relationship between immigration and social cohesion. Among those who fear the negative impact on social cohesion, some are afraid that their national identity is diluted when people from other cultures settle in their country. Others may think that immigration can erode trust and solidarity. Against these views, some argue that immigration can revitalise communities and foster a stronger sense of belonging. Empirical evidence on whether trust, solidarity and civic engagement are indeed affected is scarce.

Public attitudes towards immigration may reflect these fears. In a 2013 survey on national identity (ISSP Research Group, 2013) that was carried out in selected OECD and non-OECD countries, concerns that immigrants undermine a country's culture were relatively common (see Figure 8.6). In this sample, concerns are not related to the country's average income levels, nor to the levels of immigration that the country experiences.

The presence of refugee populations can be a particular source of social instability if the local population is unwilling to accept them. In several European countries, for example, there were protests against the arrival of refugee populations in 2015. In the longer term, countries in which refugee populations are not well-integrated can experience concentrated pockets of deprivation and societies divided along ethnic, linguistic or national lines. Fears of increasing insecurity as the result of refugee populations – whether well founded or not – can fuel anti-refugee sentiment in the host population and further foment social unrest.

Immigration may affect poverty and income inequality

Increased poverty and income inequality can be a concern among the native population when immigrant numbers rise, regardless of the actual impact of those immigrants. In OECD countries, income inequality tends to be higher among immigrants than among the native-born (OECD/European Union, 2015), but this may not be the case for developing countries (Figure 8.7).

In many cases, income inequality will go up in the short term if the composition of immigrants is skewed towards the lower end of the income distribution. This is likely to be the case if migration inflows are dominated by low-skilled immigration (Card, 2009).

In the medium term, three dynamic effects will determine the effect on income inequality. First, increased wage competition could drive down wages. Yet, as was shown in the section on the labour market, the available evidence does not support this hypothesis. Second, immigrants might have unobservable characteristics that allow them to move up the income distribution scale faster than natives. Hence, inequality may not be affected in the long term and could even decrease because of the presence of immigrants. Third, due to increased demand, enterprises might invest and increase their production. This increase in production would generate rents for capital owners and might increase inequality at the national level.

Figure 8.7. **Immigration and income inequality**

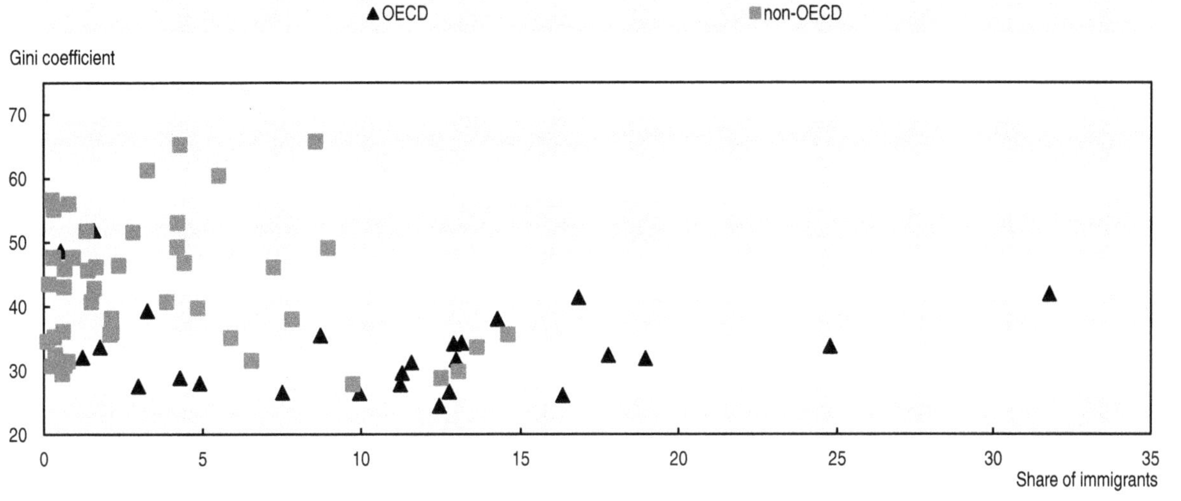

Note: The Gini coefficient is based on the comparison of cumulative proportions of the population against cumulative proportions of income they receive, and it ranges between 0 in the case of perfect equality and 100 in the case of perfect inequality.

Source: World Bank (2015), *World Development Indicators*, for latest year available, and OECD (2015), *Database on Immigrants in OECD and non-OECD Countries*, *www.oecd.org/els/mig/dioc.htm*.

StatLink http://dx.doi.org/10.1787/888933422811

In the long term, the effect of immigration on within-country inequality will depend on the economic and social mobility of immigrants. Upward mobility of immigrants would lead to multiplier effects, for instance from their consumption demand, and might augment the positive impact on the host society.

Immigration can affect the educational composition

Immigrants in developing countries tend to have lower levels of educational attainment and performance than those in developed countries. In 61 developing countries, on average 15% of international immigrants aged 15 and over had tertiary level education compared to 24% in OECD countries of destination (Dumont, Spielvogel and Widmaier, 2010). They are mostly employed in unskilled or low-skilled jobs. The results from the Programme for International Student Assessment (PISA) also confirm that immigrant students in developing countries perform less well than those in developed countries.

In most countries, a larger proportion of the native population has completed a primary education or higher, compared with immigrants (Figure 8.9). In the Dominican Republic and Ghana, almost half of the immigrant populations have not completed a primary education. About 73% of the immigrant population has completed primary education or lower in Argentina and 67% in Costa Rica. While in most countries a higher share of immigrants than native-born individuals have completed university, a greater proportion of natives in three Latin American countries has completed university, compared to the immigrant populations.

Figure 8.8. **Differences in educational attainment between native and immigrant populations**

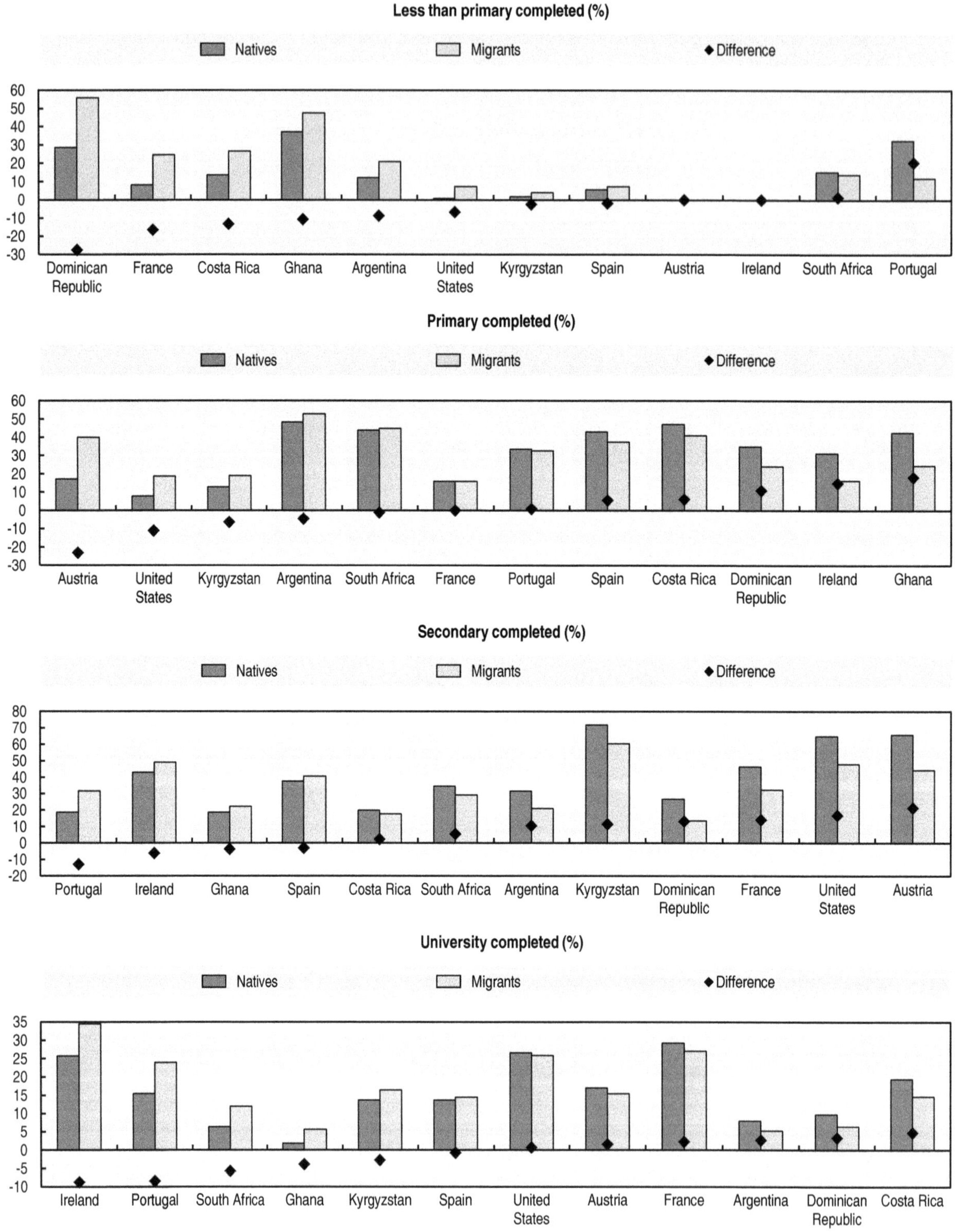

Source: Minnesota Population Center (2014), *Integrated Public Use Microdata Series, International: Version 6.3*, using countries with data after 2005.

StatLink http://dx.doi.org/10.1787/888933422828

By supplying low-skilled workers to some targeted sectors such as domestic work or care services, immigration can allow a country to release higher-skilled workers into the labour force. This may benefit female workers in particular (Tan and Gibson, 2013) and can even hold true for the inflow of refugees (Del Carpio and Wagner, 2015). The opposite may also be true: by receiving already well-educated or highly skilled immigrants, destination countries may save on education costs in the short term. However, decreased investment in public education may cause harm in the long term, although this requires further empirical analysis. Moreover, if a country uses immigrants for physical work that could conceivably be replaced by technology, the result may be a delay in innovation and technological development, as observed in the agriculture sector in many developing countries.

The overall effect of immigration on the human capital distribution in the host country depends on whether immigrants' skills are transferable and recognisable, whether their skills match the labour market's needs, whether they overlap or compete with the skills set of native workers and how long immigrants stay in the country. The relative balance of these factors can result in significantly different effects in terms of human capital.

Conditions in developing countries as destination countries may alter the effects of immigration on human capital. For example, developing countries lack school infrastructure and high-quality teachers, register lower levels of investment in human capital, through public and private education and training, and invest less in research and development (R&D). In developing countries, almost a fifth of the total population above 15 has no schooling and most are low-skilled, exhibit low productivity, and work in low-value sectors and occupations.

Immigration can affect school choice and performance among natives

Some parents may be concerned that immigrant students have a negative impact on the learning of their children. In fact, immigrant students can affect the school choice, school completion rates and school performance of native students through their impact on class sizes and class composition.

Educational performance among immigrant students is often lower than among native children (Figure 8.9). Some parents may choose to send their children to schools in other districts or private schools out of fear of potential negative effects. Some countries such as Italy have established a ceiling on the number of immigrant pupils in classes to prevent such an effect (Brunello and Rocco, 2013). However, studies on the effects of immigration on educational performance in developing countries are still rare.

Immigrant students' performance in PISA is often more strongly associated with the concentration of socio-economic disadvantage in schools than with the concentration of immigrants in itself (OECD, 2013b). Immigrants often end up in schools where the student body is made up of both immigrant students who may lack language skills and native students from relatively disadvantaged families (Brunello and Rocco, 2013). As a result the impact of immigrants on the school performance of native students cannot be treated as a causal relationship. The effect of immigrant students on reducing school performance of native children is small and varies with other factors, such as gender and the background of native parents as well as the level of segregation of immigrants in schools (Brunello and Rocco, 2013).

Immigration can also increase the level of skill premium and specialisation among natives. The skill premium can be concentrated in a specific group of occupations as natives tend to take jobs that maximise their comparative advantage in their language. It is more likely that native students will choose to upgrade their education to compete with new immigrants (McHenry, 2012).

Box 8.4. **Using PISA data to analyse the impact of immigrants in developing countries**

For most developing countries that participate in PISA, the actual number and proportion of students with immigrant backgrounds in the sample is too small for meaningful comparisons. For example, among non-OECD developing countries, there were only nine countries with an average proportion of immigrant students over 1%, with a sample size larger than 100, either in 2009 or 2012: Argentina, Brazil, Costa Rica, Jordan, Kazakhstan, Latvia, Montenegro, Panama and Serbia. Despite this limitation, PISA data are still useful to provide a general picture of immigrant students and their parents in developing countries.

Immigrant students generally perform at a lower level than non-immigrant students (Figure 8.9). However, in countries where the immigrant student population is large and highly diverse, the difference in educational performance between immigrant students and non-immigrant students of similar socio-economic status tends to be small. Immigrant students and their parents in developing countries are more likely to be from neighbouring countries than is the case in developed countries. For example, most immigrant students in Costa Rica originate from Colombia, Nicaragua and Panama. In Argentina, most immigrant students are from Bolivia, Brazil, Chile, Paraguay, and Uruguay.

Figure 8.9. **Immigrant students generally perform less well than non-immigrant students**

Difference in mathematics performance between non-immigrant and immigrant students, adjusted for socio-economic status

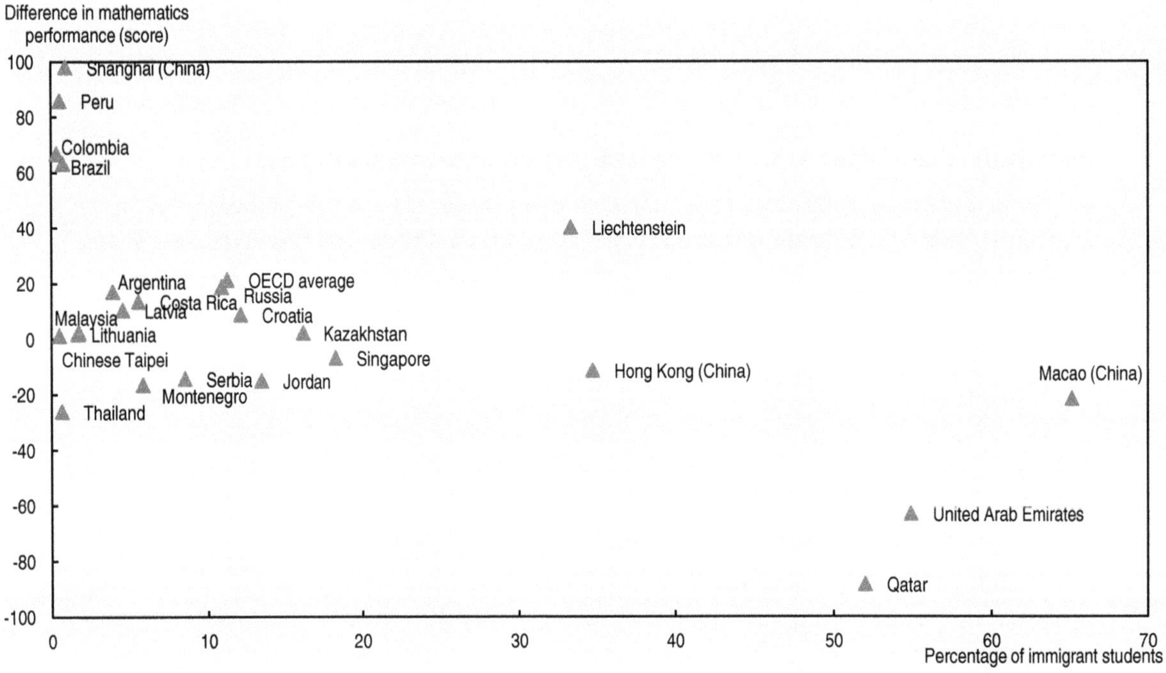

Source: PISA 2012 based on OECD (2013b), *PISA 2012 Results: Excellence through Equity (Volume II): Giving Every Student the Chance to Succeed.*

StatLink http://dx.doi.org/10.1787/888933422839

Immigrant students from different origin countries perform differently in the same destination country. For example, in Argentina, Bolivian-born immigrant students (18.4% of immigrant students) perform worse in reading, but slightly better in mathematics and science than Paraguayan-born immigrant students (11.7% of immigrant students). Native-born immigrant students perform slightly better both in Argentina and Costa Rica, yet not better than native students.

Immigrant students from the same country perform differently across countries with different school systems, meaning that education and skills systems in destination countries play a critical role in the process of integration and in the support of maintaining or gaining further skills among immigrants (Figure 8.10).

Box 8.4. **Using PISA data to analyse the impact of immigrants in developing countries** *(cont.)*

Figure 8.10. **Different destinations, different outcomes**

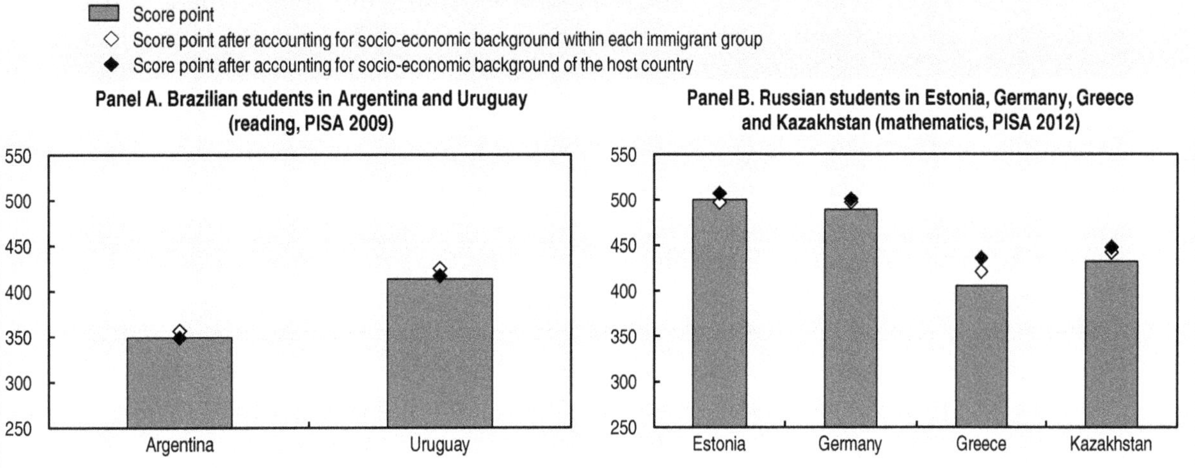

Source: PISA 2009 based on OECD (2010), *PISA 2009 Results: Overcoming Social Background: Equity in Learning Opportunities and Outcomes (Volume II)* and PISA 2012 based on OECD (2013b), *PISA 2012 Results: Excellence through Equity (Volume II): Giving Every Student the Chance to Succeed.*

StatLink http://dx.doi.org/10.1787/888933422843

The quality of public goods can be affected

While a common concern voiced in both developed and developing countries is that the availability and quality of public goods deteriorate as a result of immigration, the real impact is ambiguous. As additional users are added, roads, schools and hospitals may become crowded and the benefits that users derive may decline. On the other hand, additional tax payers may allow the government to invest in new public goods and services or to upgrade those existing.

The degree to which immigration affects the quality of public goods depends on the type of those goods, the likelihood that immigrants use them, and the reactions of the government and the native population. First, only certain goods can become "crowded". For example, on an empty road, additional drivers can initially be added without affecting the overall driving speed; but eventually, the road becomes crowded. In contrast, the quality of a country's national defence does not deteriorate with a larger population. At the opposite extreme, a public apartment can only be used by one household at a time so that some native residents may not get an apartment if an immigrant family does. Second, congestion can only increase if immigrants use the good in question. For instance, if few immigrants own cars, roads do not become more crowded. Third, the government may decide to invest in its roads, schools or hospitals and may therefore prevent any negative quality impacts. Fourth, if native citizens start to use a public good less once immigrants arrive, congestion effects may be offset. An example of such behaviour is when native citizens move their children to different school districts or private schools when the number of immigrant children in their local schools rises.

A government's capacity to undertake investment could in itself also be influenced by immigration. More diverse societies may find it more difficult to make such investment as the diversity of preferences could make it more complicated to find a political consensus (Easterly and Levine, 1997). However, this link between diversity and investment is not necessarily linked to immigration as most of the literature has focused on ethnic fractionalisation. Different nationalities do not necessarily imply different ethnicities.

Developing countries may find it particularly difficult to maintain and continue to improve the quality of their public goods and service delivery in the face of large-scale immigration. Their infrastructure and public services may already be fully used rather than being at a stage where additional users can be added without their quality being affected. Moreover, governments may not have scope within their budgets to increase investment in these goods and services. They may also not be able to increase their tax revenues.

The reception of a large number of refugees, in particular if the total rises rapidly, can test the capacity of countries to absorb them. That can be especially acute in developing countries where resources are more limited, a factor that is particularly pertinent as most refugees are accommodated in low- or middle-income countries (see Chapter 6). Host states initially need to respond to the immediate humanitarian challenge by providing shelter – either through constructing camps or finding solutions in urban areas – and food for refugee populations. In the medium to long term, the range and complexity of services required expands to include the provision of education, health and other basic social services. Provision of these services can demand substantial financial resources. As an example, Turkey had by September 2015 spent USD 8.5 billion responding to the Syrian refugee influx. This compares to the USD 470 million provided by the international community.

There is little empirical evidence on this topic for either OECD or non-OECD countries. Some limited evidence shows that immigrants are a negligible fraction of users of public housing in the United Kingdom (Robinson, 2008).

The impact of immigration on the environment is uncertain

Policy and academic debates have recently focused on the effects of the environment on migration, but there may also be effects of immigration on the environment in destination countries. These effects may occur in several areas, such as land use patterns, use of exhaustible and renewable natural resources, and pollution. The relationship between population growth and environmental outcomes is disputed. Some believe that any increase in population invariably damages the environment as humans need resources to feed, clothe and house themselves (Ehrlich and Holdren, 1971). Others argue that larger populations can generate innovations that lessen negative environmental impacts (Simon, 1990).

Empirical estimates do not give a clear answer as to which side is right. The relationship between population growth and environmental outcomes probably varies across area, time and population. For example, when the ownership of a resource is not defined, the effect of population growth on that resource may be more harmful (Robinson and Srinivasan, 1997).

It is similarly unclear whether immigrants have a more negative impact on the environment than native-born individuals. They may have a less negative impact if they consume less, if they make environmentally beneficial innovations or if they use resources more carefully (Hunter, 2000). On the other hand, immigrants may engage in more intensive and harmful agricultural techniques because they care less about the quality of resources in the long term, or because they have less knowledge of local specificities (Codjoe and Bilsborrow, 2012). They may also settle more densely. This more intense usage implies that less land gets used, but may entail environmentally damaging side effects. Empirical studies once again find differing results, suggesting that the context matters greatly.

Finally, immigration can indirectly affect the environment. For example, if immigration undermines social institutions, environmental protection efforts may decline.

Developing countries may be more affected by negative environmental effects of population growth and immigration. First, property rights for different environmental resources may be less well defined. In this case the quality or quantity of these resources usually declines more rapidly. Second, governments may have less capacity to supervise whether environmental laws are respected, also making it more likely that negative impacts will occur. While the importance of the population-environment link cannot be neglected, no conclusion can yet be drawn because of a lack of data and, as a consequence, authoritative research. Whatever the results may be in individual cases, it is, however, likely that appropriate policies can help to decouple population growth from negative environmental effects and ensure that immigration in particular is not associated with greater environmental damage than other forms of population growth.

Policies shape the development impact of immigration

Immigration and integration policies, such as those that foster circular migration, prevent discrimination and strengthen social cohesion, can maximise the contribution of immigration to development. However, non-cooperative and restrictive immigration policies come with costs and the lack of integration policies may stoke civil unrest or political crises (OECD, 2011d). This section reviews how selected immigration, integration and sectoral policies influence the socio-economic impact of immigration.

Immigration policies affect the impacts of immigration

Immigration policies can shape the composition of migration flows, but may not fully determine them, as economic, social, and other push and pull factors also affect them, as shown in Chapter 4. For example, immigration policies can promote complementary immigrant flows. To institute such policies, governments would need a complete picture of the current education and skills structure of the labour force and of current and expected skills shortages, which is not straightforward. Such shortages can also be considerable. For instance, it is estimated that by 2020, there could be a potential shortage of nearly 45 million medium-skilled workers in developing economies, or about 15% of the medium-skill demand. India, which has low rates of high school enrolment and completion, could have 13 million shortages at this level of skills (Dobbs et al., 2012).

Policy makers attempting to create complementary immigration inflows have a variety of instruments at their disposal, but the goal is difficult to achieve in most countries. Depending on a country's needs, relaxing immigration controls or providing immigration incentives can help countries alleviate skills shortages and encourage knowledge transfer. Facilitating immigration and recruitment procedures can also help. In general, policies that are driven by employer demands rather than by attempts to select immigrants based on their characteristics appear to work better, at least when it comes to high-skilled immigrants in OECD countries (Chaloff and Lemaitre, 2009). By contrast, programmes that only allow immigration into priority occupations may lead to sub-optimal results because some occupations with shortages may be neglected or the list may not be updated on a regular basis. Close co-ordination between the labour and interior ministries and employer representatives can help anticipate skills scarcities. Nonetheless, it needs to be realised that no matter what policy option is chosen, the goal of creating a perfect combination of immigrant and native skills is an unrealistic one.

Regularisation programmes for irregular immigrants can also have economic impacts. A large number of countries have enacted amnesties or regularisation processes. Among these are Argentina, Australia, Brazil, Canada, France, Italy, the Netherlands, Portugal, Spain and the United States. As a first benefit, regularised immigrants may pay more taxes, because they switch from the informal to the formal sector, because they can start a business for which they were previously not able to obtain licences or credits or because their income rises. Immigrants who are regularised generally experience rising incomes, in particularly if they are skilled (Kaushal, 2006). It is likely that these immigrants were previously employed in jobs for which they were over-qualified. Part of the increased income is then likely to lead to increased consumption, providing further positive economic impulses. Moreover, these immigrants may become better integrated economically and socially. A potential downside is that regularisation could encourage future undocumented immigration.

Immigration policies come with costs. Border protection and other enforcement policies in particular can be very expensive because they require a large number of personnel. To obtain the desired policy outcome, while keeping fiscal costs to a minimum, countries should conduct a cost-benefit analysis of different enforcement policies.

It is also important to communicate with the public so they better understand the positive contribution of immigration and to manage potential negative reactions to immigrants and immigration policies. Developing countries do not differ substantially in their views on immigration controls (Figure 8.11). The level of average support for rigorous immigration controls in both OECD and non-OECD countries shows that there are concerns and possibly public discontent with the way immigration systems work. This concern is equally present in developing and developed countries.

Figure 8.11. **Agreement with maintaining or increasing control of the entry of people**

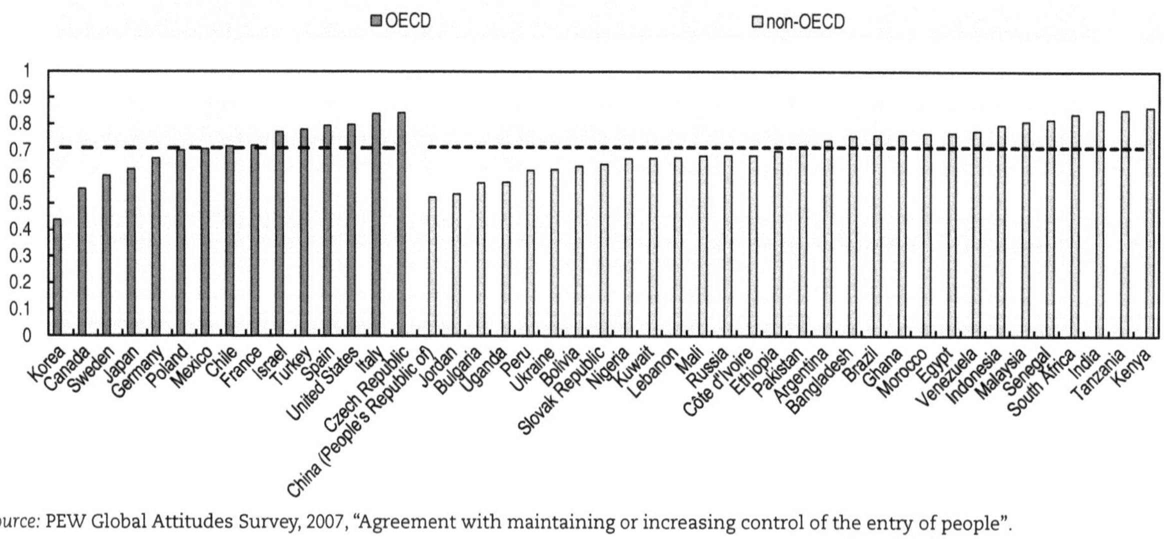

Source: PEW Global Attitudes Survey, 2007, "Agreement with maintaining or increasing control of the entry of people".

StatLink http://dx.doi.org/10.1787/888933422857

In view of such costs, international or intergovernmental co-operation can help facilitate more effective, more widely influential and less expensive migration policies (see Box 8.5). More broadly, a comprehensive governance framework is necessary when it comes to immigration policies, integrating four dimensions to maximise the benefits of international migration: international co-operation, decentralisation, inclusiveness and policy coherence (OECD, 2011d).

Box 8.5. Intergovernmental partnerships and dialogues on migration

The Rabat Process is a partnership between sub-Saharan Africa and European countries. It is funded by the European Union and implemented by the International Centre for Migration Policy Development (ICMPD) and the Fundación Internacional y para Iberoamérica de Administración y Políticas Públicas (FIIAPP).

It held four conferences in Rabat (2006), Paris (2008), Dakar (2011) and Rome (2014-17). It is currently experiencing the three-year Rome Programme, the pillars of which are:

1. organising mobility and legal migration
2. improving border management and combating irregular migration
3. strengthening the synergies between migration and development
4. promoting international protection.

This process contributed to an enhanced co-operation through the implementation of numerous bilateral, sub-regional, regional and multilateral initiatives. More specifically, it addresses border management and return policies, for example, cross-border co-operation and mobility in West and Central Africa where 23 countries are situated with 87 000 km of borders, or at the border between Burkina Faso and Mali (Hèrèmakono – Koloko) where 2 000 people cross daily. Cabo Verde, Morocco, Nigeria and Tunisia have been involved in Mobility Partnerships and Common Agendas on Migration and Mobility in the Rabat Process Region.

Source: International Centre for Migration Policy Development (*https://www.icmpd.org/our-work/migration-dialogues/rabat-process/*).

Integration policies and sectoral policies can reduce future costs of immigration

Integration takes place in three dimensions: cultural, civic and economic. It is in the interest of the receiving country to facilitate this process, since integrated immigrants can fully contribute to the country's economy and society.

Targeted integration policies as well as the degree of openness of the host society and the immigrants' own efforts influence the speed of integration. Three key programmes in this area are language instruction, skill recognition and naturalisation policies.

Insufficient knowledge of the local language has been identified as one of the major barriers for the integration of immigrants into receiving countries. Accordingly, some countries offer language courses for newly arrived migrants. Provision of language training for immigrant children not only fosters integration, but also the acquisition of skills relevant to the labour market success.

Another barrier to full integration is a lack of skills recognition. Immigrants may take up jobs for which they are over-qualified when there is no accessible mechanism for the recognition of foreign qualifications. Many regional economic communities, such as the Economic Community of West African States (ECOWAS), the Mercado Común del Sur (MERCOSUR) and the Association of Southeast Asian Nations (ASEAN), have recognised this problem. Within their frameworks on regional labour mobility, the recognition of skills is often a key priority. For example, the ten ASEAN members have developed the ASEAN Qualifications Reference Framework that will be used to relate national qualifications between member countries.

Naturalisation policies can also affect the degree to which immigrants identify with their host society and, in turn, how much they wish to contribute to civil life. Migrants who come from countries that allow dual citizenship rights opt more frequently for naturalisation (Mazzolari, 2009).

Integration policies also have an important impact on how much refugees can contribute to their host countries. Certain conditions need to be in place to increase the possibility for refugees to make a positive contribution to the host economy and society. The Ugandan experience may be instructive in this regard. There, refugees have the right to work and enjoy a significant degree of freedom of movement. This is very often not the case for refugee populations in other countries. Policies, including non-migration policies, can also have a large bearing on the social impact of refugees on their receiving country. Integration policies in particular can be fundamental to avoiding a damaging social impact. In a context where the return of refugees to their home countries is becoming less common because of the tendency for refugees to spend more time in exile, policies to support the economic and social integration of refugee populations will become more important (see Chapter 6 for further discussion of policy recommendations regarding refugees). A key to success will be a change in perspective from viewing refugees as a drain on resources to them being seen as people with untapped potential, bringing skills and expertise to their receiving countries.

Both OECD and non-OECD countries face integration challenges, but there may be some differences. For some countries, in particular in Latin America, language integration is less of a problem. For example, in Argentina and Costa Rica, among students with an immigrant background who participated in PISA 2012, more than half were born in the country while the majority of foreign-born students came from Spanish-speaking countries.[1] Some developing countries might therefore have integration advantages. Nevertheless they should not neglect the question of integration.

Education makes it easier for immigrants to integrate into the labour market in the host country and better contribute to the country's development. While immigrants tend to have poorer socio-economic backgrounds than native citizens, those with higher levels of education are better off (OECD/European Union, 2015). Programmes that target the educational achievement gap between students with and without an immigration background are therefore among the most powerful mechanisms to facilitate integration. Similarly, facilitating access to post-secondary education opportunities for immigrants is likely to aid with integration.

The fiscal effects of immigration depend on the extent to which immigrants are allowed to access the social safety nets and welfare services and how they operate to bring immigrants into the tax system as tax payers (Ratha et al., 2011).

Many other factors also influence how well immigrants can integrate and as a result how much they can contribute to their host country; and countries with a lower per capita income are often less able to provide services that can facilitate integration. In addition to targeted integration policies, policies in other areas, for instance regarding education, tax and businesses, influence how well immigrants integrate and how much they can contribute. Overall, the benefits from immigration are likely to be greatest when policies across different areas are harmonised.

Note

1. On the other hand, in PISA sample of developing countries, native students who do not speak the language of assessment at home represent a sizable proportion of the student population. These students constitute over 40% of the student population in Indonesia, Thailand and Malaysia, between 10% and 17% in Chinese-Taipei and Bulgaria, and between 3% and 10% in Kazakhstan, Lithuania, Latvia, the Russian Federation, Macao-China, Peru, Jordan and Serbia. Those who speak the language outperform those who do not speak the language by more than 10-15 score points in some countries (OECD 2013b).

References

AMERM (2008), "L'immigration subsaharienne au Maroc, analyse socio-économique", Association Marocaine d'Etudes et de Recherche en Migrations, Rabat.

Amuedo-Dorantes, C. and S. de la Rica (2011), "Complements or substitutes? Task specialization by gender and nativity in Spain", *Labour Economics*, 18(5), pp. 697-707.

Auerbach, A. J. and P. Oreopoulos (1999), "Analyzing the fiscal impact of U.S. immigration", *American Economic Review*, 89(2), pp. 176-180.

Bahar, D. and H. Rapoport (2014), "Migration, knowledge diffusion and the comparative advantage of nations", Center for International Development, Harvard University. *http://sites.bu.edu/neudc/files/2014/10/paper_108.pdf*.

Bandiera, O., M. Mohnen, I. Rasul and M. Viarengo (2016), "Nation-building through compulsory schooling during the age of mass migration", *Working Paper*. *www.homepages.ucl.ac.uk/~uctpimr/research/CSL.pdf*.

Betts, A., L. Bloom, J. Kaplan and N. Omata (2014), *Refugee Economies: Rethinking Popular Assumptions*, Humanitarian Innovation Project, Refugee Studies Centre, University of Oxford.

Brunello, G. and L. Rocco (2013), "The effect of immigration on the school performance of natives: Cross country evidence using PISA test scores", *Economics of Education Review*, 32, pp. 234-246.

Card, D. (2009), "Immigration and Inequality", *American Economic Review*, 99(2), pp. 1-21.

Carte, L. (2014), "Everyday restriction: Central American women and the state in the Mexico-Guatemala border city of Tapachula", *International Migration Review*, 48(1), p. 113-143.

Chaloff, J. and G. Lemaitre (2009), "Managing highly-skilled labour migration: A comparative analysis of migration policies and challenges in OECD countries", *OECD Social, Employment and Migration Working Papers*, No. 79.

Codjoe, S. N. A. and R. E. Bilsborrow (2012), "Are migrants exceptional resource degraders? A study of agricultural households in Ghana", *GeoJournal*, Vol. 77, Issue 5, pp. 681-694.

Collado, M. D., I. Iturbe-Ormaetxe and G. Valera (2004), "Quantifying the impact of immigration on the Spanish welfare state", *International Tax and Public Finance*, 11(3), pp. 335-353.

Collier, P. (2013), *Exodus: How Migration Is Changing Our World*, Oxford University Press, Oxford.

Del Carpio and M. Wagner (2015), "The impact of Syrian refugees on the Turkish labour market", *World Bank Working Paper*, No. 7402.

Dobbs, R., A. Madgavkar, D. Barton, E. Labaye, J. Manyika, C. Roxburgh, S. Lund and S. Madhav (2012), *The World at Work: Jobs, Pay, and Skills for 3.5 Billion People*, McKinsey Global Institute, McKinsey & Company.

Dumont, J-C, G. Spielvogel and S. Widmaier (2010), "International migrants in developed, emerging and developing countries: An extended profile", *OECD Social, Employment and Migration Papers*, No. 144.

Easterly, W. and R. Levine (1997), "Africa's growth tragedy: Policies and ethnic divisions", *The Quarterly Journal of Economics*, 112(4), pp. 1203-1250.

Ehrlich, P. R. and J. P. Holdren (1971), "Impact of population growth", *Science*, 171(3977), pp. 1212-1217.

Facchini, G., A.-M. Mayda and M. Mendola (2013), "South-South migration and the labour market: Evidence from South Africa", *Centro Studi Luca D'Agliano Development Studies Working Papers*, No. 351.

Foner, N. (2012) "The social effects of immigration", in M. Rosenblum and D. J. Tichenor (eds) *Oxford Handbook of the Politics of International Migration*, Oxford University Press, Oxford.

Gindling, T. H. (2009), "South-South migration: The impact of Nicaraguan immigrants on earnings, inequality and poverty in Costa Rica", *World Development*, 37(1), pp. 116-126.

Grimm, M., P. Knorringa and J. Lay (2012), "Constrained gazelles: High potentials in West Africa's informal economy", *World Development*, 40(7), pp. 1352-1368.

Hatzigeorgiou, A. (2010), "Migration as trade facilitation: Assessing the links between international trade and migration", *The B.E. Journal of Economic Analysis & Policy*, 10(1).

Hunter, L. M. (2000), "A comparison of the environmental attitudes, concern, and behaviors of native-born and foreign-born U.S. residents", *Population and Environment: A Journal of Interdisciplinary Studies*, 21:6, pp. 565-580.

ILO (2015), *Key Indicators of the Labour Market 2015*, International Labour Organization, Geneva.

ILO (2012), *Women and men in the informal economy - Statistical picture* (database) *http://laborsta.ilo.org/*.

IOM (2013), *World Migration Report 2013*, International Organization for Migration, Geneva.

ISSP Research Group (2013), "International Social Survey Programme: National Identity III – ISSP 2013", Gesis Data Archive, Cologne.

Kaushal, N. (2006), "Amnesty programs and the labor market outcomes of undocumented workers", *The Journal of Human Resources*, 41(3), pp. 631-647.

Kerr, S. P. and W. R. Kerr (2011), "Economic impacts of immigration: A survey", *NBER Working Paper*, No. 16736, *http://www.nber.org/papers/w16736.*

Maystadt, J.-F. and G. Duranton (2014), "The development push of refugees", *Lancaster University Management School Working Paper*, No. 66910685.

Mazzolari, F. (2009), "Dual citizenship rights: Do they make more and richer citizens?", *Demography*, Vol. 46:1, pp. 169-191.

McHenry, P. (2012), "Immigration and the human capital of natives", *Journal of Human Resources*, 50(1), pp. 34-71.

Minnesota Population Center (2014), *Integrated Public Use Microdata Series, International: Version* 6.3 (Machine-readable database), University of Minnesota, Minneapolis.

OECD (2015), *Database on Immigrants in OECD and non-OECD Countries: DIOC, www.oecd.org/els/mig/dioc.htm.*

OECD (2014), "Is migration good for the economy?" *Migration Policy Debates*, OECD Publishing, Paris, *https://www.oecd.org/migration/mig/OECD%20Migration%20Policy%20Debates%20Numero%202.pdf.*

OECD (2013a), "The fiscal impact of immigration in OECD Countries", in *International Migration Outlook 2013*, OECD Publishing, Paris, *http://dx.doi.org/10.1787/migr_outlook-2013-6-en.*

OECD (2013b), *PISA 2012 Results: Excellence through Equity (Volume II): Giving Every Student the Chance to Succeed*, OECD Publishing, Paris, *http://dx.doi.org/10.1787/9789264201132-en.*

OECD (2011a), "Migrant entrepreneurship in OECD countries", in *International Migration Outlook 2011*, OECD Publishing, Paris, pp. 139-203, *http://dx.doi.org/10.1787/migr_outlook-2011-8-en.*

OECD (2011b), *Perspectives on Global Development 2012: Social Cohesion in a Shifting World*, OECD Publishing, Paris, *http://dx.doi.org/10.1787/persp_glob_dev-2012-en.*

OECD (2011d), *Tackling the Policy Challenges of Immigration: Regulation, Integration, Development*, OECD Publishing, Paris, *http://dx.doi.org/10.1787/9789264126398-en.*

OECD (2010), *PISA 2009 Results: Overcoming Social Background: Equity in Learning Opportunities and Outcomes (Volume II)*, OECD Publishing, Paris, *http://dx.doi.org/10.1787/9789264091504-en.*

OECD (2007), *International Migration Outlook 2007*, OECD Publishing, Paris, *http://dx.doi.org/10.1787/migr_outlook-2007-en.*

OECD/EU (2015), *Indicators of Immigrant Integration 2015: Settling In*, OECD Publishing, Paris, *http://dx.doi.org/10.1787/9789264234024-en.*

Oficina Nacional de Estadísticas (undated), *Encuesta Nacional de Ingresos y Gastos de los Hogares, http://enigh.one.gob.do/.*

Ottaviano, G. I.P. and G. Peri (2006), "The economic value of cultural diversity: Evidence from US cities", *Journal of Economic Geography*, 6, pp. 9-44.

Özden, Ç. and M. Wagner (2014), "Immigrant versus natives? Displacement and job creation", *World Bank Policy Research Working Paper*, No. 6900.

Park, Y. J. (2009), "Chinese migration in Africa", *SAIIA Occasional Paper*, No. 24.

Ratha, D., S. Mohapatra, Ç. Özden, S. Plaza, W. Shaw and A. Shimeles. 2011. Leveraging Migration for Africa: Remittances, skills and investments. Washington, DC: World Bank.

PEW (2007), *Global Attitudes Survey* (dataset) *http://www.pewglobal.org/category/datasets/.*

Robinson, D. (2008), *New immigrants and migrants in social housing in England*, Local Government Association, Sheffield.

Robinson, J. A. and T. N. Srinivasan (1997), "Long-term consequences of population growth: Technological change, natural resources, and the environment", in *Handbook of population and family economics*, Elsevier B.V., Philadelphia, pp. 1175-1297.

Sautman, B. and Y. Hairong (2007), "Friends and interests: China's distinctive links with Africa", *African Studies Review* 50(3), pp. 75-114.

Shen, X. (2013), "Private Chinese investment in Africa – Myths and realities", *World Bank Policy Research Working Paper*, No. 6311.

Simon, J. L. (1990), *Population Matters: People, Resource, Environment, and Immigration*, Transaction Publishers, New Brunswick.

Tan, P.-L. and J. Gibson (2013), "Impact of foreign maids on female labor force participation in Malaysia", *Asian Economic Journal*, 27(2), pp. 163-183.

Tang, X. (2010), "Bulldozer or locomotive? The impact of Chinese enterprises on the local employment in Angola and the DRC", *Journal of Asian and African Studies*, 45(3), pp. 350-368.

Wang, H. (2014), "Recent trends in migration between China and other developing countries", presentation at the *International Organization for Migration 2014 International Dialogue on Migration, https://goo.gl/fkwgwR*.

UNHCR (2014), *UNHCR Global Trends 2014: Forced displacement in 2014* United Nations High Commissioner for Refugees.

World Bank (2011), *Migration and Remittances Factbook 2011*, World Bank, Washington, DC.

World Bank (undated A), *Enterprise Surveys* (database), *www.enterprisesurveys.org/data*.

World Bank (undated B), *World Integrated Trade Solution*, *http://wits.worldbank.org/*.

World Bank (2015), *World Development Indicators* (database), *http://databank.worldbank.org/wdi*.

Perspectives on Global Development 2017
International Migration in a Shifting World
© OECD 2016

Chapter 9

Four possible scenarios for international migration in 2030

History can teach the world about international migration in the past. But what about the future and specifically the next 15 years? This chapter presents four future scenarios for international migration. The first scenario extends the trends that are already evident today, such as slowing growth in developing economies. The second presents a more positive vision of where the world could be in 2030, using the Sustainable Development Goals as inspiration. The third scenario imagines the consequences of a global shock in the form of a financial crisis, and reveals a world in which global co-operation is effectively addressing the challenges. The final scenario shows what could happen if global co-operation deteriorates in a context of rapid automation and economic divergence. The chapter concludes by drawing lessons from the scenarios and asks what can be done to avoid the scenarios' negative aspects and advance towards the more positive aspects.

The previous chapters have shown how past and current experiences of "shifting wealth" have affected the flows of international migration and the identity of those involved in it. Lessons from the past can provide a better understanding of possible trends in the future. This is particularly relevant given the many uncertainties regarding tendencies in growth in gross domestic product (GDP), as well as of others such as those associated with demography, technology, climate change, conflict, governance and public policies.

This chapter considers the future of international migration and looks at four possible scenarios depicting its nature in 2030. The scenarios are hypothetical and are not an OECD prediction of the future. The chapter begins with a brief review of recent outlooks for international migration and highlights the main assumptions behind those outlooks. Given the interdependence between the different factors driving migration, and the uncertainties in some of the trends, the ability of forecasters to predict the future nature, direction and composition of migration using quantitative approaches and models is limited. An alternative approach is, therefore, to construct future scenarios.

Scenario-based approaches are designed to encourage open thinking to develop stories about the future and then to use these stories to make sense of a puzzling and complex situation. The aim is to analyse plausible futures that are not usually taken into account when traditional forecasting methods are used. The use of various scenarios makes it possible to investigate the complex relationship between shifting wealth and migration, as well as the factors that affect this relationship. The objectives of the scenarios are to develop a better understanding of what may affect future migration flows and improve the quality of discussions and policies about complex and interdependent factors influencing migration trends and outcomes.

Forecasting future migration patterns presents enormous problems

A number of different modelling approaches are used to forecast migration. Some models take as their basis existing statistical information. For example, gravity models, which are based on Newton's law of gravitation, are used to predict the degree of interaction between two places. These identify the main determinants of migration based on past data (seeing how factors such as wage differentials, distance and language affected bilateral migration flows or numbers) and are then fed with projections of the trends in these main determinants to produce projections of future migration (see, for example, Braconier, Nicoletti and Westmore, 2014). Other subjective expert judgement or survey results[1] are fed into forecasting models or used to produce projections (see, for example, Bijak, 2006 for a discussion of the strengths and weaknesses of various approaches).

However, migration dynamics are highly complex and include many interdependencies that models struggle to capture. Furthermore, quantitative migration projections that are based on estimates retrieved from historical data do not take into account the reality that the evolution of some trends and their interactions are difficult to predict. It is therefore questionable whether past and current relative interactions will have the same weight in the future. One alternative is to take into account different evolutions for economic, demographic and other variables (see for example, Docquier and Machado, 2014).

Poor quality or missing data can also render models less useful. Net migration is typically calculated from data about population numbers, births and deaths. This method therefore does not capture gross flows and can introduce statistical inconsistencies. Furthermore, data collection may be flawed, concepts are not always applied consistently across countries, and documentation and co-operation between countries sending migrants and those receiving them are sometimes limited. Some models are also complex and require much more detailed statistical information on international population flows than is usually available (Bijak, 2006).

As a result, migration projections that are referred to often can show very different results. For example, whereas two different models show net migratory flows increasing and plateauing for all more developed countries, projections by the UN's World Population Prospects (WPP) show a trend in the opposite direction; for the United States, different models show net migratory flows either increasing and plateauing, increasing before peaking and falling at a lower rate, or falling from 2010 (Figure 9.1). The OECD projections on migration show different trends (Braconier, Nicoletti and Westmore, 2014).

Figure 9.1. **Different methods produce very different projections of migration**

1950-2010 (actual), 2010-2100 (different projections of net migration), in millions, for more developed countries (Panel A) and for the United States (Panel B)

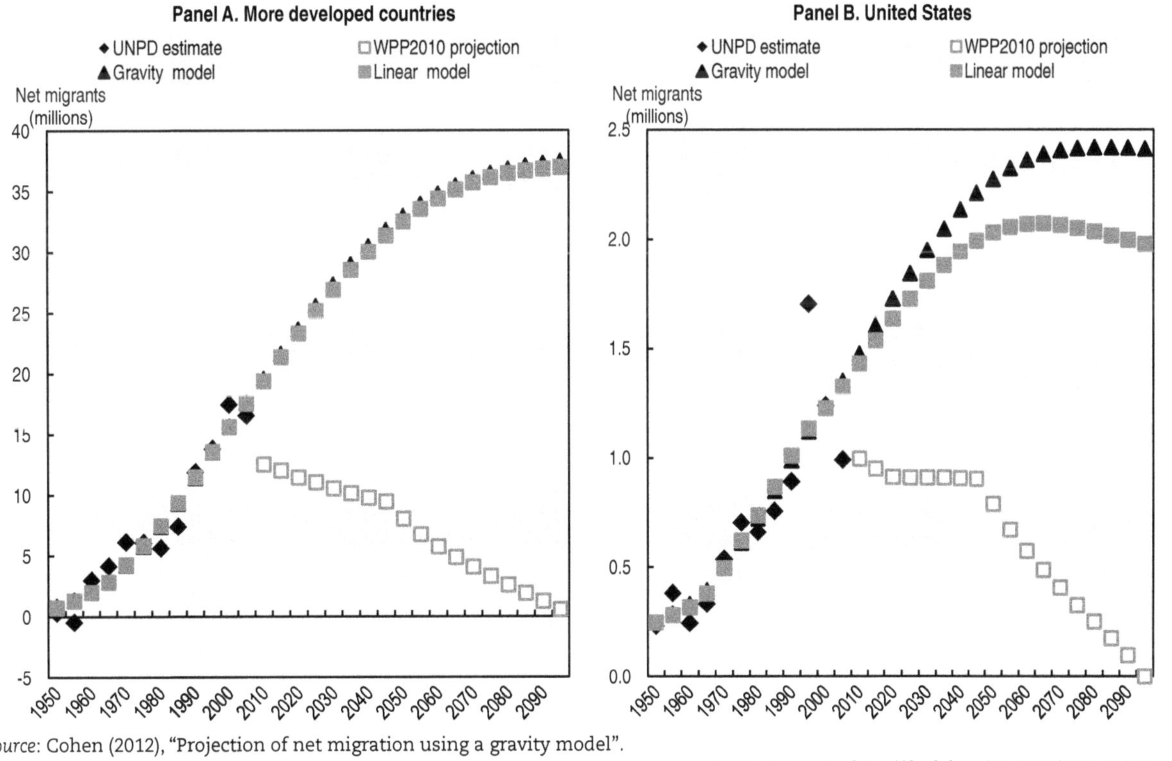

Source: Cohen (2012), "Projection of net migration using a gravity model".

StatLink http://dx.doi.org/10.1787/888933422866

Quantitative analysis inevitably omits important features of the real world and cannot deliver full conclusions on unpredictable trends. Hence, migration projections may be most useful when they are combined with a qualitative scenario exercise, as explained below.

Scenarios explore different alternative futures for migration

Scenarios are structured, well thought-out stories describing a small set of possible and different futures and how they might come about. The scenarios overlap in aspects of the future that are likely to persist, and differ in areas of uncertainty.

Unlike forecasts, scenarios are not predictions or projections, which contain implicit expectations. Rather, scenarios challenge our existing world views, mental models and assumptions to better anticipate plausible, alternative futures (Figure 9.2).

Figure 9.2. **Scenarios are not forecasts**

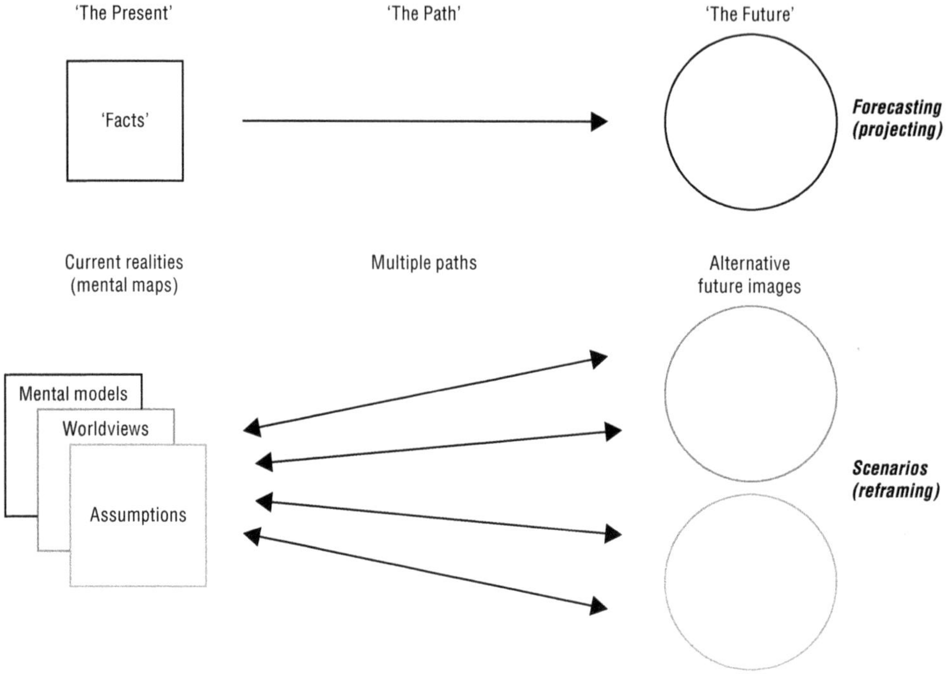

Used in a policy setting, foresight can be a way of creating a shared sense of future and of refreshing our understanding of the present. Foresight in policy is essential to anticipating global emerging issues, addressing connected challenges by using a "systems thinking" approach and enabling global collaboration. In this way, scenarios are not designed to reduce uncertainty, but to enhance our ability to operate successfully in an uncertain world, to be more proactive rather than reactive. A well-known example of a fruitful collaboration occurred in a scenario project undertaken during the post-apartheid transition in South Africa in the early 1990s (Box 9.1).

Given the political and often contentious nature of policy making on migration, and uncertainties surrounding how the drivers of migration will evolve, scenarios can be a useful tool to reframe the issue and search for solutions. Policy makers may find it useful to reflect on how the drivers of migration might develop in the future, what the important uncertainties are, and how they might combine to create a range of different possible futures (OECD, 2009).

Box 9.1. **How scenarios helped shape the political transition in South Africa**

The South African scenarios were developed to help the country make the transition from apartheid. At the time there was intense pressure for rapid land reform and other profound changes in the economic life of the country. The scenario team brought together representatives from all parts of the deeply divided South African political spectrum.

The team came up with four scenarios, none of which represented a future anyone initially wanted. One of the scenarios represented a rapid reorganisation of the economy, including extensive financial system reforms – but the team agreed that the most plausible outcome of such rapid reforms would be a fiscal crisis. The scenario was called "Icarus" after the son of Daedalus in Greek mythology whose wings melted when he flew too close to the sun. Another scenario – which eventually emerged as a desired future – was a measured approach to reforming the economic system to allow the government to be sustainable. This scenario was called "Flight of the Flamingos", because while flamingos take off slowly, they take off together.

In the decades following this exercise, the two scenarios that generated the most discussion – "Icarus" and "Flight of the Flamingos" – were alluded to in national news media, sermons and government discussions. The scenario exercise had helped provide a common language for a transformative vision of the future. And in creating the four scenarios, the diverse team established a level of trust.

Source: Kahane, A. (2012), *Transformative Scenario Planning: Working Together to Change the Future*, *www.bkconnection.com/books/title/transformative-scenario-planning*.

This chapter puts forward four scenarios of future migration that were developed through a series of workshops with migration experts and policy makers. The scenarios are hypothetical. They do not provide statements on what the OECD considers to be the future. Rather, they are designed to open up space for exploration and dialogue on migration in different contexts.

- "Slower shifting wealth" (Scenario 1) foresees business as usual, with economic convergence between OECD and non-OECD countries continuing, but at a slower pace than in the last 15 years. Global co-operation and co-ordinated action are also becoming more difficult in this scenario.
- "SDG success" (Scenario 2) presents a more positive vision of the state of the world in 2030, and assumes significant progress towards achieving the United Nations Sustainable Development Goals (SDGs).
- "Crisis with attempt for co-operation" (Scenario 3) describes a world shaken by a global financial crisis originating in the developing world, but in which countries are aspiring to co-operate to address major challenges.
- "Rapid automation and conflicts" (Scenario 4) depicts a global labour landscape drastically changed through rapid automation, and conflict-dogged countries in many developing regions.

These four scenarios illustrate possible and plausible states of the world in 2030 and how the world could move to each condition between 2016 and 2030. They are **not** predictions about what **will** actually happen. All the scenarios are written as if the year were 2030.

The description of the migration patterns resulting from and in turn shaping the different states of the world in each scenario was developed with migration experts, and the underlying transmission mechanisms from migration to the economy and vice versa are those explained in the previous chapters.

Migration is recognised as an important factor for development in origin and destination countries as well as developed and developing countries. The scenarios reveal that there are varying policy options (related to migration) that can be fostered to improve development outcomes in developing, emerging and developed economies, depending on how the world is evolving. Nonetheless, there does exist a set of migration-related polices that is likely to improve outcomes, whether the world is crisis-ridden or prospering. One purpose of the scenarios is to create awareness among policy makers that the world can move in many different directions and thus migration patterns and implications for migration-related policies may also be very different.

The scenarios are developed along three axes (see Figure 9.3), taking into account three dimensions. The horizontal axis shows economic convergence versus economic divergence in per capita incomes between OECD and non-OECD countries. The vertical axis relates to different degrees of co-operation at the international level. Global co-operation is defined as more co-operative international relations and aspiration towards global governance in several policy areas. The diagonal axis shows more open versus more restrictive migration policies. This diagonal axis is added to highlight the focus on migration in this report and to recognise the importance of migration policies in shaping different conditions of the world.

Figure 9.3. **Four illustrative future scenarios are developed along three axes**

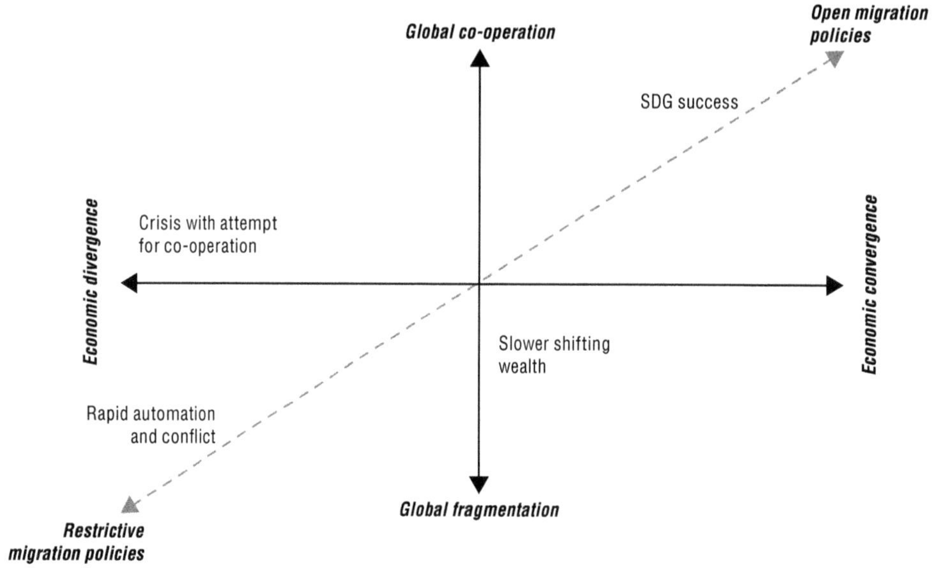

The diagram reads as follows. The point where the three axes cross corresponds to the world today in terms of convergence/divergence, co-operation/fragmentation and open/restrictive migration policies. The further away a scenario (or state of the world in 2030) is positioned from the origin, the more the world in that scenario moves in the respective directions along the three dimensions over the next 15 years.

Economic convergence versus divergence. With respect to economic convergence in per capita incomes, the world is moving fastest towards convergence in "SDG success". Most developing countries experience strong growth, while advanced countries have stable but relatively low growth rates. New growth poles, particularly in China, India and Nigeria, support growth in lower-income countries. In "Slower shifting wealth" the convergence process is still positive but slower, reflecting the current much lower growth projections over the medium term in large emerging economies compared with the 2000s.

In "Crisis with attempt for co-operation" and "Rapid automation and conflict" the convergence process is reversed because of very low, or even negative, growth in most developing and emerging economies in both of these scenarios.

Global co-operation versus fragmentation. In each scenario, the scope of global co-operation/ fragmentation is different in terms of geography and policy areas, which makes this dimension complicated and the respective specificities in each scenario require careful attention. The scenario "SDG success" describes a state of the world in which global co-operation is strongest, with countries signing and ratifying multilateral agreements across a broad range of policy areas, from trade and investment to the environment and migration. At the other end of the axis is global fragmentation, defined as conflictual international relations and an inability or unwillingness to co-operate to reach meaningful global agreements. The scenario "Rapid automation and conflicts" depicts a world where the degree of international co-operation is the weakest in all four scenarios. Countries are unwilling to reach global or multilateral agreements, and some existing agreements are ignored or even abandoned. The highest degree of co-operation that states achieve is generally at the bilateral level. The other two scenarios ("Crisis with attempt for co-operation" and "Slower shifting wealth") describe states of the world in which international co-operation falls between these two more extreme cases and patterns of global co-operation or fragmentation are different in each. For example, in "Crisis with attempt for co-operation", there is global governance in some policy areas, but this global governance is led by a small number of advanced countries. In the description of each scenario, more details are provided on what level of global co-ordination/fragmentation is in place.

Open versus restrictive migration policies. There are also specific characteristics to the migration policy dimension in each scenario (see Annex 9.A1). Overall, migration policies are much more open in "SDG success" and much more restrictive in "Rapid automation and conflict". In the other two scenarios, openness to migration is similar to today although it varies within each of these scenarios. In all scenarios, migration policies become increasingly selective and targeted, except in "SDG success", where migration is determined largely through market-led forces. While migration policy is mostly set at the multilateral level in "SDG success", regional migration agreements dominate in "Slower shifting wealth", bilateral agreements are most common in "Crisis with attempt for co-operation" and in "Rapid automation and conflict" high-income countries operate unilateral migration policies.

Beyond the economic, global governance and migration policy factors, the scenarios also explore the technological, demographic, social, environmental, conflict and political dimensions.

There are different ways to think about very negative or positive scenarios. Heaven and hell scenarios, in which everything is positive or negative, optimistic or gloomy, are intentionally avoided. In all the conditions of the world presented, both challenges and opportunities are highlighted.

Some assumptions are common to all scenarios. The impacts of climate change are a feature in each. The global mean temperature will increase by 0.5-1.2 degrees Celsius between 2015 and 2035, regardless of socio-economic trends and climate policies (IPCC, 2014). Because of this global warming, climate change will amplify existing risks and create new risks for human and natural systems. Significant sections of plant and animal species face extinction risks. The frequency of natural hazards, such as floods, droughts, typhoons and hurricanes, is already increasing because of climate change. The number of people exposed to droughts is expected to increase by 9% to17% in 2030 and 50% to 90% in 2080. The number of people exposed to river floods is expected to increase by 4% to 15% in 2030 and 12% to 29% in 2080 (World Bank, 2016). Coastal systems and low-lying areas are at increasing risk from sea level rise, which will continue for centuries even if the global mean temperature is stabilised (IPCC, 2014).

Climate change poses a significant threat to food security. Fisheries' productivity as well as wheat, rice and maize production in tropical regions will be severely challenged. Water scarcity will become an increasing problem in light of the projected reduction in renewable surface water and groundwater resources. Climate change is also expected to have an impact on human health largely by exacerbating existing health problems and diseases, such as malaria and diarrhoea. Moreover, climate shocks will disproportionately affect poorer people in developing countries because they are more exposed to such shocks, are more vulnerable to their effects and have less support to help prevent and manage these effects.

It is extremely difficult to predict the numbers of people who could be displaced because of environmental factors, and even current levels of displacement are unknown given a lack of data (Ionesco, Mokhnacheva and Gemenne, 2016). This reinforces the case for using foresight methodologies to explore different scenarios of migration that could arise as a result of environmental change and its interplay with other social, economic and political factors. The migration scenarios do not systematically explore different climate change scenarios,[2] but have some variation depending on assumptions about economic growth and global co-operation.

Demographic shifts are largely constant across all four scenarios, characterised by ageing in advanced and some large emerging economies (e.g. Brazil, China and the Russian Federation) and a youth bulge in sub-Saharan Africa, the Middle East and South Asia (Figure 9.4). For example, it is assumed based on UN population projections that the total labour force will shrink by 27 million in the European Union and by 34 million in China between 2010 and 2030, whereas in sub-Saharan Africa the working age population will increase by 288 million, and in South Asia an additional 356 million people will enter the workforce in the same time period.

Figure 9.4. **Millions more workers will be entering the job market in sub-Saharan Africa and South Asia**

Growth in working-age population, 2010-30 (millions)

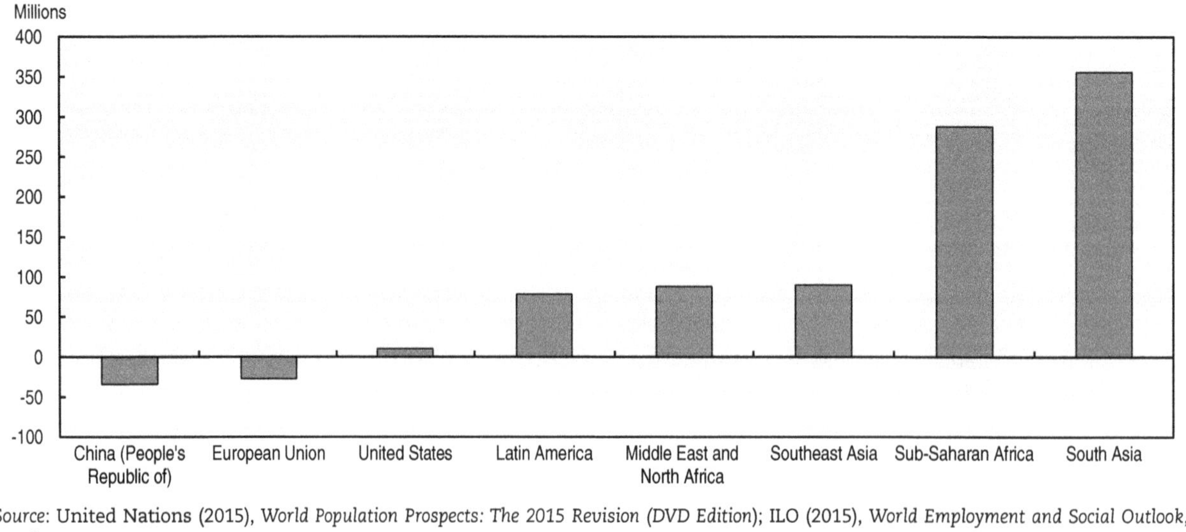

Source: United Nations (2015), *World Population Prospects: The 2015 Revision (DVD Edition)*; ILO (2015), *World Employment and Social Outlook, Trends 2015*.

StatLink http://dx.doi.org/10.1787/888933422870

Migration from countries with growing populations to those with shrinking ones can lead to large benefits for both sending and receiving countries. Sending countries will relieve some of the pressure of the youth bulge on the labour market, and also benefit from remittances and knowledge transfer from diasporas and return migration. Receiving countries will partially decrease the negative consequences of ageing populations (such as less tax contribution, increased public spending, increased costly health services and lower per capita income due to the lower workforce) by limiting the decrease of their workforce. However the youth bulge in developing countries, particularly in sub-Saharan Africa, South Asia and the Middle East, is likely to generate more potential migrants than high income countries will be able to absorb.

In all the scenarios it is assumed that very highly skilled migrants will always be sought after and face relatively fewer obstacles to their mobility than workers with lower skills. Finally, in all scenarios it is assumed that emigration rates for developing countries will increase as their GDP per capita increases.

Scenario 1: Slower shifting wealth

In "Slower shifting wealth", the global economy has moved in the direction projected by major private and public research institutions back in the mid-2010s (see for example, Braconier, Nicoletti and Westmore, 2014; IMF, 2015; and Chapter 2). Accordingly, the growth differential between OECD and non-OECD countries has narrowed further relative to the pre-2008/09 crisis period. Per capita income convergence has continued over the last 15 years, although at a much slower pace compared with the 2000s as governments failed to implement the necessary structural reforms and sufficient fiscal stimuli to relaunch strong growth. Overall, global growth performance over the last 15 years has been moderate with significant differences across the main countries and regions.

In particular, since 2016 growth in emerging and developing economies has slowed, compared with the post-2000 period. This slowdown has primarily been triggered by the weaker performance of some large emerging economies, particularly China, and countries exporting natural resources, such as Brazil and the Russian Federation.

Advanced economies have generally benefited from lower commodity prices and thereby boosted domestic demand. The United States, in particular, returned to a higher and more stable growth path driven by well-managed macroeconomic policies. Other advanced economies, particularly in Europe, are still dealing with the legacy of the crisis, including underemployed production factors and high private and public debt. In addition, European growth has slowed over the last 15 years because of the exit of some members from the European Union and increasing protectionism. This led to slower overall global growth compared with the period 2000-15.

In spite of the slower growth in developing countries, there are still many poles of growth in the developing world and global economic weight has further shifted towards the emerging world, albeit more slowly. China is now a high-income country. India is an upper-middle-income country. On the other hand, lower commodity prices over the last 15 years and political as well as geopolitical challenges have brought the Russian Federation back down to upper-middle-income status and Brazil and other Latin American countries have not reached the high-income brackets. Growth in Africa has been steady over the last 15 years. While investment in the region has increased, lower commodity prices have put a brake on exports in what is still a region very dependent on natural resources.

Adoption of new technologies in the production of goods and services (including energy) and the emergence of innovative devices and applications for consumer purposes have continued smoothly, but the scale has not been sufficient to boost global growth significantly. The trend for automation, especially of routine, manual jobs, has continued steadily, but has not dramatically changed the labour market, particularly in developing countries which remain far behind the technology frontier.

While the process of economic convergence has continued over the last 15 years, today's world of "Slower shifting wealth" is subject to big challenges regarding the dichotomy between ageing societies in developed and some emerging economies (notably Brazil, China, and the Russian Federation) and emerging youth bulges in Africa, the Middle East and South Asia – much more so than was felt in 2015. Financing pension and other social security systems is a fundamental challenge for all ageing economies. Government debt has accumulated further and is increasingly unsustainable. On the other hand, economic performance that is only moderate in regions with an increasingly young working-age population has not generated enough jobs for the millions of young people entering the job market for the first time.

In both ageing developed and emerging economies and young developing societies, moderate growth and heightened demographic challenges have led to increased incidents of social disruption and tensions over the last 15 years. In some European countries with previously high levels of welfare benefits and rapidly ageing populations, public pensions and other public goods and services have been cut in order to reduce the debt burden, which affected people in need of public support most dramatically (e.g. retired blue collar workers) and further raised inequalities within countries. These domestic social pressures in ageing societies mean that they are less willing to co-operate globally on economic issues. New forms of protectionist measures such as local content requirements, discriminatory rules for public procurement but also export subsidies are continuously implemented and extended.

Regions with emerging youth bulges have had yet more serious challenges to sustain or develop social inclusion over the last one and a half decades. Millions of young people are without jobs and remain extremely poor; many that reached the poverty threshold of USD 1.25 per day in 2015 have fallen back into poverty. Many of these people benefited from some education during their childhood and youth, which increased expectations as to what life can offer. Their frustration has resulted in increased incidents of significant social disruptions – some of them emulating the Arab Spring – over the last 15 years. This has also led to more unstable governments in these regions, and as such, to more strained, unreliable co-operation with these countries.

In the area of the environment, new but small global commitments to reduce greenhouse gas emissions and thus to diminish climate change and adapt to it have been reached over the last 15 years. China has not committed itself to globally agreed emission requirements. It does, however, engage on climate change discussions with key strategic partners, particularly the United States, and is the global leader in the production of sustainable technologies and energies. But environmental challenges remain unresolved. The most significant environmental challenges include frequent severe droughts in Africa, China, the Middle East, South Asia and the United States. Other natural disasters such as floods, typhoons and hurricanes are also very frequent. In the world's youth bulge regions, many livelihoods are based on subsistence farming but that is becoming increasingly challenging because of the problem of droughts. Larger scale farming is also seriously affected. Hunger is a rising challenge, not only for small-scale farmers but also for poor people in urban areas, as food prices increase sharply. Droughts are also more widespread in many developed regions (including the United States and Southern Europe), but these regions are managing the situation through new technologies such as desalination of seawater and infrastructure to transport water over long distances.

Simmering tensions in many youth bulge countries, in sub-Saharan Africa and the Middle East but also in some South Asian economies, combined with increasing environmental challenges in these regions have increasingly led to conflict.

Migration in this scenario

Globally, the share of migrants in the world population has not increased much beyond the 3.3% level it was in 2015 because of increasingly selective policies in most countries, although this share varies by region. The actual numbers of migrants, however, have increased in line with global population growth, increasing migration pressures.

Migration policy is characterised increasingly by regional and bilateral agreements, regulating labour migration to address the need for foreign workers for specific job categories in ageing countries (particularly in the care economy), and to ensure that sending countries benefit from the supply of workers to other countries, for example through lower costs to send remittances. There is a lack of political will and commitment to negotiate multilateral agreements on migration management as the issue is seen as too politically charged. Without more encompassing migration policies and agreements, and with increasing migration pressures, irregular migration has increased.

Migration of highly skilled workers, however, has been largely unrestricted as countries compete to attract the brightest and the best. Highly skilled migrants find it easy to migrate and move in all directions: from developed to emerging and developing countries, and vice versa. With increasing competition at the technological frontier among a larger number of highly advanced economies – now also including the BRIICS (Brazil, Russian Federation, India, Indonesia, China and South Africa), some Gulf states and other emerging economies – there is huge global competition for highly skilled and specialised workers. Even though it tends to be regionally and bilaterally regulated and partly restricted, migration has helped lend support to global economic growth and economic convergence between rich and poor nations.

The strongest labour migration pressures are from sub-Saharan Africa and Middle Eastern countries because of the youth bulge. The workforce in sub-Saharan Africa has increased by nearly 50% since 2015, but jobs have been created for fewer than 60% of the young people who have entered the labour force. Many of those who left without jobs are now trying to work abroad, mostly in wealthier neighbouring countries (e.g. Côte d'Ivoire, Nigeria, South Africa and some North African countries). However, restrictive labour regulations, particularly in South Africa, are preventing increased labour force participation and thus employment for both foreign and domestic workers. In African countries with strong economic performance and some creation of new employment, jobs have been filled mostly by the growing domestic workforce (e.g. in Côte d'Ivoire or Nigeria).

Overall, immigration of workers from the Middle East and Africa to Europe has not increased much despite the implicit labour demand in ageing Europe, as the region is increasingly closed to migration, although irregular flows are increasing. The demand for foreign workers in the developed world is severely outnumbered by the potential supply of migrants from the Middle East and Africa. What has increased is the number of migrants in so-called "transit countries". Many migrants find themselves in the countries bordering

Europe, hoping to make the final leg of their journey at some point in the future, however slim the prospects. This type of migration tends to be unrecorded, and migrants make a living in the informal sector. Sporadic crack-downs on informal settlements by the governments of these transit countries disrupt migrants' livelihoods and networks temporarily, but rarely result in migrants deciding to return to their home countries. More commonly, groups of migrants disperse and then relocate again.

Similarly, China is ageing and has the potential to absorb many of these foreign workers to keep labour costs down and to continue their development model of low cost, low value added manufacturing. However, China has a very restrictive migration regime, only granting work visas to highly specialised foreign workers, while automating many activities. With people unable to migrate to more prosperous regions, and poor economic prospects at home, there is growing social unrest in many countries in the Middle East and Africa.

As a result of limited opportunities for people to migrate from developing to developed countries, people from developing countries have increasingly been seeking work opportunities in countries within the same continent, particularly mid-skilled workers such as mechanics, plumbers or carpenters. This pattern has been driven by the continuation of the economic convergence process over the last 15 years which has been characterised by increased heterogeneity of income and wage levels between countries within regions, particularly in Asia and Latin America.

New migration corridors have emerged. In Southeast Asia, emigration rates from Myanmar have fallen substantially, reducing flows significantly in the Myanmar-Thailand corridor for example. Thailand remains an attractive destination for workers in the region however, as do Indonesia and Viet Nam. Migration patterns in the region resemble those in the European Union at the beginning of the 21st century, when countries such as Germany and the United Kingdom attracted migrants from Eastern Europe.

In Latin America, migration to resource-exporters such as Brazil has decreased as their growth prospects falter. The strong growth performance of the United States means it is still a main corridor of low- and mid-skilled migrants with migrants coming from Mexico and increasingly from other Central American countries. The United States is attractive not only for workers from South American countries, but also some African and Asian economies, particularly with respect to high-skilled migrants.

The Russian Federation is no longer an attractive destination country for migration in the Commonwealth of Independent States (CIS) region. Weak economic performance as a result of depressed oil prices has reduced opportunities and job prospects there. Many people in the CIS region instead now look eastwards to Asia for opportunities. The "One Belt, One Road" initiative, an enormous road, rail and sea port infrastructure development programme linking East Asia and Europe, started by China in the mid-2010s has strengthened the economic integration of the CIS region, driving higher rates of migration.

Although India has been booming over the last one and a half decades, it has not become an important destination for migrants. Newly created jobs in India are being filled by the growing domestic workforce, with many people migrating internally from rural areas to urban and industrial centres. The growth in the emigration rate from India is now slowing as the county has firmly established its upper-middle-income status.

The Gulf countries, once a major destination for Indian and other South Asian workers, are struggling to grow because of depressed oil prices. Consequently, the demand for foreign workers has fallen, in particular in the construction sector. There is still a relatively strong demand for care workers. Migrant workers now represent about 20% of the population of the Gulf Cooperation Council (GCC) region, compared to over 40% in the 2010s. The fall in work opportunities in the Gulf has reduced flows of remittances to South Asian countries and changed household-level decision-making and strategies. People considering migrating now look more to growth poles in the Asian region or countries with linguistic or cultural ties, for example, preferring countries of destination where English is widely spoken.

The number of displaced people has increased further over the last 15 years as a result of tensions and conflict in states with large and growing young populations and environmentally stressed areas. The European Union has been unable to agree on a system to distribute refugees among all members and countries have reinstated border controls to regulate the free movement of people across the continent: the Schengen area (with its passport-free travel) was abandoned both in practice and as a political objective by the late 2010s. Individual member states are making asylum policy decisions unilaterally, with some countries taking on more of the burden than others. In South Asia, environmentally displaced people (for example from Afghanistan and Bangladesh) are also increasingly seeking refuge in other countries, including in India. However, India itself is facing environmental challenges, and historical tensions with some neighbouring countries mean that many humanitarian migrants have been blocked from entering the country, leading to a major crisis.

Scenario 2: SDG success

Back in 2015 countries came together to pledge themselves to the Sustainable Development Goals, a new agenda for global action. That pledge resulted in the concentration of political efforts and financial resources of governments, donors and other development actors including grassroots movements on a set of 17 goals to achieve by 2030. The goals were wide-ranging, spanning targets for poverty reduction and inequality, food security, health and well-being, education, gender, environment and resource use, economic growth, infrastructure, industrialisation and innovation, cities, consumption patterns, justice, and global co-operation.

Since then, there has been, and continues to be, a growing commitment to global norms and international institutions. Countries strive to co-operate to secure global public "goods" and mitigate global public "bads" and many policy issues are governed at the global level. A large number of international agreements are struck at the multilateral level, in organisations with global mandates. For example, trade agreements are predominantly negotiated and agreed on through the World Trade Organization (WTO), rather than through bilateral channels. International tax co-operation has helped to reduce tax evasion and avoidance, boosting the resources available for public spending.

While not all the goals have been fully achieved, huge progress has been made in the last 15 years. The progress towards per capita income convergence between countries has been significant thanks to high growth rates in most developing countries, especially low-income countries, and stable but relatively low growth rates in the advanced economies. Many countries that were classified as low-income in 2015 have joined the ranks of middle-income countries. These newly middle-income countries have consequently graduated from being eligible for Official Development Assistance, but have been able to access other forms of international co-operation and finance. Some of the middle-income countries of 2015 – such as China, Colombia, Costa Rica, Indonesia, Kazakhstan, Mexico, South Africa and Turkey – are now high-income countries.

The sources of this growth have been diverse. Freer global labour mobility has boosted global growth by 10%. Massive investment in infrastructure, including regional and trans-border infrastructure, has also improved the conditions for economic development in many areas that had previously been unable fully to participate in global trade and value chains – especially least developed and landlocked developing countries. Many of these countries were thus able to jump on the bandwagon towards convergence through their economic integration with prospering growth poles in Asia (led by China and India) and Africa (led by Nigeria). These growth poles greatly supported the success of the SDGs and thus the possibilities for most developing countries to move towards convergence. Some of the boost in economic growth also came through the greater participation of women in the labour force globally, as women's rights in relation to economic resources, access to ownership of land and other assets, were strengthened through legal reforms and effective public campaigns.

Youth bulges in many countries in the Middle East, sub-Saharan Africa and South Asia have emerged. Existing demographic trends of fast population growth were reinforced as the result of improved healthcare systems in many developing countries that succeeded in significantly lowering infant mortality rates. Thanks to enhanced family planning programmes and improved levels of quality education, especially of women and girls, fertility rates are now beginning to drop in these regions which will lower population pressures in the future.

The most impressive global development achievement has been to reap the demographic dividend in countries experiencing youth bulges. Most of these countries have created millions of new jobs both in rural and urban areas. While manufacturing sectors have experienced a boom in these regions, job creation has gone beyond manufacturing. Investment in physical infrastructure for the construction of mid-sized cities, basic services (water, sanitation, basic education, health and government) created many jobs in the more rural areas. The world is also increasingly interconnected (including through the Internet) and thus opportunities for knowledge workers with very flexible skill sets have been opened up. These workers are based all over the world, including in youth bulge countries, and often provide services remotely. The expanding field of green technology is also creating large numbers of jobs. This has helped to absorb some of the youth bulge that emerged over the past 15 years.

The challenge of ageing societies in Europe and in Brazil and China has been reduced as stable growth has allowed these economies to secure public goods and services. Growth and effective government systems in these economies have also reduced social pressures.

Many of the former middle-income countries, which in 2015 accounted for most of the world's poor, put greater emphasis on inclusive growth, virtually eliminating extreme poverty. While extreme poverty still exists, today it is confined to a relatively small group of low-income countries which are dogged by conflict, especially in Central and Eastern Africa (Central Africa Republic, Democratic Republic of the Congo, Eritrea, Somalia, South Sudan and Sudan). Latin American countries which had already begun to reduce levels of inequality in 2015 have by 2030 achieved much lower levels of inequality (on a par with levels of inequality in European countries back in 2015) thanks to progressive fiscal policies. Advances in technology, in particular inclusive innovation, that address the needs of people on low incomes, has helped lower inequality by improving access to key goods and services.

Because social and economic pressures in the Middle East, sub-Saharan Africa and South Asia are lower, there are far fewer conflicts today. Conflicts that do emerge are often de-escalated through effective international co-operation, leadership, diplomacy and

  © OECD 2016

peacebuilding efforts. The threat of extremist groups globally has been fading. Nonetheless, conflicts in some African countries are proving more difficult to resolve.

By 2020 there was full implementation and enforcement of the Doha Declaration on the Agreement on Trade-Related Aspects of Intellectual Property Rights (TRIPS), which affirmed the right of developing countries to use the provision in the agreement regarding flexibilities to protect public health. This has transformed the global health landscape. Low-cost, effective treatments for AIDS, for example, are now widely available, changing the fortunes of the millions of people affected by the disease worldwide. Intensified efforts of the donor community and foundations have meant that other communicable diseases, such as tuberculosis, have been virtually wiped out and co-ordinated actions on fighting antimicrobial resistance have led to good progress.

One of the biggest challenges over the last 15 years has been to achieve the goals relating to the environment in a context of strong economic growth in developing nations. A great achievement which helped to diminish further climate change has been the expansion of access to renewable energy sources. India, for example, succeeded in its goal of creating a country-wide dedicated transmission network for power from renewable energy projects, fed by a series of mega solar power projects. China is the world leader in climate technology and pioneered the development of batteries to store solar power. Many countries have also eliminated or phased out fossil fuel subsidies. Similarly, upgrading infrastructure, retrofitting industries to make them more resource-efficient, and adopting clean technologies and industrial processes helped alleviate some of the environmental strain and reduced emissions. Massively lowered local pollution in cities has supported people's well-being in the ageing world. Transnational grassroots movements have also had huge successes in influencing consumers' behaviour towards more sustainable patterns of consumption.

However, the environmental effects of climate change that were already in motion are changing lives and livelihoods. Many areas in sub-Saharan Africa, South and Southeast Asia are now considered uninhabitable as a result of either droughts or more frequent extreme weather events. Finding solutions to water scarcity has been difficult. The increased investment in rural development and agricultural research has therefore been focussing on drought-resistant or drought-adapted agricultural systems, although the scale of the challenge is large. Many countries have also been proactively planning for such an eventuality for the last decade. Governments in countries such as China, Indonesia and Viet Nam have been resettling populations away from high-risk areas in a managed way, supported by climate change adaptation funds raised through multilateral action.

Migration in this scenario

In line with the SDGs, migration is considered as a potential engine of development in both countries of origin and destination and in developed and developing economies alike. This has led to various multilateral arrangements that facilitate and foster the regular flow of migrants at all skill levels. The stock of migrants to global population has increased to above 4% with increased circular migration. Some of the migration-specific SDG commitments have been met. For example, the cost of remittances is just 3% globally, thanks to better co-ordination and regulation. This has freed up private resources that are now used for consumption but also productive investments. Transfer of skills across countries and regions is facilitated by international curriculum standards so that the particular country in which a person is educated and acquires professional skills is now less important. Welfare provisions and pensions are largely portable across countries. In most countries, migrants have the same right to work, to education and access to healthcare as citizens.

To respond to some of the tensions that a more multicultural society can generate, governments are investing in social integration policies. Political leaders have used effective communication strategies to inform the public accurately of the economic, social and cultural contribution that migration can bring. These actions have allayed fears and eased the transition to more culturally heterogeneous societies. As a result, the welcoming culture in host countries has become more open and positive. In this way, coherent and well-managed migration policies have contributed to the process of global economic convergence.

As GDP per capita in low-income countries has been rising over the last years, emigration rates from these countries have also been rising. The share of global migrants emigrating from sub-Saharan African countries in particular – which formed the majority of low-income countries in 2015 – has therefore been increasing. This is being driven by several factors, including the changing demographics in Africa, with many countries experiencing a youth bulge; rising incomes meaning that people have more resources to finance their migration; and improved access to communication technology enabling more people to be informed about opportunities abroad, among others. Countries that were large and emerging in 2015 (e.g. China, India, etc.) now have upper-middle- or high-income status and the growth in their emigration rates has slowed. They are even seeing significant returns of their diaspora community.

With more open migration policies, flows of migration are determined largely by market forces, as migrants respond to variations in labour demand across the world. Countries also take proactive measures to attract migrants with the skills needed in their economies: jobs are advertised internationally, streamlined procedures make it easy for people to move from one country to another, and integration policies help people to settle in and feel part of the wider society. The issue of "transit countries" is no longer such an issue, as people can more easily travel directly to the intended destination country.

The share of South-South migration has increased, and in particular the share of global migration flows within geographic regions is much larger. However, in contrast to the world of "Slower shifting wealth", increased within-region migration is not a result of increased heterogeneity between front and late runners of economic development. As migration policies become more open, people take up temporary assignments in neighbouring countries, but tend to keep their country of origin as their home base. The costs associated with family disintegration – e.g. family separation, absence of parents etc. – that had previously been associated with migration are therefore lower.

Temporary work opportunities in other countries are the outcome of a work culture that is changing globally, where very specialised, but adaptable, skills may be used for a certain period and long-term work engagements are fading. People reskill themselves constantly, while developing a certain skill and work portfolio that can be put into action anywhere in the world. Moreover, with an increasing participation of women in labour markets globally, women's share in global labour migration has also been increasing. China is actively trying to encourage female immigration because of the gender imbalance in its population. Irregular migration has fallen around the globe thanks to more open and better managed migration policies that benefit from the use of advanced technological tools.

While there has been good progress in terms of economic convergence and social inclusion, pressures on the environment have increased, forcing people to relocate. Water scarcity in sub-Saharan Africa and South Asia has made small-scale farming there almost impossible. Many people in those regions have been displaced and are looking for new economic opportunities in cities and neighbouring countries. These environmental challenges have put new pressure on irregular migration flows in certain localised geographic regions, but in general more open and positive attitudes towards migration prevent people from being contained in areas where sustaining a livelihood is no longer feasible. The proactive measures of governments to resettle populations living in climate-sensitive areas averted potential crises. Furthermore, "environmental refugees" now have legal status under international law facilitating international resettlement.

The global stock of refugees is at its lowest point since the 1970s, at around 4 million. There are few remaining refugee camps. Instead, greater emphasis is placed on finding alternatives to camps, including solutions in urban areas. Furthermore, 50 countries take part in The Office of the United Nations High Commissioner for Refugees' resettlement programme to grant permanent settlement to refugees who are not able to return home.

Scenario 3: Crisis with attempt for co-operation

In this scenario, the world is still recovering from a major global economic crisis which began in the 2020s. Unlike the 2008/09 crisis, the origin of which was in developed economies, in particular the United States, this time the crisis originated in emerging economies. Given these economies' large weight in the world economy, the crisis had implications for the rest of the world. It began with the bursting of asset price bubbles, leading to a severe financial crisis which spilled over into the real economy. High levels of corporate debt in emerging economies became unsustainable and led to large capital outflows. This created problems for these countries' balances of payments and debt repayments and led to a significant economic crisis. Even though the crisis started in the developing world it had major effects on financial markets and the real economy in developed countries because of their great financial exposure in these countries, their fragile and overleveraged financial markets and their significant economic integration through foreign direct investment (FDI) and global value chains.

The crisis affected global trade, investment and consumption. Commodity prices have continued to stay low over the last 15 years, something that has created significant challenges for currency stability in countries reliant on commodity exports, such as Australia, Brazil, Canada, the Russian Federation, and many African countries.

The worst effects of the crisis were felt in developing and emerging countries. China's economic development was pushed back and so was its re-emergence as a global economic power. Today it seems far from regaining its position as a lead exporter of both lower and higher value added products and services. Beyond the challenges related to the economic crisis, livelihoods are seriously under pressure as a result of serious water shortages in some of its most populated north-eastern regions. Many countries in Africa, Latin America and Asia, but also some resource-rich developed countries such as Australia and Canada suffered a lost decade of stagnant or negative growth in the 2020s. Many people's livelihoods came under pressure in the developing world. A large proportion of the billion people living just above the poverty line in 2020 is now living in poverty.

In addition, many developing countries are dealing with huge youth population bulges, especially in the Middle East, Africa and South Asia. Environmental challenges such as droughts and floods have intensified in those regions. The accumulation of all these challenges has resulted in severe armed conflicts in many African countries as well as in South Asia.

The wage gap between advanced economies and developing and emerging economies is growing rapidly. In contrast to the great recession starting in 2008/09, during which emerging and developing countries recovered relatively quickly and many advanced economies suffered crisis legacies several years after the start of the crisis, most advanced economies recovered relatively fast from the 2020 crisis. This recovery has largely been credited to the important structural reforms and other policy steps implemented after 2010. The United States has regained its position as the biggest economy in the world, with a more stable Europe in its shadow.

Technological advances and the speed of automation have slowed with the crisis and thus economic growth in advanced economies is moderate. Moreover, growth markets in most emerging economies have to a great extent disappeared, also lowering prospects for fast economic expansion in advanced economies.

Social pressures in advanced economies intensified during the economic crisis because unemployment rates increased temporarily, but social inclusion was quickly re-established and today is not a major issue. This has partly been built on a stabilisation of sectors relying on low-skilled labour that no longer face competition from emerging markets. Also, social security systems had been renovated before the crisis and their sustainability has been proven during the recovery process.

By contrast, the crisis in developing economies has resulted in serious social instability. Populations that had benefited from two decades of relatively strong, constant growth quickly turned against their governments. This led to regime changes in many developing economies. In other developing countries, revolutionary movements have been met with heavy government crackdowns.

Just as the 2008/09 global economic crisis led to increased international co-operation, particularly the emergence of the G20 and its successful financial market stabilisation, the aftermath of the 2020 crisis also led to an increased attempt for global co-operation and co-ordination. However, in the latter, this co-operation among global powers was reduced to advanced economies, mostly the G7. US leadership was crucial in rallying G7 members to shore up the global system and provide support to China and other developing countries in deep crisis, convincing an initially sceptical public back home that such actions were in the interests of everyone. New agreements between advanced economies have also emerged. For example, the Transatlantic Trade and Investment Partnership (TTIP) between the United States and the European Union was signed five years ago, in 2025.

Economic and geopolitical co-operation among emerging and developing nations weakened, after it had gained some momentum in the 2010s. For example, institutions that emerging economies had developed to counterbalance traditional international organisations to affirm their increased relevance in global governance have scaled back their operations considerably.

Migration in this scenario

Migration pressures have increased over the last 15 years with low or negative growth in developing economies and moderate growth in the richer world translating into economic divergence and a growing wage gap. The demographic dichotomy between an ageing developed world and the youth bulge in many developing economies in sub-Saharan Africa and Asia have also increased migration pressures.

Increasing poverty in the developing world has had ambiguous implications for migration. On the one hand, it has led to increased pressure because people want to leave, but on the other, people have less money to pay for migration. Which force has prevailed has varied between countries and regions. Migration between countries within developing regions affected by the financial crisis has been reduced, including international student migration. China has seen a rapid increase in emigration following the crisis. Overall, the share of migrants of total world population has not increased much from the 3.3% in 2015, in spite of increased pressures. The number of refugees, however, has increased dramatically, with periodic peaks in refugee flows resulting from the outbreak of armed conflicts.

With the attempt for global co-operation to re-establish the global system after the 2020 crisis, many developed economies in Europe, Asia and North America engaged in bilateral agreements on selective migration at all skill levels to reduce some of the challenges related to their ageing societies. In fact, it has been empirically proven that recent inflows of migrants have considerably supported economic growth. Nonetheless, these countries have not been prepared to absorb large numbers of migrants. Bilateral agreements often stipulate that migration flows should be circular – with workers travelling back and forth between home and host countries according to the labour demand. Protecting jobs of domestic workers is a priority. Developing country governments, however, are actively promoting emigration and are keen to negotiate bilateral deals with advanced economies in the hope of boosting flows of remittances.

Given the poor economic climate in most developing regions, the proportion of migrants moving to low- and middle-income countries, whether from other developing countries or from advanced economies, has decreased. Many migrants who had been working in developing countries before the crisis have returned home, but have found little support to reintegrate into local labour markets. The supply of migrants from developing countries has increased. From the perspective of Middle Eastern, African and South Asian countries, the pressures related to their youth bulges could not be significantly lowered, despite some outflows to Europe and other developed economies. In fact, bilateral agreements with developed countries mostly made possible the selective migration of skilled people and thus these and other developing economies have experienced a wave of "brain drains", further slowing their recovery from the crisis. Some skilled migrants with sufficient resources adopt a "two-step strategy", moving to relatively more prosperous countries within their region before trying to move to work in a high-income economy in Europe or the United States. In Africa, the African Union has taken on the role of trying to help countries co-ordinate and better manage migration flows within the continent. Outflows of migrants from China and Latin American countries have also increased, and the United States, where there are large diaspora groups, remains their preferred destination. The United States remains the largest destination country for migrants globally.

Over the past 15 years, the number of refugees has more than doubled. In crisis-hit countries, social disruptions and challenges to people's livelihoods have fuelled the rise of extremist groups, led to violent government reactions against uprisings, and precipitated outbreaks of fighting. This development, combined with huge environmental stress, including droughts and other natural disasters, has led to many more people being displaced in developing countries. While many people have been internally displaced, the level of cross-border refugees has also increased. Rather than a steady increase over the last decade and a half, this phenomenon is marked by sudden, large population movements across borders in response to specific episodes of violence and conflict.

Leaders in advanced economies have engaged in impressive co-operation to deal with this humanitarian challenge. An international fund was established to which advanced countries contribute on an annual basis, in order that the necessary funds are available to support refugee populations and their initial countries of refuge (often neighbouring, developing countries) during peaks of refugee flows. Countries have also put in place systems to redistribute refugees, taking into account destination countries' populations, gross national income and other economic factors such as unemployment rates. This humanitarian mechanism is combined with skills-matching schemes designed to fast-track refugees with skills demanded by host countries. The multilateral agreement has its origins in the commitments made among EU members in the late 2010s, but now extends to all major advanced economies including Canada and the United States. The integration of refugees into their host countries is aided by full and speedy access to labour markets for those of working age, and access to schooling for their children.

Scenario 4: Rapid automation and conflict

In this scenario, global co-operation is near breaking point. Countries fail to reach new multilateral agreements under organisations such as the World Trade Organisation, and some existing agreements are routinely flouted or even abandoned. The relevance of international organisations is fading. Protectionist policies are widespread. More restrictive migration policies and an ageing society in developed and some emerging economies have triggered profit incentives to automate production processes. Developing countries are not automating. Because of the lack of opportunities for people to improve their lives many new and military conflicts emerge.

Rapid automation in high-income countries (which now include China) has led to significant job losses in many sectors in those countries. Automation has boosted productivity and thus accelerated economic growth in advanced economies, but this growth has been largely jobless or where there have been new jobs created they are biased towards very high skills. The use of robots, 3D printing, artificial intelligence, data analytics and the Internet of Things is becoming widespread. Automation is not only replacing lower-skilled jobs (e.g. in transportation/logistics, production and administration), but also high-skilled activities (including jobs in management, science and engineering, the arts, and the legal and medical fields). For example, solving a legal case or diagnosis based on a patient's symptoms is now increasingly done through "big data analytics" – applying powerful computer programmes to very large data sets. China is at the forefront of the automation revolution and invests heavily in new technologies. Even the care sector in China is increasingly automated, whereas there is more resistance to this change in other advanced economies, particularly the United States and Europe.

Advanced countries are therefore going through a painful period of adjustment. Workers are struggling to adapt given the speed of the automation process, which has been faster than previous technological revolutions which altered the jobs landscape in the past. As a result, most people whose jobs have been automated have failed to adapt fast enough and find it difficult to make a living. Some new jobs have emerged, but overall there are not enough new jobs to allow everyone to be employed. There is some demand for traditionally produced goods and services (e.g. traditionally produced agricultural goods), which has led to a re-emergence of some jobs for mid-level skills, but even many highly skilled people are unemployed.

A by-product has been soaring inequality which has not been reined in due to a failure or unwillingness to use potential policy levers. A small portion of people have captured the wealth created by automated processes. The rest make a living in a very marginal economy. With less fiscal revenue because fewer people are earning wages, and at the same time more people in need of social security support (both old and working-age people), government debt has accumulated unabated and is unmanageable. Governments struggle to finance pension and other social security systems. As a result, social unrest and protests against major corporations and the government are commonplace. Some advanced economies have tried to address this issue by introducing a guaranteed minimum income, financed by a tax on capital, but there are doubts about the efficiency and sustainability of this policy as there are signs of capital flight to countries which do not impose this tax.

The situation in newly emerging, middle-income countries is different. These countries protect their emerging markets from the automated world with discriminatory measures and thereby manage to develop new and non-automated value chains to serve regional and domestic markets. These countries are trying to catch up on the technological and productivity ladder with more advanced countries and are able to create many jobs at all skill levels. In those countries, there is some degree of automation, but to a much lesser extent.

By contrast, in many developing countries, the automation process has been much slower. These countries are therefore no longer competitive, even in low-cost, low value added sectors in value chains linked with the automated, developed world. Many activities that had been off-shored are now done by developed country firms again. There is still room for traditional economic activities, but goods and services produced by people typically serve the domestic consumer market and neighbouring markets. They may also increasingly be integrated in new, more regional value chains with emerging countries. Despite some limited opportunities, these economies are growing at a much slower rate than advanced economies and average per capita incomes are even diverging from those of fast-moving developed and automated countries. Jobs have not been created fast enough for the rising working-age population. This challenge is greatest in African, Middle Eastern and South Asian economies which face a bulge of young people entering the labour market with very limited prospects of finding decent work and improving their lives.

Environmental pressures, particularly droughts, have made life yet more difficult for people in developing countries, especially those still living in rural areas. A lack of international co-operation and solidarity with those affected has worsened the consequences of environmental changes. It has become almost impossible to survive as a subsistence farmer in many countries in sub-Saharan Africa, some parts of North Africa, India and Pakistan. Pandemics are also frequent and severe, as appropriate medication cannot be accessed. Millions of people have died due to famines and pandemics in the last decades.

The lack of opportunities for people to improve their lives is fuelling conflict. Extremist groups have gained influence in many of the most challenged developing countries as they can more easily recruit people whose alternatives and life prospects are limited. This has led to new armed conflicts in more than 20 countries in Africa and Asia since 2015. Western countries intervene in these conflicts when access to resources is in jeopardy. They use sophisticated artificial intelligence warfare systems and drone attacks, rather than risk putting troops on the ground. The real security threat for heavily tech-dependent advanced economies is now cyber-attacks, rather than traditional warfare.

Migration in this scenario

More restrictive migration policies in an increasingly xenophobic and generally less co-operative world combined with an ageing society in advanced and some emerging economies have increased firms' incentives to automate production processes. Increased inequalities as a result of automation in the richer world have further fuelled anti-migration sentiment. The total stock of migrants to global population falls below 3%.

The share of global migration from developing countries to advanced economies is falling. Although many people in developing countries have aspirations to migrate, their limited financial means prevent them from being able to turn this aspiration into a reality. Aggravating this situation, the economic context in the wealthier economies is reducing the demand for labour. Immigrants are competing for the same, shrinking number of jobs as native workers. As a result, and aided by increasingly effective hi-tech border security, both regular and irregular migration flows into developed countries have been reduced significantly. However, the share of irregular total migration flows has increased. Migration of care workers from developing to ageing developed economies (especially into the EU) has increased. Similarly, highly skilled foreign people working in programming and data analytics are increasingly recruited in advanced economies. More open migration policies narrowly targeting this type of highly skilled worker are common, while very restrictive quota systems regulate flows of lower skilled workers. Advanced economies tend to set migration policies unilaterally, rather than trying to reach bilateral or regional agreements.

The journeys of humanitarian and economic migrants attempting to enter developed countries often end in detention camps, frequently located in developing countries that border developed countries, and financed by developed countries. Applications for asylum or visas to reside and work in the desired destination country are processed slowly, and very few people are granted the right to enter. International resettlement programmes for registered refugees have effectively ceased to exist. Developed economies also give advanced border control technologies to countries that would otherwise be transit countries for large numbers of migrants, essentially extending their border control measures beyond their sovereign territory.

The share of migration between developing countries, however, has increased over the last 15 years. The poles of attraction within developing regions are those countries that are conflict free, have still relatively low levels of automation, and where there are no pandemics. These new, emerging economies attract people at all skill levels, particularly highly specialised technical experts, as firms in these countries aspire to catch up with the levels of automation taking place in advanced economies. The relatively limited capacities of national administrations, combined with a lack of international co-operation on managing flows, mean that an increasing share of migration is irregular.

In addition, skilled workers displaced by automation in advanced countries are increasingly migrating to the new emerging economies in developing regions. In these cases, migration patterns reflect historic cultural or linguistic links between countries and can be seen as a reversal in the traditional direction of migration: for example, workers from Portugal seek opportunities in Mozambique, Spanish workers go to the Dominican Republic and Dutch workers establish themselves in Indonesia. These regions in the process of automation have increased their capacities for higher education, particularly in technical fields, and are investing to attract talented foreign students.

Moving forward in 2016

This chapter has presented four future scenarios for international migration. Developed along the three axes of economic convergence versus divergence, global co-operation versus fragmentation, and restrictive versus open migration policies, they show four possible states of the world in 2030 resulting from the interplay of these different factors.

The first "business as usual" scenario extends the trends that are already evident today, such as slowing growth in developing economies, and explores the consequences. The second scenario presents a more positive vision of where the world could be in 2030, using the Sustainable Development Goals as an inspiration. The third scenario imagines the consequences of a global shock in the form of a financial crisis, and reveals a world in which global co-operation is being harnessed effectively to address the challenges. Finally, the most negative of the four scenarios shows what could happen if there is a severe deterioration in global co-operation in a context of rapid automation and economic divergence.

The scenarios are hypotheses of plausible future states of the world, not prescriptions or indications of what will or should happen. The insights gained from the scenarios test and challenge current thinking and can be used to develop policy options to address the different possible futures that may unfold. What have the four scenarios in this chapter revealed?

First, it can be seen that migration is likely to become an even more important issue in the future as the populations of many developing countries, particularly in sub-Saharan Africa and South Asia, are showing historically high growth over the next 15 years, and climate change is likely to create greater migration pressures in the longer term.

Second, three of the scenarios, including the business as usual scenario, reveal very challenging situations for the future of migration and for the issues that will need to be addressed. The more open migration regimes and effective international co-operation in scenario 2 produce several beneficial effects. The global economy is boosted thanks to a more efficient allocation of labour, with people able to move where jobs are. This is particularly important given the large numbers of young people who will enter the job market in sub-Saharan Africa, South Asia and Southeast Asia according to current demographic trends. More open regimes also prevent the containment of people in areas where they can no longer make a livelihood or worse, where their lives are threatened by armed conflict, political violence or natural disasters.

Third, these beneficial effects are able to be realised thanks to parallel efforts to foster social cohesion in migration-receiving communities and to reduce the costs of migration. Fostering social cohesion first requires political leadership, to assuage local fears about the arrival of people from other countries, perhaps with different cultures. Success is then dependent on effective integration policies, such as providing language training, tackling discrimination, supporting labour market integration and ensuring that immigrants have the same rights and access to public services as citizens. Reducing the costs of migration may include measures such as establishing low cost passports at countries of origin, a legal cap/ban on recruitment fees, double taxation agreements between countries and linking work visas to the labour demand in countries of destination.

Finally, given the international nature of migration, global co-operation is revealed to be vital to addressing the challenges in possible future worlds, and its absence leads to sub-optimal development outcomes, both at the global level and for individual human flourishing.

Notes

1. For example, questionnaires asking people about their intentions to migrate.
2. Other institutions have developed scenarios looking specifically at the impact of climate change on migration, e.g. the UK Government's Foresight Project, *Migration and Global Environmental Change* (*www.gov.uk/government/uploads/system/uploads/attachment_data/file/288793/11-1117-migration-global-environmental-change-scenarios.pdf*).

References

Bijak, J. (2006), "Forecasting international migration: Selected theories, models and methods", CEFMR *Working Paper*.

Braconier, H., G. Nicoletti and B. Westmore (2014), "Policy challenges for the next 50 years", *OECD Economic Policy Papers*, No. 9, OECD Publishing, Paris, *http://dx.doi.org/10.1787/5jz18gs5fckf-en*.

Cohen, J. E. (2012), "Projection of net migration using a gravity model", UN/POP/MIG-10CM/2012/11, 3 February 2012, presented to Tenth Coordination Meeting on International Migration, Population Division, Department of Economic and Social Affairs, United Nations Secretariat, New York, 9-10 February.

Docquier, F. and J. Machado (2014), "Revenu, population et flux migratoires au 21e siècle – Un défi sociétal pour l'Europe", *Studia Oeconomica Posnaniensia* 12.

ILO (2015), *World Employment and Social Outlook, Trends 2015*, International Labour Organization.

IMF (2015), *World Economic Outlook, Uneven Growth: Short- and Long-Term Factors*, International Monetary Fund, Washington, DC.

Ionesco, D., D. Mokhnacheva and F. Gemenne (2016), *Atlas des migrations environnementales*, Presses de la Fondation nationale des sciences politique, Paris.

IPCC (2014), "Climate Change 2014: Synthesis Report", Contribution of Working Groups I, II and III to the Fifth Assessment Report of the Intergovernmental Panel on Climate Change [Core Writing Team, R.K. Pachauri and L.A. Meyer (eds.)], IPCC, Geneva.

Kahane, A. (2012), *Transformative Scenario Planning: Working Together to Change the Future*, Berrett-Koehler Publishers, California, *www.bkconnection.com/books/title/transformative-scenario-planning*.

OECD (2009), *The Future of International Migration to OECD Countries*, OECD Publishing, Paris, *http://dx.doi.org/10.1787/9789264064126-en*.

United Nations (2015), *World Population Prospects: The 2015 Revision (DVD Edition)*, United Nations, Department of Economic and Social Affairs, Population Division.

World Bank (2016), *Shock Waves: Managing the Impacts of Climate Change on Poverty*, World Bank Group, Washington DC.

ANNEX 9.A1

Migration patterns between 2015 and 2030 in the four scenarios

	Slower shifting wealth	SDG success	Crisis with attempt for co-operation	Rapid automation and conflict
		Push/pull factors		
Demographic, combined with job opportunities	Push factors increase as a result of a large youth bulge combined with lack of economic opportunities, especially in sub-Saharan Africa and South Asia Pull factors increase due to ageing societies in developed and some emerging economies (including China)	Push factors decrease as more jobs are created and poverty in low-income countries is reduced; and in the future, falling population growth rates will also result in reduced push factors Pull factors increase due to ageing societies in developed and some emerging economies	Push factors increase due to lack of job opportunities in developing countries (including China) Pull factors increase because of ageing societies in developed and some emerging economies	Push factors increase as a result of a large youth bulge combined with lack of economic opportunities (the consequence of more widespread conflicts) Pull factors decrease as there are fewer jobs in advanced countries thanks to automation
Income inequality across countries	Push/pull factors decrease slightly as income differential is reduced somewhat	Push/pull factors decrease as the income differential is lower	Push/pull factors increase as income differentials between more advanced economies and developing world have widened	Push/pull factors increase as income differentials between more advanced economies and developing world have widened
Other factors (social, environmental and conflict)	Push factors increase as income inequalities rise, social disruptions increase, environmental stress (such as droughts, floods, etc.) increases	Push factors decrease as populous emerging economies reduce income inequality, while improved living conditions in low-income countries also reduce pressures for social disruptions, and environmental stress remains a challenge but is no worse than in 2015	Push factors increase as people's livelihoods in developing countries are at risk (economic crisis and resource constraints), also leading to more armed conflict	Push factors increase in automated economies, income inequalities increase in non-automated, developing economies leading to heavy conflicts Pull factors decrease because of xenophobia and anti-migration sentiment in developed countries
		Changes in migration flows		
Change in migration flows [This change relates to a change in the average annual global migration flows over 2015-30 as compared to 2000-15]	Increase and share of total stock to world population increases above the current 3.3% but stays below 4%	Increase and share of total stock to world population increases from current 3.3% to over 4%	Constant; share of total migrant stock to world population remains around current level of 3.3%	Decrease so share of total migrant stock to world population decreases to below 3%

	Slower shifting wealth	SDG success	Crisis with attempt for co-operation	Rapid automation and conflict
Significant changes in flows across different income groups	Developing to developed country flows continue to increase in spite of ongoing restrictive policies and are manifested in more irregular flows. (An exception is that flows to previously oil rich countries diminish because of low oil prices) Developing to emerging countries flows increase because of the difficulties of migrating to developed countries and the slower growth performance of developed countries	Flows increase among all countries	Developing to developing flows decrease because of a significant slowdown in shifting wealth Developing to developed flows increase as a result of special bilateral treaties What little developed to developing countries traffic existed decreases because of the slowdown of emerging countries	Developing to developed flows decrease because of much more restrictive policies in developed countries Developed to developing flows increase because of crisis and conflict and restricted options to migrate to developed countries
Flows of humanitarian migrants	More humanitarian migrants	Fewer humanitarian migrants	More humanitarian migrants	Many more humanitarian migrants
		Changes in migration stocks		
Migration stock (as % of global population)	Slight increase from 3.3%, but <4%	Some increase (>3.3%, but lower than 5%)	Constant (no change from 3.3%)	Decrease (<3.3%, but higher than 2%)
		Changes in migration flow composition		
Share of regular versus irregular migration flows	More irregular	Irregular decreases as a share of total	Constant or slightly more regular thanks to bilateral agreements	Irregular increases as a share of total
Share of temporary versus permanent migration flows	Constant	More temporary as a share	More circular as share	More permanent as a share
Share of female versus male migration flows	Share of female increases (care economy expands in ageing countries)	Share of female decreases (thanks to less discrimination and improved opportunities for women in home countries)	Share of female increases (care economy expands in ageing countries)	Constant or slight increase (care economy expands in ageing countries)
Share of highly skilled migrants	Increase	Decrease	Increase	Increase
		Migration regimes		
More open versus more restrictive migration policies	Similar to today	Much more open	Similar to today	Much more restrictive
More selective/ targeted policies versus market-led forces	More selective/targeted	Market-led forces rather than government quotas	More selective/targeted	Much more selective/targeted
Migration policies set at multilateral, regional and bilateral levels	Tendency for more regional agreements	Multilateral agreements	Tendency for more bilateral agreements	Wealthy countries unilaterally decide their migration policy
Agreements on humanitarian migrants	No agreement reached between countries (e.g. between EU member states), but gravity of situation forces some countries to take unilateral action to respond to the humanitarian crisis	More agreements, and not such a sensitive topic as numbers of humanitarian migrants are relatively low	More agreements as will need to absorb more humanitarian migrants and assume more global collaboration	Fewer agreements

Perspectives on Global Development 2017
International Migration in a Shifting World
© OECD 2016

ANNEX A

Classification of countries

Table A.1. **Definition of country classifications**

	Income criteria	Economic growth criteria
High Income by 1995 (HI)	Classified as a high-income country in 1995	Experienced sufficient economic growth to be classified as a high-income country in 2016
High and Sustained Growth (SG)	Not classified as a high-income country in 1995	Experienced a period of *high and sustained economic growth**
Rest of the World (RW)	Not classified as a high-income country in 1995	Did not experience a period of *high and sustained economic growth**

***Definition: High and Sustained Growth** (based on Hausmann, Pritchett and Rodrik, 2005; see Aubry, 2016 for further details):

A country is said to have experienced a period of high and sustained growth if the following four conditions hold over a period between 1980 and 2011:

1. period of rapid growth (more than 3.5% per annum for at least six years)
2. accelerated growth (the growth rate throughout the period of rapid growth must be at least two percentage points higher than in the previous six years)
3. post-growth output exceeds the output prior to the period of rapid growth (to prevent a growth acceleration episode that follows the collapse of an economy)
4. the growth must be sustained (growth rate of at least 2% during the ten years following the episode of rapid and accelerated growth).

Table A.2. **List of countries by classification**

High Income by 1995 (HI) (28 countries)	High and Sustained Growth (SG) (59 countries)		Rest of the World (RW) (57 countries)	
Asia	**Africa**	**Europe**	**Africa**	**Asia**
Hong Kong (China)	Botswana	Bosnia and Herzegovina	Algeria	Afghanistan
Israel	Nigeria	Albania	Benin	Bangladesh
Japan	Mauritius	Belarus	Burkina Faso	Cambodia
Kuwait	Angola	Latvia	Burundi	Kyrgyzstan
Korea	Ghana	Estonia	Cameroon	Lao People's Democratic Republic
Saudi Arabia†	Egypt	Moldova	Central African Republic	Lebanon
Singapore	Tunisia	Slovak Republic	Chad	Nepal
United Arab Emirates	South Africa‡	Czech Republic‡	Congo	Sri Lanka

Table A.2. **List of countries by classification** *(cont.)*

High Income by 1995 (HI) (28 countries)	High and Sustained Growth (SG) (59 countries)		Rest of the World (RW) (57 countries)	
Europe	Morocco	Lithuania	Côte d'Ivoire	Syrian Arab Republic
Austria	Sudan	Bulgaria	Democratic Republic of the Congo	Tajikistan
Belgium	**Asia**	Ukraine	Eritrea	Yemen
Denmark	China (People's Republic of)	Poland	Ethiopia	**Europe**
Finland	Armenia	Former Yugoslav Republic of Macedonia	Gabon	Romania
France	Georgia	Slovenia‡	Gambia	**Latin America and the Caribbean**
Germany	Indonesia	Hungary	Guinea	Bolivia
Greece†	Azerbaijan	Russia	Guinea-Bissau	Cuba
Ireland	Uzbekistan	**Latin America and the Caribbean**	Kenya	Guatemala
Italy	Turkey	Argentina	Lesotho	Haiti
Netherlands	Turkmenistan	Panama	Liberia	Honduras
Norway	Kazakhstan	Peru	Libya	Jamaica
Portugal	Mongolia	Chile	Madagascar	Nicaragua
Spain	Malaysia	El Salvador	Malawi	Paraguay
Sweden	Viet Nam	Colombia	Mali	Venezuela
Switzerland	Thailand‡	Uruguay	Mauritania	**Oceania**
United Kingdom	India	Mexico	Mozambique	Papua New Guinea
Northern America	Jordan	Costa Rica	Namibia	
Canada	Iran	Dominican Republic	Niger	
United States	Iraq	Ecuador	Rwanda	
Oceania	Pakistan‡	Trinidad and Tobago	Senegal	
Australia	Oman	Brazil	Sierra Leone	
New Zealand	Philippines		Tanzania	
			Togo	
			Uganda	
			Zambia	
			Zimbabwe	

Note: Countries with less than 1 million inhabitants in 1995 according to the World Bank (2016) are excluded. For the purposes of analysis, only countries with sufficient data on both GDP and migration are classified. 144 countries are included in the sample. The countries are ranked by region and alphabetical order, except for the group of SG countries. In this group countries are ranked by region and within region by decreasing magnitude of growth acceleration. †Saudi Arabia was classified as an upper-middle-income country between 1990 and 2003 by the World Bank, but the GDP of Saudi Arabia was only slightly below the classification threshold for high-income countries. Greece was not classified as a high-income country in 1995, but has been classified a high income country since 1996 by the World Bank. ‡In 2003, South Africa experienced a growth acceleration that was sustained until 2009, when the economy contracted by 2.2% before returning to an economic growth rate of more than 2% until 2011, the end of the sample data. Thailand also experienced one year of low growth in 2009, at the end of a period of high and sustained growth. Pakistan, Czech Republic and Slovenia most likely experienced a period of high and sustained growth but, due to missing data, the condition of sustained growth for ten years preceding the accelerated growth cannot be confirmed. For these reasons, South Africa, Thailand, Pakistan, Czech Republic and Slovenia have been included as countries experiencing high and sustained economic growth. The statistical data for Israel are supplied by and under the responsibility of the relevant Israeli authorities. The use of such data by the OECD is without prejudice to the status of the Golan Heights, East Jerusalem and Israeli settlements in the West Bank under the terms of international law.

Source: Author's analysis based on Feenstra et al. (2015), "The Next Generation of the Penn World Table", *American Economic Review*, Vol. 105, n°10, pp. 3150-82 and World Bank (2016), *World Development Indicators* (database), *http://data.worldbank.org/indicator;*

References

Aubry, A. (2016), "Recent economic transformations and Migration patterns", *Mimeo*.

Feenstra, R., R. Inklaar and M. Timmer (2015), "The Next Generation of the Penn World Table", *American Economic Review*, Vol. 105, n° 10, pp. 3150-82.

Hausmann, R., L. Pritchett and D. Rodrik (2005), "Growth accelerations", *Journal of Economic Growth*, Vol. 10, pp. 303-329.

World Bank (2016), *World Development Indicators* (database), *http://databank.worldbank.org/data/reports.aspx?source=world-development-indicators*.

ORGANISATION FOR ECONOMIC CO-OPERATION AND DEVELOPMENT

The OECD is a unique forum where governments work together to address the economic, social and environmental challenges of globalisation. The OECD is also at the forefront of efforts to understand and to help governments respond to new developments and concerns, such as corporate governance, the information economy and the challenges of an ageing population. The Organisation provides a setting where governments can compare policy experiences, seek answers to common problems, identify good practice and work to co-ordinate domestic and international policies.

The OECD member countries are: Australia, Austria, Belgium, Canada, Chile, the Czech Republic, Denmark, Estonia, Finland, France, Germany, Greece, Hungary, Iceland, Ireland, Israel, Italy, Japan, Korea, Latvia, Luxembourg, Mexico, the Netherlands, New Zealand, Norway, Poland, Portugal, the Slovak Republic, Slovenia, Spain, Sweden, Switzerland, Turkey, the United Kingdom and the United States. The European Union takes part in the work of the OECD.

OECD Publishing disseminates widely the results of the Organisation's statistics gathering and research on economic, social and environmental issues, as well as the conventions, guidelines and standards agreed by its members.

OECD DEVELOPMENT CENTRE

The OECD Development Centre was established in 1962 as an independent platform for knowledge sharing and policy dialogue between OECD member countries and developing economies, allowing these countries to interact on an equal footing. Today, 27 OECD countries and 24 non-OECD countries are members of the Centre. The Centre draws attention to emerging systemic issues likely to have an impact on global development and more specific development challenges faced by today's developing and emerging economies. It uses evidence-based analysis and strategic partnerships to help countries formulate innovative policy solutions to the global challenges of development.

For more information on the Centre and its members, please see *www.oecd.org/dev*.

OECD PUBLISHING, 2, rue André-Pascal, 75775 PARIS CEDEX 16
(41 2016 13 1P) ISBN 978-92-64-26253-9 – 2016

www.ingramcontent.com/pod-product-compliance
Ingram Content Group UK Ltd.
Pitfield, Milton Keynes, MK11 3LW, UK
UKHW051459290926
15471UKWH00008B/1291

9 789264 262539